ROLAND "THE HAWAIIAN" LEONG

ou Hart

Drag Racing's Iconic Owner & Tuner

CarTech®

CarTech®, Inc.
6118 Main Street
North Branch, MN 55056
Phone: 651-277-1200 or 800-551-4754
Fax: 651-277-1203
www.cartechbooks.com

Edit by Wes Eisenschenk
Layout by Connie DeFlorin

ISBN 978-1-61325-778-4
Item No. CT695

Library of Congress Cataloging-in-Publication Data Available

Written, edited, and designed in the U.S.A.
Printed in China
10 9 8 7 6 5 4 3 2 1

CarTech books may be purchased at a discounted rate in bulk for resale, events, corporate gifts, or educational purposes. Special editions may also be created to specification. For details, contact Special Sales at 6118 Main Street, North Branch, MN 55056 or by email at sales@cartechbooks.com.

PUBLISHER'S NOTE: In reporting history, the images required to tell the tale will vary greatly in quality, especially by modern photographic standards. While some images in this volume are not up to those digital standards, we have included them, as we feel they are an important element in telling the story.

All photos courtesy of author Lou Hart unless otherwise noted.

DISTRIBUTION BY:

Europe
PGUK
63 Hatton Garden
London EC1N 8LE, England
Phone: 020 7061 1980 • Fax: 020 7242 3725
www.pguk.co.uk

Australia
Renniks Publications Ltd.
3/37-39 Green Street
Banksmeadow, NSW 2109, Australia
Phone: 2 9695 7055 • Fax: 2 9695 7355
www.renniks.com

Canada
Login Canada
300 Saulteaux Crescent
Winnipeg, MB, R3J 3T2 Canada
Phone: 800 665 1148 • Fax: 800 665 0103
www.lb.ca

TABLE OF CONTENTS

DEDICATION

I am privileged to have Roland Leong as my good friend. It has been an inspiration and influence being able to have learned and shared his experiences through his passage in life. — Lou Hart

ACKNOWLEDGMENTS

My deepest appreciation goes to the following drag racing legends and personalities because without their valuable time sharing their stories and personal adventures, this project would not have been completed: Roland Leong, Don Prudhomme, Larry "Pineapple" Reyes, Larry Sutton, Mike Dunn, Johnny West, Ron Capps, Vance Hunt, Danny "Buzz" Broussard, Jim Murphy, Don Long, and Wes Hansen.

I am overwhelmed with this exceptional group of contributing photographers, illustrators, artists, historians, and great friends who allowed me the time and the use of their work, as well as input for this book: Steve Reyes, Bob McClurg, Tom West, Paul Johnson, Dale Kunesh, Tony Thacker, Phil Burgess, Dave Wallace Sr., Dave Wallace Jr., Tim Pearl, Stephen Justice, Tom Nelson, Mike Goyda, Bob McClurg, Richard Shute of Auto Imagery, Jeff Burk, Steve Delgadillo, Darr Hawthorne, Pete Eastwood, Marc Gewertz, David Beitler, Jerry Inouye, Don and John Ewald, Ross and Huey Howard, Clinton Wright, Kevin Slith of Slith Printing, Robin Millar of *Drag Cartoons*, "Big" Bob Wagner, Tal Barret, Stan Shiroma, Wendy Shiroma Hansen, Craig and Debbie Takemori, Jeff Elliker, Bill Ludewig, Bill Hilton, Marc Chezepock, and the many others who shared their experiences with Roland Leong. Also, thanks to my editor, Wes Eisenschenk.

Thank you to my immediate family, especially my wife, Dawley, and my kids for understanding the time needed to complete this book.

Lastly, I want to extend my utmost regard to Roland Leong, Susie, and the Leong family for their time, visits, and the use of Roland's personal library of memoirs. It's been an amazing journey throughout the storied life of one of my heroes in drag racing. I learned from Roland that no matter what life has in store for you, you learn from your failures first before you can succeed.

FOREWORD by Don Prudhomme

It was my first trip to Hawaii. Keith Black, Tom Greer, and I were invited by Jimmy Pflueger (owner of a Lincoln-Mercury dealership in Honolulu) to promote his newly built National Hot Rod Association (NHRA)–sanctioned drag strip: Hawaii Raceway Park. The deal included bringing the *Greer-Black-Prudhomme* car from the mainland to make exhibition runs for the grand opening. I wasn't really thrilled about going to Hawaii as a tourist; I had no desire to hang out at the beach and play in the water. My only interest was going to the strip and running the car.

I met Roland and his mom and dad, and all of us went out to dinner. Right away, there was something about Roland and me. We became instant friends, hitting it off like brothers. We were both passionate about racing and cars. We've remained good friends throughout the years.

Now, I'm not the easiest guy to know, and Roland was that way too. You had to spend time with Roland to understand him and his speaking—he had that "pigeon" English. I took to him right away, and he took to me. We became buddies. I had an older brother who passed away and didn't have any other guys who were close to me except for Roland, who became my closest friend, besides Tom McCourry.

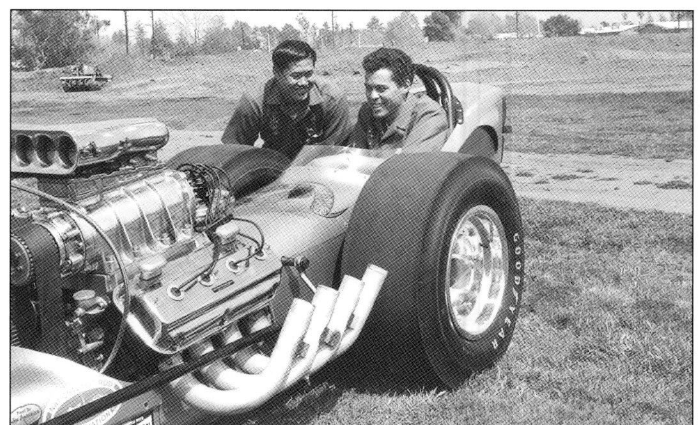

When Roland returned to the mainland, Kent Fuller finished building his Top Fueler that was a near duplicate to the *Greer-Black-Prudhomme* car. I had no reason to believe that Roland wasn't going to drive his own car. To me, running the *Greer-Black-Prudhomme* car was fairly simple because I'd been doing it for a long time. Well, maybe the word "simple" isn't accurate. I was fortunate to have a natural driving ability, even when piloting Tommy Ivo's four-engine car.

I accompanied Keith and Roland to Lions Drag Strip to

run his new dragster. We put Roland in the car and strapped him in. I had no idea that he wouldn't be able to make a successful run. Why shouldn't he? If I could do it, anyone could. That was the way I felt. While making his licensing pass, he got off the track, and I lost sight of him. Roland wound up going off the end of the track, crashing the car, and coming to a stop on the railroad tracks. He was short and sitting low in the cockpit, so maybe he could barely see over the top of the cowling. I didn't really know for sure why it happened, as I never exactly asked him what he was thinking. Fortunately, he was okay.

At the same time, I wasn't aware that Keith was fixing to hang up the *Greek-Black-Prudhomme* car and just concentrate on building engines. Keith went to Roland, sat him down, and said that Roland scared him to death when he crashed and that he wouldn't know what to do if Roland was hurt or killed.

It didn't really affect me, as drivers will crash cars. However, Roland really shook Keith up to the point that Keith told him to make the deal with me driving the car and Keith continuing to tune and maintain it. So, it didn't take long for Roland to make up his mind to put me in the car. That is how I got the ride.

After repairing the car, we returned to Lions Drag Strip in November with me driving, and Roland was working on tuning and maintaining the engine along with Keith. We won the race on Saturday night and went to Pomona the next day, also winning that race.

In February 1965, we took the car to Pomona for the Winternationals and won it all! For the Pomona win, the NHRA presented us keys to a new Ford camper pickup. Soon after that win, just the two of us went out on the road match racing across the country. That adventure was something else.

We had our neighbor build a trailer for us in his driveway. It was heavy as can be, having a steel frame with all wood. It was solid but didn't tow worth a damn! It was like having Noah's ark chained to the rear bumper. I got experience towing while on the road going around the country with Ivo. I knew what to expect when big trucks passed while towing it. Because of Roland's experience crashing the dragster, I wasn't so sure if he should be towing the rig. The only thing he was allowed to do was push-start the race car.

Anyhow, I got so tired coming home that I told him, "You're going to have to drive this thing. I can't go anymore."

I jumped into the back seat, he took off, and I fell asleep immediately. The next thing I know, I woke up, and we were going down the highway in Oklahoma.

He said, "Hey, Vipe (he always called me Vipe), I think I have a handle on towing this thing."

Just as he said that, we passed a truck, and suddenly, the car and trailer got out of control and started weaving around, moving back and forth. The next thing I know, it jacked-knifed itself. We spun around in the middle of the highway, ending up in a ditch. The trailer broke away from the car, scattering Pennzoil oil cans everywhere. We were lucky that it didn't kill us.

Truckers stopped to see if we were okay and help us. We got the trailer hooked back up to the car, but it needed welding repairs. We limped into Jimmy Nix's shop in Oklahoma City and worked on the trailer to make it highway worthy to get the car home. At that point, we stayed awake for the remainder of our journey.

I never dreamed that I would be driving for him. We got along amazingly well. If I got a big head or anything, he would say, "Oh, you're a *big shot* now." He'd call me a big shot. He'd get on me right away if I got out of line.

When we were home, we would run at Long Beach on Friday night. Then, on Saturday night, we would figure out what track to go to on Sunday. Usually, it was Pomona, Fontana, or San Fernando. We were always ready to race!

It seemed like we won everything! The *Hawaiian* was just like the *Greer-Black-Prudhomme* car. I'd say Keith Black was the guy who was most responsible, as he would set the engine up. We'd maintain it, but Keith determined the engine's cubic inches, blower overdrive, and magneto. It was really his baby, but he taught Roland how to tune it, and I drove. I wasn't as into tuning as Roland was. Keith built amazing engines. The beautiful thing was that we didn't tear them up, which was largely due to Roland. He knew how hard to run it and knew what the spark plugs were to look like and things like that.

While we were out on tour, we raced two to three times a week, many weeks in a row. Roland would change the oil, adjust the valves, and replace the spark plugs. He knew what to do, and it was the best.

I have a real soft spot in my heart for Keith Black. He's the person who gave me my start when he made the call to put me in the *Greer-Black-Prudhomme* Fueler, and he gave me the opportunity to drive for Roland. I really owe him for that!

In November 1965, I decided to go out on my own. The team was very successful, and I thought that if I ever would choose a time to leave and create my own destiny, to go out and grow, this was it. I went to Roland and told him that I was going to drive another car. I really didn't look back, and Roland never really said anything, but I think that it really bothered him.

In 1966, Roland came out with Mike Snively, and they kicked all of our asses! I thought, "Wow, maybe it isn't the driver." I realized that, perhaps, it was the car with the Keith Black engine.

How do I sum up my time with Roland? We were always close—like brothers. I was closer to him than my own brother. We spent more time together being good friends and good buddies, and we always will be!

CHAPTER 1

ROLAND LEONG: OAHU'S MOST PREEMINENT DRAG RACING LEGEND

The Leong family is shown in Hawaii. From left to right are Roland Leong's mother, Teddy; his father, James; Roland; and his sisters Jamie and Marilyn. (Photo Courtesy Roland Leong Collection)

On May 22, 1944, Roland Leong was born to parents James and Theodora "Teddy" Leong on the southern side of the island of Oahu in the capital city of Honolulu, Hawaii. Roland grew up in an affluent neighborhood with his parents and two sisters. He was a typical young lad, attending an all-boys private school from kindergarten through 12th grade.

Most of Roland's spare time as a youngster was spent playing sports and enjoying music. He especially enjoyed playing the piano and clarinet. He also played drums in the school band.

After school, he occasionally helped with the family business: the James Y.T. Leong Agency. He ran various

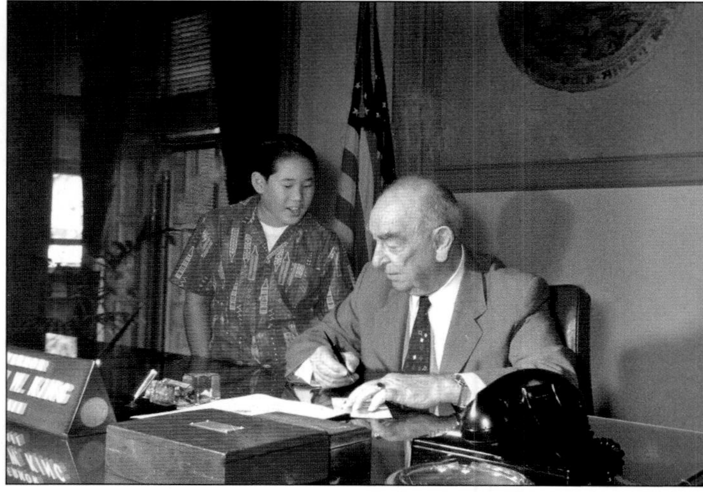
During a school field trip to the Hawaii state capital, Roland was selected to meet Samuel Wilder King, the 11th Territorial Governor of Hawaii. King served in office from 1953–1957. (Photo Courtesy Roland Leong Collection)

Roland celebrates Christmas at home in Hawaii with his sisters, Jamie and Marilyn. (Photo Courtesy Roland Leong Collection)

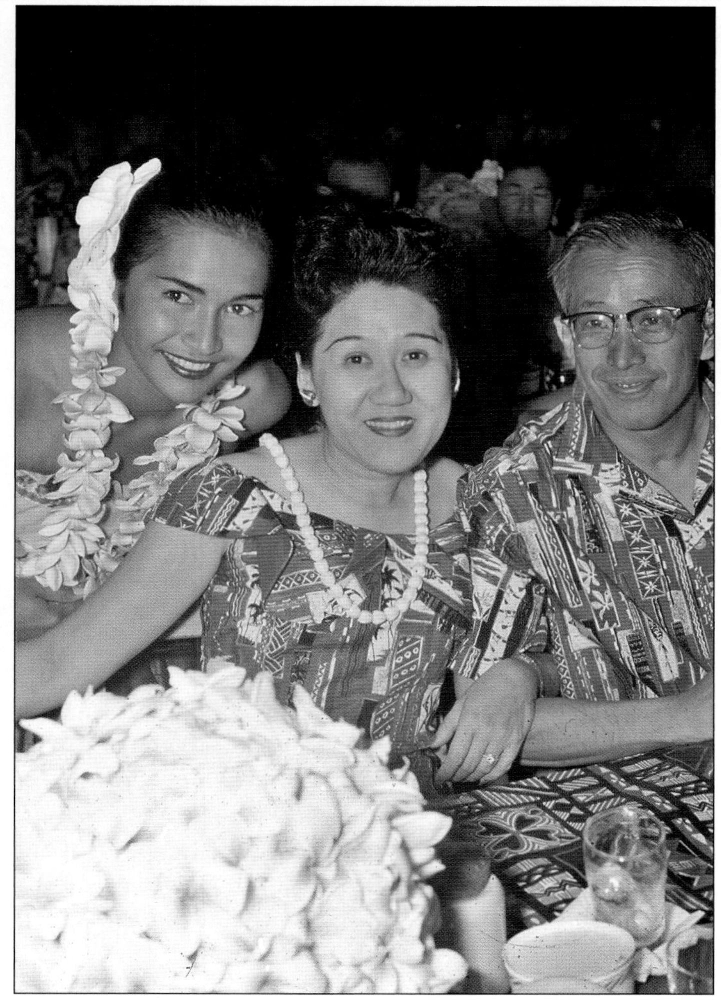

Leong's parents enjoy a Hawaiian evening at a Waikiki luau. The festive Hawaiian party features poi, kalua pua, poke, lomi salmon, opihi, haupia, and beer. Luaus also included entertainment, such as traditional Hawaiian music and hula dancing. (Photo Courtesy Roland Leong Collection)

errands, answered the switchboard, made bank deposits, and picked up around the office. Roland would take a bus home from school and from the family business, which required taking two routes. His first bus stopped at a hub in an industrial park, where he transferred to another bus.

Tunes and Tunes

The bus stop was located next to two gas stations and a car repair shop, where Roland's father took the family cars for service and repair. The buses ran on hourly schedules, so Roland often hung around the shop while he waited for his second bus home. The owner knew the Leong family and allowed Roland to stick around and learn about cars.

Roland's love of music led him to play the clarinet, drums, and piano. He played in a band during his high-school days. (Photo Courtesy Roland Leong Collection)

At the shop, a few souped-up cars and the jalopies that the workers drove really drew Roland's attention. This fueled his interest in cars, especially hot rods with polished chrome and pipes. His fascination with cars shone brightly in his future.

Roland was developing his passion for fast, loud cars, but music was still a large part of his life. He wanted to play in an organized band. The type of music that he wanted to play wasn't available at his school, so (at age 14) he connected with a few older boys from a public school who had a dance band and needed a drummer. Playing drums in this band fit Roland well, and the band performed at parties, weddings, and other social gatherings, playing all of the popular hits that were played on the radio. The trunk of Roland's mom's Oldsmobile could carry his five cases of drums, which made his commute to the performances convenient.

A "Hot Rodding" Teenager

A bonus for Roland was that the other members of his band were motor-heads. When a gig concluded, which was usually around 10 p.m. on Saturday nights, they rapidly packed up their instruments and jumped into their cars to watch the outlaw street races. This suited Roland well.

"If I didn't drag race, I would have been a musician," Roland said.

In his teenage years, Roland's interest in drag racing really took off. The Leongs were a two-car family. His dad's car was the basic, least-expensive model, while his mother, Teddy, drove their "going-out" car, which was a top-end 1959 Oldsmobile.

Before Roland had his driver's license, he borrowed his mom's car with a friend who had a license, and they took it to the drag races at Kahuku Drag Strip. At the strip, his friend coaxed Roland into racing the Olds in the stock class with his friend driving. Unbeknownst to Roland, his sister Marilyn attended the same race with several of her friends.

When he got home, he caught hell from his parents! His sister, who meant no harm, told them that she saw their car racing at the drag strip. Right away, his father banned Roland from taking the car until he had his license.

"I was continually hanging around guys older than me who were really deep into cars, and the experience that I gained in those early times served me pretty well," Roland said.

The First Hot Rod

At age 15, Roland passed his driver's-license test in the family Oldsmobile. He soon took it upon himself to "hot rod" the engine by having a roller cam installed. He lowered the front end; painted all the rims red and accented them with chrome trim rings; modified the exhaust system with sounds of a deep, throaty roar; and raced it. To make matters worse, this was the still the family's "going out" car.

Roland's Corvette

While his mother never really said anything about her car, she wanted it back to its original condition. It wasn't too long before Roland passed the local Chevrolet dealership and spotted a new 1962 Corvette sitting on the showroom floor. After several conversations with his mom about the Corvette, Roland convinced her to buy it for him. However, his mom had two prerequisites: 1) return the Olds to its original condition, and 2) he would not race the 'Vette. Roland agreed.

The second part of the agreement lasted nearly 10 months before he returned to racing at the strip.

"I lied," a smiling Roland confessed.

Roland modified the Corvette and began racing in the "B" Modified Sports class. He befriended another racer who was several years older and also owned a Corvette that he raced at Kahuku. The friend's parents owned a service station, and the Hawaii Racing Parts Speed Shop was on the same property.

Within six months, Roland's hard work paid off when he won his first race and first trophy. Roland's mother always believed in him and supported his racing but only at the drag strip—not on the streets.

Roland's First Dragster

As Roland gained experience and his love of drag racing grew, Ron Saiki, the owner of the speed shop, approached Mrs. Leong and asked if she would be interested in investing in his business. Teddy thought it would be a wise opportunity, as Mr. Saiki's business was well known and respected on Oahu. He was one of the first to advertise on the radio, selling speed parts and accessories. He scored a huge hit by introducing chrome-reverse wheels to Hawaii.

Teddy's investment profited both parties, and the idea was brought up to build a blown gas dragster to run at Kahuku. After researching the details, a call was made to Jim Nelson of Dragmasters in Carlsbad, California, for a new state-of-the-art dragster powered by a 1961 supercharged Corvette engine that delivered 500 hp. The call was made with the understanding that the car was to be driven by Saiki. The deal was struck, and construction began.

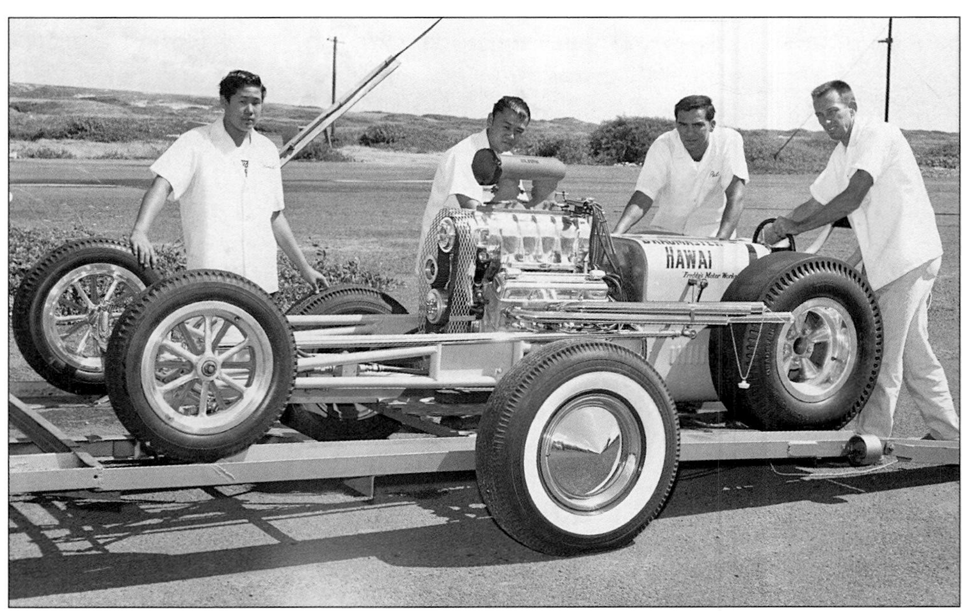

The arrival of Roland Leong's new **Dragmaster Hawaii** *blown Chevy-powered rail in August 1961 was celebrated at Kahuku Drag Strip with builder and driver Jim Nelson (far right) and crewmembers. (Photo Courtesy Roland Leong Collection)*

The Dragmaster Hawaii *crew was ready to make some noise and blast the tires of the blown Chevy-powered rail at Kahuku Drag Strip with builder and driver Jim Nelson (far right). (Photo Courtesy Roland Leong Collection)*

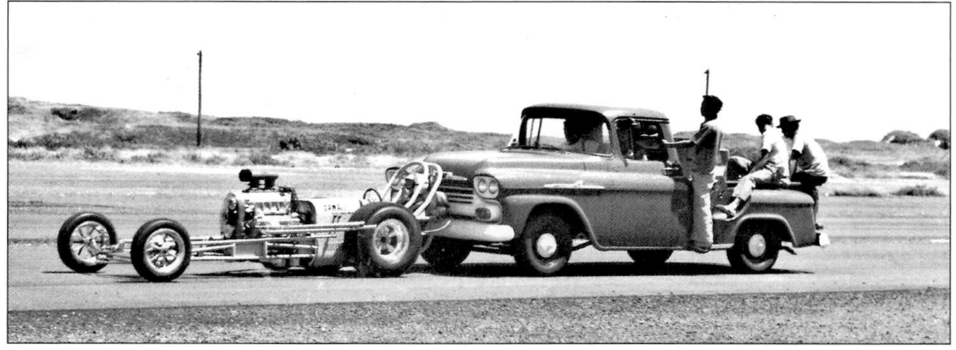

On Labor Day 1961, the new Hawaii *dragster fired up for its first run at Kahuku Drag Strip with driver Jim Nelson at the controls. The initial run netted an 8.45 ET at 163.25 mph. (Photo Courtesy Roland Leong Collection)*

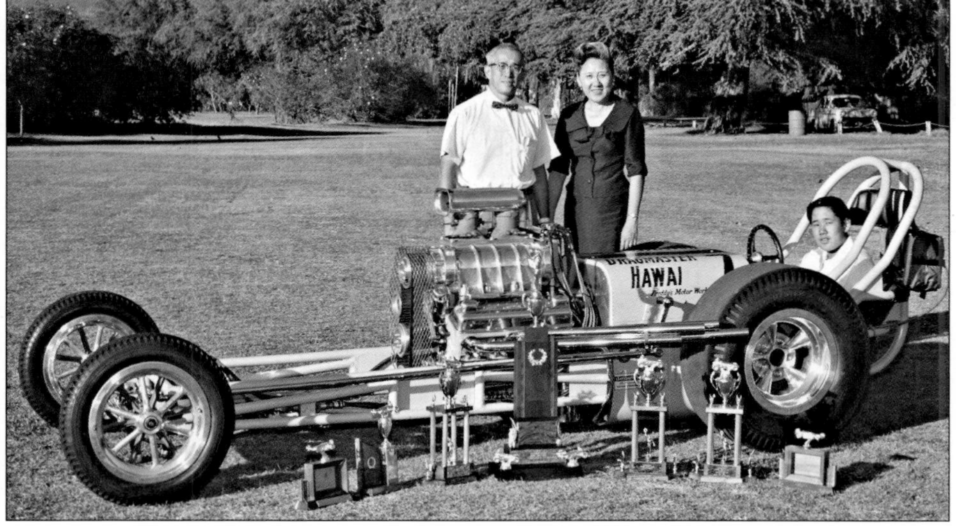

James and Teddy Leong proudly pose with Roland, who is sitting in his Dragmaster Hawaii *gas rail. Leong, a natural behind the wheel, shows off the collection of awards that he earned in the short period of time racing in Kahuku. (Photo Courtesy Roland Leong Collection)*

As the car was nearing completion, they realized that there was a minor drawback: no one had the expertise to run it. Nelson agreed to bring the dragster to Hawaii and help them get acquainted with running the car. He also made several shakedown passes at Kahuku Drag Strip.

During this time, Roland made the fateful decision to leave private school and attend public school.

Labor Day Championships

Nelson, his crew, and the dragster arrived at Oahu via a Pan Am cargo plane at the end of August 1961, just a few days before the Labor Day Drag Festival at Kahuku. The bright yellow rail arrived at the former landing strip, with Nelson set to make shakedown runs before making a full-power quarter-mile pass. Under Nelson's instructions, Ron Saiki also made a few get-acquainted runs to get the feel of driving the high-powered dragster.

On Saturday, September 2, Nelson buckled into the car and pushed off down the fire-up road for the maiden pass. The new rail ran better than expected, netting a stout run of 8.45 at 163.25 mph on pump gas. Running throughout the weekend and getting the feel of operating the dragster, both the Leongs and Saiki were ready to race.

School's Out Forever

On Tuesday, September 5, Roland was to attend his first day at his new school, but with all the excitement of racing and Jim Nelson still in town, he missed the day. On Wednesday morning, Roland walked into the classroom not knowing anyone, all eyes focused on him. The teacher asked Roland, "Who are you?" Embarrassed by the teacher's remark in front of the class, Roland walked out and dropped out of school.

When he told his mom about his decision, she said, "Okay, what are you going to do?" Roland told her that he wanted to go to California and work for Nelson's Dragmaster Company, building engines and dragster chassis for customers.

Roland's decision didn't fare well with his father, James, who graduated from Harvard with full honors, including a master's degree. Roland's mom graduated from the University of Hawaii, and his sisters earned college degrees as well. James was against Roland's decision, citing they had nothing in common with racing. Although they talked, both remained distant.

Teddy strongly believed in Roland. She made it known that he was to enroll in a trade school to continue his dreams, thinking that he would select an automotive course. Instead, Roland enrolled in the Honolulu Business School, where he took a course with IBM to learn to be a keypunch operator. This was great for Roland, as there were more girls than guys in these classes. He passed the course. He kept his promise to his mom, but to this day, he still doesn't know how to type!

During his duration at the Honolulu Business School, Roland continued racing the dragster at Kahuku and winning his fair share with the assistance of his car club members. Now an extremely capable driver, Roland was now competing on the national level in several NHRA championship events that included Indy and the major races out in California.

His once-reluctant parents, James and Teddy, were now his biggest racing fans.

"Both attended nearly every major race," Roland said. "When we raced in California, my oldest sister, Marilyn, who was attending college, occasionally drove my tow car for us. And my mother? You could see she was eager, looking over the pit crew as they worked on the car, just itching to help, from getting her hands greasy to packing the parachute, she was ready!"

Before taking on the full responsibility of running the dragster in Hawaii, Saiki decided that he didn't want to drive anymore. He offered to buy out Teddy's share of the speed shop and make the agreement that the Leongs would end up as sole owners of the dragster, now with the thoughts of Roland doing the driving.

Making a Career of It

Teddy allowed Roland to travel to the mainland, where he went to work at Jim Nelson's Dragmaster Corporation in Carlsbad, California. Leong did anything in the shop to help from painting and detailing chassis to installing engines in various cars and working on the highly promoted Dodge Charger blown Polara. There were unglamorous tasks, such as sweeping out the shop and taking out the trash. Leong was able to stay at Nelson's home to save money and go to the races.

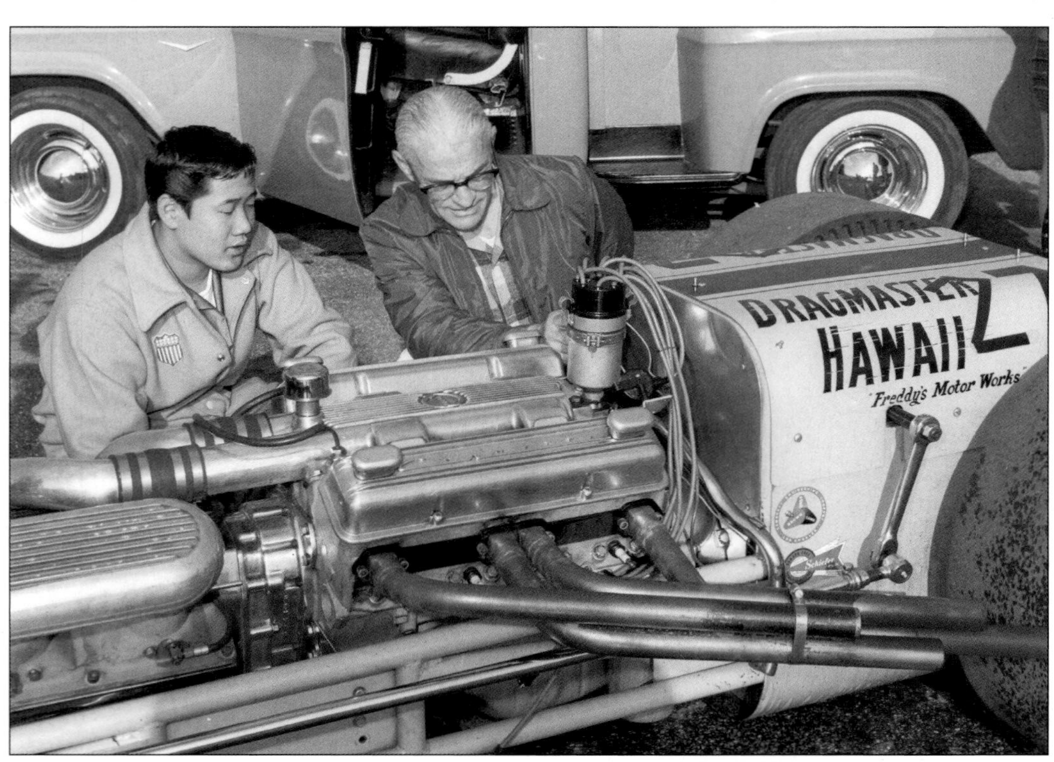

Charles Stokes of Mallory Ignition checks the magneto in Leong's AA/D Dragmaster Hawaii *at the 1962 NHRA Winternationals. The magneto worked flawlessly, as the rail ran consistent 8-second ETs. (Photo Courtesy Roland Leong Collection)*

The hardest part of adjusting to life on the mainland for Leong was getting acquainted with the food.

Leong decided to build a new rail job to race, so he spent many hours at night at the shop after working a full day. Nelson and Leong's good friend Ray Higley, the top welder at Dragmaster, helped Leong build a chassis for his new Dodge-powered gas dragster, *Dragmaster Hawaii*. Leong's first ride in the new rail took place at Riverside Raceway and wasn't all that memorable, as he ran a lowly 85 mph.

Leong's immaculate bright yellow Dragmaster Hawaii *dragster earned the Best Appearing Crew award and Long Distance award at the second-annual NHRA Winternationals. The rail ran consistent 8s at Pomona. (Photo Courtesy Roland Leong Collection)*

1962 NHRA Winternationals

In February 1962, the Leongs flew the *Dragmaster Hawaii* AA/Dragster to California to compete at the second-annual NHRA Winternationals. Leong drove his gas dragster with mixed results. Although he didn't win, he took home both the Long Distance and Best Appearing Crew awards. His oldest sister, Marilyn, who was attending college in California, occasionally helped by driving the tow car for him at the strip.

To ease up traveling between the islands and the mainland, Leong set up his base residency in Southern California. He usually lived two to six months a year in the Los Angeles area.

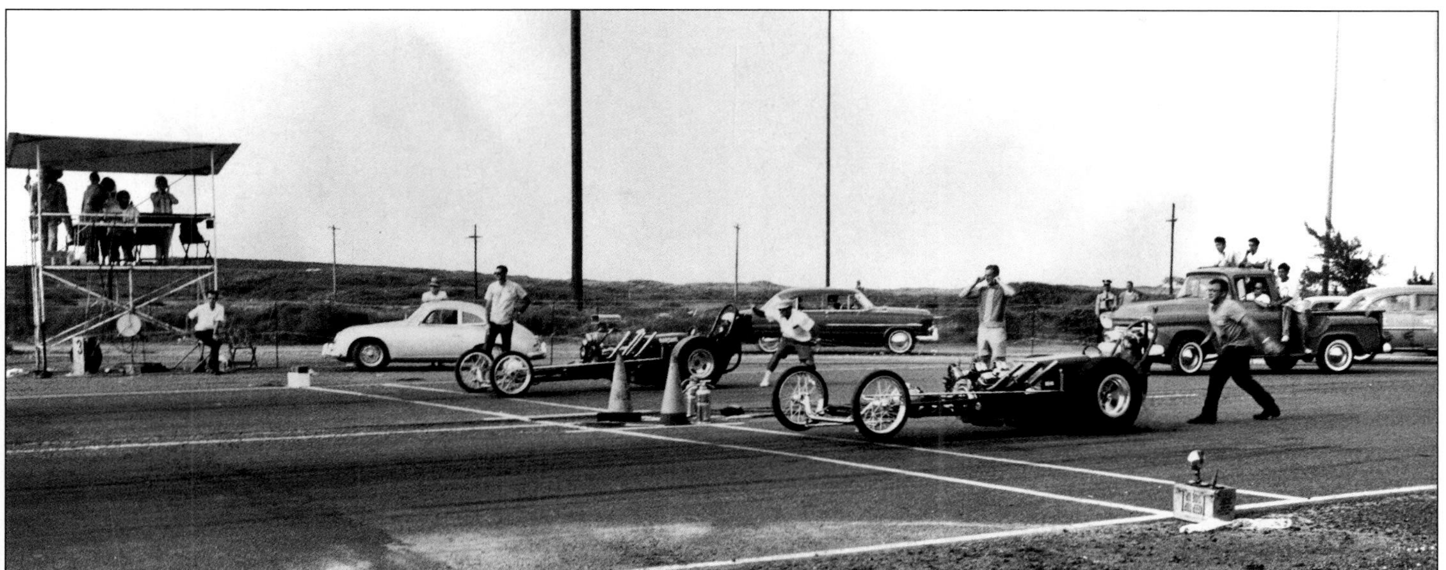

Leong (foreground) gets a hole-shot on his former business and original Dragmaster *dragster partner Ronald Saiki, who ran this blown Chevy gas dragster at Kahuku. Leong built his dragster after work hours with the help from Dode Martin, Jim Nelson, and friends at Dragmasters. Leong raced the digger in California for a few months before he shipped it over to Hawaii, racing it for nearly a year and running it either injected or supercharged. He sold the car in Hawaii before going back to work at Dragmaster. Leong went on to build his third* Dragmaster *dragster, a blown 480-ci Dodge-powered car that set both ET and top speed records at Kahuku (8.58 and 180 mph). (Photo Courtesy Roland Leong Collection)*

At the 1962 Indy Nationals, crewman Carl Wai, Mrs. Leong, Rod & Custom *magazine's trophy presenter (name unknown), Danny Ongais, and Roland were presented the Long Distance award with the* Hawaiian Dart. *(Photo Courtesy Roland Leong Collection)*

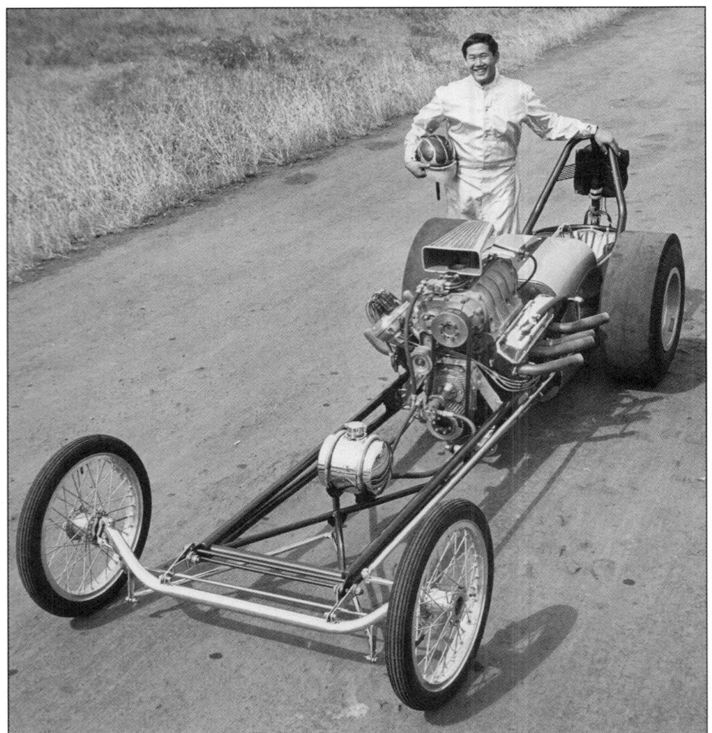

An elated Leong shows off his new Dragmaster Hawaii *dragster for 1964. Leong, Jim Nelson, and Ray Higley built the rail after hours and on the weekends at Dragmaster on the mainland in Carlsbad. Power was now provided by a supercharged Plymouth 426 Wedge engine that was punched out to a whopping 480 ci and ran on pump gasoline. Leong set both top speed and low ET at Kahuku Drag Strip. (Photo Courtesy Roland Leong Collection)*

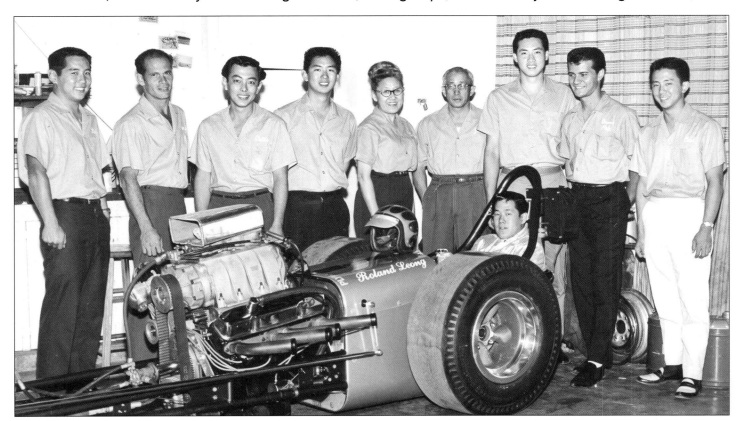

The crew of the Hawaii II, *including Leong's parents, gather around their accomplished driver at the shop in Hawaii. (Photo Courtesy Roland Leong Collection)*

On the Road and in the Sky

On a return trip back to Carlsbad, Roland Leong went on tour with Jim Nelson, taking in various strips from Oregon to Texas. In the fall of 1962, Leong brought in fellow Hawaiian Danny Ongais to assist with the expanded bookings at various strips on the East Coast in Georgia and Virginia.

Hot Rod Magazine Championships

One of the most unusual events in drag racing played out at the first Hot Rod Magazine Championships from June 12 to 14, 1964, at Riverside. Leong and Ongais showed up with the Chevy small-block-powered Dragmaster car. In the first round of eliminations, the axle snapped right off at the starting line while Ongais's opponent in the other lane disqualified himself when he red-lighted.

To take the round win, the rule book stated if the car would roll, the driver needed to get out and push the car the remaining length of the 1320. Ongais went the distance and won the round. Both Leong and Ongais advanced and wound up winning the event.

Leong slows after pulling the chute after another record-setting run at Kahuku. The former World War II airstrip provided many memorable runs and great times for Leong. The Kahuku Point Airfield was one of three ex-military airstrips at the tip of Oahu. Although the surface of the strip was bumpier than the other two fields, Kahuku had better facilities for drag racing. (Photo Courtesy Roland Leong Collection)

CARS WON AND A FRIENDSHIP LOST

Danny Ongais was a crew member for Leong and came over to the mainland with the Leongs in 1962 to drive the unblown Chevy-powered *Hawaiian Dart* gas dragster at Indy. There, they were awarded the Long Distance trophy by *Rod and Custom* magazine.

Two years later, at the 1964 NHRA Winternationals at Pomona, Ongais went on to win the Top Gas Eliminator title. That prize included taking home a brand-new Ford Falcon. A few months later, at Riverside Raceway at the Hot Rod Magazine Nationals, Ongais again won the Top Gas title with Roland's *Dragmaster Hawaii* rail, which earned him another new car.

James Leong approached Ongais and suggested that he should give them a new car, since he won two cars now with their dragster. Ongais refused to give a car to Roland Leong. He kept the dragster, thus ending their friendship and the opportunity to pilot the new *Hawaiian* AA/FD.

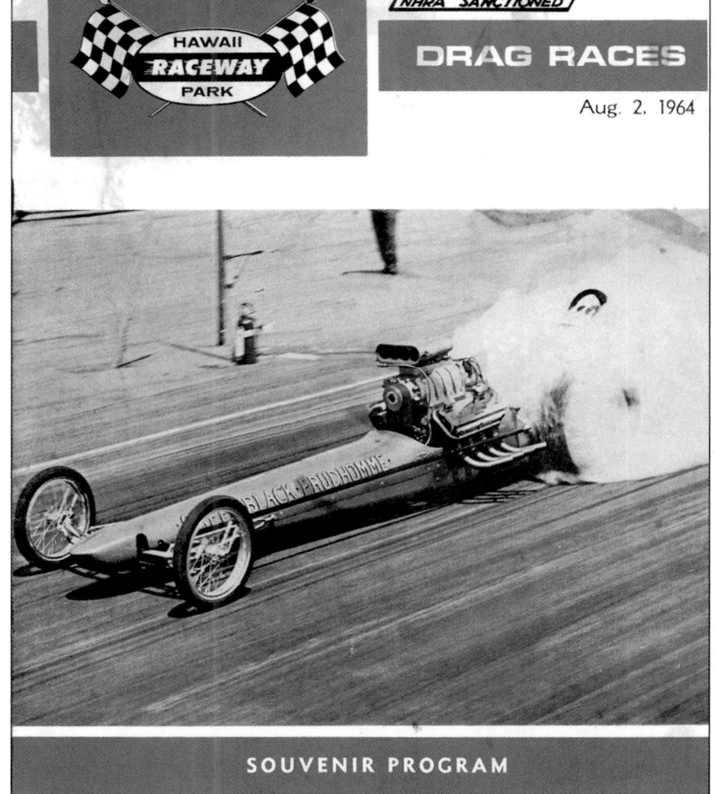

A surviving program from the opening day at Hawaii Raceway Park dated August 2, 1964, featured race coverage and results along with the special appearance of the Greer-Black-Prudhomme dragster from the mainland. The car was part of grand opening festivities at the modern, multi-functional racing facility. (Program Courtesy Roland Leong Collection)

The Leongs raced together as a family, including Roland's mother, Teddy, who was always eager to pitch in with the car, including packing the parachute brake for Roland. (Photo Courtesy Roland Leong Collection)

In 1964, Leong's *Dragmaster* rail reverted back to the Chevrolet power combination at the Winternationals. There, it won the Winternationals and Best Appearing awards. After winning the Winternationals, Ognais and Leong parted ways.

Hawaii Raceway Park Grand Opening

A memorable event for Leong was when he flew home to Hawaii to race over Fourth of July weekend at the grand opening of the new NHRA-sanctioned quarter-mile state-of-the-art drag strip Hawaii Raceway Park (HRP). The track operator and owner, Jimmy Pflueger, who also owned Honolulu's only Lincoln-Mercury dealership, was also an avid drag racer.

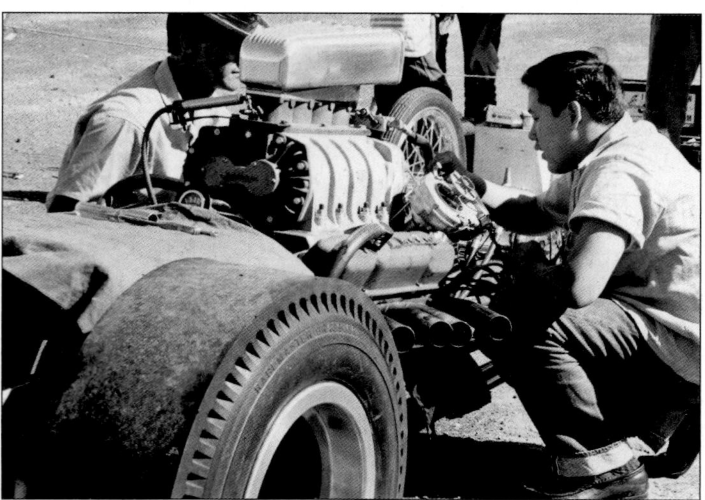

Leong examines the ignition rotor and distributor before his next pass at the new Hawaii Raceway Park. The venue opened on August 2, 1964. A crowd of 8,000 went through the turnstiles at Hawaii's state-of-the-art facility, which also included a road-course track. (Photo Courtesy Roland Leong Collection)

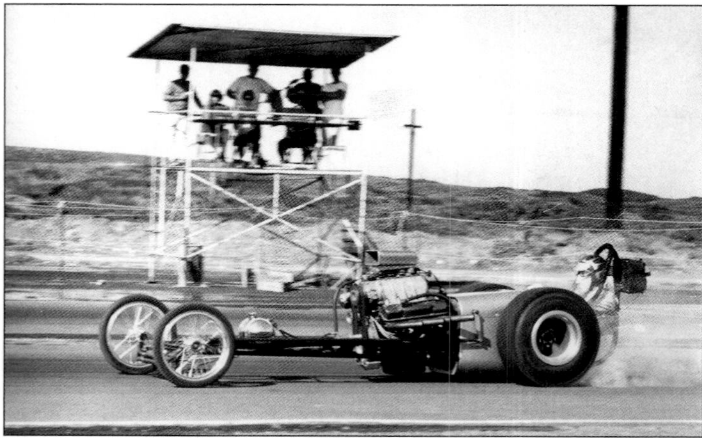

Roland found the smooth surface and traction of HRP to his liking when he won the Top Gas Eliminator title at the inaugural event. (Photo Courtesy Roland Leong Collection)

Hawaii Raceway Park Records

ELIMINATOR CATEGORY WINNERS		DATE	ET	MPH
T.E.GAS—Roland Leong		7/4/64	9.750	161.87
Comp. Elim.—Stu Copp		7/4/64	10.954	128.38
ST E—Earle "Safari" Char		7/4/64	11 793	118.57
STCK. E—Larry Megibow		7/4/64	12.349	116.12
"SPECIAL BONANZA RACE"				
1—Earle Safari" Char	Comet Wagon	7/4/64	11.813	119.36
2—Larry Megibow	Plymouth	7/4/64	12.160	117.80
CLASS WINNERS				
D/FD—Robert Stewart	Merc. Flathead	7/4/64	11.413	131.57
AA/D—Roland Leong	Plymouth	7/4/64	9.750	161.87
A/D—Miersch/Kubo	Chev.	7/4/64	10.354	154.63
B/D—Mutt's Body & Fender-Shiroma	Chev.	7/4/64	10.889	136.77
B/GS—Harold Soto	Chev.	7/4/64	15.732	89.91
A/G—Danny Vida	DeSoto	7/4/64	12.987	107.65
B/G—Rodney Chung	Ford	7/4/64	13.277	105.14
C/G—Raymond Kealoha	Chev.	7/4/64	13.739	102.15
D/G—Richard Watson	Chev.	7/4/64	15.619	85.38
E/G—Glenn Wakamatsu	Buick	7/4/64	16.536	79.22
F/G—Jack Chambers	Chev.	7/4/64	16.189	74.62
G/G—Darral Masuda	Chev.	7/4/64	15.023	92.78
H/G—John McDonald	Chev.	7/4/64	16.122	84.90
A/COM.—Alfred Nabarette	Falcon	7/4/64		
B/COM.—Melvin Teruya		7/4/64		
A/A—Stu Copp	Chev.	7/4/64	10.954	128.38
B/A—Eddie Asing	Plymouth	7/4/64	12.878	106.—
C/A—Danny Vida	DeSoto	7/4/64	12.767	106.25
AA/SR—Ivan Peroff	Chev.	7/4/64	13.411	113.35
A/SR—A/R Joseph Chir, Jr.	Chev.	7 4/64	13 991	102.38
A/FX—Earle "Safari" Char	Comet	7/4/64	11 920	115.68
B/FX—Neil Nagata	Ford	7/4/64	14.713	97 71
C/FX—Glenn Young		7/4/64	16.319	84.58
S/S—Frank Miguel	Ford	7/4/64		105.38
A/S—Brian Oba		7/4/64	14.167	98.03
B/S—Bill "Racer" Brown	Pontiac	7/4/64	14.259	95.54
C/S—Robert Yamanoha	Ford	7/4/64	14.893	94.93
D/S—Mala Acerete	Chev.	7/4/64	15.389	80.78
E/S—Kenny Otake		7/4/64	21.306	
F/S—Cullen Kasai		7/4/64	14.989	92.90
G/S—Rube Ciriacks	Comet	7/4/64	16.603	83 10
H/S—Clayton Kaichi	Ford	7/4/64	17.243	82.41
I/S—Dave Packer	Chev.	7/4/64	16.792	80.35
J/S—Miles Saito		7/4/64	17.483	64.33
K/S—Chris Lee	TR-2	7/4/64	16.942	82.79
L/S—James C. Drake	Porsche	7/4/64	16.946	79.50
M/S—Alfred Jovero	Chev.	7/4/64	18.031	72.40
S/SA—Arthur Omine	Plymouth	7/4/64	14.040	101.58
A/SA—Warren Lee	Chev.	7/4/64	15.068	92.11
B/SA—Donald Yoshikami		7/4/64	14.873	91 74
C/SA				
D/SA—David Kinney		7/4/64	16.329	86.12
E/SA—Richard Loui		7/4/64	15.312	86.87
F/SA—Edward Chi		7/4/64	16.137	84.66
G/SA—Ray Lundgren	Pontiac	7/4/64	16.958	79.15
H/SA—Rudy Higashihara		7/4/64	17.489	78.26
I/SA—TomMartin	Pontiac	7/4/64	17 168	78.26

The time sheet of class winners and performances from HRP's grand opening shows Leong as the Top Gas Eliminator, class winner, and record holder. (Photo Courtesy Roland Leong Collection)

HRP opened the gates to more than 8,000 racers and spectators, who were eager to see the top mainland drivers and dragsters, including the highlighted appearance of the *Greer-Black-Prudhomme* Top Fueler driven by Don Prudhomme. This was the first time Leong and Prudhomme met, and from then on, the two built a strong bond as friends and competitors.

Leong, in grand style, captured the Top Eliminator Gas honors at the grand opening and set the track record for both Low ET (elapsed time) (9.750) and Top Speed (161.87 mph).

Leong's racing skills had improved from his earlier days racing his mother's Oldsmobile and Corvette. He invested nearly $15,000 in constructing the three rails

Setting track records at Kahuku Drag Strip was commonplace for the Dragmaster Hawaii *team. The Leongs had one of the strongest dragsters in the state of Hawaii. (Photo Courtesy Roland Leong Collection)*

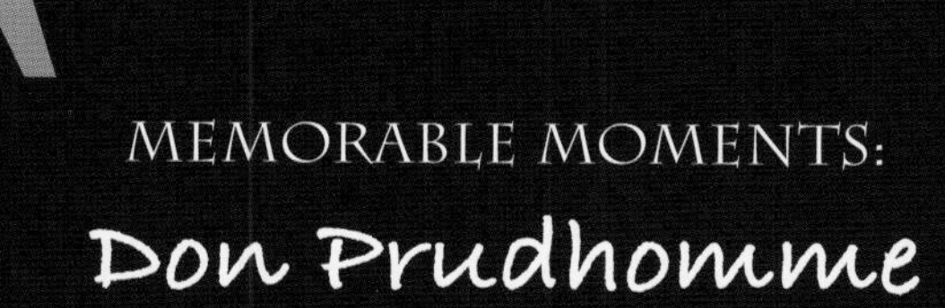

MEMORABLE MOMENTS:

Don Prudhomme

"Have you ever met someone that you became instant friends with, hitting it off right away?" Don Prudhomme asked. "That's how Roland and I were back then, and that's how it is today. At the inaugural race at Hawaii Raceway Park on July 4, 1964, Roland needed a hand to push his gas dragster back onto the trailer. He asked me to help, and I didn't hesitate to say, 'You bet!' I don't know how else to put it, we were instant friends."

The members of the Dragmaster Hawaii *proudly display the rewards from all of their hard work and dedication. The trophies were won on Hawaii and on various strips on the mainland. (Photo Courtesy Roland Leong Collection)*

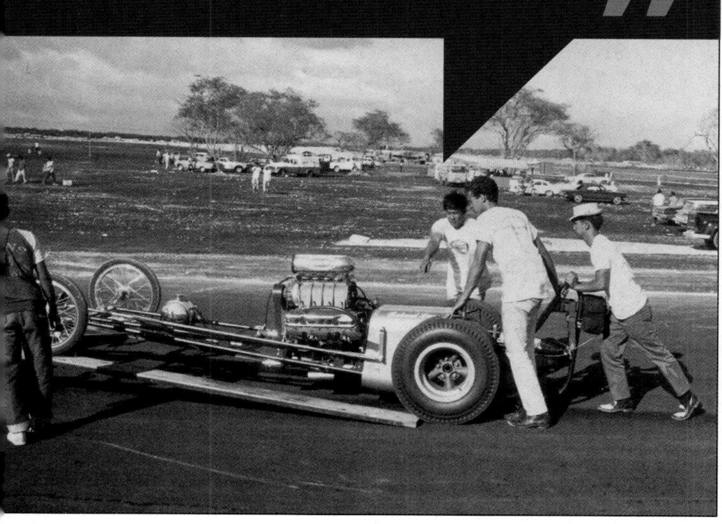

e incredible ending on opening day at HRP included Don udhomme helping to load Leong's gasoline-powered agster back onto the trailer. No one knew it at the time, but ese two future legendary greats would go on to dominate p Fuel in 1965.

How do you attract large crowds of curious race fans and pack them into the showroom at the local Dodge dealership in Honolulu? Well, ask Teddy, Roland, and James Leong and their award-winning AA/GD dragster because that's just what they did. The accomplished family proudly displayed all of the trophies that were won at Kahuku, Hawaii Raceway Park, Indy, and Pomona. (Photo Courtesy Roland Leong Collection)

At 19 years old, many young people are figuring out what path in life to take. By that age, Roland Leong already had major drag-racing accomplishments. Ray Brock, the publisher of Hot Rod *magazine, and Leong's parents, James and Teddy, celebrate the family's achievements. (Photo Courtesy Roland Leong Collection)*

built at Dragmasters. They featured a 112-inch wheelbase and weighed an average of 1,125 pounds. The first one was powered by a supercharged 400-ci Corvette engine, and the later rails had 426 Wedge engines that produced 500 hp.

He kept two of the gas rails garaged at his Hawaiian home above the unincorporated town of Pauoa in the Pacific Heights neighborhood. They were raced once a month, either at Kahuku Drag Strip or Hawaii Raceway Park. The car on the mainland won the 1964 Winternationals, taking the Top Gas Eliminator title with Danny Ongais driving. Added into the mix was Leong's stylish daily driver: a 1964 Corvette fastback.

In his first five years of racing, Leong earned nearly $12,000 in purse money and collected numerous trophies both in Hawaii and the mainland. His fastest speed in his gas dragster was more than 180 mph, which for a time stood as the Hawaii land speed record at Kahuku.

Leong even took on a new challenge in sports car racing at HRP: driving a Formula Junior car owned by Nick Senseri.

"The first time I drove, I got nowhere, but in my second race, I was running in second place," Leong said. "When going into the third lap, the left front wheel somehow exited off the car, buzzed right by me, and landed somewhere in a row of bushes. We had an awful time finding it."

Leong was now competing on the national level in Top Gas Eliminator at several NHRA championship events, including Indy, and at all the major races in California.

Top Fuel Dragster

Nitromethane had been prohibited as a fuel in drag racing since 1957, but the ban was lifted in 1963, and nitro was once again approved for the Top Fuel class. With not much more to accomplish in the Top Gas ranks, Leong sold his dragsters and took the next step toward the top of the competition ladder when he invested $10,000 to build a brand-new Top Fuel dragster.

Settling for nothing but the best available equipment, Leong enlisted Kent Fuller to build the chassis. It was a near duplicate to the *Greer-Black-Prudhomme* fuel dragster. The only difference was that the frame was stretched

With years of campaigning successful dragsters in the Top Eliminator Gas class under his belt, Leong invested a total of $10,000 in building his first Hawaiian *AA/FD. Kent Fuller did all of the chassis and steering work to nearly the same specifications of the Greer-Black-Prudhomme machine. The only difference was that the wheelbase was extended out to 136 inches, which was 4 more inches than the G-B-P car. All of the tubing was 4130 chrome-moly. The front wheels were also the product of Fuller. (Photo Courtesy Roland Leong Collection)*

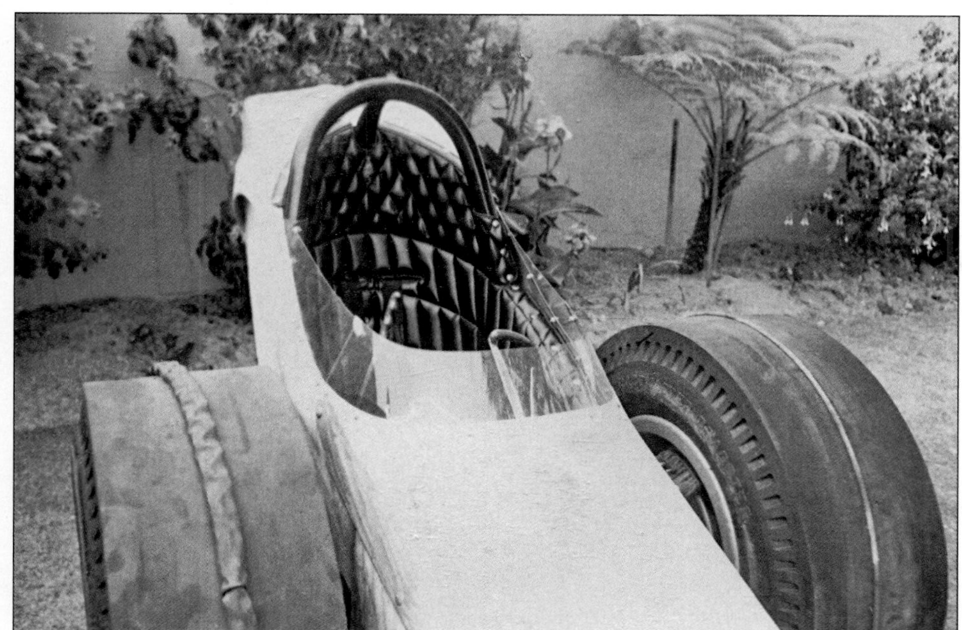

Upholsterer Tony Nancy stitched the black leather seat, which was designed to provide comfort to the driver at 200 mph. The car's final touches included the installation of a Keith Black 358 Chrysler Hemi. (Photo Courtesy Roland Leong Collection)

forward 4 inches. He searched out Wayne Ewing to fabricate the full-aluminum body, complete with a tail section.

Joe Anderson created the automotive equivalent of a classical masterpiece from the paint palette of Vincent Van Gogh. Anderson sprayed the body with beautiful sky blue Diamond Flake epoxy paint. Anderson added sculpted wood inserts made from genuine "island wood" that graced both sides of the rear tail section. The final touches to the body were the lettering finished in Bamboo Gold Leaf, giving the feeling that you were on the sandy beaches of Waikiki.

Since Leong never ran Hemi powerplants in his gas dragsters, he contacted the best in the business: Keith Black. Black built Leong's first nitro fuel–burning 358-ci Chrysler Firepower Hemi. Before Leong and Ongais went their separate ways, it was agreed that Ongais was to drive Leong's new Top Fuel car, the *Hawaiian*. When the pieces of the puzzle had fallen into place, Leong took the next steps by fulfilling his ambitions of being both a Top Fuel driver and owner.

The Unthinkable

On Saturday, October 4, 1964, after a year in the making, the long-awaited *Hawaiian* AA/FD made its debut. Leong chose Lions Drag Strip for the unveiling.

Don Prudhomme and Keith Black were there to help get Leong accustomed to the new car. As the team was busy preparing the car for Leong's Top Fuel licensing run, Black decided to be conservative by running straight alcohol in the tank. Leong thought, "What a waste."

Knowing the power provided by nitromethane, it was agreed upon by both Black and Prudhomme to be cautious, so a 40-percent nitro load was to be used. Roland measured the hydrometer several times, ending up with a 47-percent mixture that went into the fuel tank. Black checked the fuel while Prudhomme buckled Leong securely into the car. Leong was instructed to take an easy familiarization run in the new car.

When the car was pushed to life, the engine idle was way too low, and it died. After tipping more fuel into the tank and Black making a few adjustments, the car was pushed off down the strip. Leong made the turnaround

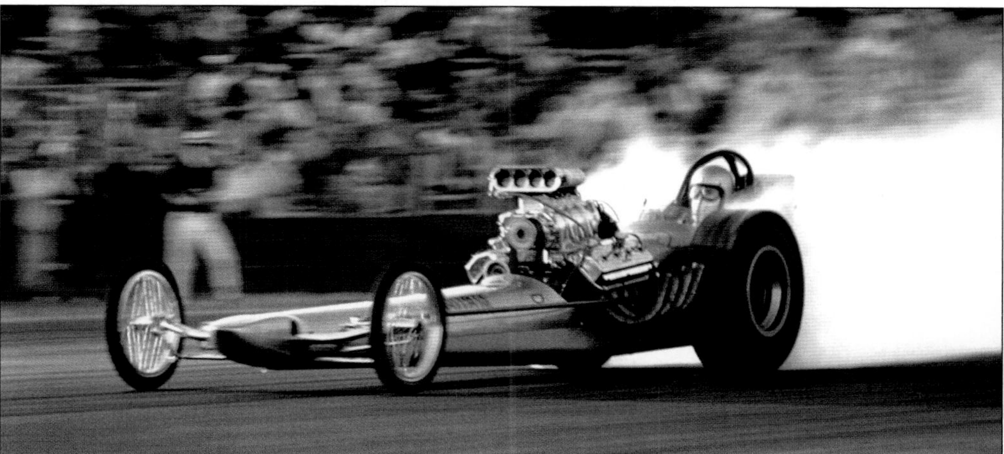

Leong made his maiden voyage in his new AA/FD Hawaiian *on Saturday, October 4, 1964, at Lions. This was the one and only time that Leong made the attempt to drive a nitro-fueled dragster, and it happened to take place on his licensing run. Under strict licensing rules, Leong was told to shut off at half-track, but he kept his foot on the gas pedal during the run, tripping the finish-line lights at more than 190 mph. The result of his mishap ended with Leong being banned from ever receiving a Top Fuel license from the NHRA. (Photo Courtesy Darr Hawthorne Collection)*

back toward the starting line. The car refired, coming to life with Leong making the sweeping turn toward the starting line.

The beautiful rail rolled into the staging beams, where Leong brought up the revs. When the tree hit green, he launched off the line like lightning, his foot burying the throttle to the floor for approximately 300 feet. After the planned throttle back off, he put his foot back into it again since it was looking to be a decent run.

In his blown gas Dragmaster cars, the chute release was located on the left side of the driver's cockpit and was pushed forward to deploy the chute. With his new fuel car, the driver needed to cross his right arm over the left shoulder to cross-pull the chute release ring. As Leong entered the traps at more than 191 mph, the car started to drift slightly to the left. It drifted farther left when Leong bumped the steering wheel in search of the chute release.

In what appeared to be slow motion, the *Hawaiian* ran off the end of the track, became airborne, turned sideways and right-side up, and came to rest way past the end of the strip on a set of railroad tracks. Huge clouds of dirt, dust, and debris obscured the view down the strip. Everyone was up on their feet with hearts in their throats. A hush fell over the stands as the crowd anxiously awaited news of Leong's fate.

Prudhomme and Black rushed to the wreck, and both were visibly shaken, thinking the worst. Leong remained conscious in the car but was obviously dazed and rattled. The only injury was seeing his new $10,000 race car suffering a badly damaged front end. The chassis buckled along with a crushed nose and lower body.

An upset C.J. Hart, the manager at Lions Drag Strip, read the follow-

MEMORABLE MOMENTS: Larry Sutton

"Here's the untold story of Roland's infamous crash at Lions," said Larry Sutton, the starter from the golden days of Lions Drag Strip. "Back in those days, we push-started the car, so when he rolled out to go down the lane, I had already been told that he was going to make a license run. I met up with him before, and I knew he liked to do his own thing. I went up to Roland sitting in the *Hawaiian* and told him, 'You must make a half pass, a half pass period!'

"Roland responded, 'Oh, okay.'

"Again, I said, 'Okay, only a half pass.'

"The push truck sent him off all the way down the strip and made the turn back toward the starting line on the return road. Roland came out of the short gate to about the 1,000-foot mark, pushing up the track. Right before the starting line, he applied the brakes, and the fuel in the tank went forward, which created an air gap in the fuel line, causing the car to lean out and die. He came to a stop and waited for the push truck to push him down again.

"Wes Hansen went to put more fuel in the tank so that it wouldn't get any more air. I went up to him again and told him again, 'Roland, you need to make a *half* pass.'

"I told Roland three different times. But I just knew that he was going to do his own thing.

"He replied 'Yeah, okay, right.'

"The push truck went back down again to the end, turned around, and came back up, this time with the engine running to the starting area, making the turn into the left lane.

"Roland pre-staged and staged the car and started his run. Going down the track he made a full run! I don't know if he got oil on his face or the deal with the parachute, but he did everything wrong, just the opposite of what I told him to do.

"The car kept drifting more and more to the left. With the fence ending on the left side, he went across into the rocks, went down the return road toward the end of the track, went up on the top of railroad tracks and somehow got turned around facing back toward the starting line. I went down there as fast as I could.

"Prudhomme was livid, he went down there as Roland was just sitting in the car semiconscious. Don was so upset that he basically started to throw up. He thought his buddy was killed. Well, later, he was okay. I cleaned up everything and went back to work.

"I told C.J. Hart that I told Roland *three* different times to make only a half pass. C.J. notified the NHRA of what happened. The NHRA called the Driver's Commission for a meeting on Monday.

"I was a Driver's Commission member for 28 years, and at the trail deal, I was called as a witness on what took place. At the time, there were three drivers in history that had been banned from driving in drag racing for life. Roland was now number-four.

"The decision was made on that Monday that Prudhomme would be doing the driving from that point forward. Soon after we revoked Roland's license, his mother sent a letter to the NHRA, thanking them for taking his driver's license away. In those days, switching over from a gas dragster to a Top Fuel dragster and driving a fuel car was more than a handful. They were dangerous.

"Roland had his mind made up on what he was going to do, and I knew it all along. Today, there is no animosity between us, and we stayed friends throughout the years. In fact, I'm just glad that he wasn't hurt, and I believe Roland was glad his license was taken away, as the outcome was absolutely a benefit for him."

ing statement to the press from the tower, "We're trying to get this driver's license program off the ground, as we tell 'em to make an easy run at 150 mph or less and shut down at half-track. No matter how much experience a driver has, they must get acquainted with a new car."

Leong smiled through a heavy dusting of sand and dirt and vowed to bring a new rail back in a few weeks. A lesser man might have been discouraged enough to throw in the towel and quit.

Leong called his mother (and sponsor) the next day (Sunday) to let her know what took place at Lions Drag Strip. After listening about the mishap, she proceeded to admonish him.

"Roland, keep in mind what you're doing," she said. "You're 20 years old, and you have a wife and newborn daughter. So, maybe it's time to reevaluate your racing career."

On Monday morning, Black called Leong into his office and said, "You scared me so bad; I wouldn't know how to explain what happened to your parents. I don't want you to get hurt or killed now that you're a husband and father. If you want to continue to drive, I won't build any engines for you."

Black strongly suggested that Leong hire Don Prudhomme to drive his car. It didn't take long for Leong to realize the dangers of driving and hang up his fire suit and concentrate on tuning and being a car owner. The newly merged team was the beginning of one of the greatest partnerships in the history of drag racing.

The "Comeback Kids" of the *Hawaiian*

On Saturday, November 28, the *Hawaiian* made its return to Lions Drag Strip after its unfortunate crash in October. Dubbed the "Comeback Kids," Leong, Black, and Prudhomme served notice when Prudhomme dropped a conservative 8.42 ET at 193.94 mph right off the trailer to qualify into the eight-car show.

In the first round of eliminations, the *Hawaiian* displayed the crushing power of giant surf thundering from a distant island beach. Prudhomme stormed to an 8.51 ET at 195.81 mph, drowning the Leffler & Woolford entry.

The semifinal round was a near duplicate run to the first round. The *Hawaiian* advanced to the finals after defeating the Duke-Ratican-Duke car. The Top Fuel final pitted the two quickest rails on the grounds: Wayne King, who was searching for his first win driving the Donovan Engineering entry, and Prudhomme, who was looking for the comeback in the resurrected *Hawaiian*.

As the two cars fired up and staged together, Prudhomme lived up to his reputation by striking first off the line. That edge led the Leong-Prudhomme *Hawaiian* to the win lights first with an 8.43 ET at 195.64 mph to King's quicker 8.38 at 191.48. When collecting the well-earned paycheck of $500 and the bonus cash, Prudhomme said, "The engine was beautiful tonight. The car handled well. It's got a 'special' Keith Black engine in it!"

Sunday's advertised Top Fuel show at Pomona was highly anticipated by many who were eager to witness record times and speeds. Sadly, subpar performances by the Fuelers were disappointing, as the big-name cars experienced blowups and breakage galore. Only five top rails made the call to the starting line, and only four officially made it off the line.

Despite all the carnage, the first-round pairing of rivals Tom "the Mongoose" McEwen, driving the purple terror *Yeakel Plymouth Special*, faced off against Don "the Snake" Prudhomme at the controls of the beautiful *Hawaiian*. Not only was this a top final round encounter and a supreme match race between two of drag racing's top drivers but it was also the battle of top West Coast tuner adversaries Jim Ward and Roland Leong.

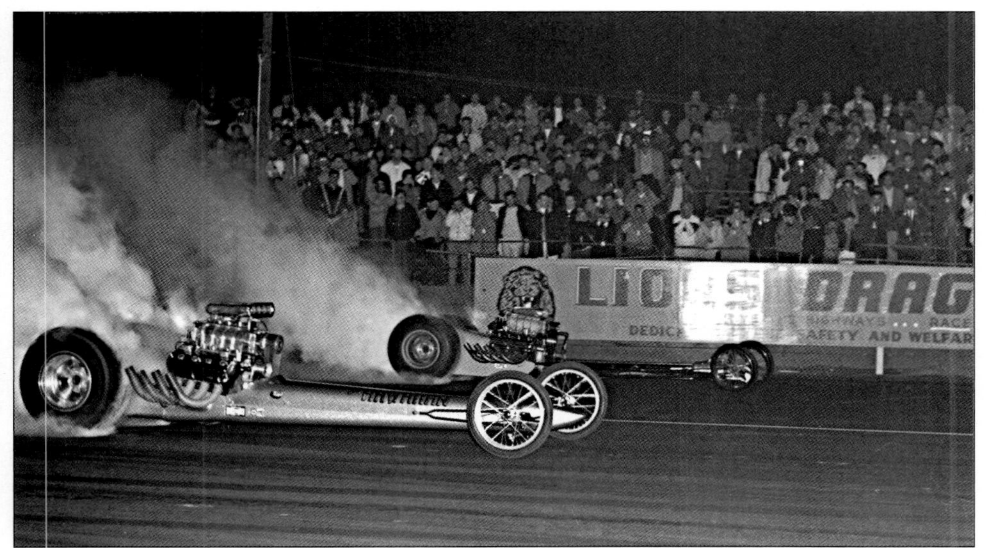

Returning to Lions Drag Strip after Leong's unfortunate crash, Don Prudhomme once again proved that he was one of the best out of the West when he drove the "revived" Hawaiian *past a powerhouse field into the winner's circle. Prudhomme didn't waste any time when he trailered Wayne King in the finals. (Photo Courtesy Tom Nelson Collection)*

Master handler Don Prudhomme is suited up and buckled into the cockpit, ready to be pushed off for a run in the Hawaiian *at Pomona. The Snake was the perfect fit to drive Leong's rail, a near clone of the Greer-Black-Prudhomme entry that Prudhomme drove to more than 250 wins. (Photo Courtesy Roland Leong Collection)*

The two race cars came to life and readied on the starting line. Prudhomme left first with McEwen behind him by the length of a wheel. The distance widened between the cars as the Snake blasted through the top end first, stopping the Chrondeks with a 7.75 ET at 202.24 mph. McEwen's race was over at the 990-foot mark when the

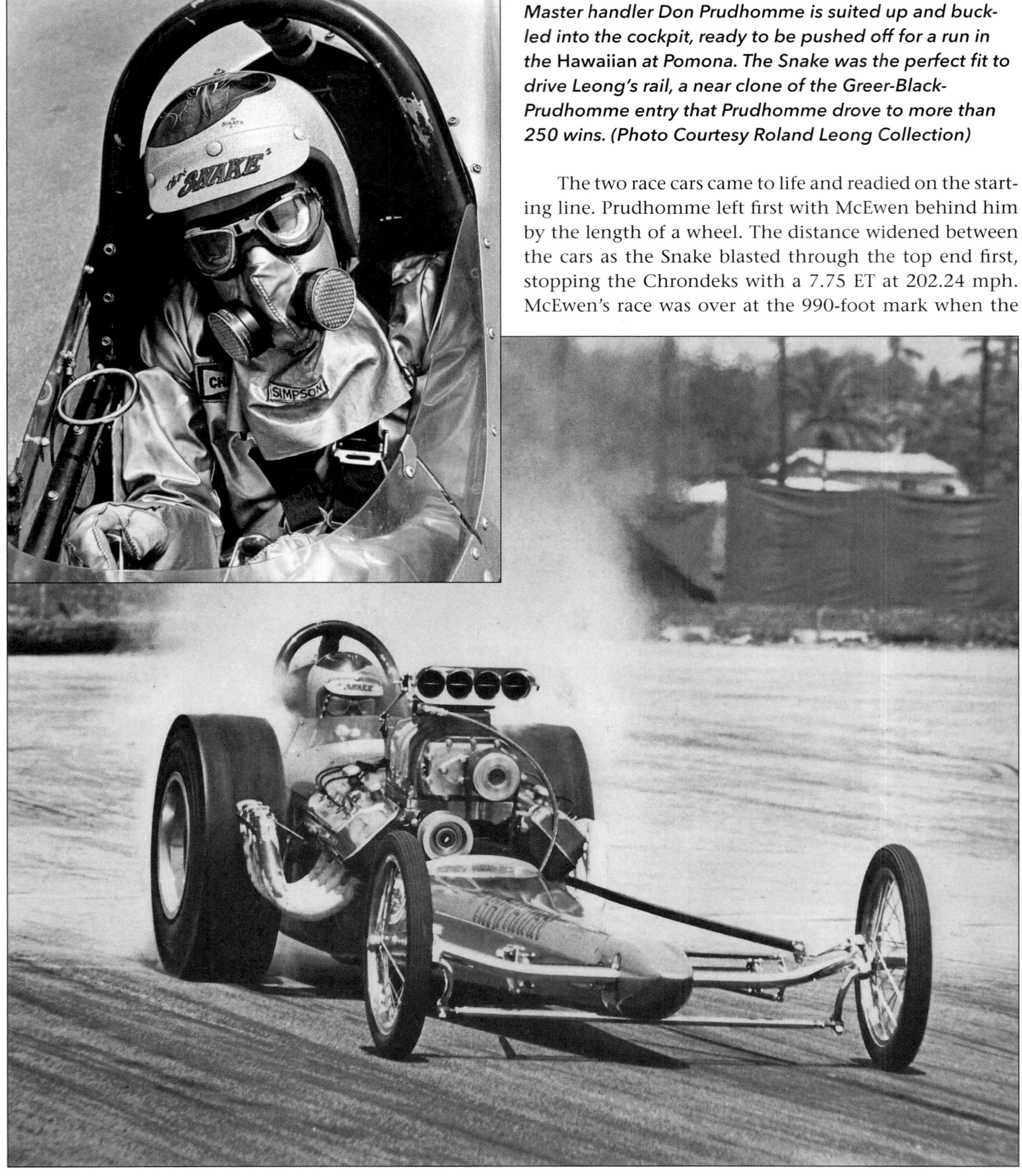

Prudhomme annihilates the M&H Racemasters en route to meeting the Chubasco *of Jack Ewell in the second leg of the Jackpot Circuit at Pomona. Local L.A. radio station KFWB created the special cash bounty for the Top Fuelers. With one Jackpot win under his belt, Prudhomme defeated Ewell in the final to earn the trophy and cash reward. (Photo Courtesy Roland Leong Collection)*

car slowed due to mechanical troubles, coasting to an 8.55 at 158.45.

This set up the finale between Jack Ewell in the *Chubasco* and the *Hawaiian*. The elimination round quickly unfolded, resembling more of a slapstick comedy routine than two highly touted heavyweight prize fighters punching it out at the ring of the bell. With engines fired up and running, both drivers simultaneously rolled their cars into the staging beams. As RPM levels increased, both engines experienced severe internal problems.

Both cars bogged off the starting line with massive clouds of smoke belching from the headers. Ewell gave up at mid-track, leaving the *Hawaiian* to crawl through the lights at a snail's pace that was too slow to register any speed. The weekend provided a glimpse of the future for the Leong-Black-Prudhomme team in the new year for Top Fuel.

The team won Top Fuel Eliminator at Lions Drag Strip and the Pomona Drags on Sunday. Pictured left to right at Pomona are Roland Leong, Wes Hansen, and Don Prudhomme. They graciously accepted the trophy and cash from the race queen at Pomona. (Photo Courtesy Roland Leong Collection)

This photo shows drag racing history in the making, as the beginning of two legendary careers is captured. (Photo Courtesy Roland Leong Collection)

The "Pineapple Express," which consisted of Roland Leong, Wes Hansen, (former crew hand of the Greer-Black-Prudhomme car), and Don Prudhomme were on the cusp of becoming the most phenomenal Top Fuel Dragster team in 1965. (Photo Courtesy Roland Leong Collection)

CHAPTER 2

1965: YEAR OF THE SNAKE

Like any professional drag racer's strategy, Roland Leong knew that he needed to combine the formula of having the best equipment, the know-how, and a driver of the highest caliber. He felt that he had that combination.

Don Prudhomme made his first appearance back at his old home track at San Fernando, simply known as the Pond. It had been nearly five years since he ran the track, and he was happy to give the spectators their first look at Leong's *Hawaiian*.

Prudhomme motored down the track through powerful headwinds in qualifying, where he ran

Car owner and super tuner Roland Leong polishes the immaculate body of his Hawaiian *Fueler that was hammered out of aluminum by Wayne Ewing, also known as the "Bonneville Body Bender." The paint was sprayed by Joe Anderson, and Jim Deist produced the 16-foot "ribbon" chute. Little did they know at the time that Leong, Prudhomme, and the* Hawaiian *would blaze a trail into drag racing's history books. (Photo Courtesy Roland Leong Collection)*

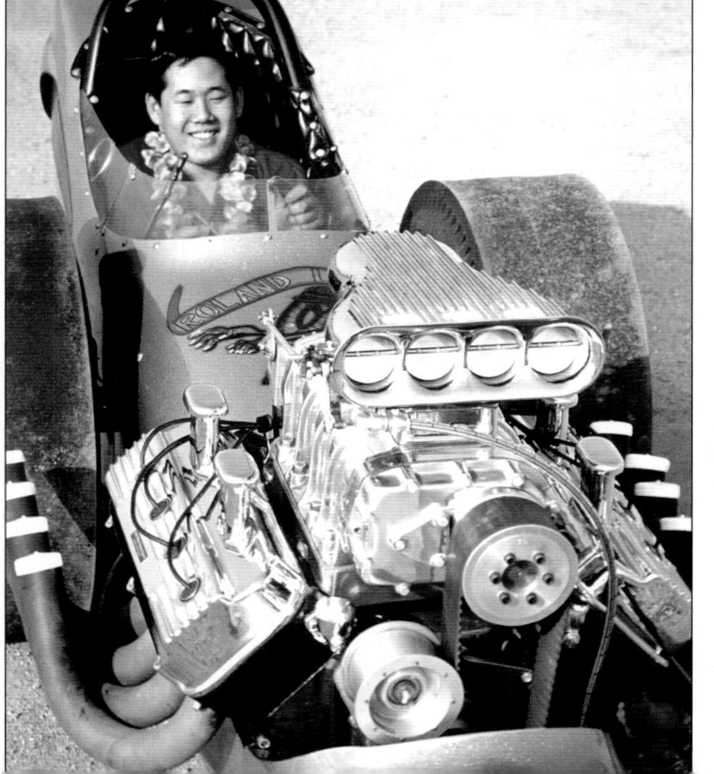

Leong checks out the view that driver Don Prudhomme is accustomed to seeing: the 1956 358-ci Chrysler Hemi that was the power and muscle behind the Hawaiian*. The Hemi was the product of mastermind Keith Black, and it packed a punch with nearly 1,200 hp. The stock-bore engine was assembled with a stock crankshaft by the Crankshaft Co. It had M/T rods, an Engle 440-5 roller camshaft, and Donovan rockers. The heads were Chrysler (ported and polished) with 2-inch intake and 11/16 exhaust valves with dual springs. The polished blower drive and intake manifold were from Cragar, and nitromethane was fed through fuel injection by Hilborn. (Photo Courtesy Roland Leong Collection)*

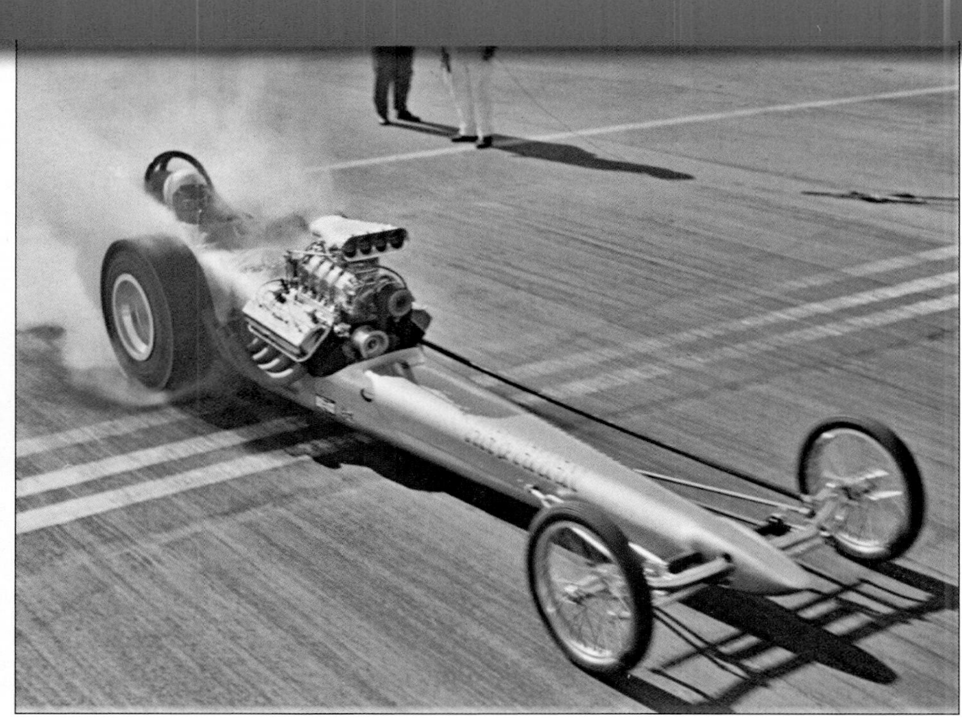

Don Prudhomme put the **Hawaiian** *through its paces at his hometown strip of San Fernando in January 1965. (Photo Courtesy Dave Wallace Sr.)*

an 8.14 ET at 196.06 mph. Bobby Tapia, "King" George Bolthoff, John Mitchell, Tony Nancy, Val LaPorte, Roger Wolford, "Wild" Bill Alexander, and the other drivers knew that it was going to be one of those days dealing with the fierce Santa Ana winds and facing the power of a Leong-tuned Keith Black Hemi.

Prudhomme and the *Hawaiian* cut through the field of competitors like a hot knife through butter. The final-round encounter faced Prudhomme with San Gabe's six-straight race champ "El Bandito" Bobby Tapia driving Jim Harbert's *Pegasus*.

Both engines were brought to life, and the cars were brought up to the starting line. As the drama set in, everyone pondered whether the six-time race champ Tapia would continue dominance or if the homecoming Snake would take center stage.

At the green, both cars moved out of the gate neck and neck until the absolute worst thing that could happen for Tapia and *Pegasus* occurred. The engine went dead silent. Prudhomme and the *Hawaiian* set a straight course toward the finish line with a 7.96 at 205.36 mph to collect the $500. With that, the *Hawaiian*'s winning streak began.

Lights, Action, and Traction

Just days before Lions Drag Strip's Saturday Top Fuel makeup event from the previous week, the strip was buzzing with the activity of a busy Hollywood television crew from Wednesday through the weekend with the filming of a handful of TV commercials. Also being shot was an episode from the popular *The Tycoon* series starring actor Walter Brennan as Dragster Andrews. The episode included the Top Fuelers of "TV" Tommy Ivo, George Bolthoff, and the *Hawaiian,* and Brennan enjoyed the time spent around the "real-action rails."

In qualifying, Prudhomme unleashed the supreme power of the 6.5L Keith Black Chrysler powerplant, careening through the traps with a 7.71 at a blistering 204.54 mph. The new track speed record at Lions Drag Strip now belonged to the *Hawaiian* of Leong and Prudhomme. By chance, a film crew from the British Broadcasting Company (BBC) was on hand

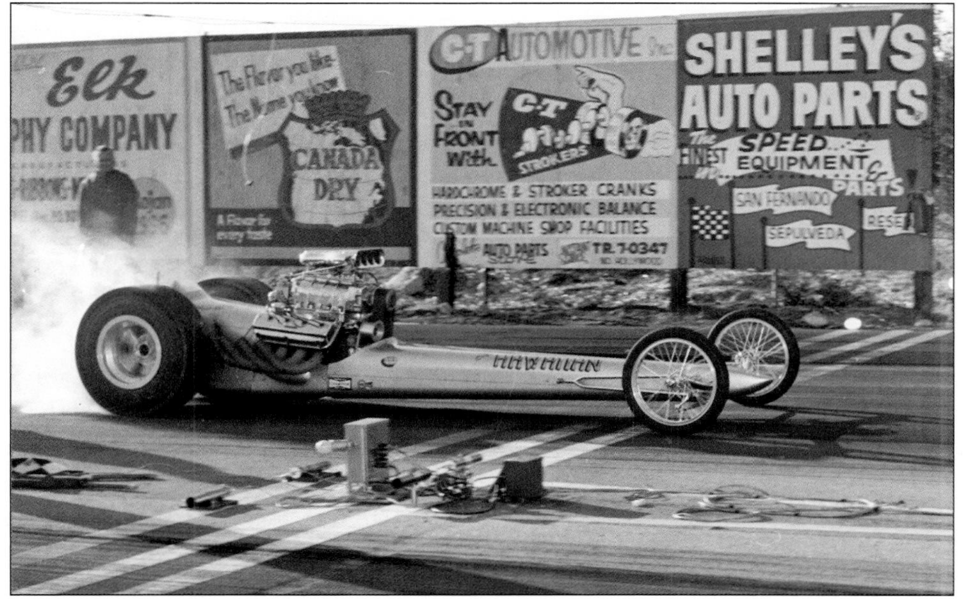

After a five-year absence racing at his home track, Prudhomme made his San Fernando return appearance one to remember. He made it look easy when he took home top honors. (Photo Courtesy Roland Leong Collection)

filming a special on the Southern California Fuelers and caught history with the 204-mph stunner.

The first round of eliminations brought the Lechien-Drake-Lear entry up to the line with Dick Lechien at the wheel facing Prudhomme. At the hit, the Snake muscled his way down to the top end, turning an 8.00 ET at 201.34 mph, which backed up the earlier 204.54.

The second round brought both local favorites to the line: James Warren wheeling the Warren-Colburn-Holloway rail against the blue islander *Hawaiian* of Leong-Black-Prudhomme. At the green, both cars left evenly, but the Snake pulled away easily for the win. Warren lost oil pressure when the oil-pump shaft sheared off the pump, demolishing the bearings.

In the money round, Danny "the Mangler" Ongais, in the seat of the Broussard-Davis-Garrison machine, faced Prudhomme. This was another first at Lions Drag Strip, as both cars and crews were running out of Black's shop. Moments before the cars were due to fire, large raindrops began to fall and became a steady downpour that lasted 45 minutes. The pits received the worst of the rain with flooding nearly forcing all the competitors out of their stalls. In the interest of safety, track manager C.J. "Pappy" Hart pulled the plug and split the Top Fuel money between the *Mangler* and the *Hawaiian*.

The "Big Go West"

The fifth-annual NHRA Winternationals drew 76 AA/FDs from all parts of the country in hopes of making it into the field of 32 at Pomona from February 5 to 7. Leong, Black, and Prudhomme arrived at the Pomona Fairgrounds, where the tipsters predicted that they had little to slim chance of pulling off the lucrative win at the giant of major winter drag events of the year. The Winternationals, known as the "Big Go West," parallels the excitement and pageantry of the annual National Championships over the Labor Day weekend in Indianapolis.

Friday morning dawned with unfavorable weather conditions, as heavy fog blanketed the entire San Gabriel Valley. Track conditions were slick and damp, and the track allowed limited qualifying runs in the Competition and Street Eliminator classes before noon. Qualifying in Top Fuel Eliminator began round 1 p.m. when the conditions improved. Right off the trailer, Don Garlits served notice as the one to beat when he charged through the top-end lights with a 7.81 ET at 206.88 mph. That speed held up throughout the weekend for Top Speed of the meet.

Next behind "Big Daddy" Garlits was the *Hawaiian,* and all eyes were focused on Prudhomme. Just as a light mist began to fall, the Snake thundered off the line, throwing thick plumes of white smoke up from the big Goodyears that shook the pavement all the way down the 1320. At the top end, Prudhomme was right behind Big Daddy's' 206-mph top speed with a 204.54 mph.

The crowd roared when it was announced over the public announcement system that the *Hawaiian* recorded the low ET of 7.80 seconds. Prudhomme edged Garlits by one tenth of a second. Some scratched their heads

MEMORABLE MOMENTS:

Don Prudhomme

"We didn't think about the money—we just wanted to go race," Don Prudhomme said. "We would have paid San Fernando to open the gates for us to go run the car. We would run at Long Beach on a Friday night, and for Saturday and Sunday, we'd find somewhere else nearby to run. We were always ready to go the next day, race wherever, and haul ass."

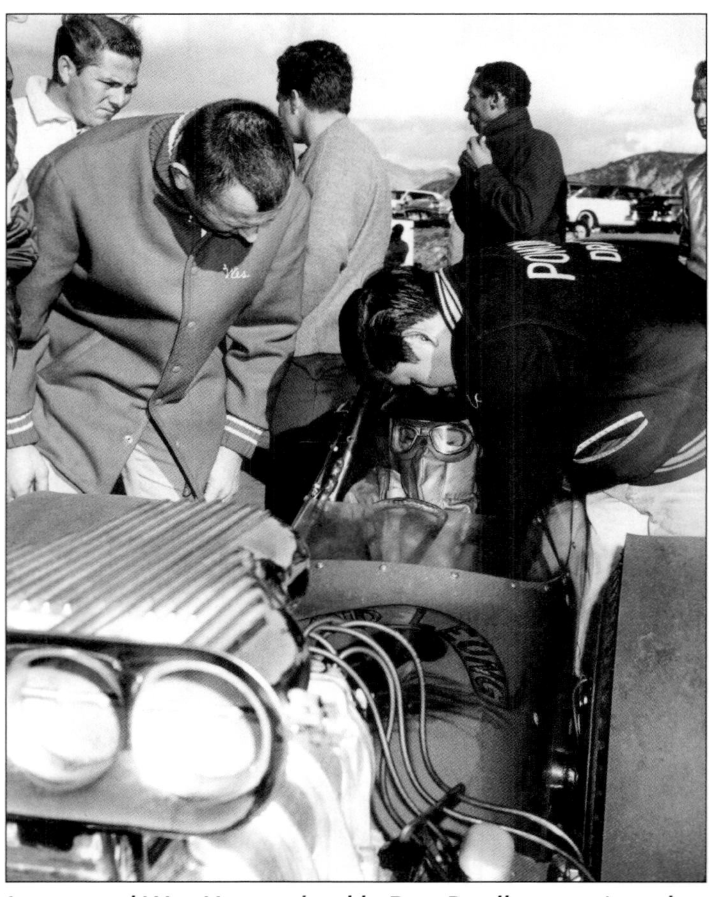

Leong and Wes Hansen buckle Don Prudhomme into the cockpit of the Hawaiian *at the Winternationals. (Photo Courtesy Roland Leong Collection)*

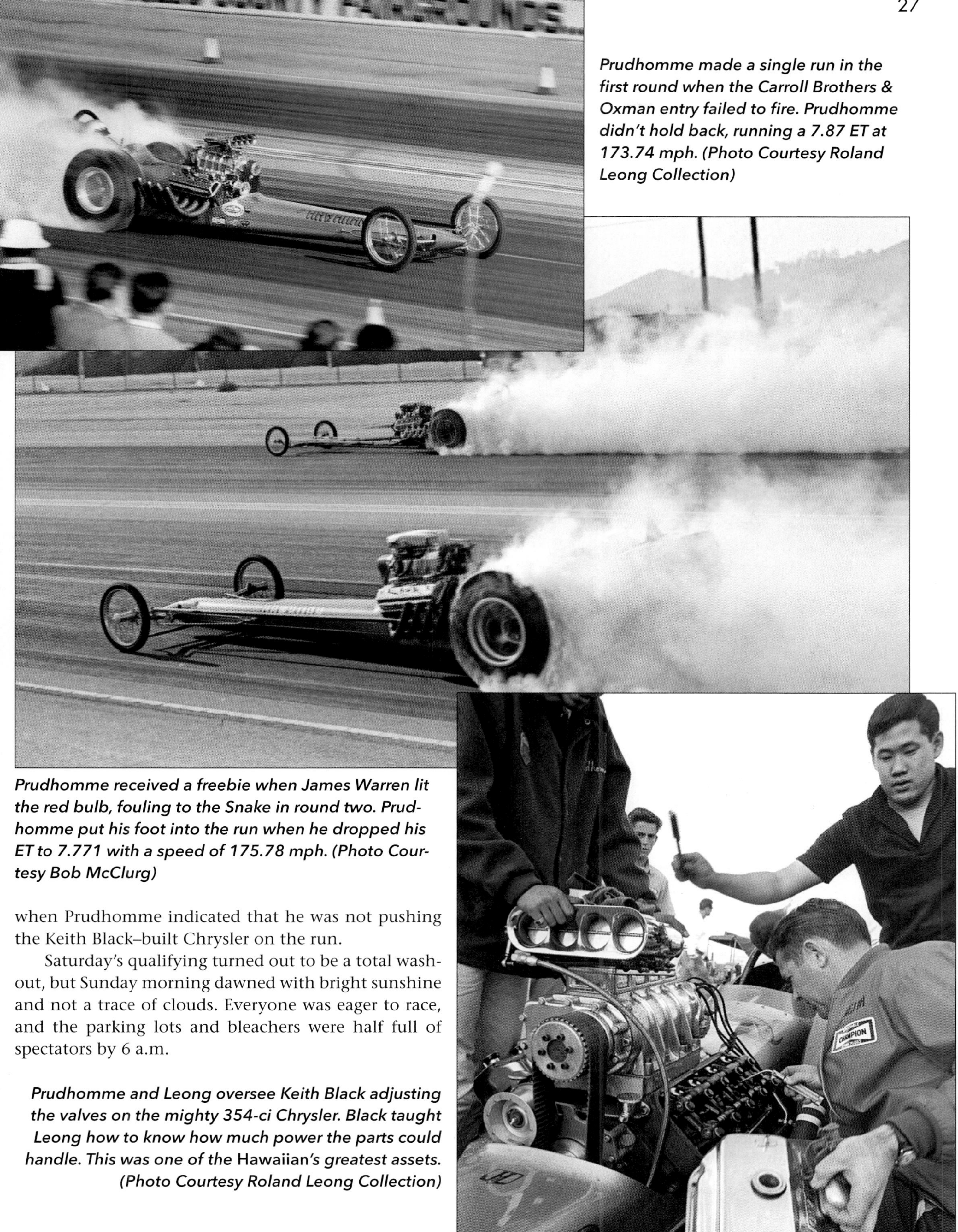

Prudhomme made a single run in the first round when the Carroll Brothers & Oxman entry failed to fire. Prudhomme didn't hold back, running a 7.87 ET at 173.74 mph. (Photo Courtesy Roland Leong Collection)

Prudhomme received a freebie when James Warren lit the red bulb, fouling to the Snake in round two. Prudhomme put his foot into the run when he dropped his ET to 7.771 with a speed of 175.78 mph. (Photo Courtesy Bob McClurg)

when Prudhomme indicated that he was not pushing the Keith Black–built Chrysler on the run.

Saturday's qualifying turned out to be a total washout, but Sunday morning dawned with bright sunshine and not a trace of clouds. Everyone was eager to race, and the parking lots and bleachers were half full of spectators by 6 a.m.

Prudhomme and Leong oversee Keith Black adjusting the valves on the mighty 354-ci Chrysler. Black taught Leong how to know how much power the parts could handle. This was one of the Hawaiian*'s greatest assets. (Photo Courtesy Roland Leong Collection)*

The fourth round at Pomona brought Rick "the Iceman" Stewart in the **Beacon Auto Special** *against the* **Hawaiian.** *At the green, it was all Prudhomme's race, as he easily disposed of Stewart with a 7.086 ET at 207 mph. The Iceman gave it his all but could only put together an off-pace 8.30 ET at 128.75 mph. (Photo Courtesy Roland Leong Collection)*

Another single pass for the Snake in round three propelled him into the semifinals. The fourth round pitted Rick "the Iceman" Stewart against the KB-powered *Hawaiian*. Prudhomme led the way to the finish line, running a 7.75 ET at 204.08 mph to Stewart's losing 8.30 at 128.75.

By late afternoon, it was time to give the command to the last remaining pair of Fuelers to send them down the push road. Both cars fired up simultaneously with the deafening sound of both thundering Hemis. Header flames and unburnt nitro were in the air as they idled toward the starting line. Not a seat was occupied from the crowd of 65,000 spectators. The crowd was on its feet, including the representatives from the three motion picture companies, the army of photographers and reporters representing numerous publications, and multiple cameramen from *ABC's Wide World of Sports*. All were anxiously anticipating the Hawaii versus California showdown between Don Prudhomme in the *Hawaiian* and "Wild" Bill Alexander in the *Alexander-Brissette* Fueler for top honors.

The field of Top Fuelers was set in place and ready to fire up. Don Prudhomme began his quest to the top in Top Fuel Eliminator with a single run of 7.87 at 173.74 mph when the Carroll Brothers & Oxman entry was unable to fire. Round two brought the *Hawaiian* and James Warren together, but Warren red-lighted away his chance to advance, giving the automatic win to Prudhomme.

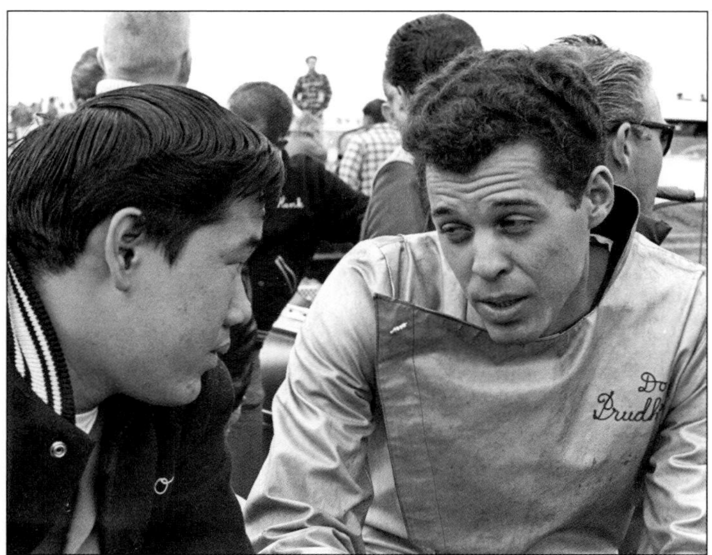

At the Winternationals, Leong listens to Prudhomme regarding the track conditions and preparing the tune-up before the final round against "Wild" Bill Alexander. Little did they know going into the final round that it would be a turning point for both of their careers. (Photo Courtesy Roland Leong Collection)

In a matter of moments, both cars rolled into the pre-stage and staged beams. Their engines revved up as the tree counted down the 3 seconds to the green. Both cars launched hard off the line like they were being shot from a bazooka! The Snake jumped out to the early advantage and never relinquished the lead. The *Hawaiian* crossed the finish line first, running a 7.776 ET at 201.76 mph to wrap up the coveted Top Fuel Eliminator title. Alexander trailed with a 7.92 at 198.22.

The unsung heroes of the NHRA need to get credit for their all-night prepping of the track, which allowed qualifying to get underway at 7 a.m. sharp. A total of 3,168 runs were made by 612 cars on Sunday in a 10-hour span. That averages 5.2 cars per minute.

As an added bonus for winning the NHRA Winternationals, Leong and Prudhomme received a brand-new Ford Camper pickup that was completely furnished, including a toilet. Both men immediately agreed to remove the toilet, as neither wanted to clean it. With the toilet gone, the truck was fitted with an auxiliary fuel tank so that they could travel farther with fewer fuel stops while on tour.

Don Prudhomme led the entire length of the track in the final round against Bill Alexander to earn the win and the coveted title of Top Fuel Eliminator. He also won a new camper Ford truck. The Snake posted a 7.776 ET at 201 mph in the triumph. (Photo Courtesy Roland Leong Collection)*

The trophy presentation at the prestigious Winternationals included Miss Winternationals, Leong's mother, Keith Black, Leong, Don Prudhomme, and Wes Hansen. (Photo Courtesy Bob McClurg)

ARTICIPANT
FIFTH ANNUAL
WINTERNATIONALS
CHAMPIONSHIP
DRAG RACES
PRESENTED BY
NATIONAL HOT ROD ASSOCIATION
A. COUNTY FAIR GROUNDS
POMONA, CALIF.
FEB. 5-6-7 1965
E— 1166

63 AA/FD
WINTERNATIONALS
NATIONAL HOT ROD ASSOCIATION
E.T. 7.876 MPH 173.74

63 AA/FD
WINTERNATIONALS
NATIONAL HOT ROD ASSOCIATION
E.T. 7.771 MPH 175.78

63 AA/F
WINTERNATIONALS
NATIONAL HOT ROD ASSOCIATION
BYE
E.T. 9.63 MPH ———

63 AA/FD
WINTERNATIONALS
NATIONAL HOT ROD ASSOCIATION
E.T. 7.806 MPH 204.74

63 AA/F
WINTERNATIONALS
NATIONAL HOT ROD ASSOCIATION
7.776 MPH 201.76
CIAL CHRONDEK TIME
LOSE ☐ WIN ☒

FIFTH ANNUAL
WINTERNATIONALS
CHAMPIONSHIP DRAG RACES
ONTESTANT
ENTED BY NATIONAL HOT ROD ASSOCIATION
NA, CALIF. FEB. 5-6-7, 1965

Post-race interviews included posing for photos from the winner's circle. From left to right are ABC television announcer Charlie Brockman, Don Prudhomme, Leong's mother, Miss Winternationals, Leong, Keith Black, and crewman Wes Hansen. (Photo Courtesy Roland Leong Collection)

The pieces of detailed history from the 1965 Winternationals show the time slips from each elimination round, as well as the participant tag and contestant sticker of the Hawaiian. (Photo Courtesy Mike Goyda/Roland Leong Collection)

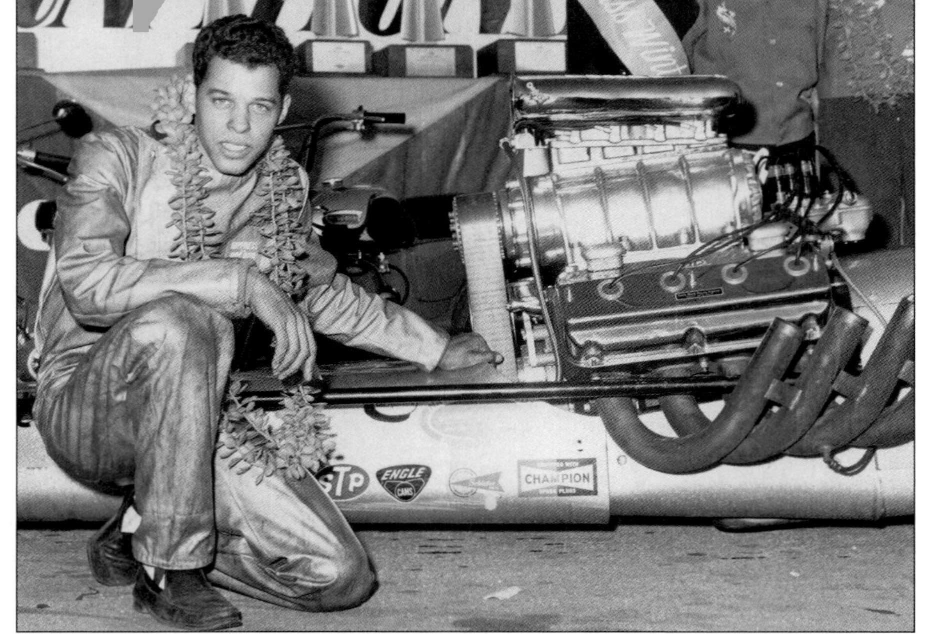

Don Prudhomme relishes the moment after winning the Winternationals. Prudhomme was at the right place at the right time when Leong crashed at Lions Drag Strip and was hired to drive the Hawaiian. *(Photo Courtesy Roland Leong Collection)*

Falling Short at Famoso

When the phrase "the greatest drag race on earth plus a little more" was heard, it wasn't taken too lightly with the abundance of Top Fuelers in attendance at the seventh-annual Smokers U.S. Fuel and Gas Championships at Bakersfield. In the field of 64 nitro rails, the *Hawaiian* qualified number-20 on Friday morning with a 7.82 ET.

Saturday's class eliminations saw Prudhomme advance out of the first round after running a 7.81 ET at 192.70 mph when Jack Ewell red-lighted. However, in round two, Tommy Ivo put the *Hawaiian* on the trailer, ending Leong's

ABC's Wide World of Sports *commentator Charlie Brockman asks Prudhomme about winning the three-day event as Leong looks on. What seemed to be an impossible dream a few months earlier, the Winternationals win layed the foundation of success for Leong and Prudhomme in the years to come. (Photo Courtesy Roland Leong Collection)*

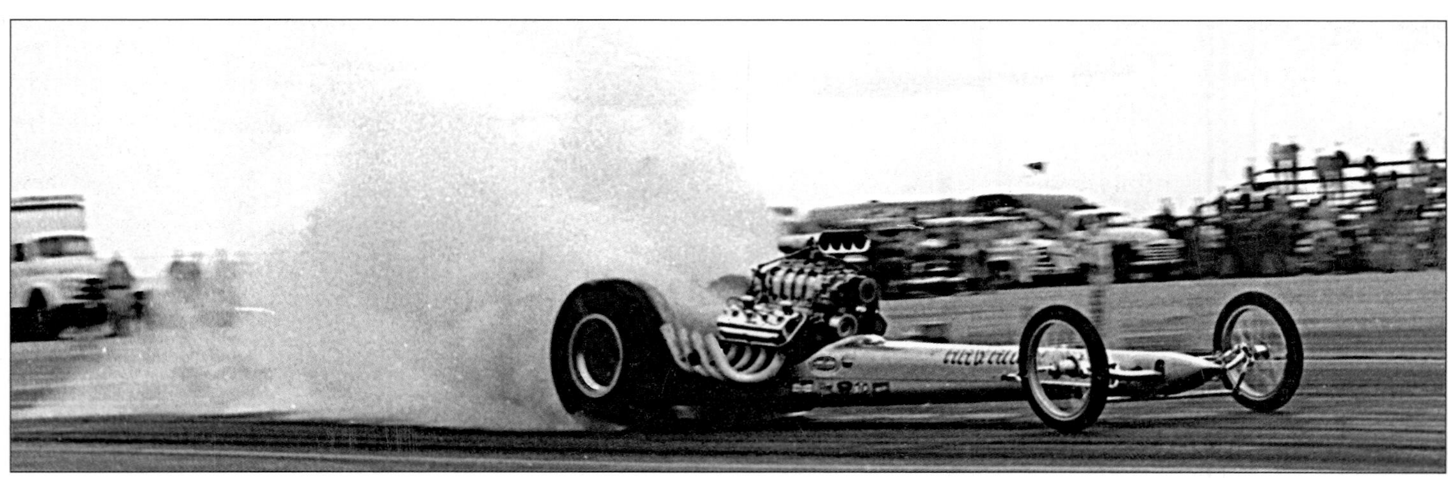

Don Prudhomme qualified the Hawaiian *in the 20th place overall in the 64-car field at the seventh-annual United States Fuel and Gas Championships at Bakersfield. Damp surface conditions from Saturday night's all-night rain delayed the start of eliminations. In the second round, Prudhomme lost a close one to Danny Ongais: 7.93 at 195.64 mph to 7.96 at 193.28 mph. (Photo Courtesy Roland Leong Collection)*

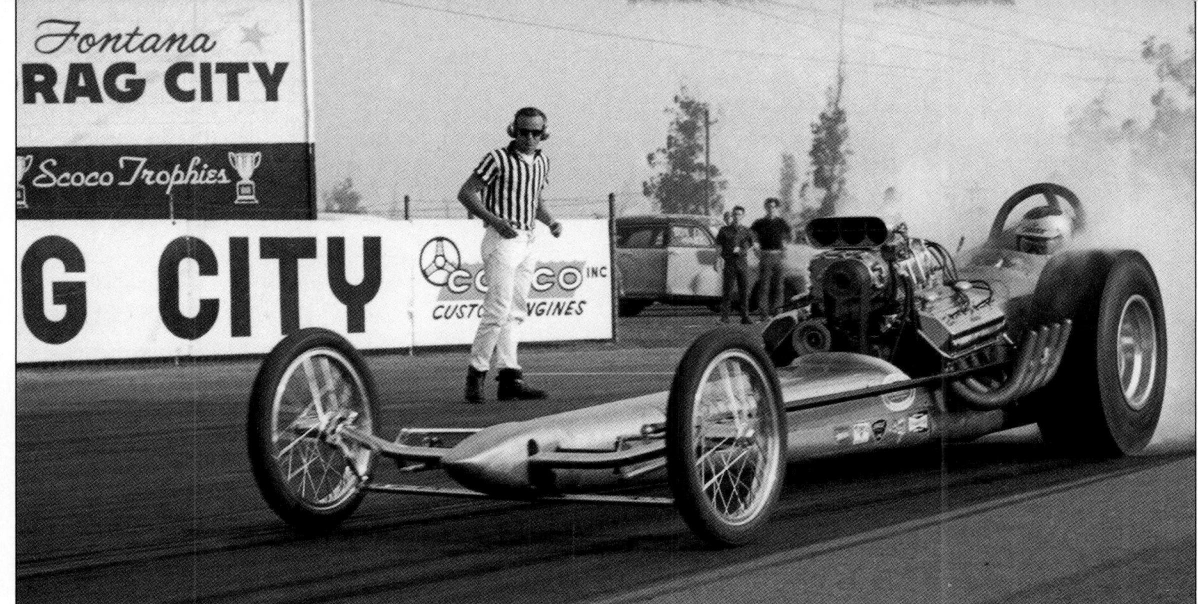

The Snake makes a qualifying pass of 7.86, which kept him into the hunt for $1,000 at Fontana's Drag City. (Photo Courtesy Roland Leong Collection)

and Prudhomme's day. During Sunday's eliminations, Danny "the Mangler" Ongais defeated Prudhomme in the first round.

Prudhomme Grabs Top Honors at Drag City

Drag racing can be described by using the following idiom: once you fall off the horse, you get right back on. It didn't take long for the *Hawaiian* gang to return to its winning ways. The Snake muscled his way back into the winner's circle on March 20 at Fontana's Drag City.

With the first day of spring and the return to Saturday-night racing, Fontana hosted 16 of the top West Coast Fuelers for a special $1,000 cash Top Eliminator prize. The *Hawaiian* breezed through the star-studded field only to have Doug "the Fatman" Robinson stand in the way. Robinson's *Horsepower Engineering* car gave it a valiant try but was sent home by the *Hawaiian* when Prudhomme unloaded a 7.76 ET at 197.80 mph to the Fatman's losing 8.08 at 189.06.

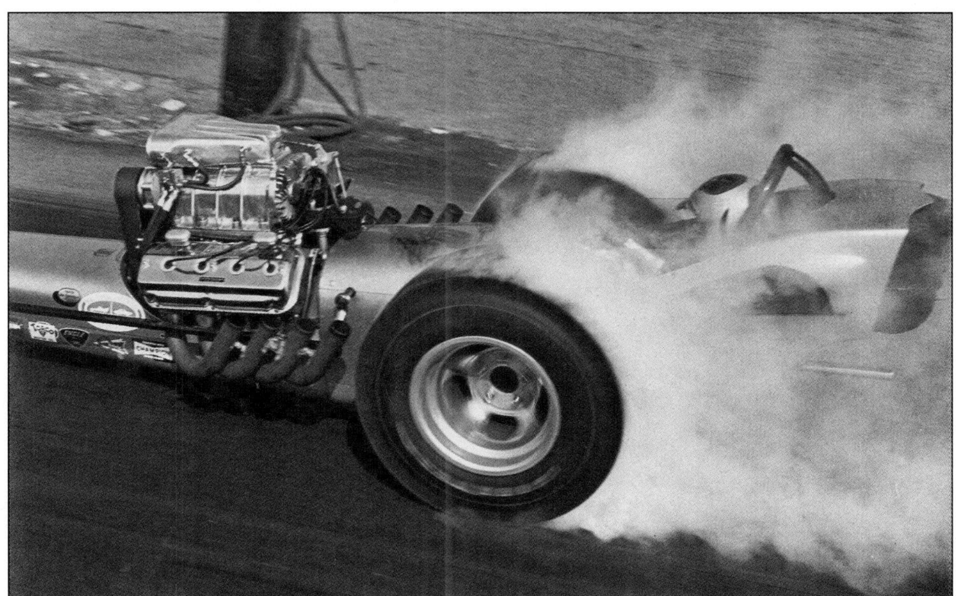

The Snake annihilates the Goodyears down the exceptional surface of Fontana. Track promoter Jack Tice couldn't have picked a better time with the weather when racing returned back to nights on the first day of spring. (Photo Courtesy Roland Leong Collection)

Don Prudhomme "pangs" the pedal on a single run at Drag City, posting a speed of 168.85 mph when first-round opposition Bill Adair lost fire. (Photo Courtesy Don and John Ewald Collection)

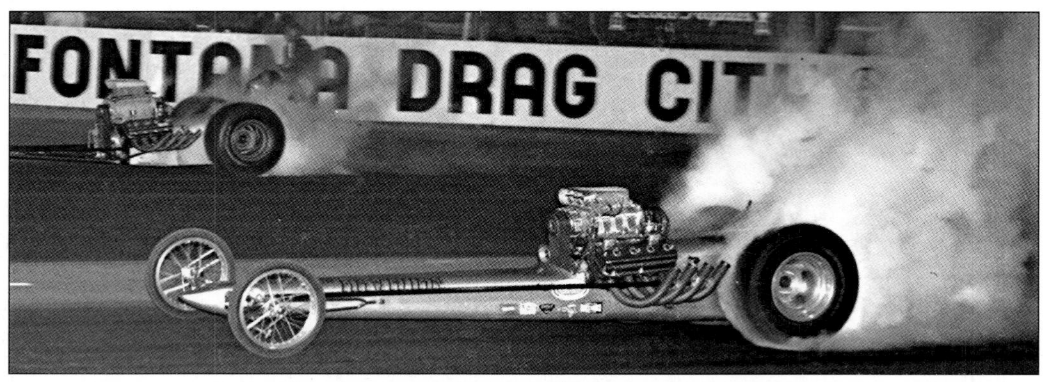

The semifinal charge of the **Hawaiian** *put another worthy opponent on the trailer when Dave Babler lost parts from the engine at mid-track, slowing to an anemic 8.82 ET at 142.68 mph. Luckily for Prudhomme, he won when he ran an off-key 7.94 ET at 171.10 mph, making it to the finals. (Photo Courtesy Roland Leong Collection)*

MEMORABLE MOMENTS: Wes Hansen

"Originally, I met Tom Greer, who had a boat (a Mandella) that he was selling," said Wes Hansen, who was a former *Hawaiian* crewman. "I bought it from him, and we became friends.

"I had a cabin at Bass Lake, and Tom and his wife would come up and visit me. After getting to know Tom, I got to meet Keith Black and was around them when they had the old *Greer-Black-Prudhomme* car. This is when I met Don. I knew Keith when he just had a van and was taking alternators, starters, and fan belts to various service stations. From there in his garage, he started to build engines and had one mechanic.

"Keith built his first blown engine for me for my boat. This was how I started with Keith and Tom to help on the dragster. I didn't have any money in the car, but I would spend time with them at the races for those years. When racing was costing him more money to race, Keith decided to stop racing to concentrate on making more money building engines. Since Keith had the best parts available, many racers wanted his engines. Keith was building his new shop when Roland came in and asked him to build an engine for his new *Hawaiian*. When Roland crashed his dragster at Lions Drag Strip, Roland hired Don to drive his *Hawaiian* under Keith's suggestion, and I moved over to help them.

"I was about 15 years older than Don and probably a little older than Roland, but I just thought about the world of the boys! I started coming down from my cattle ranch in the Hanford-Corcoran area in California every weekend and would go racing every weekend with them. In 1965, we won Pomona and then went to Indy and won the Nationals. The day after Indy, we won Detroit's All-Star Race. That was a great week!

"The following year, now with Mike Snively driving, we repeated our big wins again at Pomona and Indy. The following weekend, we went to Chicago to race, but the event was rained out. We all flew home, but I never got back much into racing because I had to take care of my cattle business and farming. My boys now were getting bigger, and I didn't want to miss any more time with them, so I kind of quit racing.

"I bought a home in Borrego Springs, and the boys came down on a weekend to play golf. 'Let's go to Pomona for the Winternationals,' I said. 'I like to see the dragsters and the Funny Cars and my old buddies.'

"They kind of looked at me, laughed, and said, 'Oh yeah, haha.'

At Pomona, we walked around, and when we got to Don's pit area, he spotted me, put his arms around me, and said, 'Come inside and sit down.'

"I got to see his wife, Lynn, as well, and she gave me a hug, asked how I had been, and said that it was great to see me. I got to meet their daughter Donna and told her (while laughing), 'The last time I saw you, you had just been born, and your mommy was changing your pants.'"

Cutting It a Little Too Close

The second-annual Hot Rod Magazine Championships were from June 18 to 20 with nearly every named rail in the country in attendance. The *Hawaiian*, *Old Master*, *Yeakel Plymouth Special*, *Frantic Four*, the *Surfers*, and the *Bounty Hunter* were just a few of the 100-plus entered for the 32-car field.

Don Prudhomme qualified number-one on Friday with a 7.65 at 207.36 mph that was the top time and speed on Friday. Sunday's first-round eliminations brought Bill Scott to the line in the Chevy-powered *Scotty's Muffler* against the Winternationals champ: the *Hawaiian*. Scott knew that he would need a miracle to overtake Prudhomme and executed a gargantuan wheelie that gave Prudhomme the easy win, but Prudhomme didn't lighten up when he pulled hard on the pass down through the lights.

"The car was really making it," said Prudhomme, who had runs of 7.54 at 211.76 mph that tied for top speed of the meet with archrival Tom "the Mongoose" McEwen.

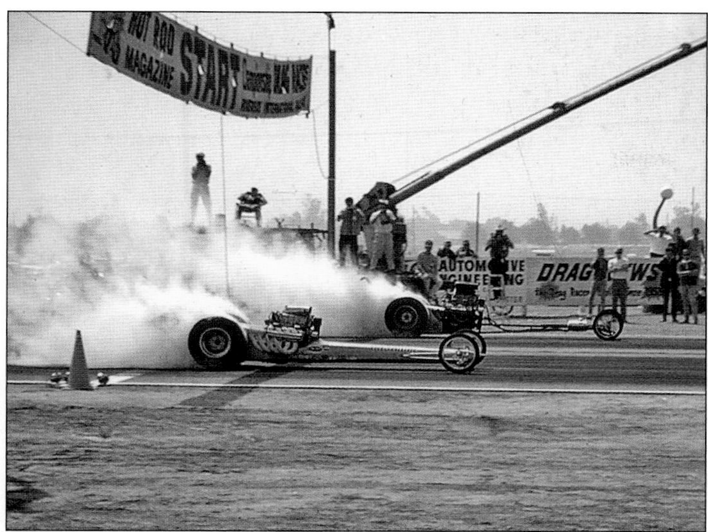

The AA/FD of Dunn & Yates jumps out of the gate first as the Hawaiian *suffers "death smoke" when Keith Black cut the injector bypass too fine, ending Prudhomme's chances to advance. (Photo Courtesy Steve Reyes)*

However, that run took its toll. The second round pitted Jim Dunn against Prudhomme. The *Hawaiian* visibly displayed "death smoke" from the engine that indicated it didn't have much life left.

CHRYSLER PARTS
MOPAR
Spark ★ Lines
PARTS AND SERVICE • VOL. 8 • NO. 7 • JULY, 1965
CHAMPIONSHIP TEAM

Chrysler's Spark Lines *monthly parts and service magazine recognized Leong, Black, and Prudhomme's* Hawaiian *on its front cover, honoring the super team for its accomplishments at Pomona and throughout the year. (Photo Courtesy Roland Leong Collection)*

Success Changed the Lives of Leong and Prudhomme

The *Hawaiian* won two Top Fuel Eliminator crowns in Southern California on its first weekend back in competition with Prudhomme in the seat. This achievement was followed by two more AA/FD Eliminator titles and four new strip records, including the new top-speed record of 204.74 mph at the American Hot Rod Association's (AHRA) Winter Nationals at Phoenix.

Now, after the performance at the NHRA Winternationals in Pomona, Leong's phone rang constantly from each of the top strip promoters and owners throughout the country. The Snake, Leong, Black, and the *Hawaiian* took on match races and competed in the major independent, big-named meets throughout the summer months. Leong indicated to the media that Prudhomme would do all the driving the entire season.

No matter how bright racing looked for both Leong and Prudhomme, there was a huge roadblock: how would Roland convince Don to quit his day job painting cars at Holiday Auto Body in the Sherman Oaks neighborhood of Los Angeles, California? There were pros and cons of being a professional drag racer. The pros included the opportunity to make a better living with larger paychecks and guaranteed income.

An early stop on the summer tour landed the Hawaiian *up in Northern California at Half Moon Drag Strip with a match race between "Terrible" Ted Gotelli and the* Hawaiian. *(Photo Courtesy Steve Reyes)*

The cons included extremely long hours, thousands of miles out on the road, traveling from state to state, and being away from family in the summer months.

It took Leong hours of convincing and persuasion with both Don and Lynn Prudhomme. They all finally agreed, and Prudhomme quit his job to become a full-time racer. This was the last time that Prudhomme and Leong ever worked a regular job.

Seeing all the possibilities in making money, Leong sat down with Prudhomme to map out their tour plans. They decided to start in the early spring in the Northern California area, stopping at Half Moon Drag Strip, Fremont, and Sacramento, and then they continued to Colorado, Texas, and more. For Leong, this was the first time he experienced seeing and driving through snow as well as traveling up the Grapevine, which is the mountain pass of the southwest end of the Tehachapi Mountains that links Southern California and the Central Valley.

East Coast Swing

The first stop was in Rockford, Illinois, to run at Rockford Dragway on July 18, 1965, to run a match race against Art Malone and his *U.S.A. 1* Jet Dragster. A stop the following weekend was at Alton Dragway under the lights against Midwest Champ Bob Murray in his AA/FD *Faifer-Murray* rail. Just like that, Leong and Prudhomme were on the road for three months as they barnstormed the Midwest and East Coast.

While in Illinois, Leong was approached by someone who asked to buy the camper, and Leong didn't hesitate to sell it. Right after, he went to Mr. Norm's Dodge Dealership, where he bought a new station wagon. It fit the bill for driving and towing the trailer.

Week in and week out, Leong and Prudhomme set ET and speed records at each venue, including Drag City's AHRA International Race of Champions, U.S. 30 Drag-O-Way's Drag News Invitational, Rockford Dragway's Drag a Go-Go Beach Party, and Cecil County's Traction Capital of the World.

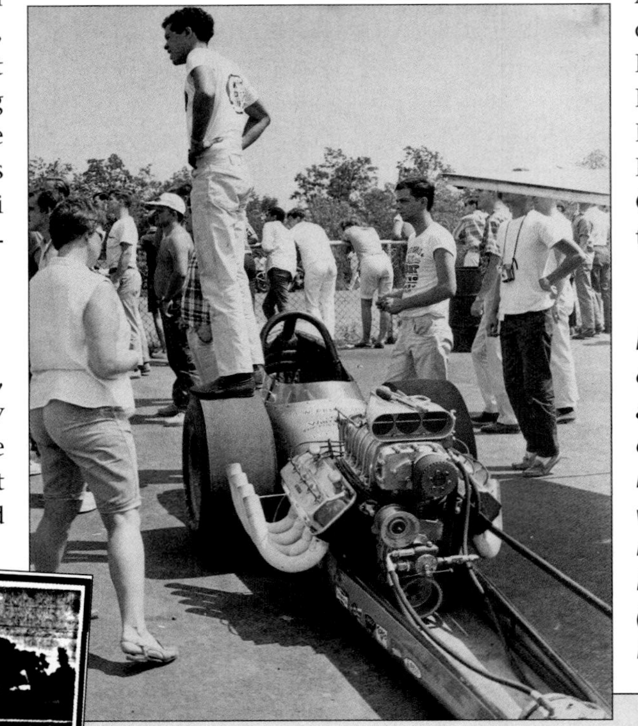

Don Prudhomme scopes out the starting-line action between rounds during the Hawaiian's *match-race encounter with Ford standout Connie Kalitta at Connecticut Dragway in East Haddam. (Photo Courtesy Roland Leong Collection)*

Jumping headfirst into match racing, the first stop was Rockford Dragway to run against the U.S. No. 1 *Jet Dragster of Art Malone.*

Connecticut strip manager and promoter Frank Maratta knew how to book in the biggest dragster personalities in the business. This included a best-of-three grudge match race between the Ford SOHC-powered Bounty Hunter *of Connie Kalitta and the authoritative Chrysler Hemi of Leong's* Hawaiian. *(Photo Courtesy Roland Leong Collection)*

MEMORABLE MOMENTS:

Don Prudhomme

"We'd win everything," Don Prudhomme said. "I mean everything! The *Greer-Black-Prudhomme* car won its share of races, and the *Hawaiian* was just like it but even better. I would say that Keith was the most responsible for the success we had and how well we ran. It was Keith who would set up the engine, the cubic inches, the blower overdrive, and the magneto. It was his baby.

"He showed Roland how to tune it, and I drove it. I wasn't into the tuning. We didn't tear anything up because of Roland. Roland knew how hard to run it just by looking at the spark plugs, pistons, and stuff like that. We'd be out on the road running three days a week with only changing oil or spark plugs, adjusting the valves, and making another run. It was just the best ever!"

Retrospectively, the *Hawaiian*'s success proved to be outstanding on its first leg of the Eastern tour. When the *Hawaiian* debuted in New York, Washington D.C., and Connecticut, crowds poured through the gates to catch a glimpse of the West Coast Top Fuel phenoms. They were the Beatles of drag racing, setting attendance, track ET, and speed records nearly every time they rolled through the gates. The high winning percentage of their races carried the California image with respect, performance, and excellence.

In the Battle of the West Coast Fuelers on August 15, 1965, Prudhomme beat "TV" Tommy Ivo in the heavily advertised match race in East Haddam, Connecticut.

On the return road back to the pits, the *Hawaiian* team was greeted by the fans in the stands with a thunderous, standing ovation and roaring cheers. No other Top Fueler in drag racing history had amassed a longer string of victories and records by a car out on tour!

The Midwest in 1965

The full summer swing brought the *Hawaiian* through the mid-section of the country when Prudhomme and Leong stopped at Detroit's Motor City Dragway, known as the drag racing capital of mid-America, on Sunday, August 22. The main event was a match race between "Sneaky Pete" Robinson, in his new Ford SOHC *Tinker Toy Too*, and the *Hawaiian*.

Fans drove for hours, coming out in droves just to see if the record-setting dragster from the West Coast could be beaten by the favored Robinson. The first round went according to plan, as the Snake took the early lead and easily ran away from the squirrely *Tinker Toy Too*. Prudhomme ran the quarter with a 7.62 ET at 196.92 mph, while Robinson shut off early due to mechanical problems, only able to muster a 10.31 at 77.92.

It was determined back in the pits that Robinson found lower bracing on the chassis that had broken the weld, which ended his racing day. Seeing that the situation could turn the crowd hostile, track operator Leo Martin sought out Maynard Rupp, who was helping with tuning for the Nationals. Both Rupp and Leong agreed to the substitution, but Rupp needed a few hours to leave the track to go to his shop and put his car together.

Rupp returned to the track with an AA/FD car called the *Prussian*, and the match racing resumed. Prudhomme took two straight from Rupp: 7.89 at 198.65 mph and 7.73 at 201.34 mph (he saved the best for last). The *Prussian* gave it a valiant effort, turning in runs of 8.13 at 183.66 mph and 7.91 at 198.65 mph.

The 1965 U.S. Nationals

The first Nationals was held at the Great Bend Municipal Airport in Great Bend, Kansas, in 1955, but since then, the Nationals relocated to Indianapolis, where the event has grown to astronomical proportions.

More than 1,300 entries from every corner of the country invaded the five-day holiday weekend that opened on Thursday with time trials and qualifying for each of the non-pro classes. On Friday, the pros took to the strip to kick off qualifying. Class runoffs were on Sunday, and overall elimination finals concluded the event on Monday.

The 1965 Top Fuel "Invincible Team" of Keith and son Kenny Black, Wes Hansen, Leong's mother, Leong, and Don Prudhomme was ready to compete at the Nationals. (Photo Courtesy Roland Leong Collection)

The Fueler class featured some of the hardest-fought competition seen in years on the Nationals' stage. During Friday's qualifying sessions, Ivo was bumped in and out of the program four times and "Big Daddy" Don Garlits sat on the bump for a time after posting an 8.03 ET, which was a far distance from the Ramchargers' Don Westerdale, who set the pace running a 7.50 ET at 210.66 mph. Sitting in the third slot was the *Hawaiian* with a 7.654 ET.

Repeat Performance

In Sunday's class finals, 38 AA/Fuelers came together for one of the wildest class runoffs that was ever seen at the Nationals. The car that won the class eliminations earned the right to sit out all day Monday until the final round to race the winning competitor who made it through Monday's 32-car field to get to the final round.

The low ET in the first round was split between the Carroll Brothers & Oxman of Texas and the *Hawaiian* of Leong-Black-Prudhomme at 7.81.

The second-round low ET was again captured by Prudhomme with a 7.68 that tied for top speed with the Westerdale-driven Ramchargers entry at 201.34 mph. The only difference was that the *Hawaiian* put the factory-backed Ramchargers on the trailer. It was also satisfactory for the non-factory-sponsored car out of the Keith Black racing stables to defeat the candy-striped rail.

In round three, the *Hawaiian* and Prudhomme were running at full steam once again, as Prudhomme set both low ET and top speed of the round, defeating Vodnik-Belfatti's *Shadow* with 7.63 ET at 202.24 mph.

The fourth round brought a pair of California Fuelers to the line: the *Mangler* of Broussard-Ongais-Davis and the fabulous *Hawaiian*. As the smoke cleared, it was the ferocious Keith Black–powered *Hawaiian* that tripped the win light, lowering the ET and top speed once more for the round at 7.59 at 204.08.

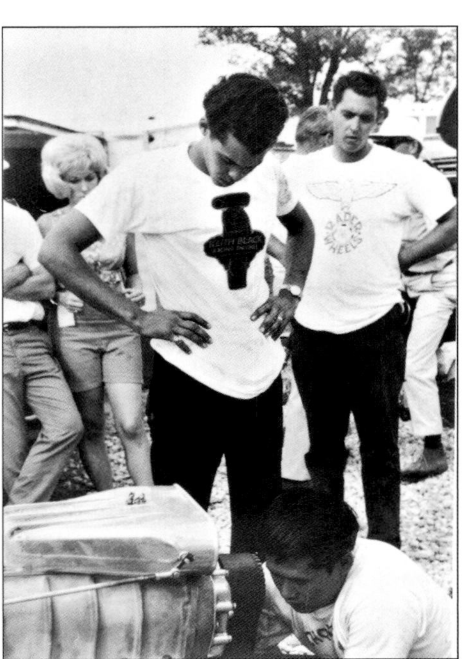

The Snake keeps abreast on Leong's preparation to the Keith Black Chrysler Hemi before Monday's final round of Top Eliminator. (Photo Courtesy Roland Leong Collection)

The stage was set for the finale showdown of Jimmy Nix and the Snake for the class honors. The highly touted run for the money and gold was over in a split second when Nix lit the red bulb and shut off, saving his engine for Monday's finals. The *Hawaiian* sent out the message that it was the car to beat, lowering the ET (7.60) and resetting the top speed of the day (205.54 mph).

The weekend performance of the *Hawaiian* was quickly unfolding into a carbon copy of the past February's Winternationals, as Prudhomme outclassed the AA/Fuel dragster field once again.

Who Can Beat the *Hawaiian*?

The pre-race buzz for Monday's overall Top Fuel Eliminator title ran rapidly through the Fueler camps. Many were wondering if the likes of the Ramchargers, Garlits, Ongais, Kalitta, or any other formable foe could put the *Hawaiian* on the trailer.

The other question came from the reporters that floated around: Could Prudhomme, Black, and Leong repeat the performances from the previous day and get the opportunity to duplicate their win at the Winternationals?

The mighty *Hawaiian* had already earned the right to sit it out until the final run on Monday afternoon. After the pre-race activities with all the pomp and circumstance and driver introductions concluded, the first round of Top Fuel kicked off without delay.

"TV" versus Hawaiian

Fellow Californian and former childhood actor "TV" Tommy Ivo waded through the tough field of the nation's top Fuelers to earn the spot to run in the final act of the day to be "the King of Indy."

As producer and director Buster Couch brought the final act up to the line, Ivo earned an audition for the role of slaying the "Eliminator Title," but Roland and Teddy Leong, Keith Black's Pineapple-juiced Chrysler Hemi, and the venomous Deist-suited Snake were ready for the call.

At the flick of the switch, the anticipated race was over immediately when Ivo turned the car sideways right off the line. Prudhomme soared through the top end with a 7.50 ET at 207.33 mph to Ivo's fruitless 7.81 at 202.71.

Prudhomme was handed the keys to a new 1965 Plymouth Barracuda as one of the added rewards in winning the Top Fuel Eliminator. Along with the money from the round, the *Hawaiian* team received a Ford SOHC 427 racing engine and more than $5,750 in cash and merchandise.

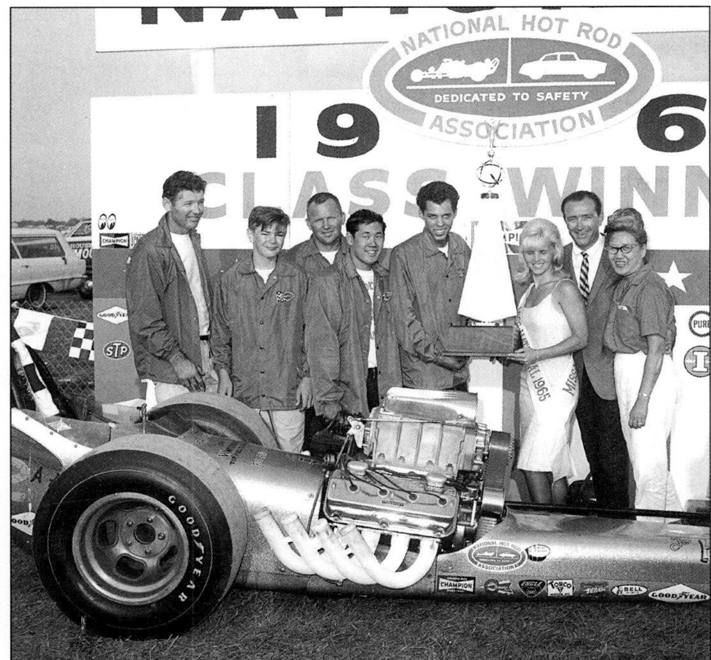

The winning crew of the Hawaiian *basks in glory after winning the prestigious Nationals at Indianapolis. Joining in the historical festivities were (from left to right) Keith Black with his son Kenny, Wes Hansen, Leong, Prudhomme, Miss Nationals,* Hot Rod *magazine's Dick Day, and Leong's mother. (Photo Courtesy Roland Leong Collection)*

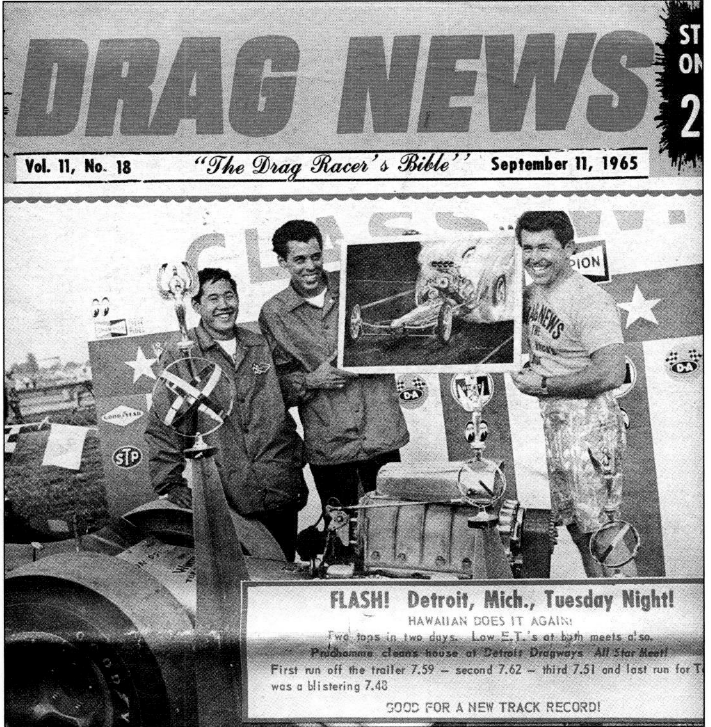
DRAG NEWS

Vol. 11, No. 18 "The Drag Racer's Bible" September 11, 1965

FLASH! Detroit, Mich., Tuesday Night!

HAWAIIAN DOES IT AGAIN!

Two tops in two days. Low E.T.'s at both meets also.

Prudhomme cleans house at Detroit Dragways All Star Meet!

First run off the trailer 7.59 – second 7.62 – third 7.51 and last run for T[illegible] was a blistering 7.48

GOOD FOR A NEW TRACK RECORD!

The cover of the September 11, 1965, issue of Drag News *celebrated the* Hawaiian's *success. The next night, at Detroit Dragway's All-Star race, the* Hawaiian *did it again, wiping out the competition while resetting the low ET track record.*

Immediately, Leong and Prudhomme decided to sell the car and use the money to go home. This was the first time in drag racing that a car owner and driver won the NHRA Winternationals and the U.S. Nationals in the same year. It should be mentioned that Leong's biggest supporter was his mother, Teddy, who attended all of the National events and traveled from the Hawaiian Islands to see the car run and helped on the car where needed.

Prudhomme Doubles Up

Just hours from their spectacular win at Indy, Don Prudhomme and Roland Leong returned to Detroit Dragway for a rare Tuesday-night appearance. They joined 14 other cars from the country's fastest machines at Detroit's fifth-annual All-Star Meet.

The old "lightning never strikes in the same place twice" cliché was proven to be wrong by Leong and Prudhomme, as Prudhomme demonstrated that the Nationals win was no fluke. His first run off the trailer netted a 7.59 ET and a win over Bud Banes and the Capitol Speed Shop Fueler out of Lansing, Michigan.

Prudhomme brought the second round to a close, running a 7.51 ET at 205.46 mph to defeat Bob Leverich's red Logghe rail. The third round was a smoky heart-stopper when the *Hawaiian* bested "Sneaky" Pete Robinson with another 7.51 ET, racking up a new track record over Maynard Rupp's 7.69 ET that was set a month earlier.

The final round was a carbon copy from June that paired Rupp and Prudhomme against each other. The fans who came out in droves to see the Summernationals Stars were not dissatisfied. The Snake pulled a hole-shot on the *Prussian* and kept on going with Rupp straining to catch up. Prudhomme saved his best for last with an incredible 7.48 ET at 208 mph, resetting the track record.

The Ramchargers End the *Hawaiian* "Hurricane" at Dragway 42

Eventually, all great things come to an end, as Don Westerdale and the Ramchargers swept Prudhomme in the finals of NASCAR Nationals on September 11 and 12. The *Hawaiian* had shaken up everything in its path on the national racing scene before losing steam at Dragway 42 in West Salem, Ohio.

Prudhomme polished off the competition at Indianapolis, swept through the fuel competition at Detroit, and cut his way in qualifying before running into Westerdale. For Prudhomme and Leong, this ended their hopes of capturing their first ever NASCAR National Championship.

This is a promotional card of Leong from the shop of Keith Black Racing Engines. (Illustration Courtesy Roland Leong Collection)

The Journey Home

The *Hawaiian*'s summer campaign across the nation was likely the most successful tour of any AA/FD team in all of drag racing. After winning the Indy Nationals (the most prestigious race on the NHRA schedule) Leong and Prudhomme loaded up the car and trailer and set a course for home, heading straight to the West Coast. When they agreed to head out on tour, the stipulation was that Prudhomme would never let Leong drive the car with the trailer hooked up to the bumper.

On the road in Oklahoma, Prudhomme was at that point where he could no longer keep his eyes open. No matter how much coffee and caffeine pills he ingested, he was totally exhausted. It was time for Leong to take over and drive.

"Not to worry," Leong told Prudhomme. "I'll keep to the right, staying only in the slow lane."

Prudhomme told Leong to be careful going next to the big-rig trucks, as the trailer was notorious for getting the air sucked out, causing the trailer to get squirrely and possibly come around.

Prudhomme immediately fell asleep in the back seat. Leong figured out that when the semis would come around and pass to the left, he would activate the rheostat for the trailer brake to steady the trailer. This worked well for Leong, but later Prudhomme woke up and checked with Leong on how he was doing.

"I'm sure I have this handled," Leong replied.

Just then, a tractor trailer rolled by on their left, causing the trailer to weave around, swinging side-to-side. Suddenly, the trailer came around and jack-knifed, detached the trailer from the bumper, and forced the wagon off the highway.

Several cases of oil and tools spewed onto the side of the highway, and some debris ended up in the ditch. Both Leong and Prudhomme were fortunate that they weren't seriously injured or even killed. Many good Samaritans stopped to see if they were okay. They helped them to hook the trailer back to the bumper, but the trailer was too damaged to continue all the way to California.

They made a call to Jimmy Nix, who told them to drop by his shop in Oklahoma City to make the necessary welding repairs to the trailer and get them back on their way home. After the ordeal, they stayed awake for the entire trip home.

Don Prudhomme also provided an account of this event in the foreword of this book.

Prudhomme Hits the Jackpot

Prudhomme had one of the hardest-working weekends at Pomona on November 27 and 28 when he won both legs toward a "Jackpot Circuit" grand slam.

The newly formed Top Fuel Jackpot Circuit was a local Southern California race event. It was sponsored by radio station KFWB during the traveling Drag Festival series, and it gave an extra bonus of $1,100 to the

WHAT SAYS THE MONGOOSE ?
1."I am the World's Record Speed holder at 214.78 m.p.h.--"
2."I'm not gonna red light, just leave on the early green!"
3."I'll blow him off in two straight and run faster & quicker than he does"
4."Prudhomme has had a very successful year, he's done done everything important but beat me"
5."I started off a good year by shutting down the Snake, I'm gonna end it the same way!"
WHAT SAYS THE SNAKE ?
1."I am the top speed king at 215.m.p.h., have a better E.T. record of 7.40"
2."My Lions track record of 7.53 has not been touched in a year"
3."The Snake is interested only in national events - sometimes we leave the smaller, less flashy meets to McEwen"
4."I ended his year about 8 months ago, he must realize, it's the year of the Snake!"
5."Tell the Mongoose to read one of the latest drag magazines, the Snake is polled number one on the West Coast"
Don "SNAKE" Prudhomme and the Leong- Prudhomme "HAWAIIAN" will race.....
Tom "MONGOOSE" McEwen and the Yeakel Plymouth Special
AT
LIONS
DRAG STRIP
223RD & ALAMEDA, WILMINGTON
$2.00 ADMISSION
PHONE 424-09[illegible]1
AHRA SANCTION
SAT. NITE DEC. 4th

Rivals Tom "the Mongoose" McEwen and Don "the Snake" Prudhomme traded hilarious pre-race barbs in a highly advertised match race on December 4 at Lions Drag Strip. This was the last match race that the Snake drove the Hawaiian, *closing out an incredible year with numerous record wins, ET records, and top-speed records.*

winner. The top prize of $500 was awarded to the victor for winning the scheduled race, plus the extra Jackpot bonus dough for the winner.

Prudhomme swept through the competition at the festival with consistent 7.30, 7.66, and 7.65 ETs, running identical top speeds of 205.46 mph. The final round was the moment of truth for the *Hawaiian* when the Snake matched up against a young John Mulligan in the Adams & Warye digger. Mulligan got the jump on the national champ, out-blazing Prudhomme to an event-best 7.61 ET at 205.97 mph. However, it was all for naught, as he had fouled coming off the line. Pomona brought in a record number of 8,953 spectators for the two-day festival!

Rumblings from the Jungle: The Snake versus the Mongoose

The highly touted match race and verbal war of the year, which featured Tom "the Mongoose" McEwen verses Don "the Snake" Prudhomme, was like taking a page right out of Nobel Prize–winning writer Rudyard Kipling's *The Jungle Book*.

Ralph Guldahi caught up with the two for the December 30 issue of *Drag News*. The Mongoose stuck out his chest, boasting, "Snake's going out in two, as we have a party to go to early tonight. I got a little somethin' for him tomorrow at Bakersfield."

Over in the *Hawaiian* camp, Prudhomme declared, "Tell Mongoose [that] it won't affect me that much if I lose, my income tax bracket is a little bit high. It's best if he wins tonight, as I'm dropping the nickname 'The Snake' and going back to Don Prudhomme—the name known as Top Fuel Champion. I've just been keeping the name 'the Snake,' supporting him on somethin' to go on, [because] if there's no Snake, there's no Mongoose!"

After the afternoon trial run of 7.95 at 202.70 mph by McEwen in Lou Baney's *Yeakel Plymouth Special*, the car and team were spotted leaving the front gate to go back to the shop for repairs. At first, it was thought that something seriously broke or it was a prank of physiological overtones.

"We were trying to run careful and went back to check everything out," Baney explained. "Everything looked good."

The battle of the minds took to the strip, as Prudhomme clocked an 8.09 ET at 207 mph as the three-week-old Scott injector on McEwen's car failed to

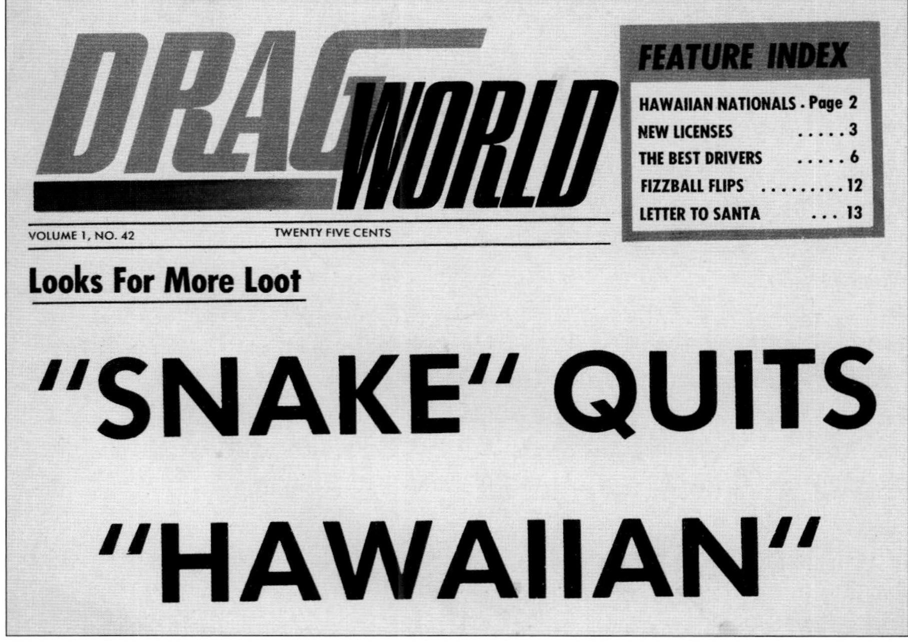
DRAG WORLD

FEATURE INDEX
HAWAIIAN NATIONALS . Page 2
NEW LICENSES 3
THE BEST DRIVERS 6
FIZZBALL FLIPS 12
LETTER TO SANTA ... 13

VOLUME 1, NO. 42 TWENTY FIVE CENTS

Looks For More Loot

"SNAKE" QUITS "HAWAIIAN"

The headline on the December 14, 1965, issue of Drag World, *proclaimed that current (at the time) NHRA Winternationals and Nationals Champion Don Prudhomme had parted ways with Roland Leong and Keith Black on friendly terms. Prudhomme decided to venture out on his own with Bob Spar's B&M Torkmasters rail. (Illustration Courtesy Steve Reyes Collection)* fire the engine. Prudhomme went on to take down the Mongoose Saturday night.

Sunday at Famoso, the fog and damp grounds forced the postponement of the Jackpot Pro Circuit. So, Prudhomme and the *Hawaiian* remained the ones to beat at the next meet, and they continued as the reigning prize money leader at $2,200.

A question that Prudhomme had been asked constantly was, "How did the *Greer-Black-Prudhomme* dragster compare with the *Hawaiian* with the better Goodyear tires and advanced engines?"

"Well, the orange car would run good, but not as good as this one," Prudhomme said.

Roland Leong and Don Prudhomme ran the most successful campaign by any Top Fuel team in the early history of drag racing. But with every dawn comes a new day, and for Leong, the next one shook the world of drag racing.

Although they went their separate ways, Leong and Prudhomme stayed good friends. (Photo Courtesy Roland Leong Collection)

The End of an Extraordinary Run

In late December, the *Drag World* racing publication broke the news with the stunning headline "Snake Quits *Hawaiian*." Don Prudhomme would no longer drive for *Hawaiian* owner Roland Leong and was going out on his own with an AA/FD Ed Pink–powered rail.

The 25-year-old fuel dragster driver Prudhomme felt it was time for a change and confirmed that there were no hard feelings.

"There are certain things about dragsters that I like, and I figured it out," Prudhomme said. "It's about time [that] I got a new car for myself and do everything the way I would like it."

Following its victory at the Winternationals earlier in the year, the *Hawaiian* dragster embarked on a 50,000-mile tour of nearly 100 strips in the United States. It wound up in Indianapolis for the "grand daddy" of all big meets: the NHRA Nationals. Leong and Prudhomme had accomplished everything. Now that the pair had split, there could only be one dominant force for 1966. Who would it be?

MEMORABLE MOMENTS:
Don Prudhomme

"I had such a great time [competing] with Roland," Don Prudhomme said. "It's hard to put into words how we won the Winternationals and then Indy in the same year. I kept pinching myself to see if it was real. Just seeing our names in the papers was unbelievable. The *Hawaiian* took on the character with the names "Hawaiian" and "Roland Leong" on it, and it was very popular. We were both kids that didn't amount to much. We both dropped out of school, and all we thought about was cars. We were in love with what we were doing, traveling down the road, being our own bosses, just having great times."

CHAPTER 3

1966: THE HAWAIIAN'S IMMINENT RISE TO DRAG RACING STARDOM

When Roland Leong reintroduced his *Hawaiian* in late 1964, he was met with outstanding success. He maintained a championship reputation by winning multiple Eliminator titles at NHRA national events, setting and then resetting the bar for greatness. This year's *Hawaiian* would achieve that same excellence.

Leong reloaded for 1966, making a few minor changes to the record-setting car. First, he did so by extending the chassis to a 136-inch wheelbase. Gene Whitfield refurbished the body in spectacular metalflake blue. The *Hawaiian*'s combination of power and durability was again supplied by one of the best in the business: South Gate's Keith Black.

How did Roland Leong step up from his record-setting year in 1965 without seasoned expert driver Don Prudhomme? Leong sent his car to Kent Fuller's shop for a re-fronting of the chassis, which was lengthened to 136 inches. Gene Whitfield applied fresh blue metallic paint, and Leong hired new driver Mike Snively to occupy the cockpit. The wizardry of Keith Black helped power the Hawaiian.

The most glaring difference was the hiring of Mike Snively to fill the driver's seat. Snively provided experience, having fared quite well in such dragsters as Ed Pink's *Old Master*, the Scotty's Muffler entry, the Blair and Hanna car, the Beacon Auto A/GD, the Heidelberg Roadster, and Bill Martin's *400 Junior*. Tony Nancy restitched the seat leather for a safe and comfortable fit to Snively's "office" at over 210 mph.

Right out of the gate, the new combination of Leong, Black, and Snively was tested at the United Drag Racers

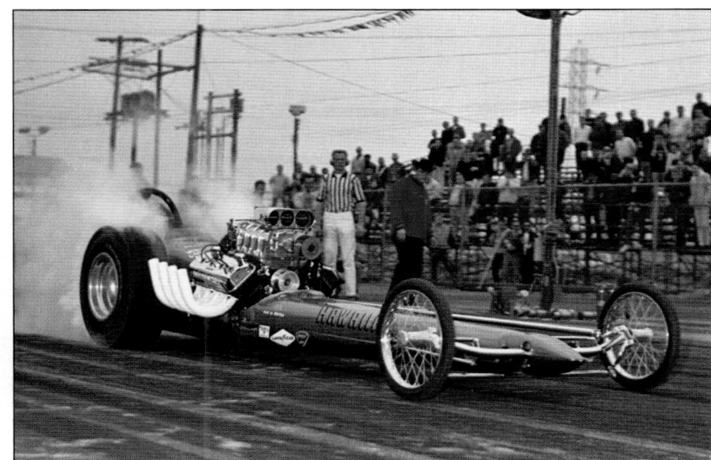

Mike Snively spent a mere two weeks getting accustomed to the seat of the Hawaiian *before the "Big Go" at the NHRA Winternationals. Many thought that the* Hawaiian *wouldn't be a serious contender with Snively as the driver, but Leong, Snively, and the wizardry of Black had a different forecast. (Photo Courtesy Roland Leong Collection)*

Association (UDRA) Winter Nationals at Lions Drag Strip on February 5 and 6. After a single time-trial run, the angry skies opened up with record amounts of rainfall that postponed the weekend event until February 26.

The Great *Hawaiian* Sit-Down Strike

The following week was the seventh-annual AHRA Winter Nationals at Irwindale Raceway, located in the heart of the San Gabriel Valley. Snively qualified the *Hawaiian* into the field of 32 nitro Fuelers anchoring in the fifth slot with a 7.61 ET at 209.30 mph. Controversy arose in the first round of eliminations against Bob Downey in the A&W Root Beer entry. Snively was disqualified (red-lighted) by track officials when it appeared that he took too long to bring the car into the staging lights.

The upset Snively slowly drove down the strip and stopped abruptly before the traps, with Roland, Black, Snively, and the crew all refusing to move with a "sit-down" protest that delayed eliminations. The track dispatched a tow truck along with several of Irwindale's finest police officers to remove the protestors and car off the track. After the team voiced their opinions about the incident, the "sit-down" ended peacefully, and the racing continued.

Doubling Up at Pomona

Crew chief Keith Black, Leong, and Snively regrouped at the sixth-annual NHRA Winternationals Championships at the Los Angeles County Fairgrounds in Pomona. The "Big Go West" was exactly that, with 102 quarter-mile fuel stormers on the premises vowing to earn a spot in the elite field of 64. A reported 90,000-plus fans were in attendance for the three-day drag-in to witness if there would be a repeat performance by the *Hawaiian*.

"Mr. Consistency" Mike Snively didn't disappoint the crowd. He made five runs in the elimination rounds that averaged the time of 7.57 seconds with the lowest at 7.54 and speeds ranging from 208.08 to 209.78 mph.

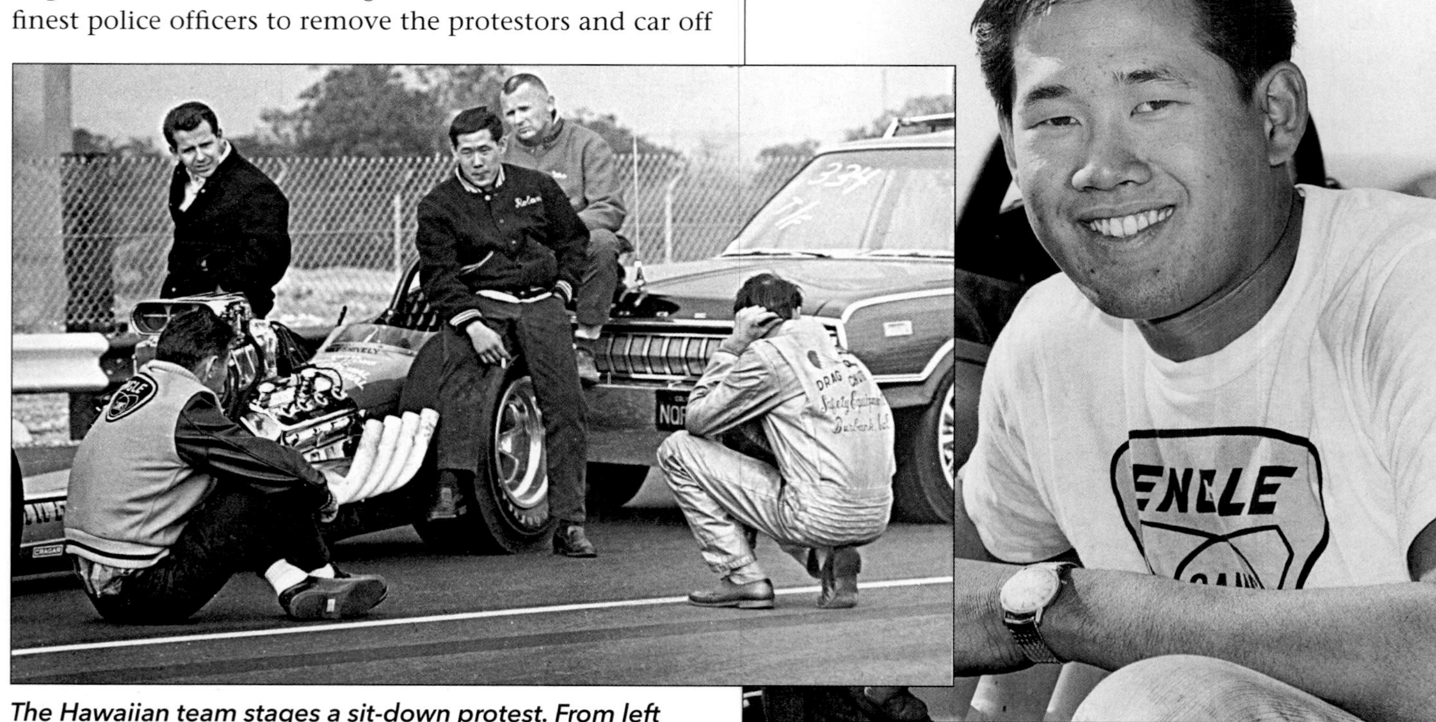

The Hawaiian team stages a sit-down protest. From left to right are Keith Black (sitting in the foreground on the left), an unidentified man (sitting behind the engine), Roland Leong (sitting on the tire), Wes Hansen (sitting on hood behind Leong), and Mike Snively (on the far right). The team refused to exit the track during the 1966 AHRA Winter Nationals at Irwindale Raceway after the officials disqualified Snively for not staging in a timely matter. An on-duty tow truck was dispatched along with uniformed police and track personnel to remove the protestors. The truck stopped within feet of the car as the group expressed their opinions to management about the ordeal. The team then exited the track peacefully. (Photo Courtesy Roland Leong Collection)

Tuning wizard Roland Leong pauses at Pomona, hoping for a repeat Top Fuel Eliminator title with Keith Black muscle, driver Mike Snively, and the revamped Hawaiian dragster. (Photo Courtesy Roland Leong Collection)

MEMORABLE MOMENTS:

Don Prudhomme

"When Roland hooked up with Snively, they were tremendous," Don Prudhomme said. "I felt I shot myself in the foot. I felt so down, and, of course, Tom Ivo called me, laughing at me, telling me what a big mistake I made, leaving the car that kept on winning."

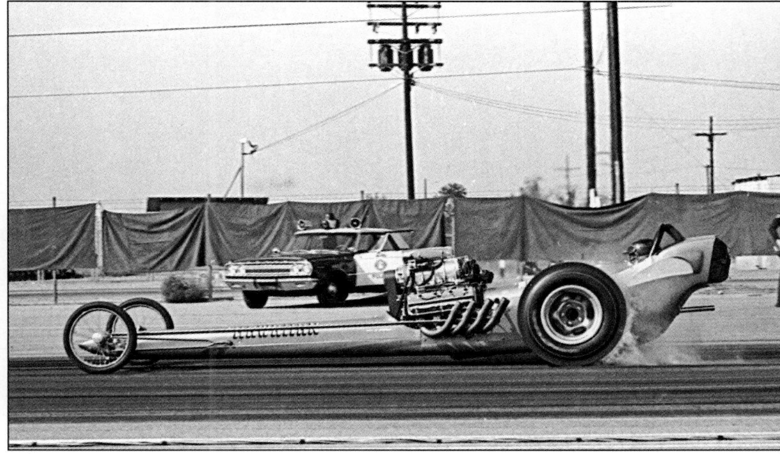

Mike Snively found the surface of Pomona to his liking when he posted five consecutive runs in the 7.50 range during elimination rounds. His consistency earned Leong and the **Hawaiian** *a second consecutive Winternationals Top Fuel Eliminator title, which was a first in NHRA history. (Photo Courtesy Bob McClurg)*

Snively's quickest run of the event (7.52) came in the final against Jim Dunn in the Yates & Dunn entry, putting the *Hawaiian* back in the winner's circle. Leong and Black became the first car owner and crew chief ever in NHRA history to win back-to-back Top Fuel Winternationals Eliminator titles.

Mike Snively dropped a perfect hole-shot on a quicker James Warren to take the semifinal win at the "Big Go" in Pomona. Snively defeated the quicker Warren (a 7.59 ET at 204.54 mph to a 7.58 at 209.78). (Photo Courtesy Stephen Justice Archives)

MEMORABLE MOMENTS:

Wes Hansen

"I went to the March Meet at Bakersfield with one of my sons for Nostalgia racing, and I found out that Roland was there running and tuning one of the nitro cars," Wes Hansen said. "I walked around, and there was Roland, working his magic on the car.

"The crew was making everyone step back out of their way to fire the car for the warmup. When the car shut off after the warmup, Roland looked around and looked right at me. I yelled, 'Wong (I always called him Wong), what are you doing?'

"He smiled, came running over to me, and we put our arms around each other. It was like old times being together as we talked and reminisced over the glory days. It sure brought back some of the best memories.

"On another note, I always have had a deep admiration for his mom, Teddy. She would always come over from Hawaii to support and be with him at the big races."

Mike Snively and Roland Leong accept the contingency check from the Hurst Corporation representative Miss Linda Vaughn for winning the Winternationals. Contingency money brought in as much or more than winning a national meet from a sanctioning body. (Photo Courtesy Roland Leong Collection)

Keith Black and Roland Leong listen in to ABC's Wide World of Sports *announcer Charlie Brockman interviewing an ecstatic Mike Snively on what it meant to win the prestigious Winternationals. (Photo Courtesy Roland Leong Collection)*

MEMORABLE MOMENTS:

"When Prudhomme left to go out to run his own car, I made the calls to the drag strip promoters for bookings for the upcoming summer," Roland Leong said. "They told me, 'Sorry, we're going with Prudhomme.'

"As soon as we won again at Pomona, they were now calling me back constantly, day and night, nonstop. Dealing with all the track managers and the companies that were into drag racing really helped me, but I was pretty intimidated for a long time because of my ethnic status."

The Fuel Duels

The early spring months between March and May were active times at the strips before many of the local West Coast Fuelers hit the road during the summer's touring season across the country. Several teams usually participated in match races or competed in either 8- or 16-car fields up and down the West Coast. Leong often booked the highly demanded *Hawaiian* into these highly competitive match races, including an advertised best-of-three match race at Irwindale with the Fuel and Gas Champions, Mike Sorokin and the Surfers.

Although the results might have been unfavorable, Sorokin unloaded on the *Hawaiian*, taking all three

Mike Snively powered the Hawaiian *into the fourth slot of the field of 64 of the nation's Top Fuelers with a strong 7.49 ET at 200.64 mph during qualifying. Snively's weekend at the eighth-annual U.S. Fuel and Gas Championships at Bakersfield came to an end in the third round when the "Famoso Terror" James Warren, defeated the* Hawaiian *with a 7.40 ET at 202.70 mph to Snively's losing 7.57 at 201.78.*

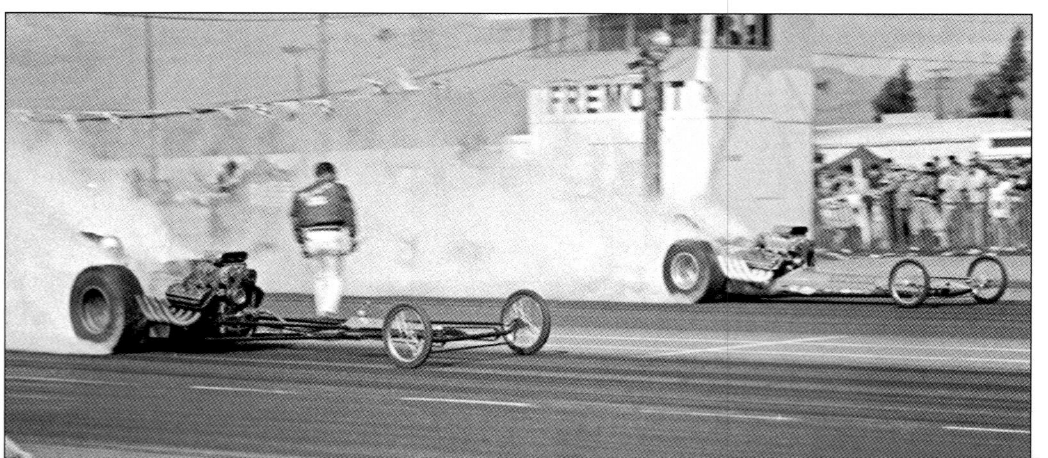

A quick weekend trip up the California coast with a stop at Fremont on Saturday set up Don Cook versus the Hawaiian *in a best-of-three match race. The* Hawaiian *prevailed by taking two wins from Cook. (Photo Courtesy Steve Reyes)*

Wes Hansen and Roland Leong wipe the impurities off the Goodyears prior to meeting Don Cook in the second round of their highly billed match race at Fremont. (Photo Courtesy Steve Reyes)

rounds. A week later and back at Irwindale, the tide quickly turned. Snively and the *Hawaiian* struck back, dissecting their way through the 16-car field to meet the *Wilmington Special* of Danny Ongais in the final.

Snively came out of the gate blazing and never backed down. The *Hawaiian* stopped the clocks with a 7.61 ET at 205.97 mph to Ongais's 8.28 at 140.46 when he shut off early due to handling problems.

A week later, a trip up to Fresno Dragway in April brought a mixture of the best equipment from all points in California. This included the South (Tommy Ivo, the *Hawaiian*, the Surfers, and Warren-Miller), the North (Ted Gotelli and Jim Davis), and from the Central area (Mark Danekas and the injected Chevys of the *Valley Muffler Special* and Jack Childers).

In the qualifying rounds, Leong's *Hawaiian* had low ET of the meet with a 7.14 at 212.26 mph for a new AHRA track record. During eliminations, Snively defeated Ivo in round one. In round two, he lost on a hole-shot from James Warren, ending the day for the *Hawaiian*.

Irwindale held three weekends of consecutive Top Fuel shows from mid-April to the first weekend in May. There, Leong was able to test out several equipment changes that would work for any track conditions.

Snively also tested M&H's new slicks, but the team elected to stay with the Goodyears, as their best times and speeds (7.14 at 212.00) were had on that rubber. This was also the time Leong announced that they would be starting their tour on May 26, with their first booking in Texas. The tour would take them to many strips in

Up the coast from Fremont, the second stop in Northern California was at Half Moon Drag Strip with another best-of-three match race with "Terrible" Ted Gotelli and his driver Kenny Safford. Half Moon Drag Strip was located on the outskirts of South San Francisco and was the largest drag strip in Northern California. The highly acknowledged powerhouses each won a round, but the overall victor went to mother nature, as the rains washed out racing for the day. (Photo Courtesy Steve Reyes)

Tom Hanna examines the damaged body pieces of the **Hawaiian** *after an unfortunate accident in the California desert. The tow car and trailer were forced off the highway when a truck towing another race car tried to pass the rig on a narrow bridge. (Photo Courtesy Roland Leong Collection)*

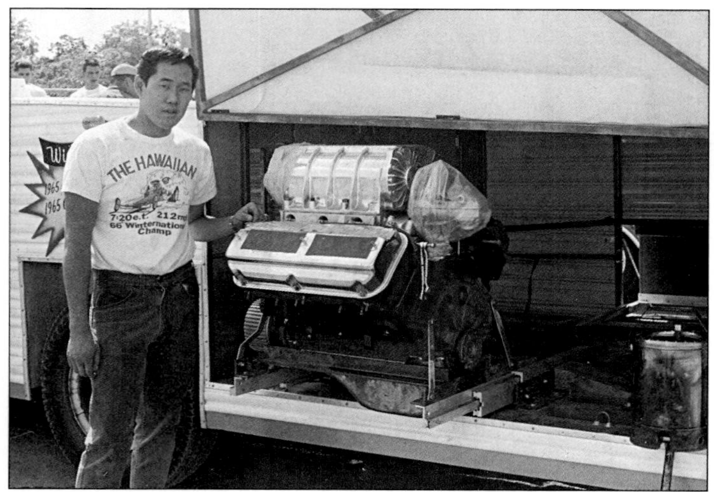

During the **Hawaiian's** *return trip to Connecticut prior to the NHRA Nationals, Leong came well-armed with a spare Keith Black 392-ci engine for the match race against Connie Kalitta. Leong had the unique gift of understanding engine "dialogue," knowing how not to damage or destroy parts, including heads and blocks. (Photo Courtesy Roland Leong Collection)*

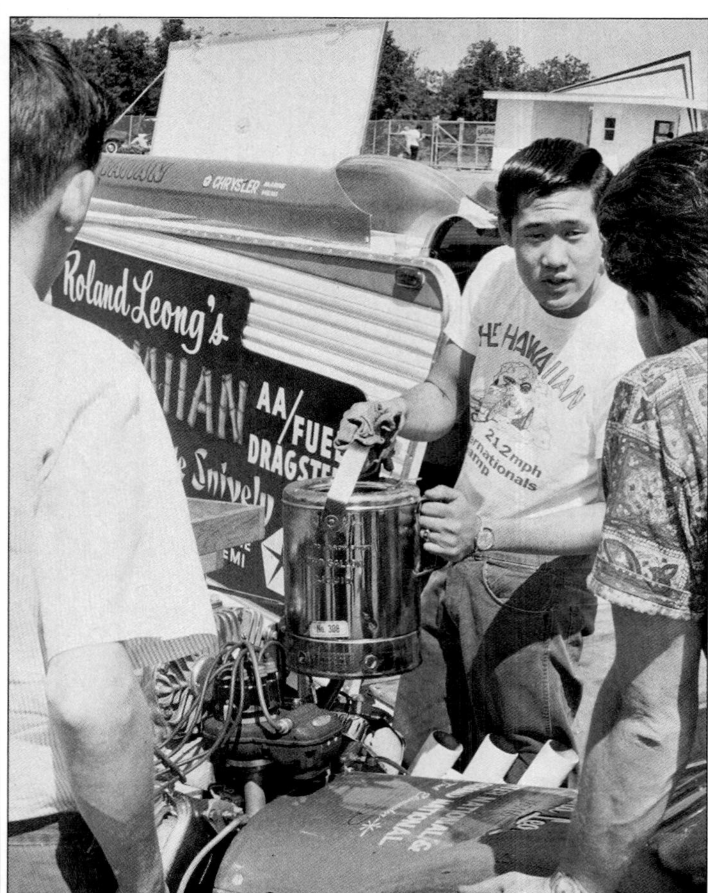

Between rounds at Connecticut Dragway, Leong performs routine maintenance to the engine and engages in "bench racing" stories with one of the greatest legends of the sport of drag racing: Chris "the Golden Greek" Karamesines. (Photo Courtesy Roland Leong Collection)

the South, Midwest, and Northeast. They'd finish up in Maine before the Nationals over the Labor Day weekend.

As Leong, Snively, and Danny "Buzz" Broussard headed out of town to Amarillo, Texas, for the first leg on their eastern tour, the *Hawaiian* ran into an unfortunate situation. Snively was driving through the California desert in the middle of the night with Broussard sitting in the passenger's seat and Leong sleeping in the back seat. Along came a truck behind them, towing (of all things) another race car: a '57 Chevy. The driver decided to pass them on the left and pulled into the opposite lane, not knowing that there was a narrow bridge coming up.

The Leong station wagon and trailer were clipped in the left rear of the trailer. This caused the trailer to swerve, come around, and crash, separating the car from the trailer. The tow car rolled over, coming to rest on its roof. The trailer was sent off into the pitch-black desert, where it couldn't be seen.

Snively and Broussard were shaken, but each was able to climb out on his own through one of the broken side windows. Leong thought he was dreaming and woke up, realizing he was laying upside down on the roof. He heard someone calling his name as well as a crying baby (from the other vehicle) as he crawled out of the mangled station wagon, dazed and confused from the accident. The only window that wasn't broken out was the one Leong was next to.

Leong, Snively, and Broussard returned the next morning with a new station wagon and spotted the trailer out in the desert. It was approximately a quarter mile from the road, mangled and resting upside down.

The trailer and the race car were destroyed. Everything on the car and the trailer needed to be rebuilt or replaced. The crew left to finish the tour. The remaining portion of the tour ran smoothly due to the hospitality and help shown by various manufacturers and generous people.

Leong rechecks the adjustments on the Keith Black Chrysler Hemi before the first round of Sunday's class runoffs at Indy. (Photo Courtesy Roland Leong Collection)

The *Hawaiian* Drops Garlits in Two

One of the most heated rivalries in 1966 unfolded at Aquasco Speedway in Maryland between the top runner from the Southeast, "Big Daddy" Don Garlits with his *Wynn's Jammer*, and the West Coast powerhouse, the *Hawaiian*, operated in the capable hands of Mike Snively. Spectators filed through the gates with the expectations of thunderous, tire-smoking 210-mph blasts on Aquasco's "Super Traction" surface.

The crowd was on its feet in round one with both Chrysler Hemis making tumultuous noise rolling into the staging beams. Both cars were deadlocked off the line when Snively started to put daylight between the cars and Garlits suddenly slowed. The *Hawaiian* tripped the win light with a 7.19 ET at 209.36 mph to Garlits's off-pace 7.67 at 195.83.

Round two was nearly a repeat performance of round one. Both launched from the line, but Snively took a commanding lead to the finish stripes when the crossed-up Garlits shut it off.

The *Hawaiian* Scores Four in a Row

Labor Day weekend had become the NHRA's largest event in the history of drag racing. Close to 1,500 entries took part at the 12th-annual Nationals at Indianapolis. Qualifying started early on Thursday morning, and by Friday night, more than 2,397 runs were completed down the quarter mile.

Mike Snively drove the *Hawaiian* to low ET with a 7.46. The rest of the 15 qualified Fuelers included Don Prudhomme, Don Westerdale in the Ramchargers entry, John Mulligan at the wheel of the Adams-Warye-Mulligan entry, Vic Brown, Marvin Schwartz, and Tommy Ivo.

Top Fuel qualifying for Sunday's class runoffs continued Saturday morning. Connie Kalitta's *Bounty Hunter* dropped a blistering time on the field, wheeling a 7.39 ET at 209.78 mph for the number-one spot. When the sun rose on Sunday morning, a total of 36 nitro rails were assembled to take a shot at winning the tournament, earn the right to sit out Monday's eliminations, and only make the run for the overall title.

Snively's impressive round wins came over Marvin Schwartz, Fred Swanda's *Spoiler*, A. J. Gilardi's *Mafia*, and Don Garlits. A bye in the fifth round sent the *Hawaiian* into the final round against Nick Marshall and Dick Vermilya. A red-light foul by Marshall gave Mike Snively the right to sit out until Monday night's finale.

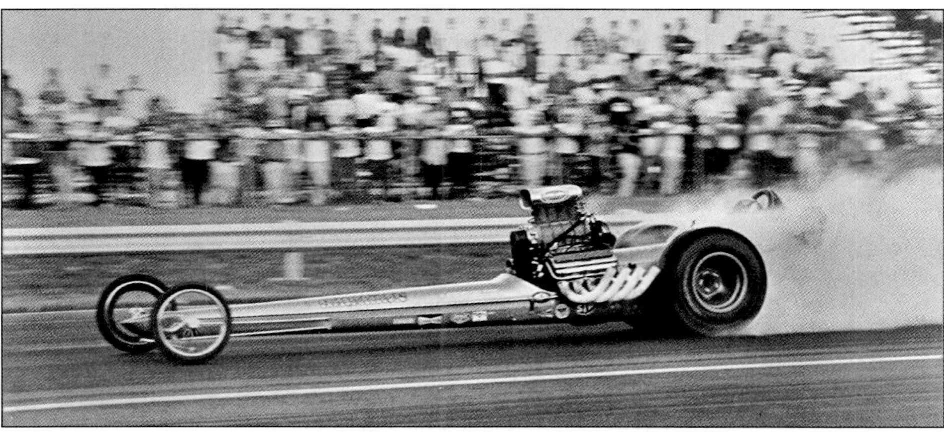
Mike Snively kicked off Thursday morning's qualifying session at the 12th-annual Nationals in Indy with a right-off-the-trailer 7.46 ET. It held up as the number-one time through the end of the Friday night session. Snively ended up in the fifth overall position after Saturday night's final qualifying round by posting a 7.544 ET at 212.76 mph.

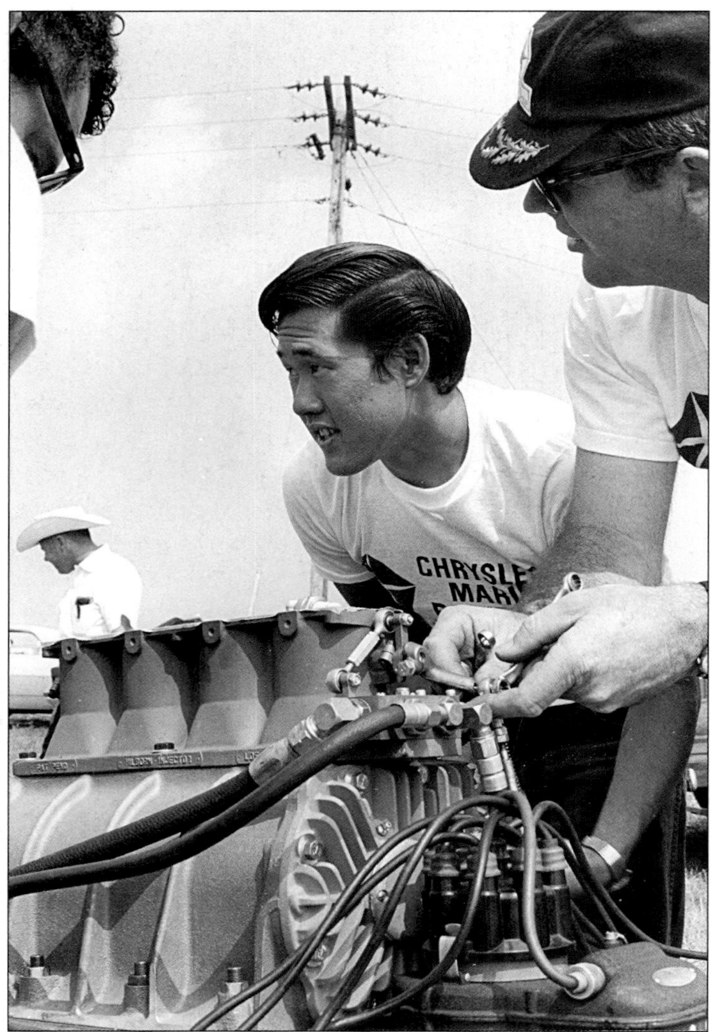

Roland Leong and Keith Black worked their magic, making the right adjustments to qualify them in the fifth overall position with a 7.454 ET at 212.28 mph. Consistency paid dividends for the Hawaiian *round by round of Sunday's runoffs. (Photo Courtesy Roland Leong Collection)*

Mike Snively, Keith Black, and Roland Leong showed the world why they were the kings in Top Fuel Eliminator when the phenomenal *Hawaiian* prevailed over the fastest and most talented field ever assembled at the annual Big Bash.

Top Fuel Eliminator

Monday's Top Fuel Eliminator saw the first position taken by Don Westerdale (Ramchargers). The 17th slot was occupied by stand-by Don Garlits. He moved up when Snively earned the sit-out position by winning Sunday's

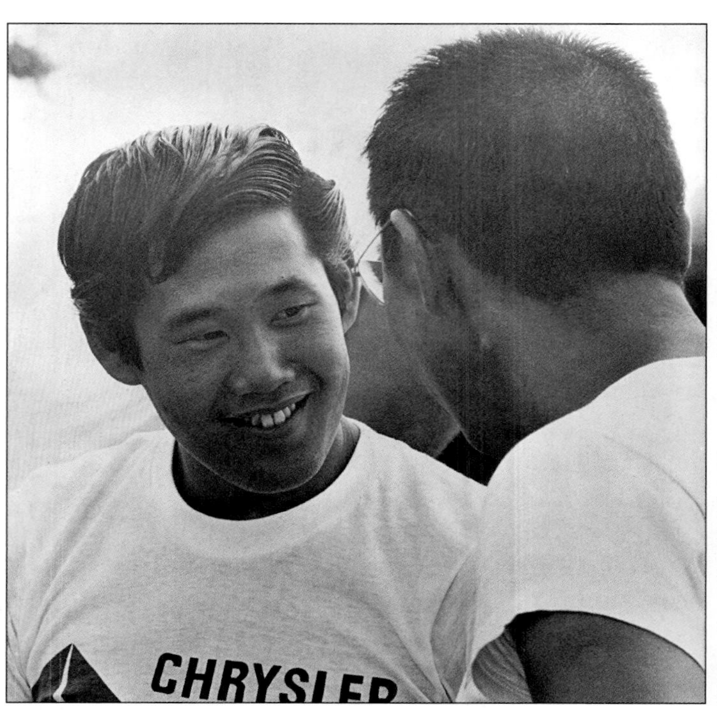

A confident Leong displays his calm, nerves-of-steel smile without showing signs of stress at the Indy Nationals. The 22-year-old dragster owner was the only owner who had won the Nationals three consecutive times, and he was hoping for his fourth title. Leong and Snively waited patiently for the outcome of Monday's Top Fuel elimination rounds to see who their final round counterpart would be. (Photo Courtesy Roland Leong Collection)

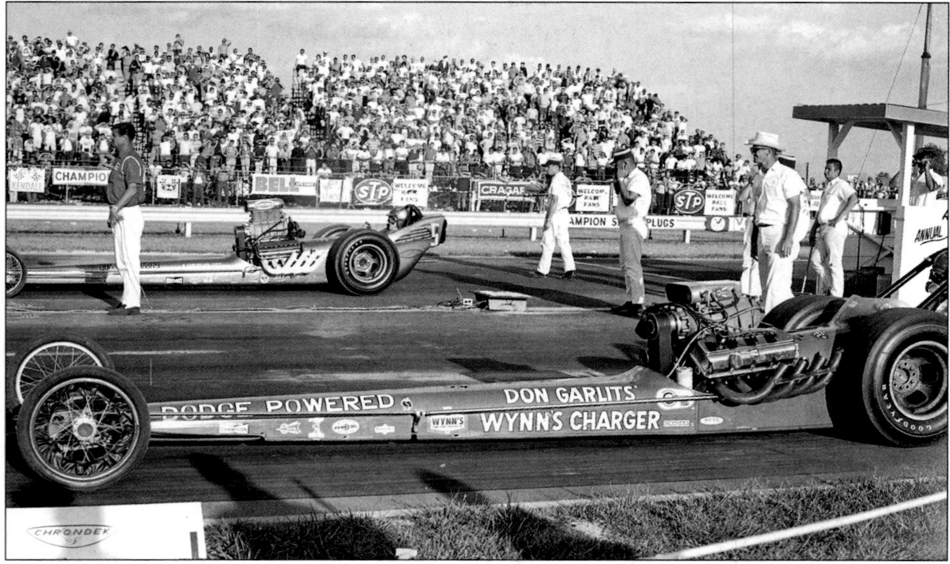

Sunday's class runoffs in the fourth round put the Hawaiian *up against "Big Daddy" Don Garlits. Snively worked out a 7.41 ET at 199.87 mph to dump Garlits and advance to the final round against Nick Marshall. (Photo Courtesy Roland Leong Collection)*

class runoffs against the loaded 36-car field.

It all boiled down to rival and fellow Californian Danny "the Mangler" Ongais and Snively for all the gold, glory, and money. At the hit, Ongais took a commanding lead, but he was unaware of his red-light foul, which ended his chances for the Eliminator title. Snively caught and drove by Ongais with a 7.32 ET at 215.82 mph to the Mangler's losing 7.44 at 208.32. The Leong-Black machine became the first to win four national titles in a row.

As a sidenote, Snively's task was a little more difficult due to heavy cross-winds gusting across the track on Monday, which hindered many of the drivers.

Never before in Nationals history had one owner, one engine builder, and one car dominated the Top Fuel class.

Snively's class win on Sunday earned the Hawaiian *the opportunity to sit out until Monday, when he met rival Danny Ongais in the all-important final for the prestigious Top Fuel Eliminator title. In the final, smoke obscured the air up to the 660-foot mark, and Snively charged to a historic 7.32 ET at 215.82 mph for a victory over the* Honda of Wilmington *entry of Ongais.*

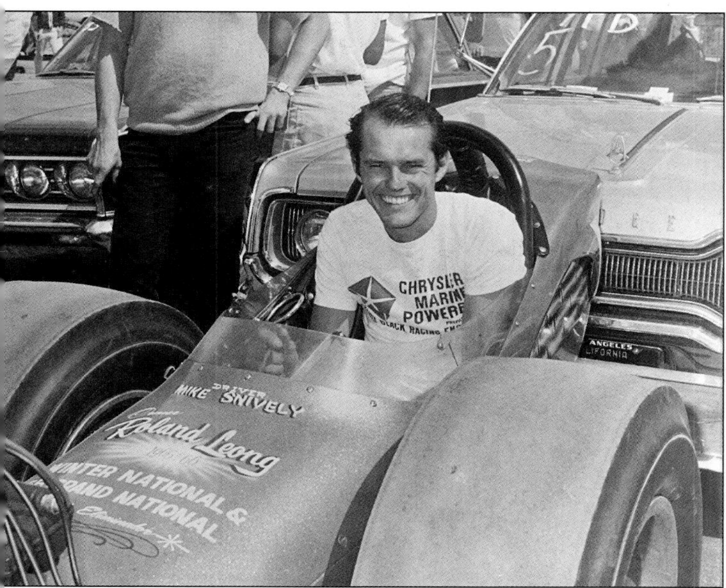

Mike Snively's victory extended the string of Roland Leong's Kent Fuller–built cars with Keith Black's Chrysler engines to four in a row at the NHRA National Championships.

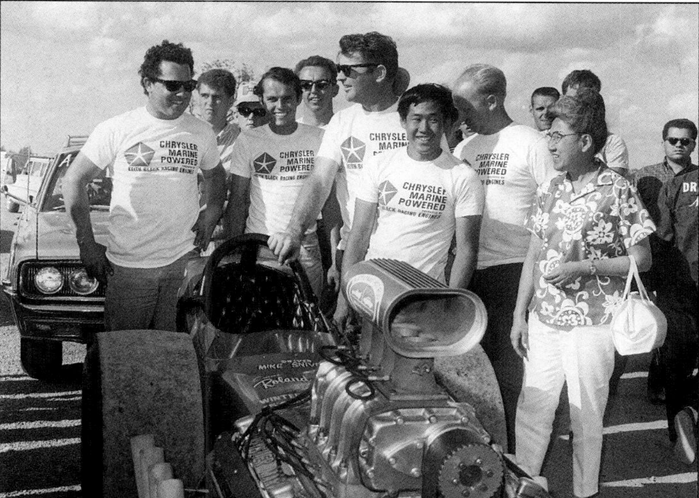

Making it back into the familiar confines of the winner's circle, the elated crew of the Hawaiian *rewrote drag racing history by winning back-to-back Top Fuel Eliminator titles at Pomona and Indy. The "Chrysler Marine" bunch consisted of (left to right) Danny Broussard, Mike Snively, Keith Black, Leong, Kent Fuller, Leong's mother, and the historic* Hawaiian. *(Photo Courtesy Roland Leong Collection)*

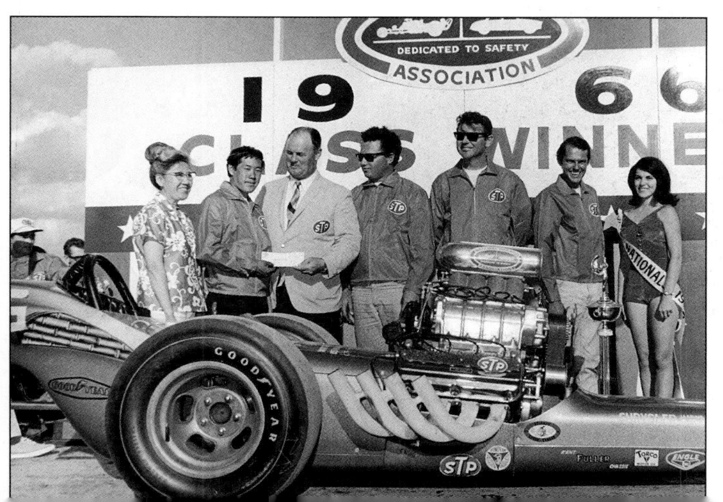

Contingency awards from sponsors were a bonus for both racers and corporations. They included apparel and money for the winning crew. Stickers from those corporations were slapped on the sides of the winning car to promote their products. Here, the crew of the Hawaiian *dons its new STP jackets as Leong graciously accepts the award check from an STP company representative. (Photo Courtesy Roland Leong Collection)*

Leong and Snively share the prized Top Eliminator trophy for photographers after winning the Nationals at Indy. (Photo Courtesy Roland Leong Collection)

Route 66's Big Texas Showdown

Within days of winning their second consecutive NHRA Nationals at Indy, Leong and Snively headed home toward the West Coast. First, they made a stop at Ern Walker's Amarillo Dragway in Texas for the "Texas Style-Texas Giant" NHRA Division 4 World Points Final.

All eyes were on the *Hawaiian*, as Snively thundered to a 7.66 ET in qualifying for the number-one position.

Billed as "David versus Goliath," the *Hawaiian* battled the favorite Wayne Burt from Tulsa, Oklahoma, in the first round of eliminations. Snively's hopes for advancing into the second round ended abruptly when Burt dropped a hole-shot that gave him the win when he ran a 7.80 to the *Hawaiian*'s quicker 7.76 ET.

WORLD CHAMPIONSHIP SERIES

STRIP NOISE

THE WORD! FROM AMARILLO DRAGWAY FOR THE BIG RACE SATURDAY & SUNDAY SEPT. 17&18TH

WHERE THE BIG ACTION IS!!

CAN THE HAWAIIAN BEAT THE "SPOILERS"

The "Hawaiian" Roland Leong owner, Mike Snively driver, are looking forward to their attempt at the "World's Land Speed Record" in ¼ mile DRAG RACING at the Sept. 17&18 event

1966 WORLD-RECORD CHAMPIONSHIPS

NHRA'S MAJOR DRAG RACING EVENT

IT'S HERE AGAIN . . . the hard nose racing for those hard earned points and a real choice purse. This will be our only 2-day race of the season. In order to check in all the entries and give everyone a chance for plenty of time trials and record runs we will open the track Saturday at 11 A. M. and be open until 6 P. M. So let's get those cars in here early. The complete NHRA team will be on hand and we're shaping up the track for a real swinger of an event. All eliminators will be run according to the book — this includes competition eliminators.

Class eliminations will begin at 11 A. M. Sunday morning at which time all entries will be closed. We will begin elimination rounds at 2 P. M. Sharp, Sunday.

RACE CAR TECHNICAL INFORMATION:
Chuck Nelson - 806 FL 5-6856

PURE STOCK CLASSES!
All you pure stockers are invited to be on hand for this big race, with large championship trophies going to all class winners. Also you fellows will be competing to set a new Amarillo Dragway Class Record. All manual and automatic transmission cars will compete in separate classes.

AMARILLO DRAGWAY

Front-page headlines from Amarillo Dragway's Strip Noise *highlighted the* Hawaiian*'s assault on the World's Land Speed Record at the 1966 World-Record Championships. The NHRA Nationals champs fell victim to the Spoilers' hole-shot with a first-round loss that ended their day. (Illustration Courtesy Roland Leong Collection)*

A Rocky Mountain High

Roland Leong and Mike Snively dropped in at Continental Divide Raceway for a highly advertised best-of-three match race. Leong's *Hawaiian* was up against Colorado's land-speed-record-holder Ernie Spickler's Chrysler-powered AA/FD.

In the first round at the drop of the green, both cars were even out of the hole. Snively opened a lead with a distance of 100 feet before Spickler got crossed up and shut down. Snively tripped the win lights with a 7.69 ET at 184.80 mph, while Spickler coasted through at less than 70 mph.

The cars switched lanes for the second round. Snively pulled into the west lane while the Colorado giant lined up in the east.

At the second-round green, both rails lit the tires down the length of the quarter. Spickler dropped a hole-shot on Snively, taking the win running a 7.81 ET at 197.36 mph to the *Hawaiian*'s 7.44 at 176.86. Each car

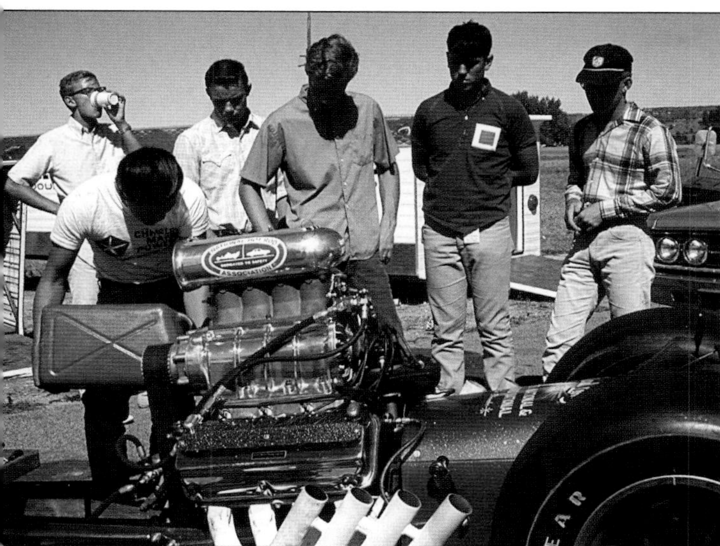

Preparing a Top Fuel car for a match race is tough business for a crew chief, as adjustments need to be made for the track conditions, altitude, air density, and fuel jetting. These fans watch Leong tip the can into the fuel tank for Snively's first-round encounter against Colorado's land-speed recorder holder Ernie Spickler. (Photo Courtesy Roland Leong Collection)

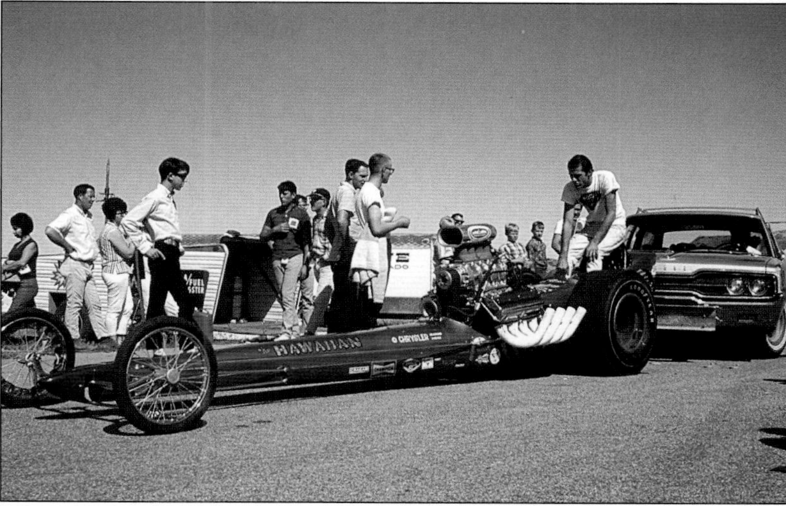

The back-to-back NHRA Nationals Top Fuel Eliminator* Hawaiian *rolls out of the pits, heading toward the starting lanes for the first run in the best-of-three match race between Mike Snively and Ernie Spickler. (Photo Courtesy Roland Leong Collection)

now had one win each going into the rubber match.

Most Coloradoans figured that Speckler had this locked into his favor due to the altitude because the *Hawaiian*, with respectable ETs, wouldn't be able to make the high speeds. In round three, Speckler nipped the *Hawaiian* off the line. Everyone thought that Speckler had this in his pocket, but the relentless *Hawaiian* came on strong before the top end. Snively took the race with a fine 7.70 ET at 200 mph to Speckler's 7.95 at 193.54.

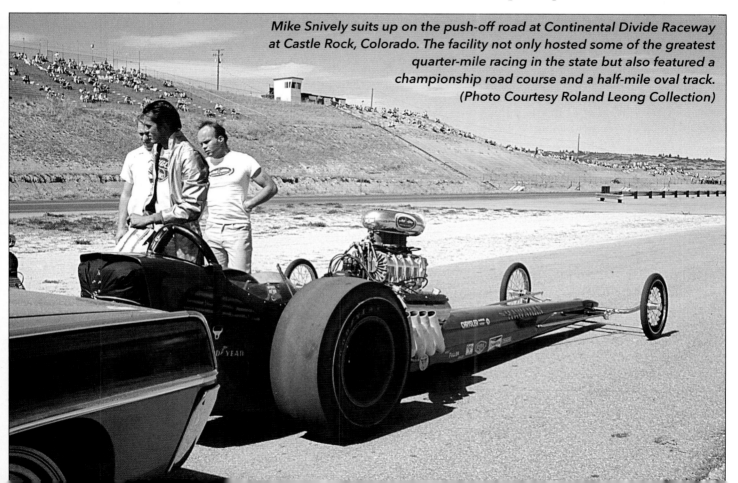

Mike Snively suits up on the push-off road at Continental Divide Raceway at Castle Rock, Colorado. The facility not only hosted some of the greatest quarter-mile racing in the state but also featured a championship road course and a half-mile oval track. (Photo Courtesy Roland Leong Collection)

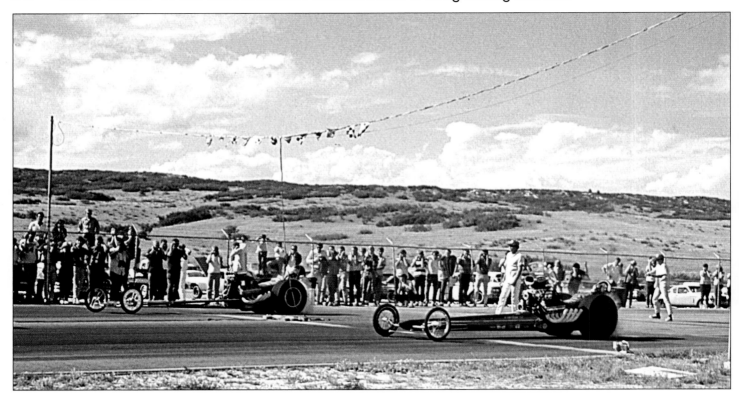

Most of the Colorado faithful figured that the local favorite, Ernie Spickler, who held the state's land speed record, would make easy work of Leong and Snively, but you can't ever underestimate the power from the Keith Black Hemi. Spickler jumped to an early lead, but the* Hawaiian *came on strong for the finish, as Snively tripped the win lights with a 7.70 ET at 200 mph to Speckler's 7.95 at 193.54. (Photo Courtesy Roland Leong Collection)

Hawaii's Annual Hot Rod Show Closes Out 1966

Leong and his mother, Teddy, were honored at a special dinner hosted by Hawaii Raceway Park (HRP) for their fuel dragster's accomplishments of winning the Winternationals and Nationals in two consecutive years along with their record-setting runs throughout the mainland. In addition to the black-tie ceremony, Hawaii Raceway Park brought Dragdom's top rail to Hawaii for Hawaii's annual Hot Rod Show, which was December 1 to 3 at the Honolulu International Center.

Along with the annual Hot Rod Show, a special best-of-three match race was held at HRP with another top Mainland fuel dragster: the *Frantic Four* of Dennis Holding, Norm Weekly, Jim Fox, and Ron Rivero. Both cars were displayed in the arena along with the drivers, the owners, and the crews that held court, promoting professional drag racing while taking questions and signing autographs.

The *Hawaiian* and the *Frantic Four* were billed as the main headliners at the show, but both lost some thunder when the *Bat-Cycle* and Bat sidecar from the popular television show *Batman* were on hand. The Bat cars held live demonstrations with a stunt look-alike of Robin, showing how the actor was ejected out of the sidecar.

Hawaii Raceway Park honored Roland Leong and Teddy Leong in Honolulu with a formal dinner. They recognized the* Hawaiian*'s accomplishments of winning four consecutive NHRA Top Fuel Eliminator titles at Pomona and Indianapolis in 1965 and 1966. (Photo Courtesy Roland Leong Collection)

Leong and Snively crated up the Hawaiian *for a flight to Maui from the mainland for a best-of-three match race with the* Frantic Four *AA/FD. Leong proudly presented the* Hawaiian *in front of King Kamehameha's historical landmark, which prominently stands in front of the Ali Iolani Hale building in Honolulu, Hawaii. (Photo Courtesy Roland Leong Collection)*

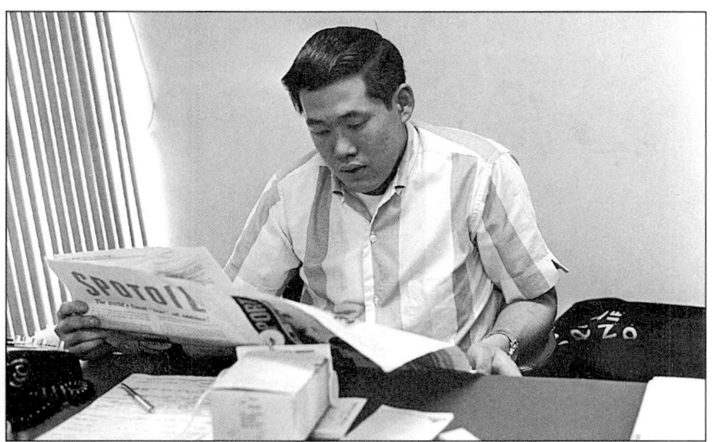

With repeated Top Fuel Eliminator titles won at both Pomona and Indy, Leong's successful tour throughout the country didn't skip a beat when the Hawaiian *won nearly 80 percent of all of its races. Back at his desk at Keith Black's building, Leong reads the latest issue of* Speed Sport News. *(Photo Courtesy Roland Leong Collection)*

The next day was Sunday at the strip, and more than 12,000 fans attended. Leong and Snively, in typical fashion, took two straight rounds from the *Frantic Four* en route to setting the new Hawaii Raceway Park ET record with a 7.37.

Leong was asked what made the *Hawaiian* the top AA/FD of its time. He said, "One, you need a good car; two, a good motor; three, a good driver; and last, great luck—heavy on the luck."

Onward and Upward

Looking back, many thought that the Prudhomme and Leong campaign was just a fluke, a one-and-done, flash-in-the-pan year. But Leong, Snively, and Black proved them wrong. They never looked back, and never eased off the pedal. The *Hawaiian* only surged ahead, raising its performances to a whole new level.

We would like to take this opportunity, appropriately during the holiday season, to extend a hearty thank you for your help in making the year 1966 a successful one for the Hawaiian dragster.
On behalf of all our crew members and our driver, Mike Snively, Best Wishes for a very Merry Christmas and a Prosperous New Year.

Roland Leong

Mele Kalikimaka

Hauoli Makahiki Hou

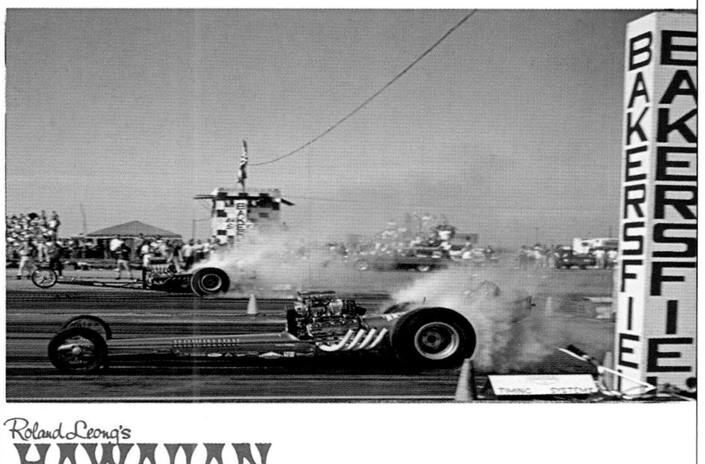

How cool would it have been to open up your mail during the Christmas season and receive a Christmas card from Roland Leong? (Photo Courtesy Roland Leong Collection)

CHAPTER 4

1967: THE PERFECT STORM

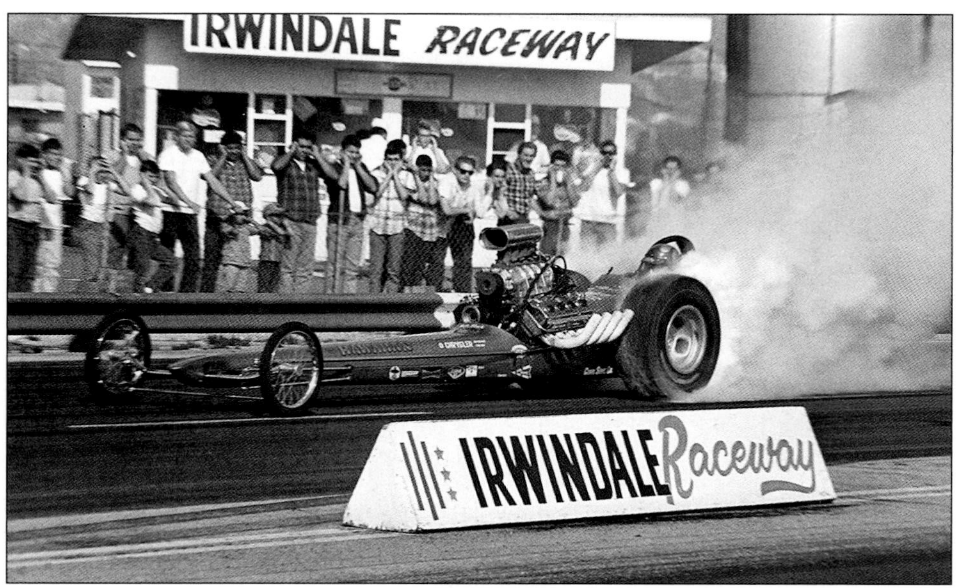

The United Drag Racers Association (UDRA) returned to Irwindale Raceway for 1967. Once again, Snively retained his dominance at the pedal when he added another win to the Hawaiian's *impressive list of achievements.*

The technical data of the 1967 *Hawaiian* was exceptional. The race car was based on a plain and simple 136-inch-wheelbase frame designed and fabricated by Kent Fuller. The car featured 1¼-inch chrome-moly tubing fitted with a Wayne Ewing body that was sprayed a vibrant metalflake blue by Gene Winfield. Tony Nancy stitched the leather seat that gave Snively quality comfort at over 210 mph.

The continued success behind the *Hawaiian* was the power supplied by one of the best in the business: Keith Black Racing Engines. Black built two different engine combinations for Leong's dragster: 1956 and 1957 Chrylser Hemi engines with displacements of either 354 or 392 ci. Both were tuned and maintained by Leong.

In Like a Lion

By 1967, Roland Leong's *Hawaiian* dragsters had won more major events and Top Fuel Eliminator titles than any other fuel dragster in drag racing history. Keeping up the pace with a wide-open pedal, Roland Leong, Mike Snively, and Keith Black proved that there was no letting up. It seemed to be that the closer the Winternationals drew near, the more unbeatable the *Hawaiian* became.

Celebrating the return of the UDRA to Irwindale Raceway in late January, Snively once again dominated Top Fuel, adding another win to the

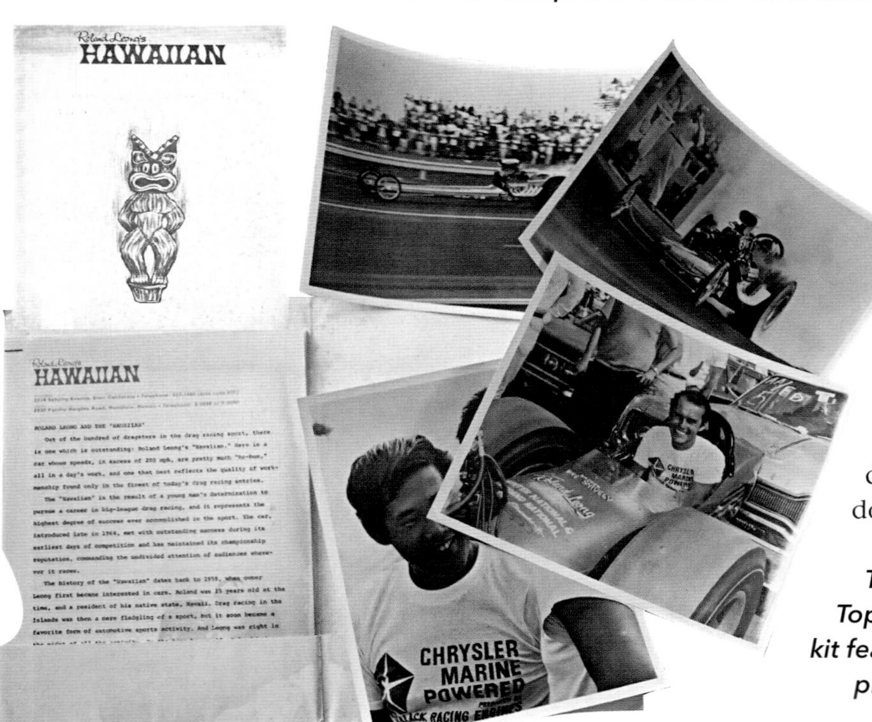
Roland Leong's HAWAIIAN

ROLAND LEONG AND THE "HAWAIIAN"

Out of the hundred of dragsters in the drag racing sport, there is one which is outstanding: Roland Leong's "Hawaiian." Here is a car whose speeds, in excess of 200 mph, are pretty much "ho-hum," all in a day's work, and one that best reflects the quality of workmanship found only in the finest of today's drag racing entries.

The "Hawaiian" is the result of a young man's determination to pursue a career in big-league drag racing, and it represents the highest degree of success ever accomplished in the sport. The car, introduced late in 1964, met with outstanding success during its earliest days of competition and has maintained its championship reputation, commanding the undivided attention of audiences wherever it races.

The history of the "Hawaiian" dates back to 1959, when owner Leong first became interested in cars. Roland was 15 years old at the time, and a resident of his native state, Hawaii. Drag racing in the Islands was then a mere fledgling of a sport, but it soon became a favorite form of automotive sports activity. And Leong was right in

This could possibly be considered the "Holy Grail" of Top Fuel memorabilia. The 1967* Hawaiian *AA/FD press kit featured pages of original literature, a set of four press photographs, and the original folder that featured the Hawaii tiki caricature for Luck.

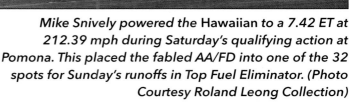

Mike Snively powered the Hawaiian to a 7.42 ET at 212.39 mph during Saturday's qualifying action at Pomona. This placed the fabled AA/FD into one of the 32 spots for Sunday's runoffs in Top Fuel Eliminator. (Photo Courtesy Roland Leong Collection)

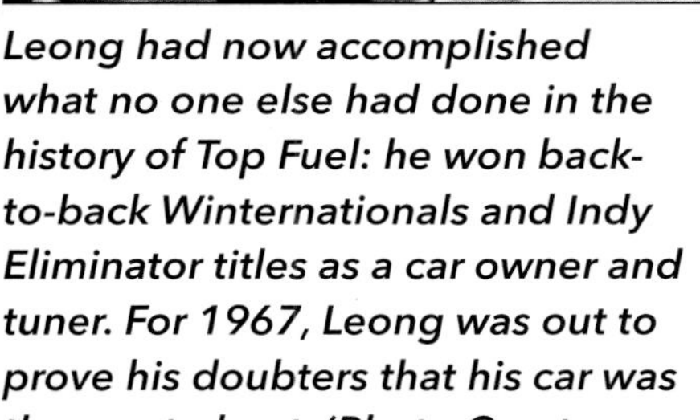

Leong had now accomplished what no one else had done in the history of Top Fuel: he won back-to-back Winternationals and Indy Eliminator titles as a car owner and tuner. For 1967, Leong was out to prove his doubters that his car was the one to beat. (Photo Courtesy Roland Leong Collection)

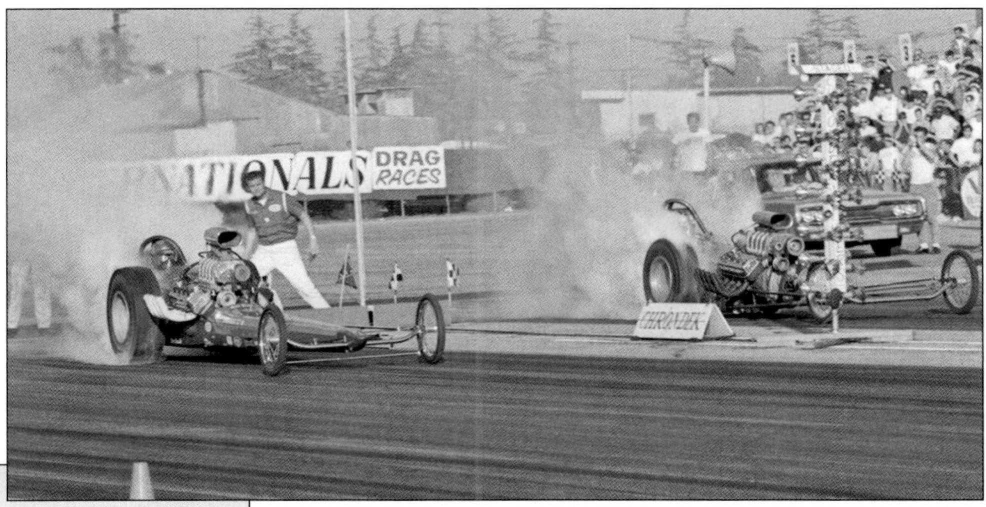

Mike Snively and Rick "the Iceman" Stewart compete during qualifying at Pomona. (Photo Courtesy Steve Reyes)

Roland Leong keeps a sharp eye on Connie Kalitta maintaining his 427-ci SOHC Cammer before Friday's time trials at Pomona. It didn't take long for Leong to find out how well the Ford performed when his Hawaiian lost to the Bounty Hunter in the second round of eliminations, thus ending his chances to three-peat. The rest of the competition also found out how Kalitta's Cammer performed when he won the Winternationals crown. (Photo Courtesy Steve Reyes)

Mike Snively, the defending Winternationals champion, freewheels the Goodyears during Friday's attempt to qualify at the seventh-annual NHRA Winternationals. (Photo Courtesy Steve Reyes)

Hawaiian's long list of amazing achievements. Snively defeated Bob Muravez (also known as Floyd Lippincott) in the Don "Beachcomber" Johnson entry in the final run to take home the Top Fuel purse. Snively's 7.34 ET at 213.76 mph bested Muravez's fine 7.36 at 214.28.

The *Hawaiian* Falls Short

A crowd of more than 70,000 fans packed the L.A. County Fairgrounds on February 4 and 5 at the seventh-annual NHRA Winternationals. They were there to see if Leong and Snively could pull off the three-peat in Top Fuel Eliminator.

In the first round of Sunday's eliminations, Snively disposed of the Waterman-Hampshire entry. He then drew the number-one qualifier, Connie Kalitta, with his potent SOHC Ford in round two. With one of the closest races of the day, Kalitta crushed the hopes of many when the *Bounty Hunter* denied the *Hawaiian* the chance to return to the winner circle. Kalitta ran a 7.24 ET at 214.58 mph to Snively's 7.35 at 212.26.

Many showed displeasure toward Leong for not winning his third consecutive NHRA Winternationals in 1967. However, there are 7, 15, 31, or 63 losers and only one winner at these meets. That's the name of the game . . . Top Eliminator!

Connie Kalitta prevented Top Fuel's first three-peat winner when his Bounty Hunter dropped the Hawaiian in round two at the Winternationals. Kalitta's 7.24 ET at 214 mph was too much for Snively's 7.35 at 212.26. (Photo Courtesy Steve Reyes)

This was round one of eliminations on Sunday at Pomona, as the Waterman-Hampshire entry faced Snively and Leong. Snively drove past Hampshire to take the win. (Photo Courtesy Steve Reyes)

The *Hawaiian II* Debuts

Imagine being a Top Fuel driver as the car is rolling into the staging beams. Then, when you glance over into the next lane, you see that your head-to-head encounter is against the *Hawaiian*. Now, visualize the added distress of the opposing drivers and teams when the realization hits that there are two *Hawaiians*!

Well, that's what happened when Leong and Black rolled onto the grounds at Bakersfield for the ninth-annual U.S. Fuel and Gas Championships on February 18 and 19, 1967. The nightmare became a reality when the team brought its one-two punch to Bakersfield with the famed original *Hawaiian* driven by Mike Snively and their latest experiment, the *Hawaiian II*.

Many eyebrows were raised from the curious onlookers during Mike Sorokin's first ever pass in the *Hawaiian II*. He went straight down Famoso's fabled quarter mile with a shattering 7.16 ET at 212.00 mph.

In the opening round of Top Fuel, Snively kicked it off when he ran a 7.28 ET at 206.20 mph to overcome a hole-shot by Texian Dan Rightsell, who cut the losing round of 7.70 at 196.92. Also sandwiched into the field of 32 diggers was Leong's brand-new *Hawaiian II*, which was piloted by Mike Sorokin. Sorokin dropped a hole-shot on Tommy Allen and cut a fine 7.46 ET at 192.54 mph.

After two torrid days of qualifying for a spot in the 32-car field, the action at Famoso resulted in the quickest Top Fuel field ever assembled in the sport of drag racing. Among the leaders in the field were Snively and Sorokin, averaging 7.20 ETs at 210 mph throughout the weekend. The magic continued to the semifinal heats with both *Hawaiian* entries leading.

The bubble soon popped for Sorokin, as a hole-shot win by Dave Beebe upset the works. Snively advanced to face Beebe when "Sneaky" Pete Robinson fouled with the

DOUBLE THREAT: THE HAWAIIAN II

Weeks before the seventh-annual Winternationals at Pomona, an announcement was made from Marysville, Michigan, by Joseph D. McCarthy, who was president of the Chrysler Corporation's Marine Division. McCarthy announced that Keith Black was appointed to concentrate on the 426-ci Chrysler Hemis for flat-bottom boat racing.

The first late-model marine engine was implanted into Barry McGowen's drag boat with Black, Gene Mooneyham, Danny Broussard, and others on hand for the maiden run. Unfortunately, the test session ended abruptly when the boat lost control and flipped over. After the incident, Black, McCarthy, and the Chrysler group decided that the marine engine and its funding would be applied to a Top Fuel dragster that would be campaigned by Leong, appropriately named the *Hawaiian II*.

The chassis was built by Don Long. It was originally built for the H&A Processing Company (Marshall & Vermilya) with the new-fashioned 426-ci Chrysler Marine Hemi mounted between the pipes.

Leong tabbed good friend Mike Sorokin of the Surfers AA/FD fame to drive for him with the hopes of taking the Top Fuel troupe by storm. Added to the team was Danny "Buzz" Broussard to assist with the tuning and maintenance on the Chrysler Hemi. Broussard earned the nickname "Buzz" from Leong when Leong had difficulties pronouncing "Broussard."

Mike Sorokin waits for the command to push out in the new* Hawaiian II *at the ninth-annual U.S. Fuel and Gas Championships at Bakersfield. Bolted between the rails was Keith Black's latest engine: a 426-ci late-model Chrysler Marine Hemi. (Photo Courtesy Steve Reyes)

Pit space was at a premium at Bakersfield. The* Hawaiian *team of Leong, Black, and Broussard settled for a patch of weeds against a fence, which proves that anyone can thrash on a race car on any surface and win the event. (Photo Courtesy Roland Leong Collection)

unwanted red-light. Snively and Beebe staged in the final for the nearly $4,000 cash purse. Snively was declared the easy winner when Beebe had a misadventure and completely crossed up the car and got out of shape.

Nearly all of the spectators showed their appreciation with a standing ovation to Roland Leong, Mike Snively, and company for their performances in winning Top Fuel. Since the first of the year, the team had won three other Top Fuel shows, had been runners-up at two other meets, and had run every big meet in or out of town.

Sorokin Beats the House

Fresh off their Smoker's victory from the previous week at Bakersfield, Leong's team arrived in Las Vegas, Nevada. The team was the wily tipster's favorite to win it all at the Stardust Raceway National Open on February 25 and 26.

Balancing out the adjustment ratios for the 2,300-foot altitude, La Mirada fireman Jim Dunn led the charge in Saturday's qualifying. Dunn ran a 7.36 ET at 211.26 mph for the number-one overall position in the open field of 16. Mike "Snipe" Sorokin held down the third slot with a 7.40 ET in the *Hawaiian II*. Snively followed Sorokin's lead, hitting a 7.52 ET in the *Hawaiian*.

In the first round, Sorokin made easy work by disposing of Steve Carbone in Dave McKenzie's rail with a 7.31 at 206.88 mph blast. The second round was a little tougher for Sorokin against Danny Ongais's Honda

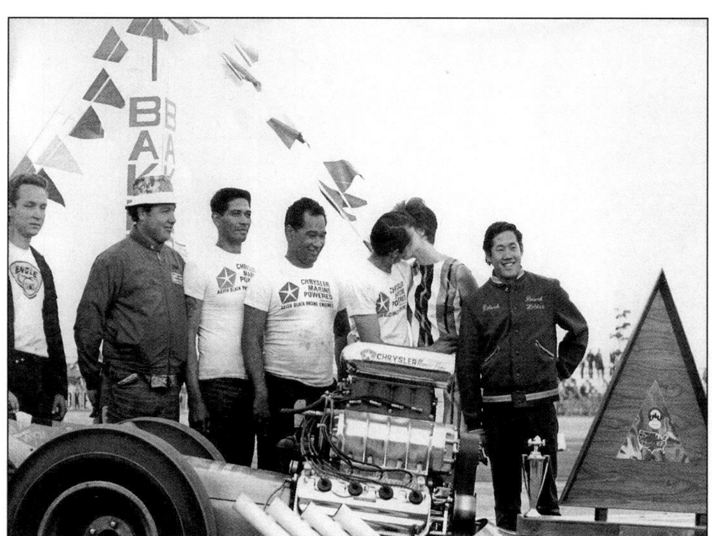

The jubilant crew of the* Hawaiian *joins in the winner's circle celebration after winning the ninth-annual U.S. Fuel and Gas Championships at Bakersfield. Danny Broussard, Lawrence Kaanapu, Smokey Kanehailua, and Roland Leong look on as Mike Snively collects the congratulatory kiss from race queen Linda Rickman. (Photo Courtesy Roland Leong Collection)

Mike Sorokin erupts off the line in the* Hawaiian II *at Stardust Raceway's National Open in Las Vegas. Sorokin beat the odds and took home all the chips when his final-round foe James Warren red-lit, which gave the* Hawaiian II *the win. Despite knowing that he'd already taken the win light, Sorokin didn't hold back as he sped to the best time and speed of the day: 7.23 at 206.78 mph.

of Wilmington entry. The horsepower from the Black Elephant 426 Hemi powered the *Hawaiian II* past Ongais and opened the door to the final round against James Warren.

In what appeared to be the battle of California heavyweights, Warren jumped the gun and fouled his chances away. Sorokin took advantage of Warren's foul but still gave the fans their money's worth when he put his foot to the wood and ran his best time and speed for the day: 7.23 at 206.78 mph.

The New Dragster Debuts

With the venue changed to Riverside Raceway for April 7, 8, and 9, the mood of the weekend crowd at the fourth-annual Hot Rod Magazine Championships indicated that the sport of drag racing was alive and well. Friday's rain delays didn't dampen the highly spirited atmosphere leading up to Sunday's elimination runoffs. Once again, the invincible team of Roland Leong, Keith Black, Mike Snively, and Mike Sorokin was the one to beat.

While it took on the appearance of another easy win for the team, it took the strength of a 7.07 ET along with a huge amount of good fortune in the final round for Snively to put away the underdog-turned-crowd-favorite Glen Brown from Phoenix, Arizona. Brown's home-built, outdated 136-inch car had not been raced for several years. To Brown's advantage, he was quick on the lights, cutting 7.40s with his low-budget Chrysler.

When Brown qualified into the show with a 7.44 ET,

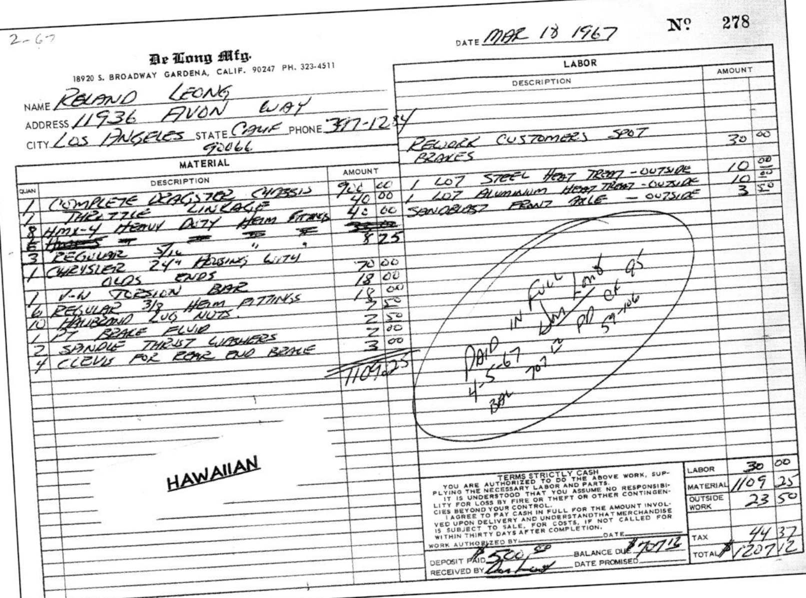

2-67

De Long Mfg.
18920 S. BROADWAY GARDENA, CALIF. 90247 PH. 323-4511

DATE MAR 18 1967 №. 278

NAME ROLAND LEONG
ADDRESS 11936 AVON WAY
CITY LOS ANGELES STATE CALIF PHONE 317-1284
90066

MATERIAL

QUAN	DESCRIPTION	AMOUNT
1	COMPLETE DRAGSTER CHASSIS	900 00
1	THROTTLE LINKAGE	40 00
8	HMX-4 HEAVY DUTY HEIM FITTINGS	40 00
3	REGULAR 5/16 " "	8 25
1	CHRYSLER 24" HOUSING WITH OLDS ENDS	70 00
1	V-W TORSION BAR	18 00
6	REGULAR 3/8 HEIM FITTINGS	18 00
10	HALIBRAND LUG NUTS	7 50
1	PT BRAKE FLUID	2 50
2	SPINDLE THRUST WASHERS	2 00
4	CLEVIS FOR REAR END BRAKE	3 00
		1109 25

LABOR

DESCRIPTION	AMOUNT
REWORK CUSTOMERS SPOT BRAKES	30 00
1 LOT STEEL HEAT TREAT - OUTSIDE	10 00
1 LOT ALUMINUM HEAT TREAT - OUTSIDE	10 00
SANDBLAST FRONT AXLE - OUTSIDE	3 50

PAID IN FULL 4-5-67 Don Long 707 pd ck 95 59-106

HAWAIIAN

TERMS STRICTLY CASH
YOU ARE AUTHORIZED TO DO THE ABOVE WORK, SUPPLYING THE NECESSARY LABOR AND PARTS.
IT IS UNDERSTOOD THAT YOU ASSUME NO RESPONSIBILITY FOR LOSS BY FIRE OR THEFT OR OTHER CONTINGENCIES BEYOND YOUR CONTROL.
I AGREE TO PAY CASH IN FULL FOR THE AMOUNT INVOLVED UPON DELIVERY AND UNDERSTAND THAT MERCHANDISE IS SUBJECT TO SALE, FOR COSTS, IF NOT CALLED FOR WITHIN THIRTY DAYS AFTER COMPLETION.
WORK AUTHORIZED BY ______ DATE ______
DEPOSIT PAID $500.00 BALANCE DUE $707.12
RECEIVED BY Don Long DATE PROMISED ______

LABOR	30 00
MATERIAL	1109 25
OUTSIDE WORK	23 50
TAX	44 37
TOTAL	$1207 12

In 1964, the original Hawaiian *AA/FD was built by Kent Fuller. The car sent Top Fuel Eliminator onto a whole other level, winning nearly everything in sight and rewriting numerous speed and track records whenever the car rolled onto a drag strip. The* Hawaiian *now was almost three years old. The car had been unloaded and loaded at every race, towed thousands of miles from coast to coast, and run several times a week. It had survived two crashes, been re-fronted and stretched forward several times, and it was now considered outdated. Leong decided to contact Don Long Manufacturing and ordered a brand-new car to replace the original. This was the last* Hawaiian *dragster for Leong. (Invoice Courtesy from Pete Eastwood/Don Long)*

Three great friends (from left to right) Roland Leong, Tom "the Mongoose" McEwen, and Ernie Hashim of M&H Racemaster tires pose for Drag News *photographer Alan Earman before the roar of excitement runs rampant at the fourth-annual Hot Rod Magazine Championships. (Photo Courtesy Roland Leong Collection)*

Mike Sorokin boils the Goodyears during the first round of eliminations at Riverside. In a close heat, Sorokin took down the reigning NHRA Winternationals champ, Connie Kalitta, with a 7.36 ET at 191.88 mph over the faster Kalitta's 7.37 at 211.78. (Photo Courtesy Roland Leong Collection)

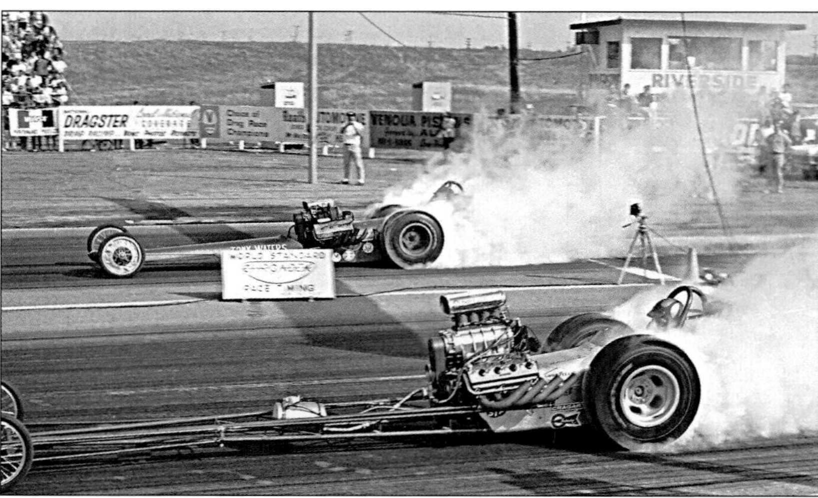

In the third round, Snively faced John Edmunds. It was Snively's first run after the improvements to the new Hawaiian*, and his ET was reduced by three-tenths of a second to an unbelievable 7.13 ET at 218 mph. (Photo Courtesy Paul Johnson Collection)*

Unheralded Glen Brown and the favored Mike Snively were the last pair of Top Fuel dragsters remaining to close out the fourth-annual Hot Rod Magazine Championships at Riverside Raceway. Brown and Snively took a different approach on how to win, but Snively's plan worked, as he set Riverside's ET and speed records: 7.07 at 221.66.

he had to borrow fuel from other racers to keep racing. Snively's slower time of 7.45 in qualifying put the *Hawaiian* behind Brown, as Leong and Black faced a situation that they'd never experienced running the car.

In the first round of competition, the week-old *Hawaiian* turned in an unimpressive win with a 7.43 ET at 206.88 mph over Tom Toler, who ran quicker with a 7.41 at 212.76. Both Leong and Black realized that these times wouldn't hold back the rest of the competition.

A second-round win over Steve Carbone resulted in the identical time (7.43) from the previous round. Mulling over the situation to improve, the decision was made before the third round to take a hacksaw and cut off the main rail braces on both sides of the new chassis. This was the team's attempt to increase traction and add more flex to the chassis. The results drastically improved in the third round when Snively dropped the ET three-tenths of a second from the previous round to run an unbelievable 7.13 at 218 mph and beat John Edmunds.

In the semifinals against Tom McEwen in the Bivens-Fisher entry, Snively once again lowered his ET by disposing of the Mongoose with a record blast of 7.07 at 218.44 mph to McEwen's 7.35 at 217.38.

Brown and Snively faced off in the final round. Strategies resembled a high-stakes poker game when the heavily favored Snively had to retain his blistering pace and not red-light. In the other lane, Brown, the underdog, had to beat the light and "dump the can" to have a chance at the title. Brown cut a nearly perfect light off the tree when he jumped from the line first, giving him the lead. However, the hard-charging *Hawaiian* caught and passed Brown at mid-track and opened a two-car lead at the lights.

Snively completed his dominance while setting both ends of the time and speed records: a 7.07 ET at 221.66 mph to Brown's plucky 7.42

It took more than just driving and tuning to win the fourth-annual* Hot Rod Magazine *Championships. It was a meeting of the minds that made the right combination of modifications to the chassis to put the new* Hawaiian *into the winner's circle.* Hot Rod *editor Bob Green awards Mike Snively and the exhilarated* Hawaiian *crew* Hot Rod*'s piston plaque trophy. (Photo Courtesy Roland Leong Collection)

at 213.76. Mike Snively once again downed the competition and earned $3,000 for the *Hawaiian* trio, celebrating another major eliminator title.

Northern California fans were treated to the finest and fastest drag racing event ever in that region. Lodi's Kingdon hosted its version of East versus West Championships with a bevy of California's top rails up against a collection of the country's finest iron.

Leong, Snively, and Leong's mother pose for photos holding the coveted **Hot Rod** magazine championship trophy after their hard-fought win over 64 of the nation's best Top Fuelers. (Photo Courtesy Steve Reyes)

Hawaiian II Success

Irwindale Raceway hosted one of its Saturday-night Top Fuel cards with local talent that had the characteristics of a top national event. The competition supplied big numbers of what the touring pros would offer, including Warren-Colburn-Miller's whopping 7.19 ET at 224 mph. Right behind Colburn was Mike Sorokin in the *Hawaiian II* with a 7.22 ET at 201.78 mph.

Sorokin began his night by taking down Butch Maas driving Bill Crossley's *Crusader*. He then bumped out Kenny Safford in round two when Sorokin motored Leong's late-model Chrysler Hemi past the Ted Gotelli entry, turning a 7.14 ET at 205.46 mph. Gearing up for the final round against the track's new top-speed record holder, James Warren, Keith Black proceeded to make the

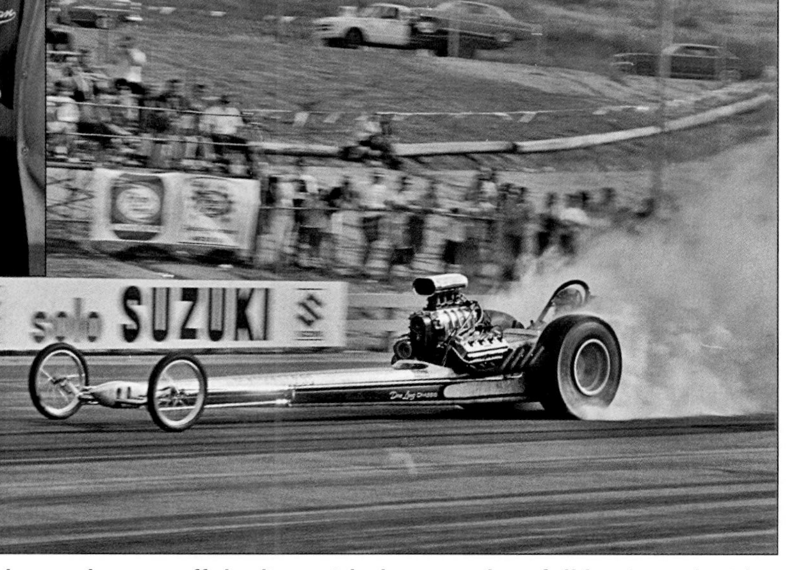

Mike Snively accelerates off the line with the complete full body and with a reliable 392-ci Chrysler engine that was prepped by Keith Black and maintained by Leong. (Photo Courtesy Roland Leong Collection)

BEST COVERAGE OF HRM CHAMPIONSHIPS - - PART ONE

NATIONAL DRAGSTER

IN THIS ISSUE

EDITORIAL	Page 2
BITS FROM THE PITS	Page 2
NHRA SIGNS CECIL	Page 3
HRM BREAKDOWN	Page 5
MEANWHILE IN ENGLAND	Page 17
DRAG MART	Page 19
NATIONAL RECORDS	Page 21

APRIL 14, 1967 ★ ★ ★ JOURNAL OF THE NATIONAL HOT ROD ASSOCIATION ★ ★ ★ VOL. VIII – NO. 6 25c COPY

HOT ROD'S Believe It Or Not . . .

HAWAIIAN III

This misleading headline from **National Dragster** *congratulates the* **Hawaiian III** *of Roland Leong and Mike Snively for the win at the fourth-annual Hot Rod Magazine Championships. According to Leong, there was never a third Hawaiian. His new Don Long car replaced the well-traveled, four-time national-event-winning car, and the* **Hawaiian II** *was a test vehicle for Black's late-model 426 Chrysler Marine program.*

adjustments on his experimental toy for Sorokin. Sorokin cut low ET of the night: 7.11 at 215.82 mph. Unfortunately for the Ridge Route Terrors, a rod exited from the block before the 660-foot mark, ending their chances to reset the top-speed record.

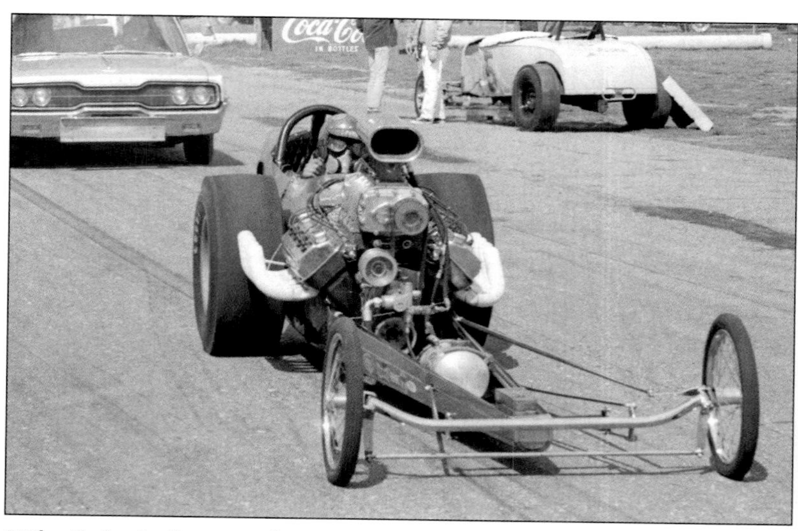

Mike Snively fires up the Hawaiian *at Kingdon on the push-off road, checking out the oil pressure and the tune-up before eliminations. (Photo Courtesy Steve Reyes)*

Leong-Black-Snively Continue Unbeaten

The first of numerous stops throughout Northern California was at Half Moon Drag Strip with a match race against Ken Safford and the "Terrible" Ted Gotelli's Speed Shop digger. Safford and Gotelli picked the wrong weekend to try out their new car, as they tackled the virtually unbeatable team of Leong-Black-Snively and their famed *Hawaiian*.

While Safford rewrote the track top-speed record for the strip at 214.78 mph, Snively put Gotelli's entry away in the first round on two straight passes, running a 7.19 ET at 213.28 mph. The second time around, it was a hole-shot for Snively that gave the *Hawaiian* the big win when Snively shut off with a 7.42 ET at 193.12 mph to Safford's 7.27 at 212.76.

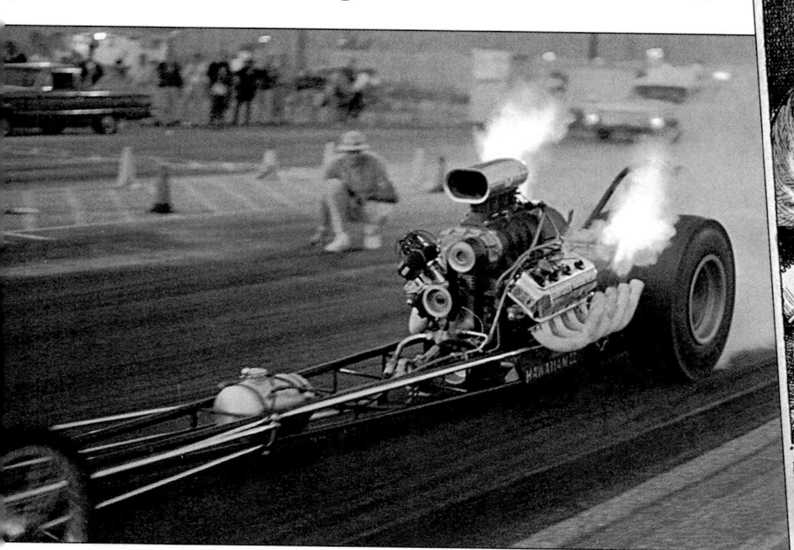

Nothing was more exciting at dusk than seeing the 6-foot flames blasting out from the zoomie headers, especially when Mike Sorokin unleashed the power of the Keith Black "Elephant" 426-ci Hemi in Roland Leong's Hawaiian II *at Irwindale.*

Pete Millar's Drag Cartoons *ran a series of exclusive cartoon features in several issues of* National Dragster *on the jesting humor of Leong and Black with the rival engine builders. (Photo Courtesy of Robin Millar/Drag Cartoons)*

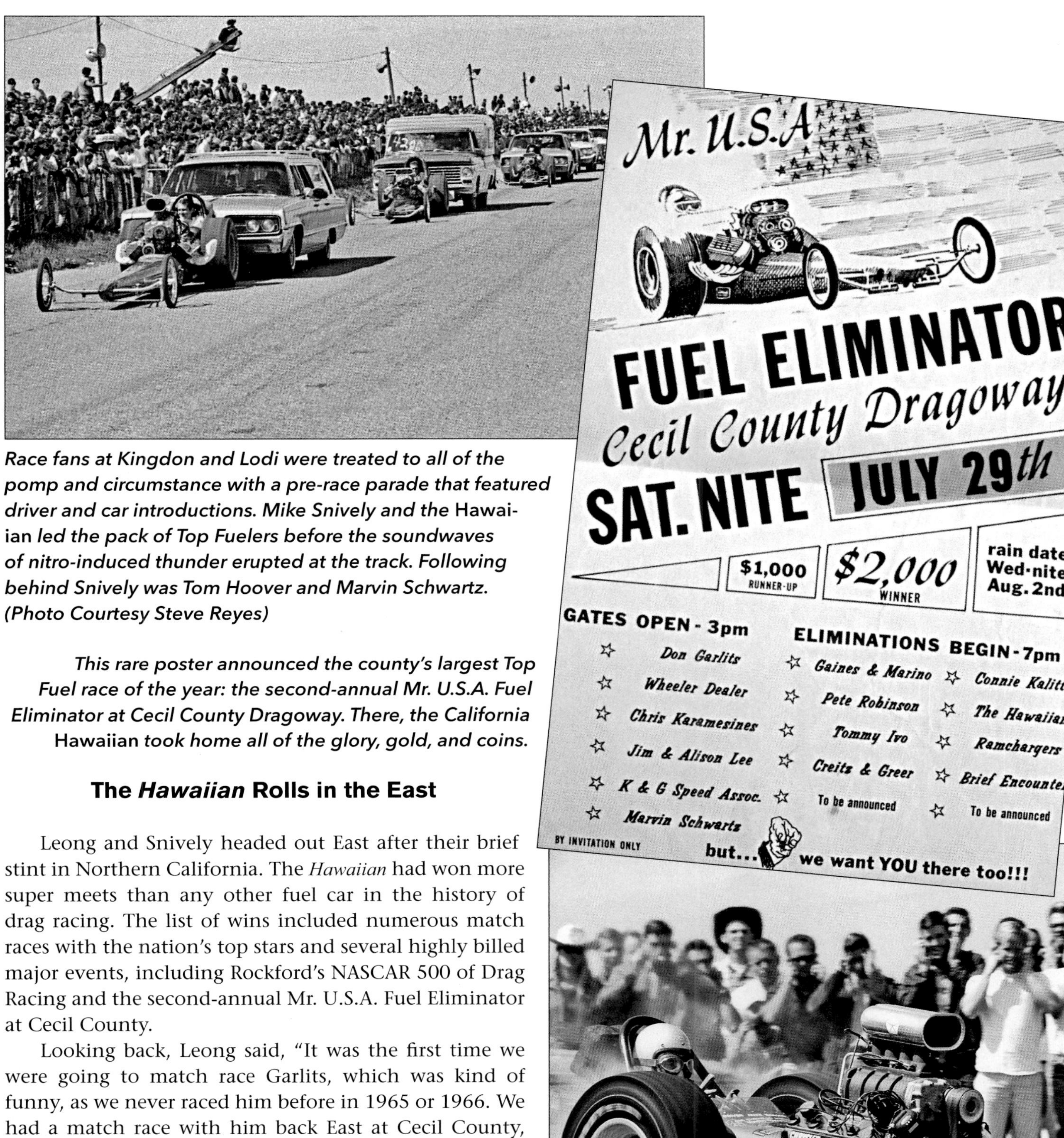

Race fans at Kingdon and Lodi were treated to all of the pomp and circumstance with a pre-race parade that featured driver and car introductions. Mike Snively and the Hawaiian *led the pack of Top Fuelers before the soundwaves of nitro-induced thunder erupted at the track. Following behind Snively was Tom Hoover and Marvin Schwartz. (Photo Courtesy Steve Reyes)*

This rare poster announced the county's largest Top Fuel race of the year: the second-annual Mr. U.S.A. Fuel Eliminator at Cecil County Dragoway. There, the California Hawaiian *took home all of the glory, gold, and coins.*

Mike Sorokin unleashes the noise from the experimental 426 Chrysler Marine Elephant built by Keith Black. By the reaction of the fans, they are impressed with the performance of the Hawaiian II. *(Photo Courtesy Roland Leong Collection)*

The *Hawaiian* Rolls in the East

Leong and Snively headed out East after their brief stint in Northern California. The *Hawaiian* had won more super meets than any other fuel car in the history of drag racing. The list of wins included numerous match races with the nation's top stars and several highly billed major events, including Rockford's NASCAR 500 of Drag Racing and the second-annual Mr. U.S.A. Fuel Eliminator at Cecil County.

Looking back, Leong said, "It was the first time we were going to match race Garlits, which was kind of funny, as we never raced him before in 1965 or 1966. We had a match race with him back East at Cecil County, Maryland. I took the car apart to check over everything before making a test run before racing Don. In those days, you match raced two out of three, so if you won the first two, you didn't need to run the third one, which would save us money. But, who thought about the money then? We just wanted to win.

"I remember that we went out and made a test run to check everything. At race time, we beat Garlits two straight! When we went up to pick up the money, the track manager said, 'Garlits was so mad, he didn't even stop by to pick up his money. He grumbled and said just to send it to him!'

"This was the first time ever that he left the track without getting his money!"

Wipeout at Indy

If the number 13 proved to be superstitious for Leong, the 13th-annual NHRA Nationals turned out to be very unlucky for both *Hawaiian* cars in eliminations. After both Fuelers qualified strong in the field of 32, Snively in the seventh position (6.955 at 214.78 mph) and Sorokin in eighth (6.970 at 218.44 mph), both were defeated by the eventual winner, "Big Daddy" Don Garlits.

Snively fell victim to Garlits in round one, when Garlits ran a 7.067 ET at 216.86 mph to put Snively on the trailer with an off-pace 7.256 at 215.30. Sorokin advanced to the second round after dropping Fred Welshman Jr. from Milwaukee, Wisconsin, in the opening frame. Snively lined up against Garlits, but he left too soon, handing the win to Garlits and ending Leong's reign at the U.S. Nationals.

At the 13th-annual NHRA Nationals at Indy, Leong, Buzz, and Mike Snively found time for a Hot Rod *magazine media and photo session. Keith Black provided the 1,500-hp 392 Chrysler Hemi. Tom Hanna handcrafted the aluminum body and wrapped it over the Don Long 178-inch-wheelbase frame. George Cerny sprayed the beautiful blue and "cobwebbed" white paint. (Photo Courtesy Roland Leong Collection)*

Car Craft Magazine's All-Star Drag Racing Team

In 1967, the brass at *Car Craft* magazine honored drag racing's top performers with the first-annual *Car Craft* magazine All-Star Drag Racing Team awards. A banquet was held during the week of the 13th-annual NHRA Nationals on Labor Day weekend in Indianapolis, Indiana.

The awards were broken down into five divisions: Competition, Match Race, Stock, Manufacturer of the Year, and Man of the Year. One of the most highly recognized achievement awards voted on by the readers of *Car Craft* was for the Crew Chief of the Year. It was presented to 23-year-old Roland Leong.

Leong was the heavy favorite when he outpolled several outstanding nominees. In the balloting, he ended

Car Craft *magazine's first-annual All-Star Drag Racing Team award was determined by popular vote from participating readers of the drag racing magazine. Readers selected from a list of nominees from two divisional categories. The lineup of honorees that are sitting at the table were the Competition winners. From left to right, they are Top Fuel driver Connie Kalitta, Gas driver "Ohio" George Montgomery, crew chief Roland Leong, engine builder Keith Black,* Car Craft*'s managing editor John Raffa (standing), chassis builder Woody Gilmore, Competition sponsor Lou Baney, and Fuel and Gas match-race drivers "Dyno" Don Nicholson and Ronnie Sox. Each award member received a bounty of goodies that included a custom All-Star chronograph wristwatch, two pairs of Levi's Sta-press dress slacks; a Westinghouse travel clock radio, distinctive All-Star blazers, two special All-Star shirts, over-the-head lightweight yellow jackets, a custom* Car Craft *award plaque, and an array of decals for their vehicles and race cars. (Photo Courtesy Roland Leong Collection)*

Leong receives his Car Craft *magazine' Crew Chief of the Year gold ring from Jackie Hart, daughter of NHRA event director Jack Hart. (Photo Courtesy Roland Leong Collection)*

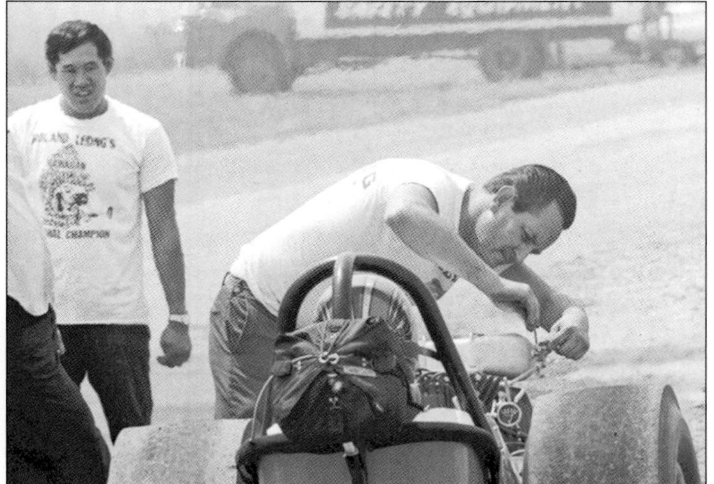

Leong sees Bob Creitz adjusting the throttle linkage on the borrowed original Hawaiian *during Goodyear's new-compound tire-testing session at Lions Drag Strip. Leong loaned Creitz his dragster after Creitz's car crashed a few weeks earlier at a drag strip in Wisconsin. Leong didn't take the compensation paid from Goodyear and let Creitz use the money toward the purchase of a new chassis from Don Long. (Photo Courtesy Steve Reyes)*

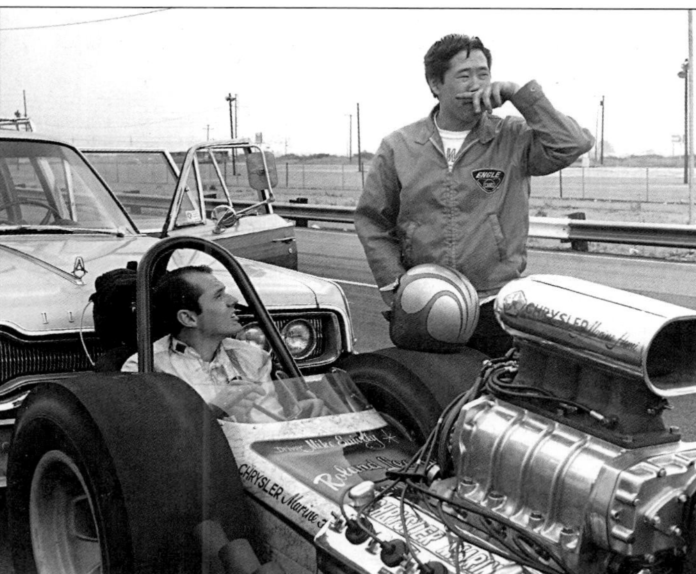

Leong, Snively, and Ed Pink had fun teasing each other. It was a way of trying to stay steps ahead of their cat-and-mouse games and secrets. Racers, owners, engine builders, and parts and component suppliers were serious rivals on the track, but they also were a fraternity that had a side of humor and kindness. They were always first to lend a helping hand or loan parts to help others compete. (Photo Courtesy Roland Leong Collection)

up with more than 15,000 votes from the readers of the magazine. The *Hawaiian*'s spectacular and steady performances in winning back-to-back Winternationals and Nationals Eliminator titles for 1965 and 1966 were the main reasons behind Leong's winning the Crew Chief of the Year award and Keith Black being the recipient of the All-Star Completion Engine Builder award.

Rewriting a Mile-High Record

Completing the back end of the long summer touring season and heading west for home, Leong, Snively, and the record-setting *Hawaiian* made a stop in Albuquerque, New Mexico. They arrived several days before the highly touted match race at Albuquerque Raceway, so Leong and Snively gave their unlimited support promoting the races. They both appeared on several Albuquerque radio and television programs along with displaying the record-winning *Hawaiian* dragster at a local car dealership.

The special Top Fuel "Texas verses California" event featured a best-of-three match race against the "fastest in the Southwest" Vance Hunt entry, with driver Watus Simpson from Dallas, Texas.

The first race was a real nailbiter for the spectators, as the cars exchanged leads back and forth, streaking side by side from the starting line down to the traps. At the end,

"We had run Snively and Roland at Albuquerque Raceway, New Mexico, in a big, advertised Texas versus California match race, where they outran us twice and beat us, as my car just couldn't cut it on top of that mountain," said Texas Top Fuel champion Vance Hunt. "Snively told me while we were sitting on my tailgate, 'Vance, let me tell you, if you had our clutch, you would have beat us. You had more power than us.'

"I asked Mike, 'How's that?'

"Mike mentioned that the *Hawaiian* had a new three-disc-clutch package with adjustable springs to adjust the fingers, weight, and height. Mike gave me the independent clutch builder's number, and the following week, I had one in my car. It dropped my time a tenth or two.

"Roland and Mike both helped me get the right clutch. I had a lot of wonderful times and met a lot of wonderful people that always helped me in the early days. Drag racers were pretty nice people and watched out for one another. That was Roland and Mike, they were in this group."

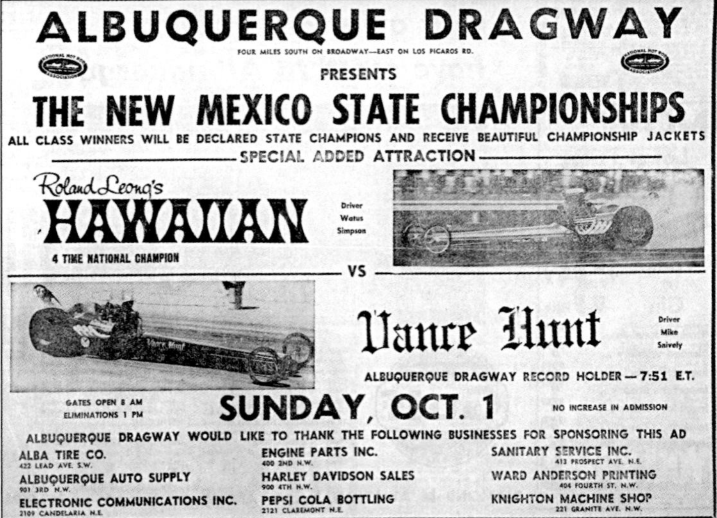

***Drag racing's equivalent to two champion heavyweight boxers battling for supremacy was the highly touted Texas versus California best-of-three match race. It was between Vance Hunt and his driver, Watus Simpson, from Dallas, Texas, taking on the* Hawaiian.**

it was Snively by a front wheel for the win. The *Hawaiian* ran a respectable ET of 7.53 (just 0.02 second off the track ET record set just the month before by Hunt and Simpson) at 213.03 mph for a new strip record. Simpson trailed with a 7.82 at 212.84.

Round two was all Simpson. The Texas slingshot drove past Snively, resetting both ends of the strip records with an unbelievable 7.19 ET at 219.78 mph to the *Hawaiian*'s strong 7.54 at 216.76.

Both Leong and Hunt went through their cars, trying to get the best that each had to offer for all of the money and bragging rights. Both cars launched evenly off the line through all the noise and haze of smoke, but Snively repeated his first-round win, crossing the line first with a 7.27 ET to a 7.34, the length of a spoked front wheel.

Snively also broke the speed record again with an incredible 221.34 mph top speed for the mile-high record. Leong and Snively packed up the car and trailer and drove through the gates, heading west for the trip home. Just as they hit the highway, they noticed the Albuquerque Dragway's "Home of 200 mph Racing" entrance sign leading into the track. Snively brought the station wagon to a stop and grabbed a roll of duct tape from the toolbox in the back and rewrote the sign with the tape to read "Home of 220-mph Racing."

Consecutive Streak Snapped

The quickest field of fuel dragsters in the history of Irwindale Raceway heated up the crowd on a chilly November 4 night. A crop of more than 40 Fuelers attempted to qualify for a coveted slot in the 16-car program.

It was one of the few times that Mike Snively, Roland Leong, and the *Hawaiian* failed to make the show during Snively's second qualifying pass. The engine coughed in the lights and let go, spraying hot oil onto the facemask of Snively. He veered off the asphalt course and down the left side of the track, where he flew in the air several times and brought the car to a stop right-side up without serious injury or damage to the car.

The following week at Orange County Raceway, 47 Fuelers invaded the premises for a scheduled 16-car Top Fuel Eliminator program. It had one of the quickest fields assembled for the three-month-old facility: a total of six cars qualified under 7 seconds, including Stan Shiroma in the "borrowed" original blue *Hawaiian* with a 6.97 ET.

Seeing how the older car performed, many were left wondering if the car had a newer, tricked-out chassis underneath it. The only difference was that Shiroma removed Leong's Keith Black–built powerplant and replaced it with his own engine.

One interesting sidenote is that at the closing of qualifying, Shiroma put the original "old blue car" into the show by bumping out Snively in the orange *Hawaiian II* at the last moment. Shiroma put the fabled Fueler to the task, winning the first round with a 6.93 ET but wasting

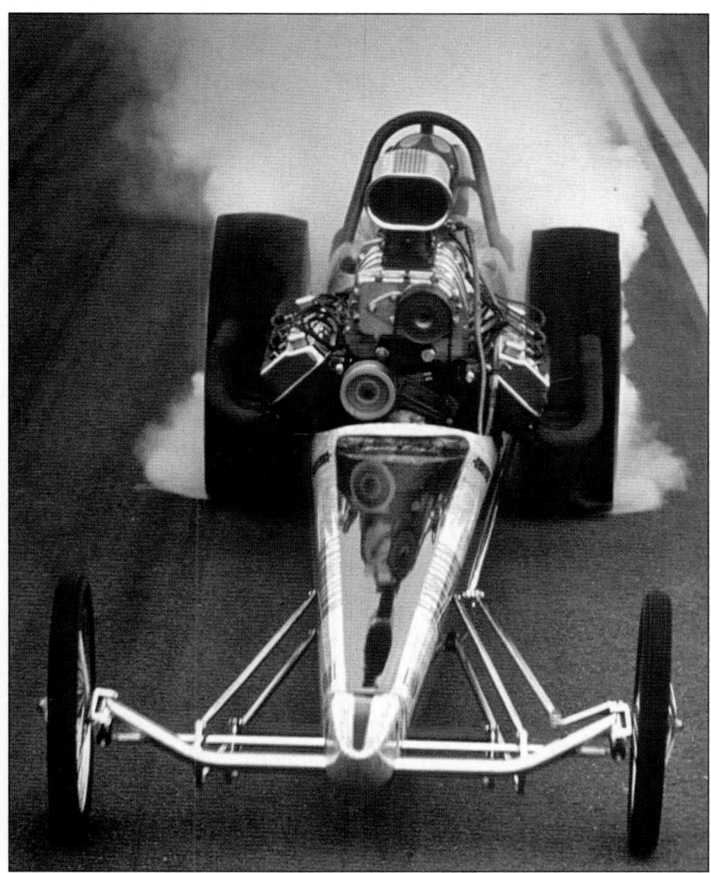

Mike Snively's qualifying streak at Irwindale was snapped during this second-pass attempt, when the engine coughed in the lights and blew hot oil from the engine and onto his goggles. His impaired vision caused him to go off the end of the strip. Although missing the show, both Snively and the rail were unharmed. (Photo Courtesy Roland Leong Collection)

the engine driving through the last light, melting several pistons in the process and ending his march for the crown.

Fire Brewed Racin'

On December 4 at Lions Drag Strip, Hart procured a unique mystical formula that consisted of four AA/Fuelers, a pinch of two fuel roadsters, a dash of Junior Fuel, and the twist of Top Gas. It was the best concoction of pure excitement that was ever staged.

Not only did the large crowd of spectators go wild over the sight of the smaller Jr. Fuel rail trying to chop down on the mighty Top Fueler but the drivers were also nearly executing cartwheels when Hart raised the round money to $110.

The extravaganza commenced with the fabled *Hawaiian* taking on the *Wailer* of Hays and Walsh.

Snively, a top driver in anyone's league, dashed to a 7.25 ET at 208.32 mph when his competition fell from contention with engine difficulties. Mike Sorokin, now driving Tony Walters's relatively new mount, fell to the *Outcast*. (Let it be noted, Mike Sorokin moved on to wheeling Tony Waters's latest Fueler when Chrysler ceased funding the Chrysler Marine experiment, parking the car).

As the smoke cleared, two Top Fuelers remained to collect the big bucks: John Mitchell in the *Red Mountain Boys* entry and Mike Snively. At the hit, the *Hawaiian* torridly jumped out ahead without smoking the tires, leading the way to the timing traps ahead of Mitchell, who was plagued with severe traction problems. Snively won

Mike Snively flexed the power of Roland Leong's **Hawaiian** *at Irwindale, setting low ET and top speed in late December at the Top Fuel finale for 1967. He blasted to a 6.90 ET at 229.24 mph from the 426-ci* **Black Elephant***, but all hope was lost when Snively wasted a 7.03 ET at 216.34 mph in the second round of eliminations when he cut the light too soon, setting the tree red in his lane against the overall winner Bob Downey.*

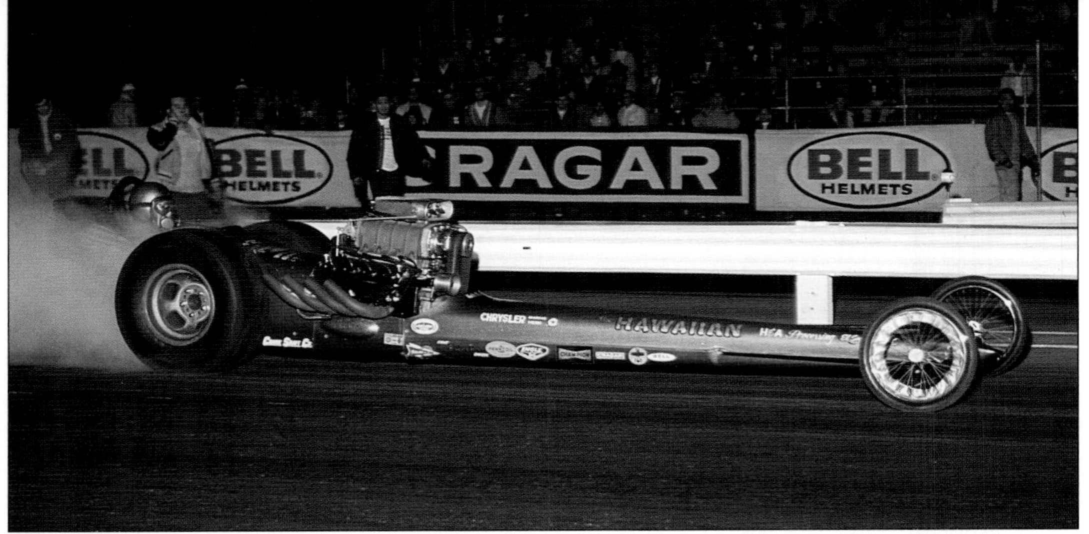

Stan Shiroma smokes the Goodyears under the lights at the County. The Honolulu-born racer, who was a championship-winning circle-track star in Hawaii, worked for Keith Black and had been friends with Roland Leong for years. After Shiroma left the Mr. Ed *Top Fuel ride, he borrowed Leong's legendary* Hawaiian *and planted his engine into the well-traveled rail for this round win. The historic Fuller-built* Hawaiian *would soon see less action and would later retire from drag racing in 1968. (Photo Courtesy Tim Pearl Collection)*

the special one-time event and also carded low ET and top speed of the show: 7.08 at 217.38 mph.

Another Dominant Year

Leong had won every major title in the sport of drag racing, including the only back-to-back victories at the Winternationals and the Nationals in the same years. For 1967 alone, Leong's *Hawaiian* dragsters had won several top major events, including the Smokers March Meet at Bakersfield, the Stardust National Open in Las Vegas, the Hot Rod Magazine Championships at Riverside, the NASCAR 500 of Drag Racing in Illinois, and the Mr. U.S.A. Fuel Eliminator at Cecil Cox, Maryland.

SILENCED COCKPIT: DECEMBER 30, 1967

Always seen with a serene smile that accented his warm personality, the shining light of 28-year-old budding superstar Mike Sorokin was dimmed when his car's clutch violently exploded at Orange County Raceway, claiming his life.

Leong had hired Sorokin (the ex-Surfers driver and the previous year's U.S. Fuel and Gas Top Fuel Champion) to pilot Keith Black and Leong's 426 Chrysler Marine Hemi-powered test and research dragster, the *Hawaiian II.* The idea of having two dragsters, especially one that was funded by Chrysler, excluding nitro, looked like a successful plan on paper, but overall, the project never panned out.

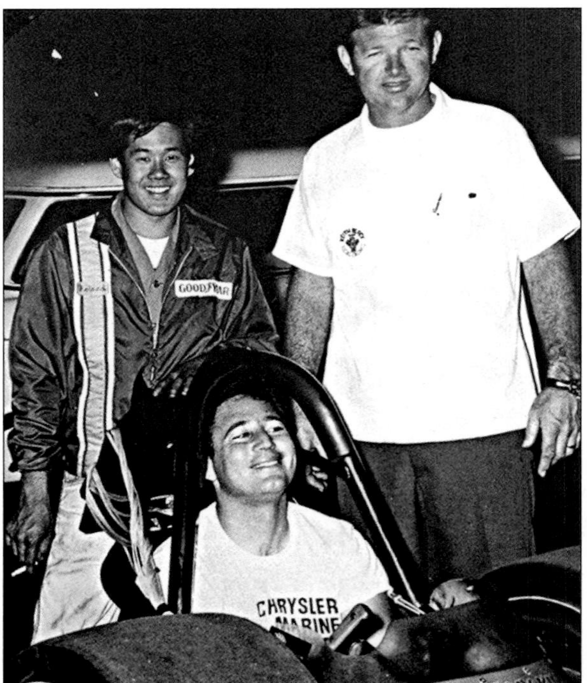

Mike Sorokin's trademarks were his smile and warm personality. He raced by this motto: "Try hard, play fair, and you'll win your share." Leong said, "He was a contributor to the team. He was sincere. He meant it." (Photo Courtesy Roland Leong Collection)

There were a few stellar moments for the *Hawaiian II* with Sorokin driving, including winning the Stardust Nationals in Las Vegas early in the year. With Leong and Snively out on their Eastern tour with the 392 Hemi-powered Top Fueler that Leong referred to as his "money maker," Mike Sorokin, Danny "Buzz" Broussard, and tuner Keith Black pocketed several wins on the West Coast, racing at the local Southern California strips.

"Mike was a good friend," Leong said. "We were neighbors. The night Mike was fatally injured, we talked for roughly five minutes before he got into the car that he drove that night. Our test program with the new 426 Hemi was stalled, so it didn't bother me for him to drive another car. We lived a few miles from each other, so I knew him and his family really well, so it wasn't a big deal for me. He was there to make a living."

CHAPTER 5

1968: THE TWILIGHT OF A PHENOMENAL RUN

After another successful year, Roland Leong and Mike Snively were eager to get the new season under way. Concentrating now on running only one dragster, Leong basically left the car untouched, only making a few minor modifications, including new paint colors and chassis refinements.

The most noticeable factor in 1968 was the increasing popularity of Funny Cars. Track promoters were offering larger payouts for the Funnies from round wins to event wins, as spectators increased in attendance at Funny Car shows. Overall, the fuel dragsters were still the kings in the quarter mile, but the Funnies were rapidly gaining ground on their thunder and glory.

In late January, Mike Snively was back in action at Irwindale after recharging the batteries during a well-earned vacation. Snively ran a 7.136 ET at 214.28 mph in qualifying that slotted him number-two in the field of eight. (Photo Courtesy Paul Johnson Collection)

Return to Irwindale

With the return of the top fuel dragsters after a six-week absence, Irwindale provided some of the best traction and top times for its eight-car season opener. Mike Snively showed no signs of being rusty when he qualified the *Hawaiian* in the second position, posting a strong 7.136 ET at 214.28 mph, which was right behind Frank Pedregon driving the *Ernie's Camera Special*.

Snively's day ended quickly in round one when Tom "the Mongoose" McEwen defeated the *Hawaiian* with a 7.21 ET at 215 mph to Snively's losing 7.12 at 222.22.

The AHRA Winter Nationals

Roland Leong and Mike Snively made the stop in Scottsdale, Arizona, for the AHRA Winter Nationals from January 19 to 21 at Bee Line Dragway. The drag strip was resurfaced over the winter with the hopes for quicker ETs and top speeds during the AHRA opener, but many Fuelers couldn't get traction on the new surface during qualifying on Friday and Saturday.

Snively's run on Friday placed the *Hawaiian* in the show with an ET of 7.45. In the first round of eliminations, the *Hawaiian* sailed by easily, running a 7.16 ET at 216.37 mph, as the Fisher & Greth rail lost fire off the line. Keith Black had the *Hawaiian* moving in the second round with a 7.27 at 222.22 win over Tom Hoover's 7.42 at 210.28.

Round three brought two grizzled veterans, Mike Snively and Vic Brown (handling the Creitz & Greer entry), up to the line. Snively's 7.30 ET at 209.78 mph disposed of the quicker Creitz & Greer. In the fourth round, two old friends faced each other: Don Prudhomme and Roland Leong. When the smoked cleared, the Baney-Pink-Prudhomme entry sent Prudhomme's old friend home with a 7.27 ET at 222.76 mph to Snively's quicker 7.15 at 226.76.

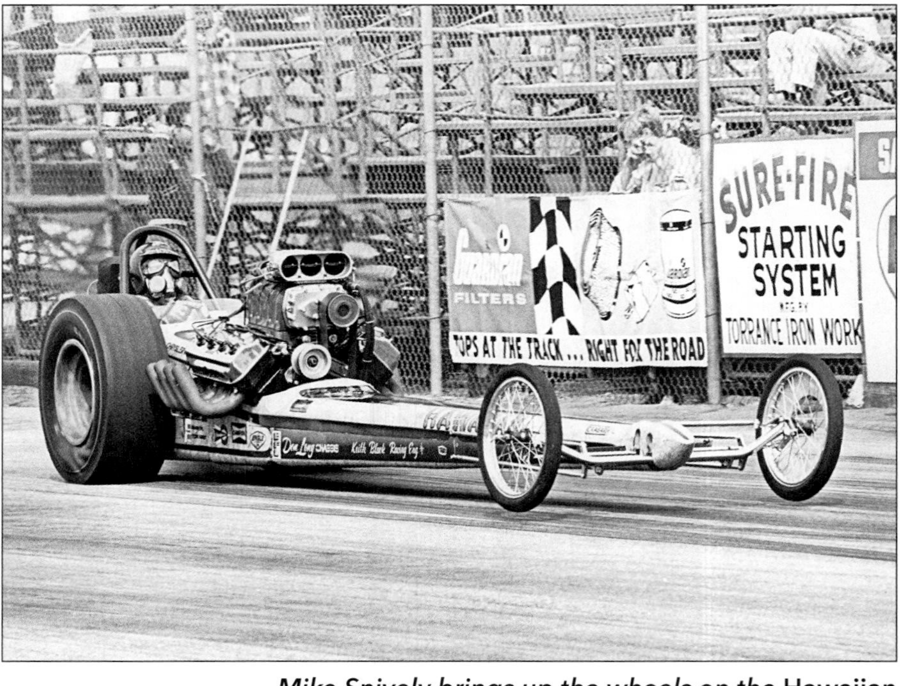

Mike Snively brings up the wheels on the Hawaiian *during a magazine feature shoot at Lions Drag Strip. Depending on track and weather conditions, Leong had options, running either the Elephant Hemi or the smaller-cubic-inch Hemi. (Photo Courtesy Roland Leong Collection)*

The NHRA Winternationals

The eighth-annual Winternationals kicked off the NHRA season over the weekend of February 2 to 4 with more than 720 entries from all areas of the country, including Alaska and Hawaii. Top Fuel qualifying was underway Friday

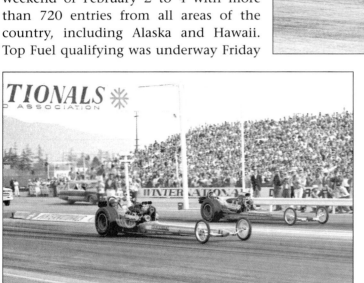

First-round action at the NHRA Winternationals in Pomona had Mike Snively out ahead in the Hawaiian *against John Mulligan, who was driving Beebe & Mulligan's* Fighting Irish *Fueler. Snively kept his lead through the top-end lights with a 7.08 ET at 219.59 mph to the Mulligan's quicker but losing 6.967 at 222.76. (Photo Courtesy Steve Reyes)*

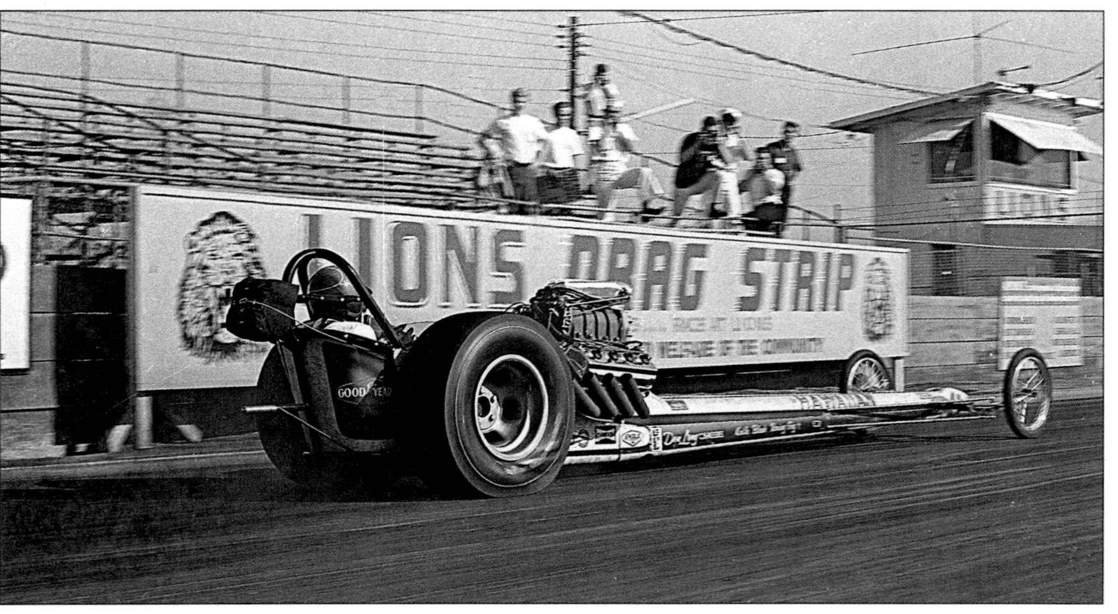

Mike Snively led the Hawaiian *on a run past a group of media journalists and photographers, showing what a ground-pounding, 220-mph charge to the top end at Lions Drag Strip looked like. The thundering sounds from the fuel cars on a Saturday night could be heard all the way down to the Pike, which was located on the shoreline just south of Ocean Boulevard. (Photo Courtesy Paul Johnson Collection)*

morning with more than 60 Fuelers jostling for a spot in the 32-car field. Sitting comfortably in the third position was Mike Snively and the *Hawaiian* with a strong 7.037 ET at 223.32 mph.

Snively advanced to round two on a hole-shot over his first-round opponent, John Mulligan. The Beebe & Mulligan entry ran a quicker 6.967 ET at 222.76 mph to the *Hawaiian*'s slower but winning 7.08 ET at 219.59 mph. The second round was over for Snively before it started, as he red-lighted against the *Bounty Hunter* of Connie Kalitta.

Members of the media were wondering if the *Hawaiian* would repeat its winning ways of 1966 and 1967. Leong's group was picked to have its best year yet by the writers, tipsters, and journalists due to its knowledge, experience, and Keith Black running the Chrysler 426 Hemi.

The First Tournament in the Sport: The PDA

On March 3, Orange County International Raceway (OCIR) kicked off the Professional Dragster Association (PDA) Classic with 80 "everybody who was anybody" fuel burners that were all hopped up on large dosages of nitro. The cars represented locations such as Oklahoma, Florida, Washington, Washington D.C., Georgia, Michigan, California, etc. Some sources mentioned that 2,000-plus fans were turned away at the gates on Saturday night, one-and-a-half hours after the gates had been shut off for the day.

An unlucky mechanical misfortune occurred for the *Hawaiian.* Snively experienced a bitter defeat in the first round when a cracked head gasket resulted in water being sprayed onto the left slick that retired the car (taking the freewheeling route). It was also devastating for his foe, Watus Simpson, who was driving for Texan Vance Hunt. Simpson couldn't fire his car after officials allowed two attempts to push-start the car up and down the strip. Bad luck also plagued Hunt and Simpson when it was determined that a broken magneto rotor was the culprit.

Mixing Good with Bad

The trip in mid-March up to the Bay Area at Fremont's West Coast's Fuel and Gas Championships was shortened due to rain all day Saturday that canceled qualifying. The action began Sunday morning at 8 a.m. sharp with many runs by the pros before eliminations at 11 a.m. Leong had the *Hawaiian* pointed in the right direction when Snively set the new speed record at 225.54 mph, and that top speed was backed up with a 222.76-mph blast. The *Hawaiian* advanced to round two, but Snively fell short of advancing further when Dennis Baca beat him with a 7.05 ET to Snively's 7.10.

MEMORABLE MOMENTS:

Vance Hunt

"My best memory was when we ran Snively in Roland's car, the Hawaiian, at the PDA Classic at Orange County," Vance Hunt said. "We paired up against Snively in the first round, where we couldn't start due to a broken rotor in the magneto.

"Simultaneously, I knew that Snively was having troubles as well, so the officials told us to go back down the fire-up road, turn around, and come back up and try again. Again, same results, I couldn't get it to run!"

Trying for a team *Hawaiian* repeat win at the Stardust International Raceway at the Las Vegas Open, Mike Snively set low ET in the third round but lost to Vic Brown in the Creitz & Greer entry from Oklahoma. Snively ran a 7.02 ET at 210.76 mph.

Even with threatening weather, more than 375 machines of all types filed into "Famous Famoso" for the fabled March Meet at Bakersfield from March 8 to 10. Stan Shiroma qualified Leong's original *Hawaiian* into the show, where he paired up with Dave Babler in the first round. Shiroma showed the crowd that the "old" *Hawaiian* still had plenty of pop when he ran an unreal 7.01 ET at 212.26 mph while Babler hit the kill button.

Fuelers versus Funnies

On April 20, Irwindale Raceway promoted its first-ever gathering of four 225-mph Top Fuel dragsters versus four 7-second Funny Cars. A one-second handicap round-robin series made for three full rounds of the wildest racing on the West Coast.

The "Action Strip" hosted 5,000 avid drag racing enthusiasts who cheered on their favorite type of car. The Top Fuel team consisted of current and former Winternationals champions Warren-Colburn-Miller and the *Hawaiian*, Beebe and Mulligan, and the Irwindale Grand Prix champs Larry Stellings and Butch Maas's *Silver Fox*.

The hopes of the Funny Car team relied on the Fords of Gas Ronda and Dick Loehr as well as the Blair's Speed Shop Camaro and the Keith Black–powered *Imperial Kustoms* Dodge Charger, which were both driven by Steve Bovan.

The *Hawaiian* represented the Top Fueler team well, winning two out of three rounds. Snively set low ET and

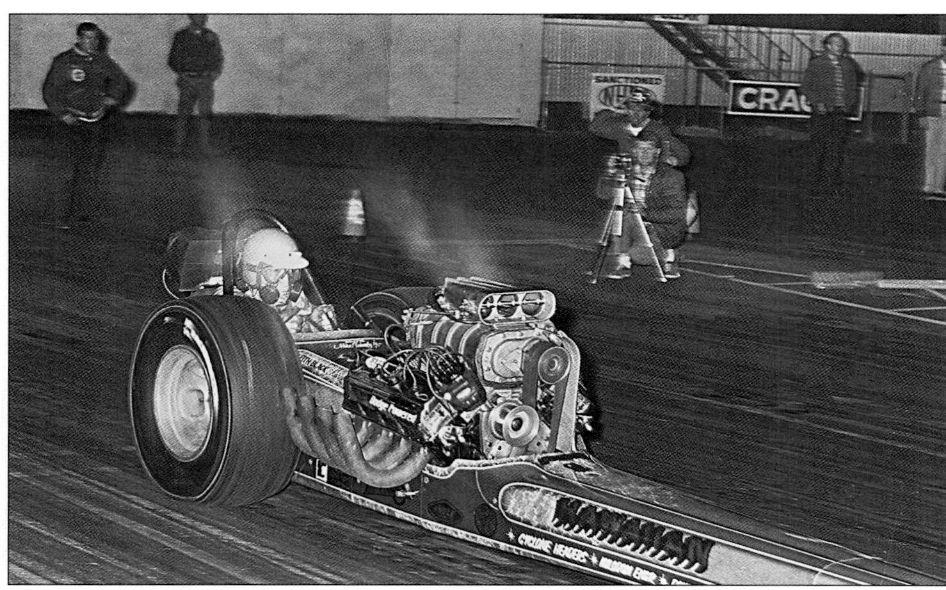

Irwindale Raceway pulled out all of the stops with its first-ever challenge of four Top Fuel dragsters against four 7-second Funny Cars in a special handicap match race for three full rounds of side-by-side racing. Funny Cars were given a full second head start to balance out the speeds of a 220-mph Fueler. Heading the dragster attack team was Snively, who set both top speed and low ET while winning two out of three races. (Photo Courtesy Paul Johnson Collection)

top speed in the show all in the first round (7.14 at 228 mph) to defeat Bovan's Camaro.

A loss in the second round to Dick Loehr led to a third-round matchup of the Keith Black–powered machines of Leong and Nelson Carter. Snively took advantage of Bovan's loss of traction.

Fuel Dragsters at the Super Track

On April 24, 26 Top Fuel dragsters were entered into a creative, unique program that guaranteed each participant a spot in the 16-car field. The rules stated that there would be no qualifying. Instead, all cars entered in the meet would run in the first round. The eight low-ET winners advanced to the second round. The next eight low ETs from the first round received first-round money: win, lose, or draw.

When it was all said and done, Snively outran 25 of the top crop of the West Coast Fuelers. The *Hawaiian* returned to its winning ways in May at OCIR after a three-month dry spell visiting the winner's circle.

In eliminations, Snively defeated John Martin in the Ewell-Bell-Stecker car in the opening round, Fred Farndon in round two, and Jim Dunn wheeling the Ayres and Crossly entry in the semifinals. He met archrival James Warren in the final.

The finals were interesting to watch, as the *Hawaiian* had been struggling for a legitimate win for months. On the other hand, the *Rain for Rent* Warren-Colburn-Miller entry was the favorite to win and had been looking strong, steamrolling through competition in the previous weeks.

As Black and Leong were rapidly changing the injector readings and making fuel and jet changes in the pits, a confident James Warren answered questions in a live track interview. From all indications, Warren had the definite edge for the win. When the smoke that was steaming off from the slicks had cleared, both Warren and Snively were running flat out. Then, the *Hawaiian*'s 5-foot flames went out momentarily but instantly rebloomed. With Warren having the upper hand with a solid one-car-length lead, Snively drove past the 1968 Winternationals champ for the all-important win, running a 7.32 ET at 231.36 mph to a losing 7.75 at 139.79.

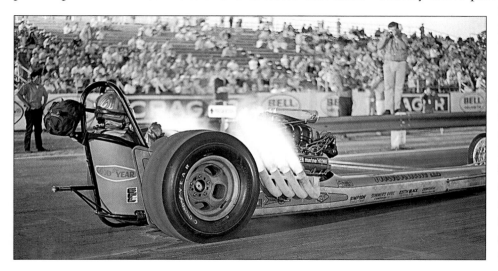

Roland Leong and Mike Snively made the return to the winner's circle after a three-month drought when the Hawaiian *won "Fuel Dragsters at the Super Track," which was a first-time event. All cars ran in the first round of eliminations without any qualifying, but only the quickest eight cars advanced into the next round. (Photo Courtesy Paul Johnson Collection)*

Big Horn's Big Noise

Making its annual spring and summer migration tour throughout the nation, the *Hawaiian* made a stop in Greybull, Wyoming. The team raced on Mother's Day in 1968 at Big Horn Dragway, saluting the drag strip's last year of operation. This gave Leong the opportunity to test out his Keith Black "Super Slipper" clutch assembly for higher-altitude racing. Leong proved the clutch's dependability, as Snively set both the strip's top speed and ET records: 7.21 at 212 mph.

AA/Fuel Dragster The Hawaiian

First time in Wyoming! The Nation's Top Fuel Dragster, direct from Los Angeles

Making a Greybull stop during a nationwide tour!

SUNDAY, MAY 12 GREYBULL WYOMING

Don't miss your chance to see the nation's No. 1 Fuel Dragster in action. It will be the first time this outstanding racer has appeared in Wyoming. This fuel dragster is owned by Roland Leong and driven by Mike Snively (see below) and has an outstanding record on drag strips.

Big Horn Dragway

DRAG RACES

ALL CLASSES WILL RUN

Time Trials at .... 9 A. M.

Eliminations at .... 1 P. M.

One of the Hawaiian's *rarest advertised racing posters was the announcement of the car's first-ever appearance at Big Horn Dragway on Mother's Day 1968 in Greybull, Wyoming. It was something for the area fans to see the number-one Top Fueler in drag racing make an appearance at a smaller, remote drag strip such as Big Horn. Track manager Red Lindsey drew several top performers, including Kenz & Leslie and the Colorado and Wyoming state record holder, Ernie Speckler, to the South Big Horn County airport facility, but there was none larger than Leong and Snively.*

Calm, Cool *Hawaiian* Enjoys Hot Summer Times

Memorial Day Weekend at Great Lakes Union Grove, Wisconsin, had both Leong and Snively lighting up the scoreboard when the *Hawaiian* was the only Fueler to run ETs in the 6s: 6.91, 6.98, and 6.88 for a new track record with each run. The *Hawaiian* set track records at each stop on its Eastern tour.

Mike Snively experienced the feeling of what it was like to be shot from a cannon against the Creitz-Greer-Donovan rail with a carnival-like atmosphere during this match race at Southwest Raceway in Tulsa, Oklahoma. (Photo Courtesy Darr Hawthorne Collection)

Zigzagging throughout the country, the *Hawaiian* made a stop in Tulsa, Oklahoma, for a match race against the Oklahoma champs Creitz & Greer. Mike Snively said it felt like being "shot from a cannon" when he ran against the Creitz & Greer rail in a highly advertised match race at Southwest Raceway in Tulsa, Oklahoma.

The New York Championships

The dragsters poured through the gates on the weekend of June 7 to 9 in Center Moriches, Long Island, New York, for the 10th-annual Smokers Fuel and Gas Championship at New York National Speedway. The overflowed pits made it nearly impossible for cars to maneuver up to the starting line. This was the first time that Smoker's Inc. relocated from Bakersfield, California, to its new permanent location at New York National.

Bakersfield was now considered only as "the March Meet." It was the second stop of the big three events in Southern California: the Winternationals, Bakersfield, and *Hot Rod* magazine's event at Riverside. Then, the racers headed to the events in the East.

The action was hot and plentiful for the nitro rockets. The entries included nearly every big name, including McEwen, the Ramchargers, Ivo, Kalitta, Baney, Prudhomme, Leong, Snively, etc.

Friday night opened the three-day marathon with the Ramchargers setting low ET of the meet and winning the first leg of the weekend. Saturday and Sunday's eliminations were owned by Roland Leong, Keith Black, and Mike Snively.

The *Hawaiian* opened Saturday's eliminations by setting top speed of the weekend in the first round with a 6.74 at 230 mph, defeating Bernie Schacker. Snively's next victim in round two was the *A & B Speed Special*. In the semifinals, the *Hawaiian* put Tony Passalarqua on the trailer with a 7.54 ET at 226 mph.

The finals brought Fred Forkner and Snively to the line for the $4,000 purse. The crowd was on its feet as both cars came off the line. Forkner briefly held a lead by only a few feet when the *Hawaiian* dug in and laid down a pair of smokeless tracks all the way down to the top end, winning with a 7.32 ET at 230.70 mph.

The first race on Sunday was the biggest upset of the day. East Coast regular Biddy Windward slayed the West Coast champion Tom McEwen with a 7.06 ET at 275.78 mph to McEwen's 7.32 at 211.26.

Knowing what took place, Leong took no chances with the *Hawaiian*. It showed when Snively dropped a 7.00 ET at 225.56 mph over Robinson Auto. Next up was Norm Weekly, but he blew the clutch when the *Hawaiian* rocketed to an unreal 6.79 ET at 227.27 mph. Snively had a bye run in the third round, but Leong didn't hold back as Snively dropped his ET with a 6.76 at 218.96 mph.

The semifinal round was a repeat from Saturday night's finale with the new East Coast "folk hero" Fred Forkner meeting the *Hawaiian* for the right to advance to take on Don Prudhomme in the *Shelby Super Snake*. Unfortunately for Forkner, death smoke emitted from the engine, forcing him to shut off. The fans recognized the performance by Forkner with a standing ovation.

Leong versus Prudhomme

Snively advanced to meet Prudhomme on a single run. With the crowd on its feet, the *Hawaiian* and *Super Snake* carefully rolled into the staging beams. The tree lights counted down, and both cars left together on smokeless runs. Prudhomme pulled away early, and Snively was coming on strong when Prudhomme's supercharger exploded into a ball of fire. The *Hawaiian* took the win with a 6.92 ET at 227.84 mph to the *Snake*'s 6.98 at 198.22. During the post-race interviews, Leong, Black, and Snively all agreed, "The bite here was unbelievable."

National Championships

The Eastern tour continued for Leong and Snively with a stop from June 28 to 30 at the National Championships at Union Grove, Wisconsin. Snively drove the *Hawaiian* to a runner-up position against Jim Nicoll's *Der Wienerschnitzel*.

The Eastern swing continued at the Super Bowl for fuel dragsters at Pittsburgh International Dragway on July 28. The onslaught of the *Hawaiian* continued when the Leong-tuned and -maintained Keith Black Hemi set low ET of the meet (7.10). Superstars Pete Robinson, the Ramchargers, "Big Daddy" Don Garlits, Tommy Ivo, Connie Kalitta, the "Golden Greek" Chris Karamesines, and a cast of others competed for the Top Eliminator trophy.

During his illustrious career, Leong received a combined total of five Car Craft All-Star Crew Chief awards, which were voted on by the readers of the popular magazine. Instead of plaques, the 1968 recipients received the "Ollie" All-Star trophies that resembled a starting line Christmas tree. (Graphics Courtesy Ross Howard)

Leong Takes Home the "Ollie"

Mike Snively made a quick exit from competition at the Nationals. In the first round, he rattled the tires coming off the starting line, which crossed him up completely, and he got out of shape.

The weekend wasn't a total loss for Leong, as he won his second consecutive *Car Craft* magazine All-Star award for Dragster Crew Chief of the Year. The *Car Craft* All-Stars were formally recognized with a banquet dinner and awards ceremony prior to the NHRA Nationals in Indy. Several changes and new awards for the year included unique Christmas tree "Ollie" trophies that were awarded to all deserving All-Stars.

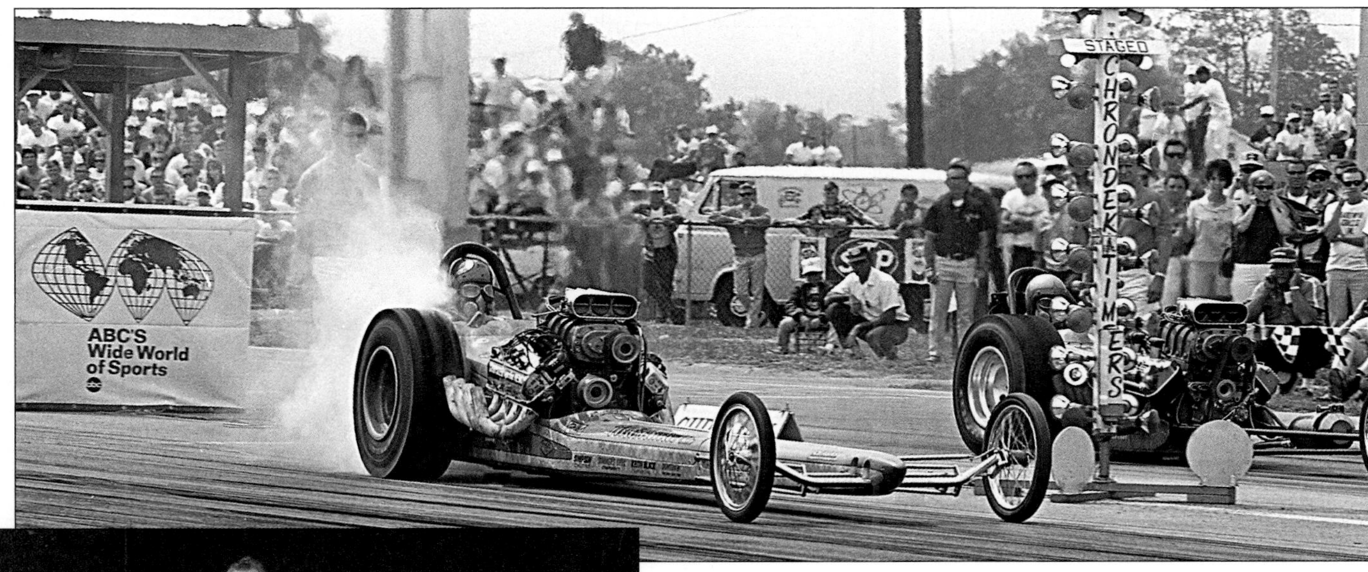

The first round at Indy was one that Snively wanted to take back. He went in deep, staged against Chuck Kurzawa, and had to hold, waiting for a good green. At the hit, the Hawaiian *launched too hard and ended up going sideways. Snively had to lift and finally shut it down with an 8.431 ET at 165.44 mph to Kurzawa's winning 7.32 at 216.34, which ended Snively's hopes for a repeat Indy title.*

Roland Leong and Keith Black had been accustomed with winning multiple back-to-back Eliminator titles at both the Winternationals and the Nationals. Now, they added back-to-back Car Craft *magazine All-Star awards for both 1966 and 1967. The duo was honored at a formal ceremony prior to the NHRA Nationals in Indianapolis along with all of the other deserving All-Stars in their perspective categories. Those pictured include Don Garlits (Man of the Year, Top Fuel Driver, and Dragster Chassis Builder), Bill Tola of Gratiot Auto Supply (Competition Sponsor), Joe Mondello (Competition Engine Builder), Ed Iskenderian of Iskenderian Cams (Dragster Sponsor), George Montgomery (Competition Driver, fendered), Bill Jenkins (Super Stock Driver and Stock Engine Builder), Angelo Giampetroni of Gratiot Auto Supply, Roland Leong (Dragster Crew Chief), Jack Chrisman (Funny Car Engine Builder/Crew Chief), and Willie Borsch (Competition Driver, nonfendered), Ben Wenzel (Stock Driver), Logghe Brothers with Jay Howell accepting (Funny Car Chassis Builders), Don Nicholson (Funny Car Driver), Doug Thorley of Doug's Headers (Competition Sponsor), Mr. Jim Musser/Chevrolet Motor Division (Stock Automotive Manufacturer of the Year), Dick Landy (Super Stock Engine Builder), Gordon Collect (Top Gas Driver), Buddy Martin (Super Stock Crew Chief), Mr. B. F. Boehm Vice President of Valvoline Oil (Super Stock Sponsor), George Hurst of Hurst Performance Products (Manufacturer of the Year), Keith Black (Dragster Engine Builder), John Mazmanian (Competition Crew Chief), Paul Harvey (Stock Crew Chief), and Milt Schornack of Royal Pontiac (Stock Sponsor). (Photo Courtesy Bob McClurg)*

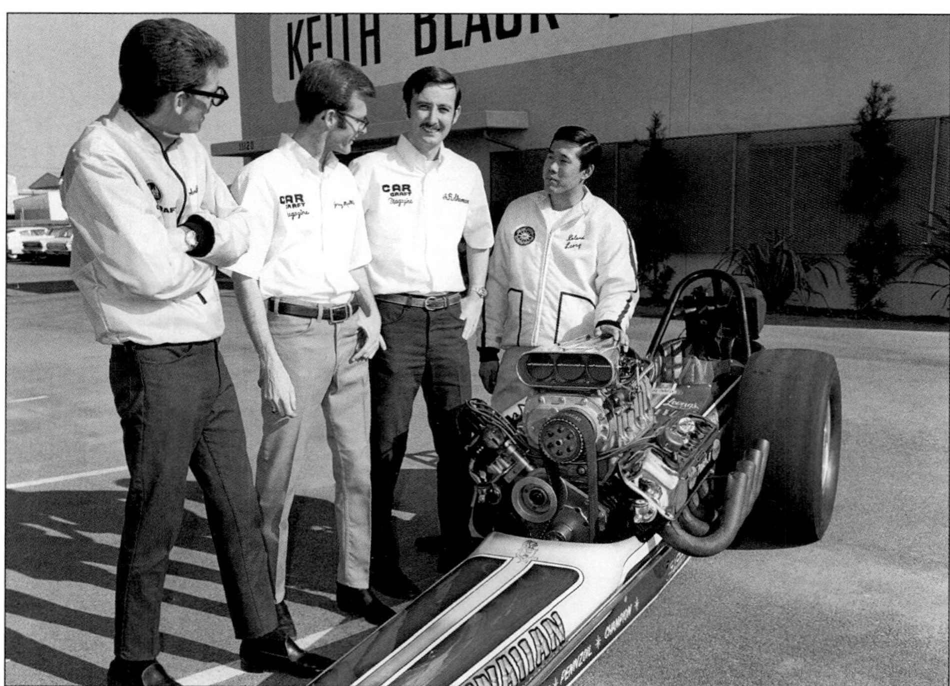

Car Craft **magazine editor John Raffa, associate editor Jerry Mallicoat, and technical editor A.B. Shuman stopped by the shop and offices of Keith Black to present Leong with his new** *Car Craft* **magazine All-Star Drag Racing Team Crew Chief of the Year award for 1968. Missing from the photo was Keith Black. (Photo Courtesy Roland Leong Collection)**

The first round brought the *Hawaiian* and Stan Shiroma in Ed Willis's *Mr. Ed* Fueler up to the starting line. With Snively already fired up and off the rollers, a noxious, repugnant blue smoke poured from the Sure-Fire electric starter motor. It put a temporary halt to the firing up of the *Mr. Ed* car. The chief honcho and starter at Lions, frantically gave the shut-off sign to Snively. The already "amped up" Snively jumped from the cockpit and pulled off his helmet and face mask, his face livid with anger. Getting the explanation from Larry Sutton, a much calmer Snively told the *Drag News* reporter, "It's a good thing the weather was cold."

After repairs to the Sure-Fire starter system, Sutton gave the command to fire. With both cars coming off the line, Shiroma found the track to his liking, taking the win over the *Hawaiian* with a 7.03 ET at 224.18 mph to Snively's 7.26 at 222.22.

Drag News All-Pro Championships

On October 26, Lions Drag Strip hosted its second-annual Drag News All-Pro Championships. It featured 60-plus of the nation's top-running fuel stars trying to earn a spot on the ladder of 32. Leong and Snively pulled out all the stops, placing the *Hawaiian* into the fifth overall spot of the field, running a 6.97 ET at 221.29 mph.

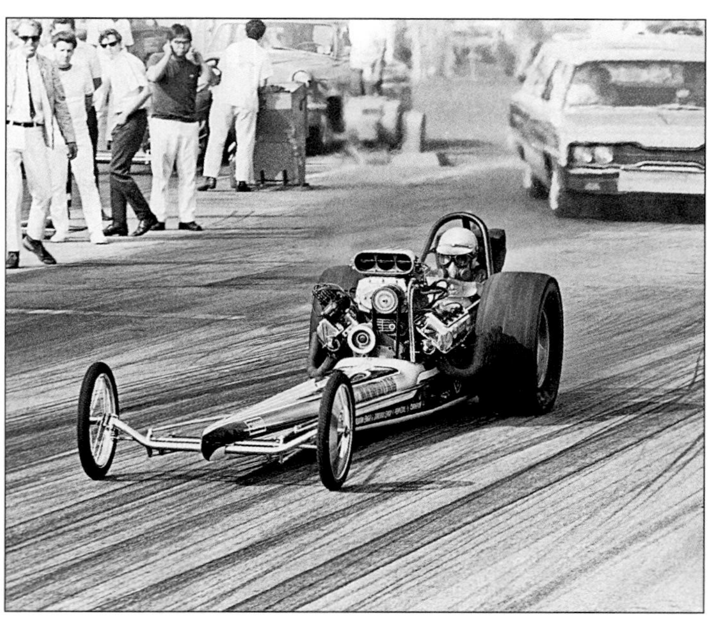

The *Hawaiian* Goes the Funny Route

With the 1968 racing season winding down, Leong ordered a new dragster chassis from Don Long for the 1969 campaign. With OCIR hosting a combined Top Fuel/Funny Car card, Leong noticed the fans' excitement and reactions to the loud, brightly painted fiberglass-bodied muscle cars that emitted huge clouds of tire smoke from their long, smoky burnouts. He realized that the popularity of the fiberglass cars was really taking off.

Pondering how much money he could earn running a Funny Car locally and on tour, Leong decided to make the change. He sold his unfinished chassis to his longtime friend, Don Prudhomme, who had just inked a lucrative sponsor package from the Wynn's Friction Proofing Company.

Leong swapped out the reliable 392 Chrysler in favor of the 426 Marine Keith Black Hemi at the Drag News All-Pro Championship. More than 60 Top Fuelers were contending for a spot in the 32-car field. For Leong, the track conditions were favorable for the reliable 392, but in time trials, the engine emitted clouds of death smoke that resulted in a rush to change the engine plate to accommodate the late-model Hemi. (Photo Courtesy Paul Johnson Collection)

Planning and researching for the best products available, Leong reached out to Jay Howell, the general manager of the Logghe Stamping Company, for a new chassis. With Leong's long association with Keith Black and Chrysler, it was an easy choice for the engine supplier and manufacturer to use.

With word getting out about Leong making the shift over to floppers, other top-notch drivers were busy filling out applications. Leong's decision was made roughly around the first week of December, when he hired the experienced Larry Reyes to handle the driving chores. Reyes immediately sold his current supercharged mount, a 1969 Barracuda-bodied Funny Car. By December 14, the car had already been booked at 60 different tracks in about 30 states.

The deteriorated condition of the "Holy Rail" remains on display in Italy. While the Hawaiian *was never restored, it remains in the same condition after its final run, when it was loaded up and locked away in the trailer for nearly 60 years. Back in the day, Leong was approached by Ray Brock, editor of* Hot Rod *magazine, and asked if he wanted to sell the car to a car show promoter in Europe just as the way it sat without the engine. Leong accepted the offer, and the rail was sealed up into a container and shipped off to Italy to its new home. (Photo Courtesy Tony Thacker Photography)*

A Sad Goodbye for the Original *Hawaiian*

After a spectacular and historic career in American drag racing, Ray Brock, the editor of *Hot Rod* magazine, approached Leong to see if he would be interested in selling his fabled Kent Fuller–built *Hawaiian* to a European car promoter, complete, as it sat. When Leong agreed to the terms, it was like saying good-bye to an old friend. Leong watched his famous car get loaded and locked into a shipping container to take the journey to its new home: the Carlo Biscaretti di Ruffia Museum in Turin, Italy. Today, the car rests in a deteriorating state and is in need of a complete restoration.

Leong campaigned his original Hawaiian *dragster from late 1964 through early 1967 with drivers Don Prudhomme and Mike Snively. He also loaned the car to fellow* Hawaiian *native Stan Shiroma for Shiroma to race using his own engines. The original car was one of the most recognized Top Fuelers that blazed a trail in drag racing history. The car has been on display in the Carlo Biscaretti di Ruffia Museum in Turin, Italy. There have been countless attempts to bring the piece of American automotive history back to the United States, but miles of red tape have thwarted the efforts. Italian law says that it cannot export any object over 50 years of age if it is classified as a cultural asset. (Photo Courtesy Tony Thacker Photography)*

KEITH BLACK: THE ENGINE MASTERMIND BEHIND THE HAWAIIAN'S SUCCESS

Success for any athlete requires preparation, proper training, and devotion, but the most critical factor is the coach. This also holds true for a race car. Its success depends primarily on the engine.

The modest and unassuming Keith Black had been the "coach" and premier engine builder since 1954. Black built entire engines, aside from the camshafts, rocker arms, valve springs, superchargers, and fuel injectors.

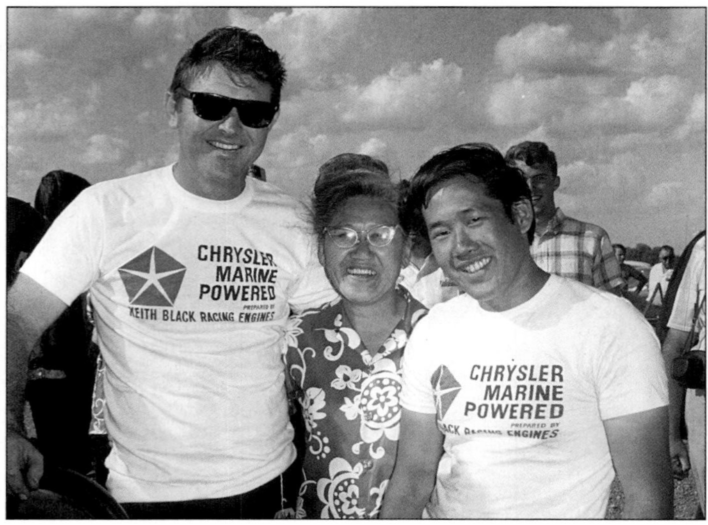

Behind the success of the Hawaiian *were the roots of Keith Black and Teddy and Roland Leong. The trio dominated NHRA competition with first-class equipment and the determination of champions. (Photo Courtesy Roland Leong Collection)*

Roland Leong, the 1967 Car Craft *All-Star Crew Chief of the Year, and Keith Black, Competition Engine Builder of the Year, receive their well-merited award plaques from* Car Craft *editor Dick Day and Teddy Leong. Leong and Black provided a successful one-two punch in the Top Fuel battles. (Photo Courtesy Roland Leong Collection)*

Roland Leong and Keith Black shared close ties in their early days before Leong crashed in his one and only time driving his Top Fuel dragster. They connected like father and son, where Black gave his advice to Leong, and positive results followed. (Photo Courtesy Roland Leong Collection)

Keith Black Engines

Keith Black was a no-nonsense, inquisitive-minded man behind the magic of the Chrysler Hemi. A question that Black has been asked several times is, "How did a drag racing engine builder get involved putting engines together for boats?"

Boats were the first serious work for Black. He built a boat, built an engine, and put himself into the seat. He went on to build a hydroplane because it was easier to make the engine perform with that kind of hull. Black went on to race for some time before the inevitable happened: someone asked if he could work on their boat. Reluctantly, he did, and it ran better than it had previously.

When the word spread, more and more people reached out to Black to work on their boat engines. One day, Black was in a boat when he lost control and crashed. He admitted that the accident didn't

Presenting Keith Black with his 1967* Car Craft *Competition Engine Builder of the Year jacket was Jackie Hart, daughter of NHRA event director Jack Hart, and Tom Shedden of the Peterson Publishing Company. (Photo Courtesy Roland Leong Collection)

Keith Black holds court in the pits at OCIR's Manufacturer's Funny Car Championships with long-time customers "Big" John Mazmanian (second from left) and Roland Leong. (Photo Courtesy Steve Reyes)

force him out of the seat, but he felt for a long time that the boat was doing things that he realized he had no business in doing.

The boat work wasn't his main form of business. Selling wholesale auto parts during the daytime was his bread and butter. Putting together boat engines at night kept him busy.

When Black decided to get into drag cars, Kent Fuller built him a rail with the understanding that Rod Stuckey was to drive. However, Black could see that Stuckey was going to have troubles right away.

Seeing the situation, Fuller suggested that a young Don Prudhomme would be the right fit, so Black terminated his agreement with Stuckey and asked Prudhomme if he would be interested in the job. The two worked out a deal that started their illustrious careers together in drag racing. It wasn't an instant success, but they built on their mistakes along the way and learned together.

Then, the Leong situation occurred. Danny Ongais ordered a car from Kent Fuller for Leong with the condition that it would be an exact duplicate of Black's "orange car," and Black was to build the engines for it. One of the best-kept secrets was that Ongais was groomed to drive the car, but as the rail neared completion, the Leong-Ongais connection dissolved.

With the car completed, Leong took it upon himself to drive, but he crashed on his first try in the cockpit. Black told Leong he needed to give up driving and concentrate solely on tuning and being an owner. Under Black's advice, Leong hired Prudhomme to drive. Leong now was transformed from just an ordinary customer to more of a friend, a member of the Black family.

Black continued to build boat engines. In fact, Black thought that the car engines were more of a sideline than the boats and never actually sold engines for dragsters. With more orders coming in, construction soon began for an 11,000-square-foot facility that housed dyno equipment, an engine shop, a harbor for budding *Hawaiian* cars, and massive storage bins for Mopar performance parts.

Black believed that to have a successful operation work well, everyone had to be on board, including both the driver and owner. Everyone should agree on any changes before anything was to be altered or changed during a race or on the race car. He also talked to the driver if he needed to with "no chewing out, just only straight talk," as Black noted in a 1966 *Hot Rod* magazine interview.

Black recalled that Mike Snively was having trouble

KEITH BLACK CONTINUED

during the 1966 Winternationals. He was new in the car and felt pressure with everyone, especially Leong, expecting him to win. Many told him that it was the driver that won and not the car. Black pulled Snively aside after the third round of eliminations on Sunday and said, "Mike, you already saved us. You drove past three cars. Now, go back out there, have fun, and enjoy yourself. Whatever you felt you needed to prove, you did!"

Keith Black was one of the top iconic engine builders in drag racing and drag boats. He was well known for making tremendous horsepower from both the 354 and 392 Chrysler Hemi. He also developed his trademark 426 "Black Magic" Elephant Chrysler Hemis that powered dragsters and Funny Cars into the winner's circle. Anyone's who's ever drag raced has heard of a Keith Black Hemi.

Snively was filled with confidence, and the string of *Hawaiian* wins grew. He went out and drove two more rounds to end the day with a perfect slate, winning his first Winternationals title.

Over Labor Day weekend, Black was asked this question by a local reporter during a pre-race interview at the Nationals in Indy: "What do you do differently when you go out to a strip with Roland with any or all of the *Hawaiian* cars? How about an example of what you've done in the past?"

After a brief pause, Black replied, "Alright, let's take a look at the '66 Winternationals for an example that should give you an idea. We'd slowly raised the nitro percentage after the first round of Top Fuel. Track conditions change by getting slicker as the day goes on. You drop tire pressure and bump the magneto back by a hair. As you have seen, the results were rewarding. The car simply has to be tuned for the current track conditions."

After the *Hawaiian* won its second straight Nationals, Black was asked what he thought about the other engine builders. Black took his time to respond.

"I don't know much of anything about them," Black said. "Someone once told me if you follow somebody around to see what others are doing, you're only going to wind up following them to the finish line. I figure the best thing to do is just keep tryin' to win because every time you do, it just makes it that much tougher for the storytellers."

The *Hawaiian* became its own character along with the names of Roland Leong, Don Prudhomme, and Keith Black. It was very popular everywhere they raced. They were practically faultless. Black just kept building tough engines and was not finished making his indelible mark in the library of performance engine building.

Keith Black passed away on May 13, 1991, after a battle with brain cancer. He was 64.

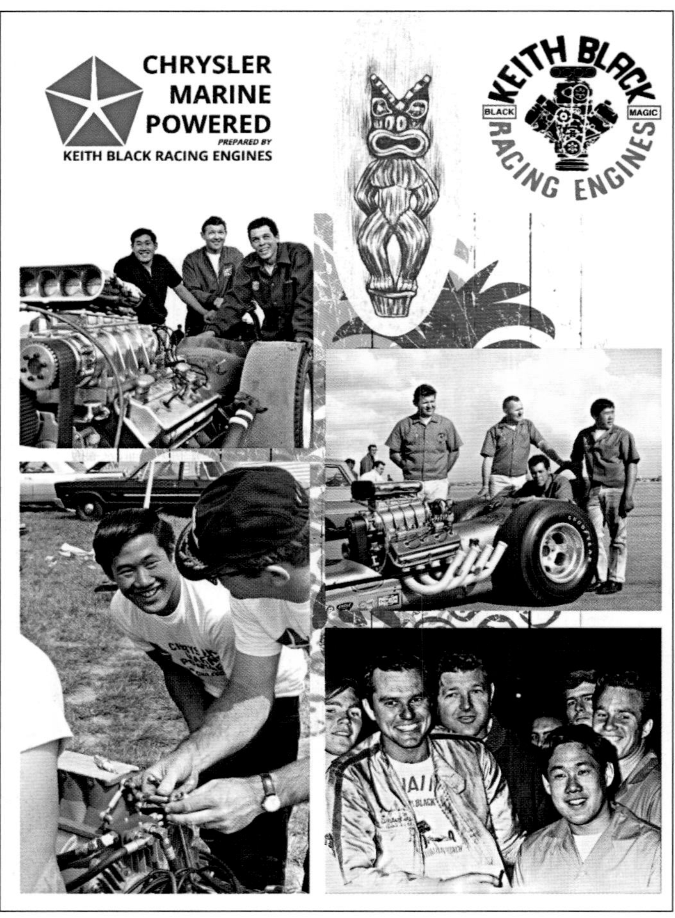

A fitting salute to the success behind the Hawaiian was made possible with the magic of Keith Black. (Graphics Courtesy Ross Howard)

CHAPTER 6

1969: RIDING THE WAVE INTO THE FUNNY-CAR ERA

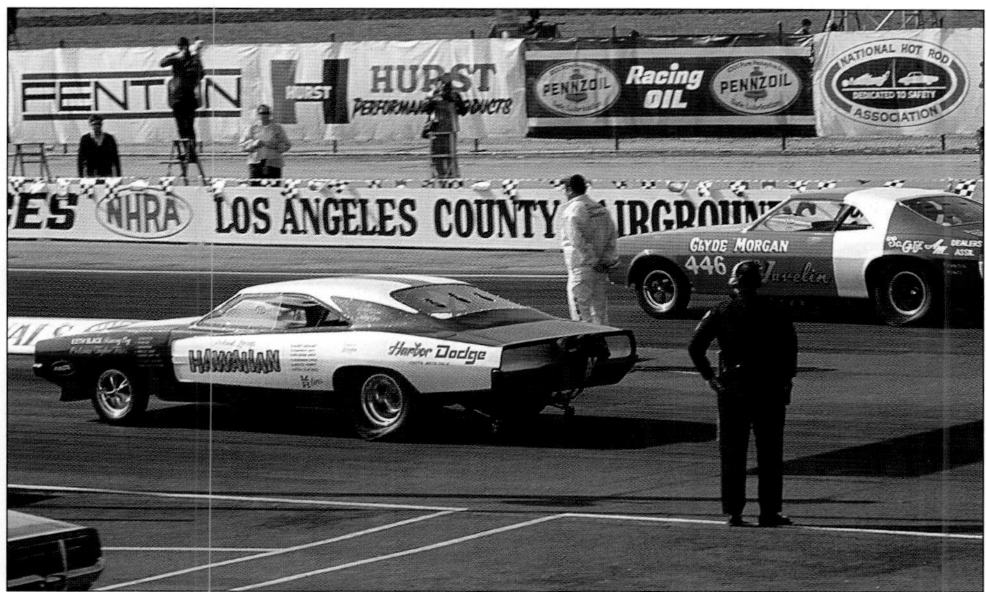

The Hawaiian's first-ever full quarter-mile run was Friday morning in the first qualifying session at the Winternationals in Pomona. This photo shows the long, wide, full-size Dodge body that lifted up at the front end. Under a recommendation from Chrysler's engineering department, a spoiler to provide downforce for speeds above 190 mph was unnecessary for the 1969 Chargers in NASCAR and NHRA Funny Cars. Leong incorporated three pineapple motif cutouts into the rear Plexiglas window to relieve air pressure in the driver's compartment. The Hawaiian's first full charge down the quarter-mile happened on Friday morning during the first qualifying secession at Pomona.

By 1969, Funny Car had become the most exciting class in drag racing. Awarded with their own NHRA Eliminator class, these gypsy-like touring professionals traveled across the country with wild fiberglass replicas of Detroit's finest muscle. As with any other racing class, Funny Cars required hard work and produced both good and bad results.

At the end of the 1968 touring season, Leong noticed how Funny Cars ushered people to the drag strip in droves. Fans wanted the noise; the bright, fluorescent, hallucinogenic colors; and ground-pounding, smoky burnouts that brought the peak of excitement up several levels. Funny Car drivers and owners were also paid large amounts of cash, especially for the big names. They were here and not going away, so Leong ended his eight-year run with both Gas and Top Fuel dragsters.

Leong made a call to Gene and Ron Logghe for a new Funny Car chassis, which put the wheels in motion to have the new flopper built in time for the Winternationals at Pomona. Keith Black once again did the engine work, and Fiberglass LTD molded the full-size Charger 500 body. The paint was the product of the talented Tom Kelly, who also designed the island theme in the front grille area.

Leong Tabs Reyes to Drive

Leong's association with Chrysler and Keith Black dated back several years, so the decision was clear for him to stick with success. Leong ordered a 1969 Dodge Charger 500 body with a Keith Black 426-ci Elephant Hemi between the rails of the Logghe tubular frame.

As the car neared completion, Leong had numerous inquiries from several top drivers, including his latest dragster pilot, Mike Snively, about inhabiting the seat in his new car. One particular driver, "Pineapple" Larry Reyes was leaving Bill Taylor's ride in the *Super Cuda* and was unsure what was next for him. Reyes was at Black's shop getting parts and struck up a conversation with Gene Snow. Snow mentioned that Leong was looking for

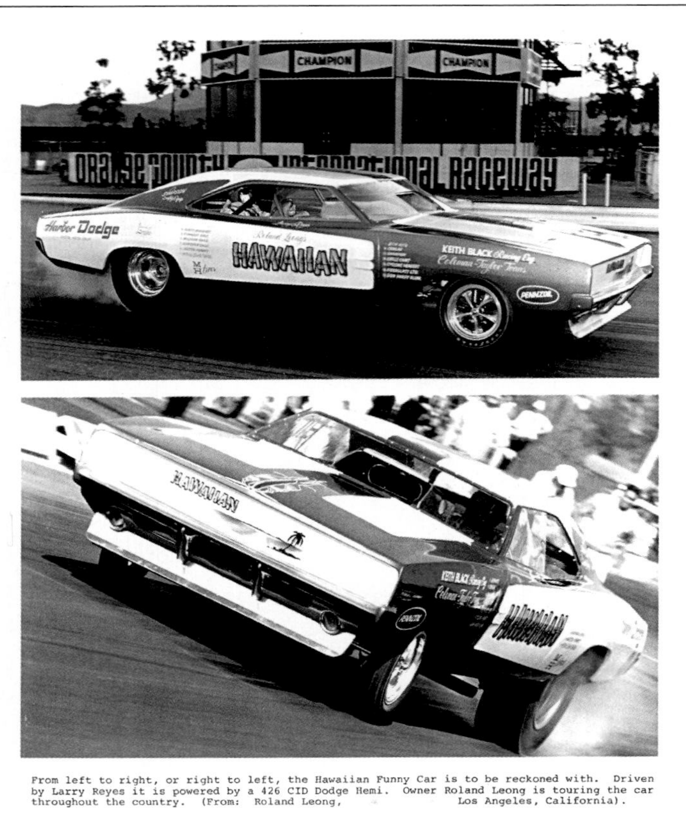

CHAMPION
HAWAIIAN
Harbor Dodge
From left to right, or right to left, the Hawaiian Funny Car is to be reckoned with. Driven by Larry Reyes it is powered by a 426 CID Dodge Hemi. Owner Roland Leong is touring the car throughout the country. (From: Roland Leong, Los Angeles, California).

This is an original Roland Leong promotional handout for the first* Hawaiian *Funny Car.

a driver. Reyes happened to see Leong in the parking lot, and Reyes walked over and introduced himself.

After their brief visit, Reyes went back home to Memphis, Tennessee, for the holidays. Word had it that the new car was already booked into 60 different tracks in 30 different states for the 1969 season. Leong made his selection official when he called Reyes, who had five years of Funny Car driving experience, and offered him the job to drive the *Hawaiian*.

In the early weeks of the new year, the new, untried Dodge was brought out to OCIR for a publicity shoot with the media and for the Chrysler representatives. Reyes performed only a few burnouts and short bursts to get accustomed to the car without making any wide-open runs.

"Man, at the beginning, I just never felt right being in the car," Reyes said. "The car was so big, like a boat, and I didn't feel right in the seat. The steering was hard to turn, and the brakes were just terrible. I didn't like it, and I felt Roland thought the same too."

Hawaiian Funny Car Debuts at Pomona

Excitement at the ninth-annual Winternationals at Pomona brought out the much-anticipated debut of Roland Leong's beautiful blue and white *Hawaiian*. When the big Dodge Charger rolled out onto the launch pad, the fans on the grounds made tracks to the grandstands to watch the car's first-ever run on the strip.

At the hit, Reyes wrinkled the M&H Racemasters, "flat bladin'" the butterflies. At about the 1,000-foot mark, the front of the car started to wander and skate around when, simultaneously, the rear of the car lifted slightly. Reyes pulled one of the chutes early and corrected the Charger from coming around.

Oddly enough, the run qualified him first into the field. Friday's second session getting down the track was a near carbon copy of the morning's attempt. Again, at the 8-mile mark, the car once more fishtailed, wanting to lift and come around when Reyes clicked it off, deploying the chute once again.

On Saturday morning, the team made several adjustments before the early and late afternoon rounds in qualifying. The results replicated the performances from the previous day. After the last run on Saturday, the car was quickly loaded back on the transporter and taken to Black's shop. Jay Howell, Ron Logghe, Leong, and Black spent the night going through the car, trying to solve the mystery of why the car wanted to track so poorly.

On early Sunday morning, Reyes returned to the shop, and Howell told him that it was fixed and ready to race. At this point, the new car had only made a total of four full quarter-mile passes in the three days of qualifying. It was anyone's guess if the handling issues were solved.

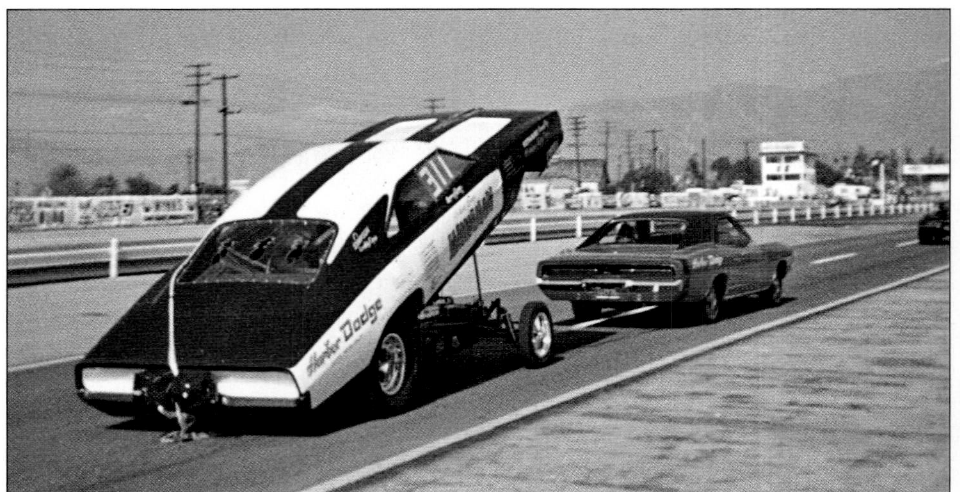

The trip back up the return road was a memorable one for Leong and Reyes after the* Hawaiian*'s first full quarter-mile pass nailed down the number-one spot in Friday's qualifying round. (Photo Courtesy Dale Kunesh Photography)

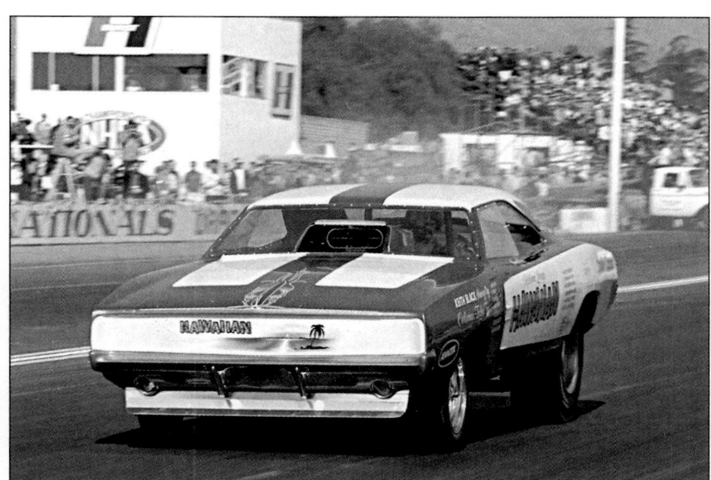

Photographer Steve Reyes caught Larry Reyes (no relation) having difficulties with the steering, fighting it off the line in round one of eliminations against Mike Hamby in Larry Christopherson's Chevy II flopper at Pomona. Right after Reyes took this photo, the* Hawaiian *started to come around and lift. It went airborne before the chutes were deployed and ended up rolling upside down. (Photo Courtesy Steve Reyes)

In the first round of Funny Car eliminations, Reyes was matched up against Mike Hamby, who was driving Larry Christopherson's Chevy II. At the hit, the Charger left straight off the line ahead of Hamby, but just before the top end stripes, the *Hawaiian* started to lean in a little, pulling hard and wanting to come around. Reyes entered through the top-end and stopped the clocks with a decent 8.14 ET at 181.45 mph when the car suddenly lifted high off the track, rolled over so that it was facing the starting line, turned upside down, and took flight for nearly 200 feet down the strip! The Charger crash-landed hard on the asphalt surface and broke apart. The car came to a stop, staying upright.

Reyes remained conscious and was quickly removed from the car by the NHRA Safety Safari. Arriving immediately on the scene was Roland Leong, Don Prudhomme, Keith Black, Jay Howell, and the crew from Logghe.

Reyes was shaken up, receiving only bruises and contusions from the safety harness and belts. For safety concerns, he took an ambulance to the hospital. The car's body was a crumpled mass of broken fiberglass, and the chassis was bent and broken, but the roll cage stayed intact, protecting Reyes from serious or fatal injuries.

What remained of the car was cleared off the track, loaded up on Tom Smallwood's ramp truck, and hauled back to Black's shop in South Gate. Logghe was already in the process of constructing the first Mini-Charger Funny Car for the Castronovo family car. Reyes went back to Logghe to get fitted for a new car, where he ran into Jay Howell and Tom Prock, who were going into the building.

Photographer Lane Evans captured Larry Reyes just before the* Hawaiian *crash-landed before the lights at Pomona. The new Dodge Charger was mangled beyond repair after only making its fourth pass ever down a drag strip. (Photo Courtesy Roland Leong Collection)

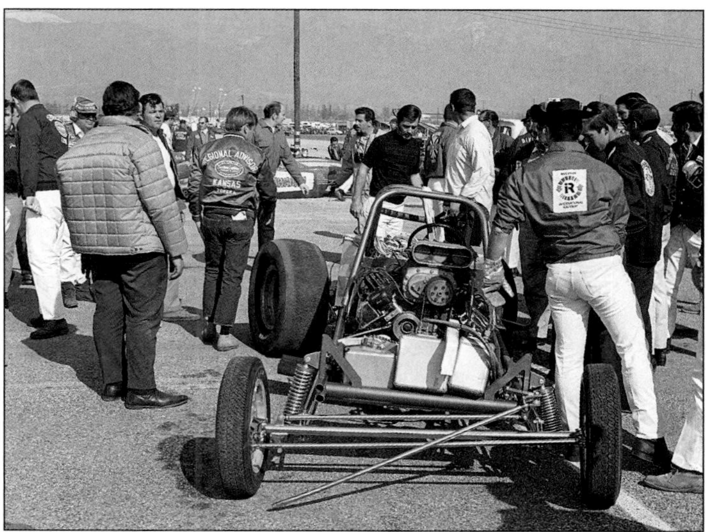

NHRA regional directors, track officials, equipment manufacturers, and safety personal examine the bent and broken chassis and the damage to the fiberglass body from the devastating crash.

Reyes, Howell, and Prock weren't aware that Leong had jumped ahead in getting their car that had already been started. This gave Reyes and Leong a head start to

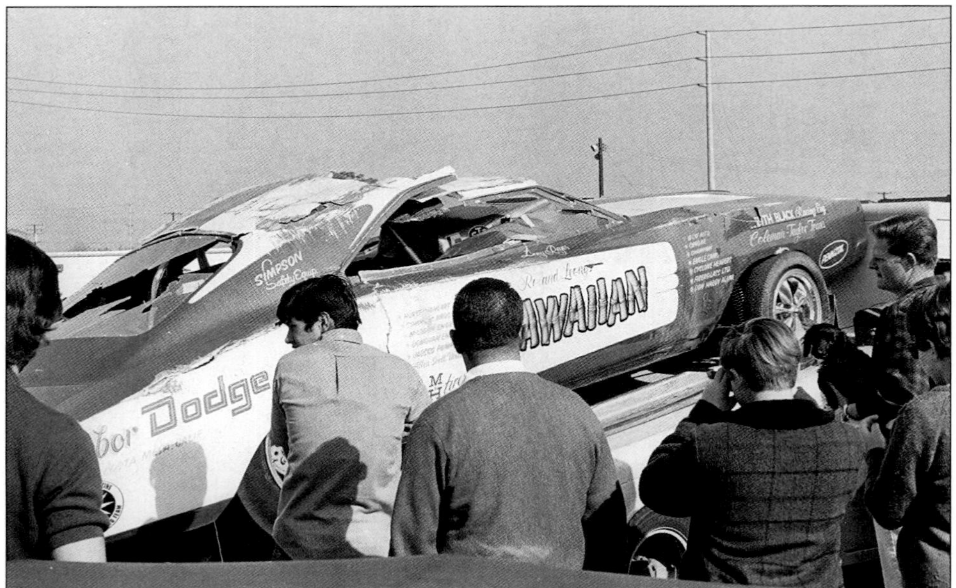

A group of curious spectators gather around T.B. Smallwood's ramp truck to catch an up-close glimpse of the broken carnage of the* Hawaiian*'s shell and mangled frame. (Photo Courtesy Steve Reyes)

The remains of the* Hawaiian*'s chassis rest atop the pulverized Charger body that sits behind Keith Black's building. Most importantly, the roll cage did its job and kept driver Larry Reyes from serious injury. (Photo Courtesy Paul Johnson Collection)

be ready in time to race by Memorial Day. Even though Reyes and Leong took their car, they have all remained great friends!

No Spoiler Needed

Leong was asked why the original *Hawaiian* didn't have a rear spoiler to aid with any downforce.

"I had no idea, as I had never ran a Funny Car [at that time]," Leong said. "Chrysler said we didn't need one because the NASCAR Chargers didn't have them and they were running over 200 mph on the speedways.

"Well, two things that were a lot different that the engineers didn't figure on were: 1) NASCAR Chargers sat much lower than the Charger-bodied Funny Cars; and 2) the NASCAR Chargers were twice the weight of what we were running, which is why I think it made the difference.

"After that, we added a smaller spoiler on the back on the new Mini-Charger, and from then on, we didn't have any trouble. As time went on, you wonder whether it would have made a difference if the early car had one, but we just didn't know, as we didn't have a wind tunnel to test them."

Although the potential of the car had never played out, the complexity of the accident and the way the car was demolished, were the deciding factors in not duplicating the original design. Several safety improvements were used in the newer Logghe "Stage II" chassis. Leong decided on a smaller, more aerodynamic Dodge Charger body instead of a full-size model. He also wanted the wheelbase tread ratio, which measured 118 inches, changed to the size of the Mustang, Camaro, and Firebird class.

Leong and Prudhomme Temporarily Reunite

With the new car ordered, Don Prudhomme reached out to Leong to have him assist with Prudhomme's new *Wynnswinder* Top Fueler until the new *Hawaiian* was completed. Larry Reyes didn't stay idle either. Just weeks after the crash, he spent time on the East Coast driving Larry Coleman's Super Torino, racing in New York and Long Island.

With Leong and Prudhomme together again, the duo began to reap the benefits right out of the gate, just like old times.

Leong helped the Snake win the Stardust Nationals at Las Vegas. The following weekend at Fremont's Two-Day Top Fuel Championships, Prudhomme took home the gold along with setting the top time and top speed of

MEMORABLE MOMENTS:
"Pineapple" Larry Reyes

"I was in my home state of California for the Manufacturer's Race at Orange County International Raceway, and I dropped by Keith Black Racing Engines to pick up some parts and visit the guys in the shop," "Pineapple" Larry Reyes said.

"As I was putting the parts in my truck, Roland Leong walked to the parking lot where I was, and [we talked]. Off the cuff, he mentioned that he was looking for a driver for a new Dodge Charger that he was building and wanted to know if I would be interested.

"Later, I found out that Gene Snow, who was also in the shop, told Roland, 'There's the guy you need to get to drive the new car.'

"I was taken aback that having just met Leong, he would ask me to drive his new car. Approximately a week later, I responded to him that I would be interested, as my time as driver for the *Super Cuda* had ended amicably.

"After a trip back to Memphis, Roland contacted me by phone and said the car was almost ready. A trip to Texas was necessary for the aluminum work. After the car returned to Keith Black's, a flurry of work started to try to get the car ready for Pomona. After wiring, painting, and plumbing the car, we headed to OCIR to shoot magazine photos of the car. A few days later, we were off to Pomona for the 1969 Winternationals.

"From the very beginning, the car was ill handling. The steering and brakes were the major problems. The car was not a comfortable fit for me. I couldn't see the Christmas tree very well.

"I lined up for the first round of the Winternationals. The instant I left the line, I knew the car still wasn't right. As I was nearing the finish line, the car took off and flew. I remember seeing the crowd while I was upside down, and I remember thinking the last thing I want to do is go up into the crowd.

"The car slammed back down to the ground on its roof and flipped over right-side up. The next thing I knew, Prudhomme, Ron and Gene Logghe, Keith Black, and Roland were all around me and making sure I was okay. I was walking around, and Prudhomme asked me to sit down because he feared that I would go into shock. The ambulance arrived and the medics placed me on the stretcher. I was checked out in the emergency room and released.

"I wasn't back in Memphis very long before I was summoned to Logghe's shop in Detroit to be fitted for the new car. In the meantime, the NHRA had changed the rules for the dimensions of Funny Car bodies. The bodies were now allowed to be shorter and narrower than their stock counterparts. The new *Hawaiian* was the first Mini-Charger. Then, the body went to Al Bergler's shop then back to Keith Black's for completion.

"The car won three races over the Memorial Day weekend and the rest is history."

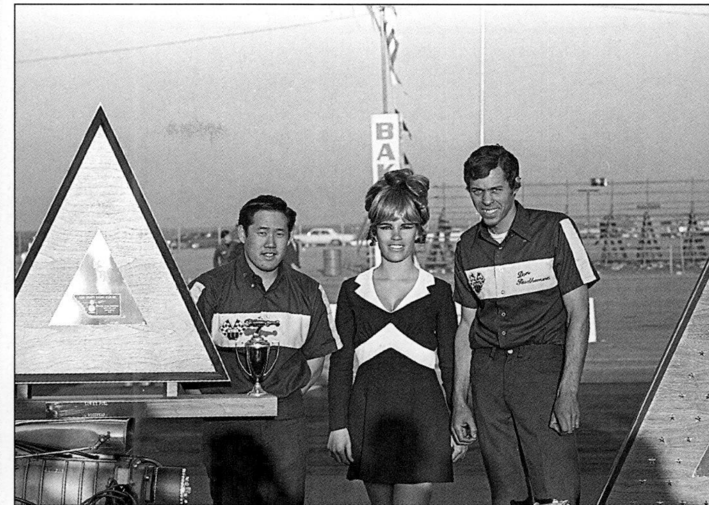

Days after the horrific crash at Pomona, Don Prudhomme reached out to Roland Leong to see if he would assist with running the Snake's Top Fuel dragster while Leong's new replacement Funny Car was being built. Just like their earlier racing days, the dividends paid off quickly for both Prudhomme and Roland when Prudhomme won the Las Vegas Stardust Nationals. At Bakersfield, the Snake took home low ET honors (6.75) at the March Meet. (Photo Courtesy Paul Johnson Collection)

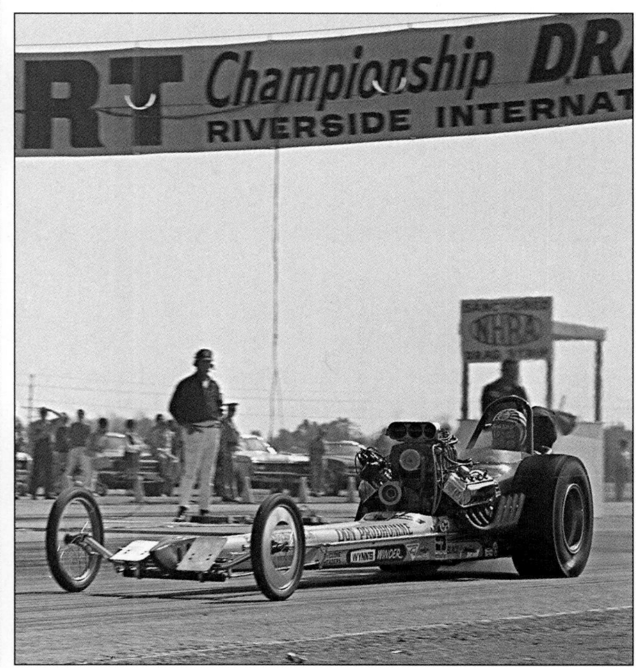

Prudhomme and Leong kept putting the pressure on the competition with wins and top performances, including Fremont's California Championships, the All-Pro series finale at OCIR, Lions Drag Strip, and this semifinal finish at the Hot Rod Magazine Championships.

MEMORABLE MOMENTS:

Don Prudhomme

"I guess at the time when I got back with Keith Black, Roland was into Funny Cars," Don Prudhomme said. "I didn't think much of them, in fact, I really didn't like them. They were big, heavy things, 'leakers,' having automatic transmissions in them. They were the worst thing in the world, but the fans loved them! I was more of the Don Garlits kind of guy, running Top Fuel dragsters.

"I came to find out that the spectators liked them. They were colorful, although not the fastest or quickest but the ones who put out the most smoke. Racers like the *Chi-Town Hustler* and 'Jungle' Jim Liberman got a lot of attention.

"When Roland crashed his Funny Car at Pomona, I was right there. Roland called me right away, and I gave him parts and whatever I could to help. In fact, I asked him to come help me on the dragster while he built a new car, as back in those days, you couldn't build a new one overnight because there's a lot of bulls–– on a Funny Car.

"When he came over to help me, we had a lot of fun. I had just the best time running the dragster with him, running the late-model Hemi with 100-percent nitro in it. We were kicking ass really well and having a great time. When his second Funny Car was done, he seemed disappointed, and he wasn't that pumped about going back to racing it. But as a pair, we won the 1970 U.S. Nationals again–but this time in my dragster."

the weekend (6.98 at 223.32 mph). Then, at the March Meet, the Snake ran low ET of the meet (6.75) again with Leong. Together, they turned in a consistent month of performances against the nation's top runners.

"When I decided to run a Funny Car, Prudhomme got a new sponsorship with Wynns," Leong said. "I sold him my new chassis that I had ordered from Don Long for the 1969 season with a late-model Hemi built by Black. After the Funny Car crashed, Don asked me if I could help him run his dragster until he went out on tour, which would be around the same time the new Funny Car would be ready with the new downsized Charger body. I couldn't run the car at any NHRA national event due to the size, so I helped Don run his car at Indy and won. It was a pretty good year after all!"

Relaunching the "New" *Hawaiian*

Ron and Gene Logghe, Jay Howell, Tom Prock, and Al Bergler rushed to put the unfinished car together and had it loaded up and driven back to California by one of Reyes's friends from Memphis. The car returned to Black's shop with the body and the chassis left unpainted. The body needed the correct mounting nuts and bolts and adjustments to fit properly to the frame. The underbody tin also needed slight alterations to both the body and the chassis for a correct fit.

Pressed for time to make the scheduled bookings, Leong loaded up the car and sent it from Black's shop in South Gate over to Ronnie Scrima's Exhibition Engineering in Van Nuys for completion. With the repairs completed (except for paint and lettering), the new car passed through the gates at Lions Drag Strip on May 24. The car rolled up to the starting line with a patchwork team consisting of crew chief "Big" John Mazmanian, Doug

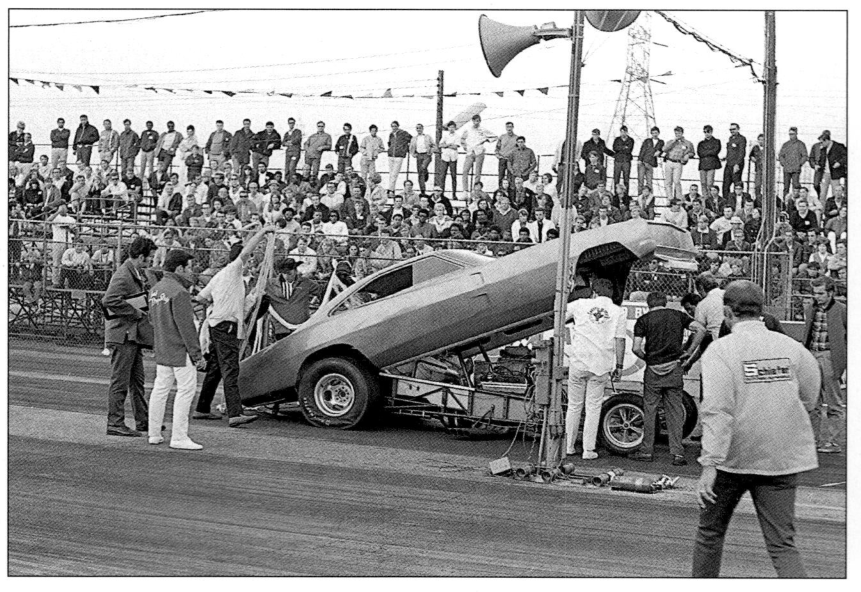

The rushed Hawaiian *made its debut at Lions Drag Strip on May 24, three months after Larry Reyes and the original* Hawaiian *took flight at Pomona. Pressed to assemble a full crew, Keith Black recruited the help of "Big" John Mazmanian, who volunteered his tow rig and his crew (known as the Armenian Army) to aid Roland and Larry Reyes. When Reyes fired up the car on the starting line for its maiden run, the vibrations from the Keith Black Elephant shook so hard that the parachute-pack release cable popped open. The chute came out onto the starting line, causing Reyes to shut off the car. Shown here untangling the parachute was starter Larry Sutton with help from the Army crew. (Photo Courtesy Paul Johnson Collection)*

With the chute repairs completed, Larry Reyes exited the water box with the* Hawaiian*'s first attempt back on the strip. The easy shakedown pass netted the Mini-Charger an 8.92 ET at 160.05 mph. (Photo Courtesy Paul Johnson Collection)

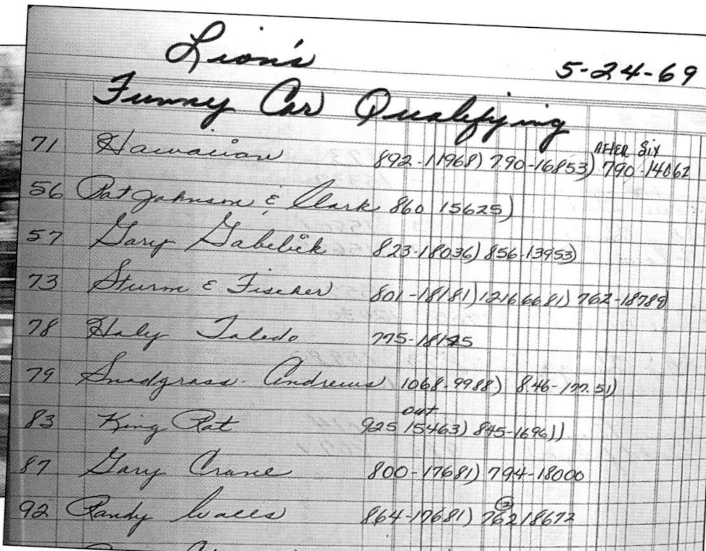

Lion's 5-24-69
Funny Car Qualifying

71 Hawaiian 892-1(1968) 790-16853) AFTER SIX 790-14062
56 Pat Johnson & Clark 860 15625)
57 Gary Gabelick 823-18036) 856-13953)
73 Sturm & Fischer 801-18181) 1216 6681) 762-18789
78 Haly Toledo 775-18175
79 Snodgrass Andrews 1068-9988) 846-177.51)
83 King Rat out 925 15463) 845-16961)
87 Gary Crane 800-17681) 794-18000
92 Randy Walls 864-17681) 762 18672

Pam Sutton, wife of Lions Drag Strip starter Larry Sutton, was the official "Hot Car" recorder for Lions. She logged many years of every pro car that made a run down the fabled strip. This page details Leong's new* Hawaiian*'s return with the three qualifying runs, the best one was 7.90 at 168.53 mph. (Time Sheet Courtesy Darr Hawthorne Collection)

"Cookie" Cook, Stan Shiroma, and Mazmanian's "Armenian Army."

Reyes fired up the car and rolled into the bleach box, activating the pre-stage and stage lights. At the green, the Mini-Charger launched off the line and eased down the strip with a respectable 8.92 ET at 160.05 mph on the initial run. With several more impressive but softer identical 7.90 ETs, the *Hawaiian* was in the show holding down the eighth and final spot. A last-second charge by Dale Armstrong in Gary Cranes's *Travelin Javelin* recorded a 7.85 ET, which knocked Reyes out of contention and spoiled the debut of the new *Hawaiian*.

The Learning Curve of Perfection

The following Friday night at Irwindale on Memorial Day weekend, Roland Leong, "Big" John Mazmanian, Keith Black, Holly Hendrick, Doug "Cookie" Cook, Stan Shiroma, and the Armenian Army returned to iron out the kinks of the new Charger. Now sporting white shoe-polish lettering over the blue gel-coat body, Leong instructed Reyes to be cautious and take it easy. Reyes lost in the first round but was able to return in the second round via the break rule, and it was the opportunity that the team needed. The car hooked up and ran like a rocket all night long.

Advancing to the final round, Reyes took out Ron Leslie in the Kenz & Leslie *High Country* Cougar to take home the $1,000 prize. The night was not quite over yet when Irwindale issued a $250 "winner take all" challenge to John Peters, owner of the twin-engine *Freight Train* dragster along with his driver Bob Muravez, for a one-round, non-handicap race against the Funny Car champs. With both owners and drivers accepting, the pair left evenly on the green. The *Hawaiian* kicked it in high gear, and Reyes never looked back, taking home the additional cash.

On Saturday (the next day) at the Hang Ten Funny Car 500 Championships at OCIR, the Armenian Army unloaded the car. Right out of the trailer, Reyes proceeded to run a 7.40 ET at 200.00 mph that put him into the low-qualifier position. For his efforts, he pocketed the $1,000 bonus for low ET put up by the track officials. Reyes added an additional $500 from sponsor Hang Ten for running a super quick 7.38 low ET in the first round.

The night concluded with the *Hawaiian*'s army and El Cajon's Randy Walls facing off in the finals. Up for grabs was the $1,000 purse to the winner, but it was Reyes's

Saturday at OCIR, Larry Reyes ran low ET of 7.40 at 200.00 mph right out of the transporter. The run earned him OCIR's $1,000 bonus for setting low elapsed time of the meet. An additional $500 bonus was paid out from event sponsor Hang Ten.

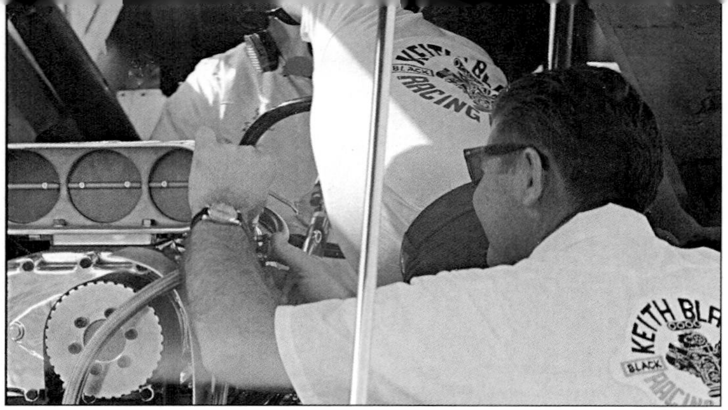

Keith Black adjusts the barrel valve while Holly Hendrick checks the safety restraints, checking in with Reyes to make sure that he's okay in the seat.

night. He abruptly disposed of Walls, who suffered from transmission woes.

The weekend concluded with Sunday's Caper at Carlsbad. The Super Team hit the trifecta when the *Hawaiian* "hailed down pineapples" on the entire field! Reyes unloaded a 7.37 that was good for low ET of the meet, taking home all honors including the extra cash. Overall, Leong bankrolled more than $6,000, which was not bad for the three days' work.

Doug "Cookie" Cook and Leong make last-minute adjustments before the all-important final-round meeting with the Chevy-powered Super Nova II of Randy Walls. (Photo Courtesy Auto Imagery)

CHEESEBURGER?

Roland Leong was questioned about the reason behind the bumper sticker "Cheeseburger" that was adhered to the front spoiler of the car. After being asked in several interviews over the years, Leong doesn't recall who, how, or why it was placed there. It might have been one of Mazmanian's crewmembers' shenanigans for fun. To this day, the unsolved mystery continues. No matter, it brought the team three days of good fortune over the weekend.

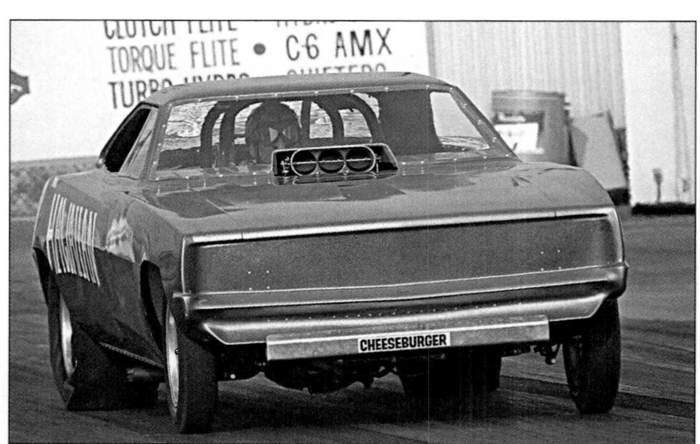

The Memorial Day weekend kicked off with three continuous days of racing: Friday night, May 30, at Irwindale; Saturday at OCIR; and Sunday at Carlsbad. Reyes placed the new unfinished Mini-Charger into the show, but he lost in the first round. On the breakage rule (if the winning driver from the previous round breaks, that allows the loser back into the show), Reyes was reinstated to run in round two. That was the spark he needed, as he never let up and mowed down the rest of the competition.

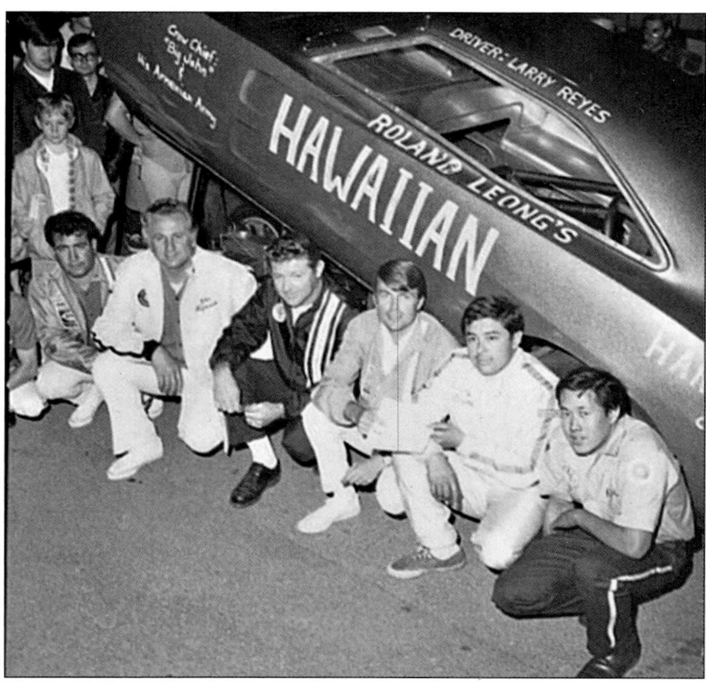

The "Super Crew "of Ruben, Mazmanian, Black, Reyes, and Leong share the laurels, collecting the $2,500 check from OCIR track manager Mike Jones for dominating the Hang Ten 500 Funny Car Championships. (Photo Courtesy Auto Imagery)

The finished product of the painted and detailed Stage II Logghe chassis of the* Hawaiian *was completed for the summer touring season from the reworked tin down to the correct nuts and bolts.

"That was better than Vegas, any time," Leong said.

Meanwhile, Back at Black's

Roland's "Home of the *Hawaiians*" was located in the network of several individual shops that were under one roof at Keith Black Racing Engines in South Gate, California. The facility was 12,000 square feet. It housed many of Black's customers and was shared by many of the fall and winter touring pros who experimented with new parts and engine combinations.

The shop spaces were large enough for racers, including Leong, to completely strip down the car to the bare chassis to make the necessary repairs and modifications. Those in the facility could also tear down and overhaul their Black Elephant 426 Hemi engines, with Black supplying a vast inventory of parts and aluminum blocks.

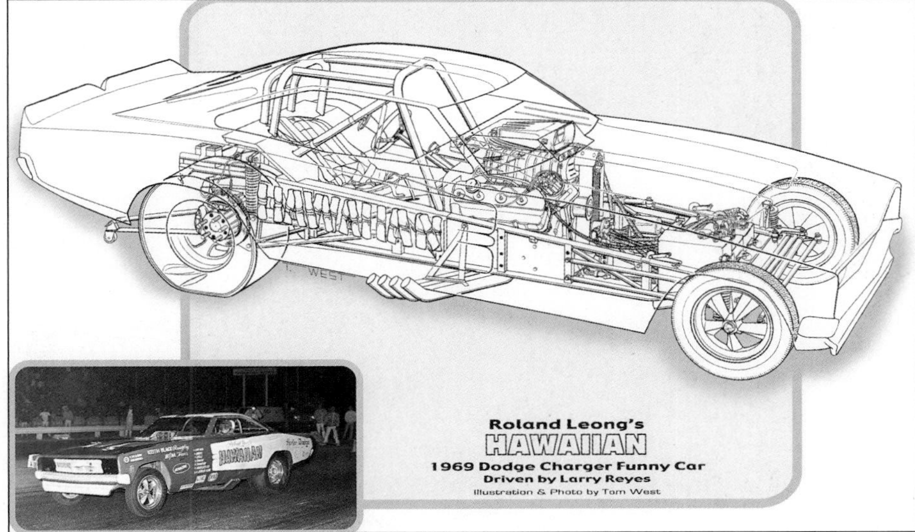

Roland Leong's
HAWAIIAN
1969 Dodge Charger Funny Car
Driven by Larry Reyes
Illustration & Photo by Tom West

Photographer and illustrator Tom West was an expert in highlighting the precise details with his X-ray drawings of race and show cars. His comprehensive version of the* Hawaiian II *highlights the Logghe Stage II chassis; the Fiberglass LTD Mini-Charger body; and all the hardware, plumbing, wiring, and details of the Keith Black 426-ci Elephant Hemi.

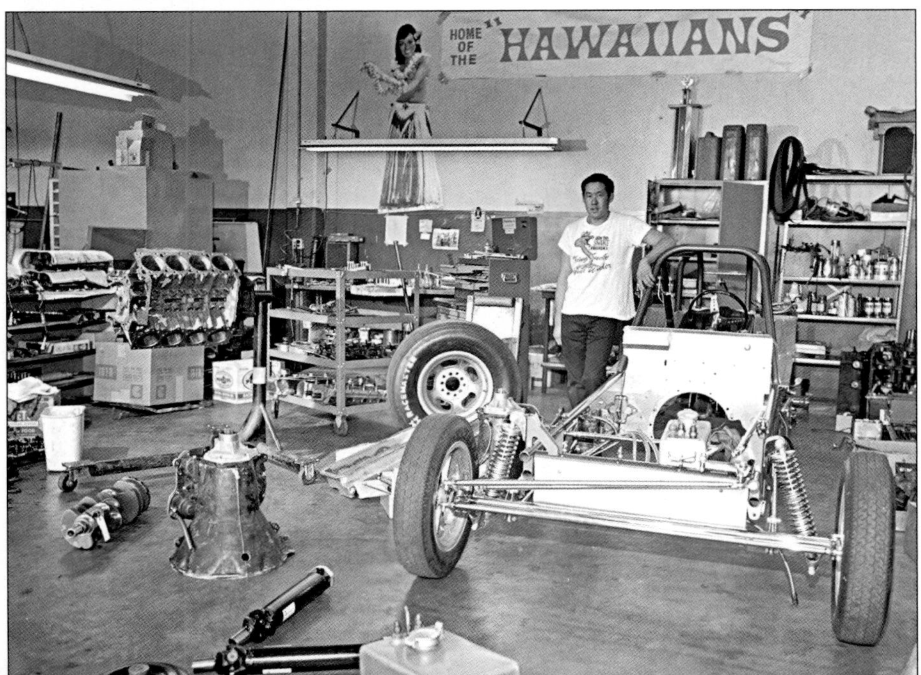

The state-of-the-art facility at Keith Black Racing Engines was a modern 12,000-square-foot building that was a tribute to the phenomenal growth of Black's modest operation. Black's engines had set more than 50 world records. The consistencies of winning both on land and water had made the performances and power legendary. (Photo Courtesy Roland Leong Collection)

Preparing for his upcoming summer tour, Leong torques down the main cap bearings to spec on his current 426-ci Keith Black Hemi. Leong was one of the best to get the most power and performance out of a Hemi engine without damaging or wasting parts and engines. (Photo Courtesy Roland Leong Collection)

SPIR hosted some of the best racing out on the West Coast with ideal weather conditions in the Bay Area that often had Funny Cars and dragsters resetting low-ET and top-speed records. This was a fan-favorite pairing that featured "Jungle" Jim Liberman versus the Hawaiian *and Larry Reyes. (Photo Courtesy Steve Reyes)*

SPIR "Points" the Way

With a purse of $20,000 up for the taking, Sears Point International Raceway (SPIR) compiled a select group of Funny Car stars for the annual North versus South Bash with 24 entries. Competition was understandably rough, as many of the entered machines were sidelined due to breakage. Performance numbers were off due to struggling traction issues, but only two drivers were able to solve the grip of the surface: Gas Ronda (7.61) and the talented Larry Reyes (7.56).

The consistency of the *Hawaiian* and Ronda brought them to meet in the finals. What looked to be a great finish ended before both cars staged. The *Hawaiian* suffered the misfortune of snapping off a sway-bar mount on the burnout and had to shut off.

Ronda's Mustang labored as well. He tried to keep it running and was awarded the win because his car was able to roll up to the line and leave under its own power. It was a somewhat confusing ending to the day, but Reyes was credited with both the top speed and low ET of the day (7.56 at 198.76 mph).

The Summer of '69

Making the stop at Suffolk, Virginia, in July for a best-of-three match race between the brother and sister team of Bernie and Della Woods, the *Hawaiian* swept all three encounters against the *Funny Honey*. Della broke the rear end coming off the line in round two.

New York National Speedway hosted the American Hot Rod Nationals, which was considered one of the top races on the East Coast. The three-day extravaganza attracted more than 69,000 spectators to the Long Island, New York, facility. They were there to see which of the 22 supercharged fuel coupes would etch their names into the record books.

The lone fuel-burning entry from west of the Colorado River was the *Hawaiian* Charger. Leong found all the right combinations to outperform the troops from both the East and Midwest states.

Friday's rainout limited the racing to a two-day affair with Sunday's finalists meeting for the title and cash. After a brief rain delay, Don Schumacher's *Stardust* Barracuda and Larry Reyes in the *Hawaiian* squared up together in all-important final. After both cars fired up and exchanged a couple tire heaters, the stage was set to go. Unfortunately, Reyes was a bit over-eager and rolled

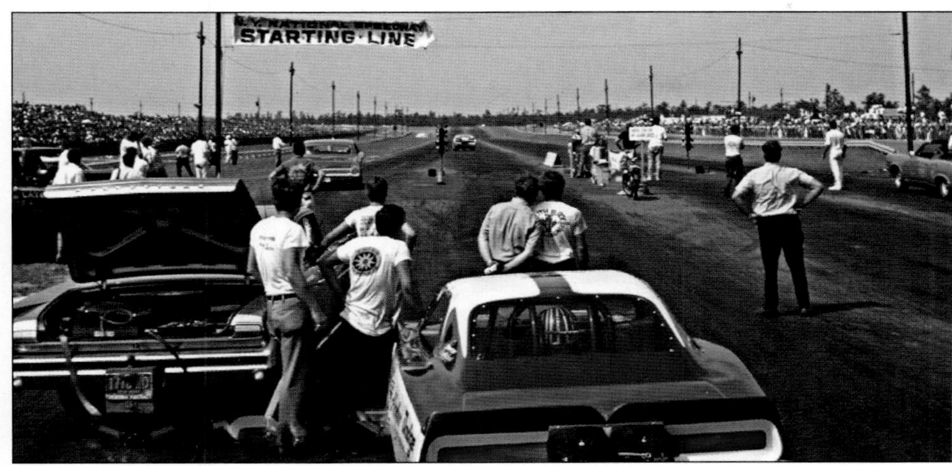

Roland Leong and crew watch the action before facing a formidable foe at the AHRA Nationals at New York National Speedway. More than 60,000 fans filed into the facility for the three-day Big Sound on Long Island festival. Sunday's final pitted East versus West with Don "the Chicago Kid" Schumacher and "Pineapple" Larry Reyes. Unfortunately for Reyes, he rolled through the staging beams, where he was stopped in his tracks by the red light. Schumacher took the win, but it proved costly, as his engine coughed up the blower and blew the roof off the Barracuda. (Photo Courtesy "Big" Bob Wagner)

out of the staging beams early, tripping the red-light foul and handing Schumacher the win.

With the NHRA still not approving the downsized Mini-Dodge Charger bodies to run at national events, Leong opted to help Don Prudhomme once again. This time, they paired up at the annual Indy Nationals while Reyes took the *Hawaiian* to Detroit Dragway and represented the West Coast for an eight-car Funny Car Spectacular with several of the nation's top floppers.

Reyes joined the list of entries that included both of Arnie Beswick's GTOs (the new *Super Judge* and his 1968 GTO), Connie Kalitta's SOHC Ford Mustang, "Jungle" Jim Liberman, the *Super Cuda*, Bill Lawton's Tasca Ford Mustang, Roger Lindamood, and the Wahley Brothers' *Warlord* 'Cuda. Reyes paced the *Hawaiian* to low ET honors of the show with a 7.44, winning all three rounds before he met the undefeated *Color Me Gone* Dodge of Roger Lindamood for the cash and bragging rights. Unfortunately, the weather didn't cooperate, as rain halted activities for the night.

The touring pros made the bulk of their living at various strips throughout the summer, racing sometimes four or five times during the week. Some would run at sanctioned national events on the weekends to go after and collect the elusive points, which often was more valuable than purse money. One of the favorite stops out on the road was at Maple Grove Raceway, which was on the outskirts of Mohnton, Pennsylvania.

Larry Reyes is literally blowing the competition into the weeds during this stop at Detroit Dragway, which featured an eight-car invitational field against the "Beasts from the East." Among the invitees of the Eastern stars was Bill Lawton's **Tasca Ford, *Connie Kalitta's*** **Bounty Hunter, *Terry Hendrick's*** **Super Shaker, *Arnie Beswick's pair of Pontiac GTOs, Roger Lindamood, and "Jungle" Jim Liberman. The*** **Hawaiian, *the lone representative from the West Coast, set low ET of the meet with a 7.44 in three rounds of round-robin competition. Just when the unbeaten Reyes and Lindamood were ready to compete for the top honors, the skies let go, washing out the last round. They ended up splitting the cash.***

MEMORABLE MOMENTS:

Roland Leong

"If you haven't struggled, then you haven't been in racing long enough," Roland Leong said. "No matter how successful you are, at various times, if you don't change your combinations, other racers catch up. You're always constantly finding a different way or better way to make the car perform quicker and faster. Anytime you change something different, you'll always go through that learning curve, as nothing ever stays the same."

Welcome Home

The team returned back home after the lengthy, strenuous summer tour going from state to state and logging tens of thousands of miles on open interstates and back-country roads. It wasn't glamorous, but the money made was worth the travel. It

Match racing was the bread and butter of drag racers. The races could be booked into tight schedules (sometimes three to five times during the summer), and racers could make more money than if they actually won a national event. One track that was a must stop on tour was at Maple Grove Raceway. Located just outside of Mohnton, Pennsylvania, Maple Grove hosted some of the Northeast's finest racing. One highly touted East versus West match race was the "Best from the West" Hawaiian, *mixing it up with the "Beasts of the East" and the* Frantic Ford *Mustang. (Photo Courtesy Paul Johnson Collection)*

was also time for the team to race back at its favorite local strips, such as venues in L.A., Orange County, and San Diego.

A Record-Setting Day

Promoter Don Kruse ignored the dark, ominous skies to stage the second-annual Professional Driver's Association (PDA) Race of Champions at Carlsbad in front of 6,000 faithful San Diego–area fans. The *Hawaiian* established another new track record over a crack field of the nation's elite floppers that included Terry Hendrick, Farkonas-Coil-Minnick's *Chi-Town Hustler*, "Jungle" Jim Liberman, Gene Snow, Ron O'Donnell in the Greek's 'Cuda, and Danny Ongais.

The final round was well worth the cost of admission with Don Schumacher and Larry Reyes meeting up in the finals. This was not a typical nailbiter. The Shoe's starting-line tactics resulted in an unbelievable hole-shot, leaving Leong to cover his eyes as Reyes set out on a fruitless attempt. But, once again, the power of the "engine whisperer" propelled the *Hawaiian* to a ruthless top-end charge, reeling in the *Stardust* just before the lights with a 7.46 ET at 195.27 mph to the runner-up's 7.84 at 166.66. The talented Reyes joined the Top Fuel Race of Champions in the winner's circle after a resounding victory in the Funny Car class.

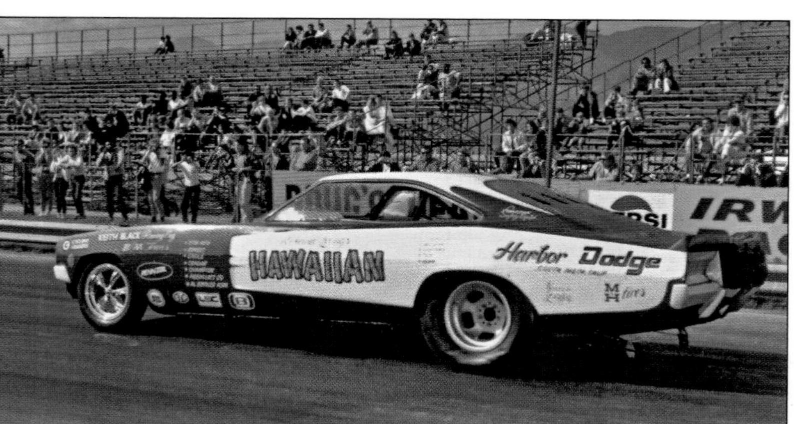

Irwindale Raceway's East versus West Funny Car All-Star Championships were witnessed in front of 12,681 faithful Funny Car fans. Time trials kicked off the afternoon festivities with Reyes posting a quick 7.51 ET. Reyes later fell victim to the slippery bite of the track in the second round, losing to Frankie Pisano and the Italian Army.

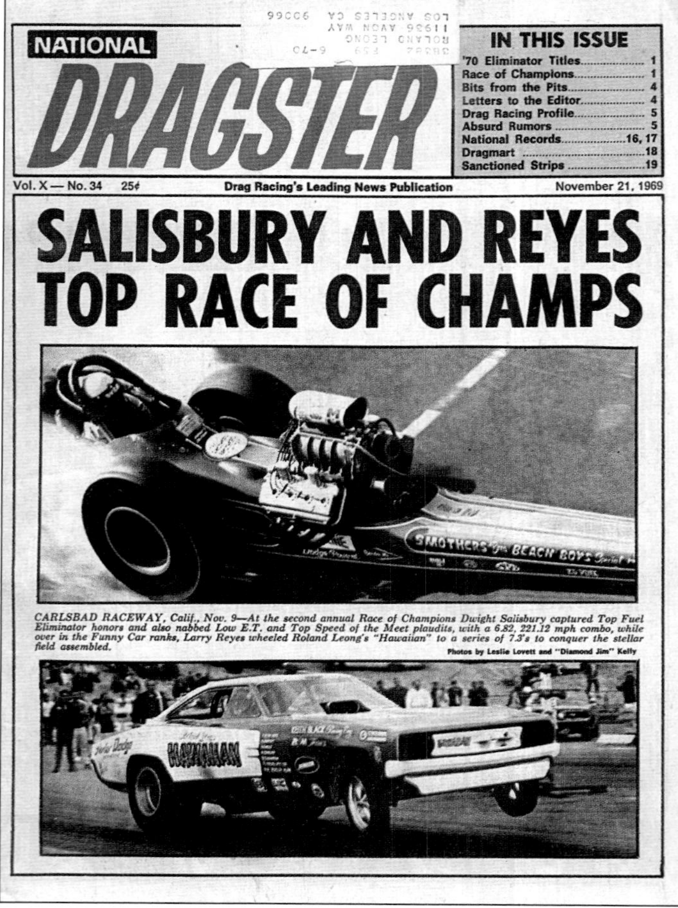

NATIONAL DRAGSTER

IN THIS ISSUE

'70 Eliminator Titles	1
Race of Champions	1
Bits from the Pits	4
Letters to the Editor	4
Drag Racing Profile	5
Absurd Rumors	5
National Records	16, 17
Dragmart	18
Sanctioned Strips	19

Vol. X — No. 34 25¢ Drag Racing's Leading News Publication November 21, 1969

SALISBURY AND REYES TOP RACE OF CHAMPS

CARLSBAD RACEWAY, Calif., Nov. 9—At the second annual Race of Champions Dwight Salisbury captured Top Fuel Eliminator honors and also nabbed Low E.T. and Top Speed of the Meet plaudits, with a 6.82, 221.12 mph combo, while over in the Funny Car ranks, Larry Reyes wheeled Roland Leong's "Hawaiian" to a series of 7.3's to conquer the stellar field assembled.

Photos by Leslie Lovett and "Diamond Jim" Kelly

The Hawaiian *was constantly making headlines in the weekly drag-racing publications in 1969, including this copy of* National Dragster. *It covered the* Hawaiian *winning the PDA at Carlsbad with record-setting performances and the domination of both Larry Reyes and Roland Leong.*

The "Beach" hosted its popular East-West Funny Car Extravaganza with a select cast of Eastern stars versus their West Coast counterparts, which included the Hawaiian *fresh off its successful summer tour. (Photo Courtesy John Ewald Photography)*

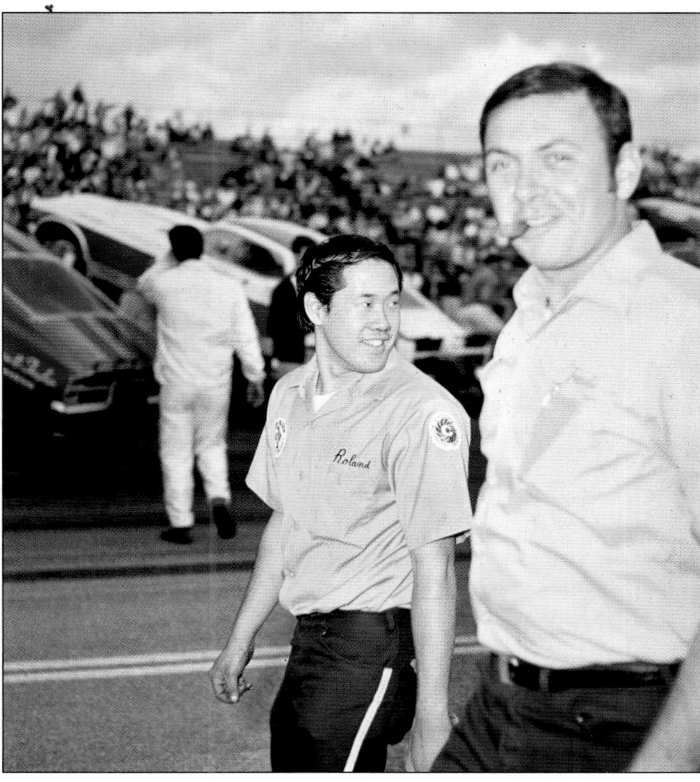

Pre-race activities were an added highlight that were enjoyed by all who attended the Funny Car Manufacturers Team Championships at OCIR. In addition to seeing marching bands, spotlights, and driver and team introductions, having all the cars lined up on the strip with their bodies raised was quite the sight. Taking in the pre-race pomp and circumstance were Chrysler teammates Roland Leong and Paul Candies, seen here taking a walk down the strip. (Photo Courtesy Roland Leong Collection)

The *Hawaiian* Dominates December

Lions Drag Strip hosted the two-day PDA Funny Car Nationals with 42 of the nation's top cars scrambling to crack into the field of 16 to see who would run on Sunday. There were 8,000 fans on hand Saturday night to witness the field battle for the top eight positions.

Among the top performers were "Jungle" Jim Liberman in the top spot with the unheard of time of 7.08. Pat Minnick's *Chi-Town Hustler* held the number-two slot with a 7.24 ET, while the local-favorite *Hawaiian* was right there with a 7.24 ET. Sunday's eliminator runoffs in the first round proved to be too costly for Reyes and the *Hawaiian,* as the Dodge Charger had problems with the bite. It went up in smoke, running an uncharacteristic 15.66 ET at 48.88 mph against Jess Tyree driving the *Bad Bascomb's Ghost* Chevy II.

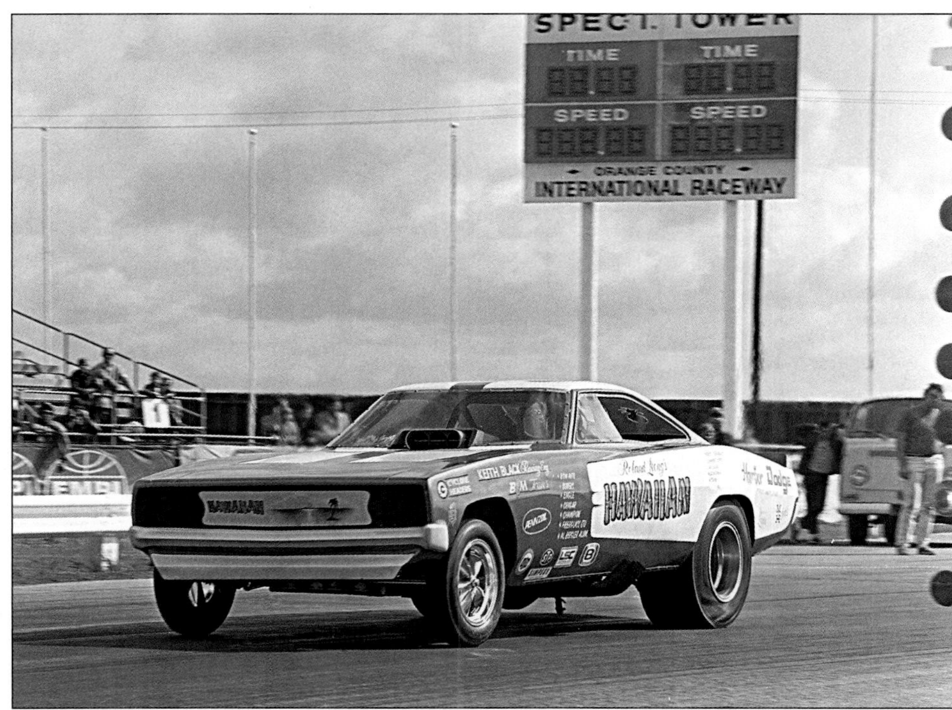

The 1969 Manufacturer's Funny Car Contest was the highlight of the year out on the West Coast. That year's unpredictable weather came into play with a weeklong delay due to rain. Racing was underway a week later on a sunny, cloudless Sunday morning that started early and concluded well into the night hours. Irvine's farm-fresh air was interrupted by the Hawaiian's *right-off-the-trailer 7.26 ET that set the tone for team Chrysler.*

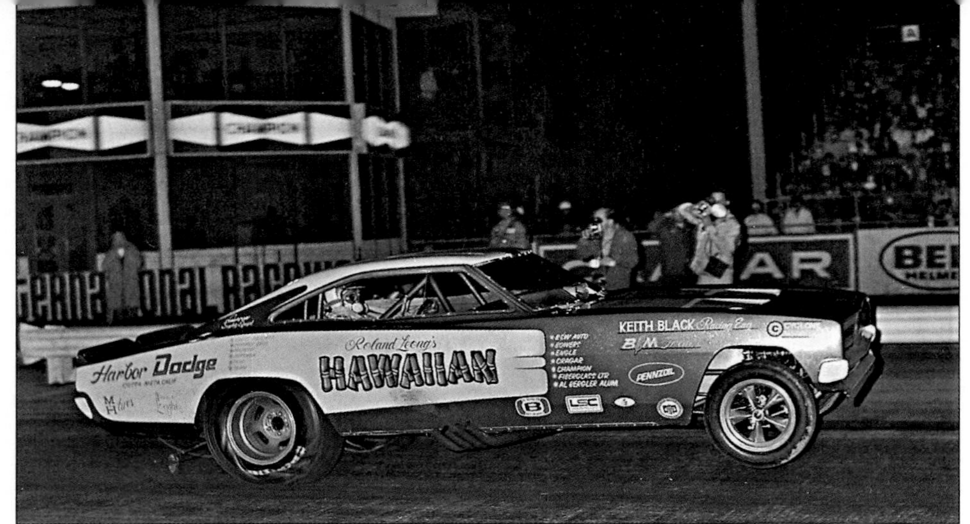

Larry Reyes propelled the Hawaiian *to all three round-robin wins, running over the 200-mph mark every time. Shown here in the third and last round of round-robin action, Reyes carries the front wheels in the* Hawaiian *en route to another win for the Chrysler camp.*

Records Fall for the *Hawaiian* at OCIR

The final 1969 drag race at OCIR featured an eight-car open that drew no less than 20 competitors who were determined to land one of the elite starting births. It turned out to be an old-fashioned free for all.

For Larry Reyes, consistency was the key when the *Hawaiian* blazed a record path to winning OCIR's finale of the year. Reyes began his quest in qualifying by unloading a phenomenal 7.20 ET at 202.70 mph for the number-one slot.

A first-round win with a 7.26 ET at 200.89 mph dropped Dave Beebe, the semifinal ET of 7.53 at 195.22 mph knocked out Randy Walls, and the final-round effort of 7.34 at 200.44 mph sent out-of-shape Pat Foster in the *Beach City* Corvette onto the trailer. The Leong-Reyes team dominated the eight-car field, setting the new Funny Car ET track record with a 7.20 and resulting in a $1,000 victory. It was noted that the *Hawaiian* had more runs below 7.30 than any other Funny Car at OCIR.

Reyes Resets Irwindale's Track Records

The week after setting the new ET record of 7.20 at OCIR, team *Hawaiian* picked up where it left off. This time the team was at Irwindale, when "Pineapple" Larry Reyes simply dominated the eight-car field by setting both low ET and top speed of the meet with a 7.27 at 195.94 mph to conclude the year on a winning roll.

Initiating a Learning Curve

Leong began the 1969 campaign in a different class with a new, untested race car that had logged less than 1 mile on the track, which was showcased in the destructive crash at Pomona. Leong never looked back after the setback. He persevered and returned three months later with a vengeance.

Team *Hawaiian* marched through the competition from the Memorial Day weekend to December. It ended a very successful year with numerous wins and track records across the nation.

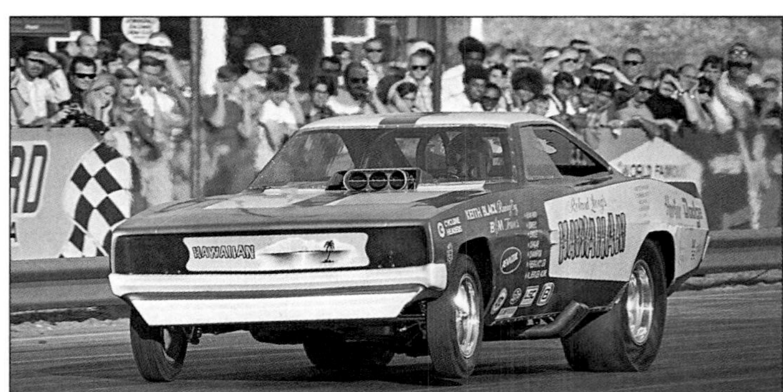

Irwindale's first-ever closed 32-Funny Car Invitational ran without anyone making qualifying runs. When Larry Reyes laid down a 7.43 ET, it served as a notice of things to come. Reyes went on to run low ET and top speed of the show with a best of 7.38 at 207.84 mph. Racing Dave Beebe in the quarterfinals, the racing ended for the Hawaiian *when a throttle-linkage clip broke off during the burnout.*

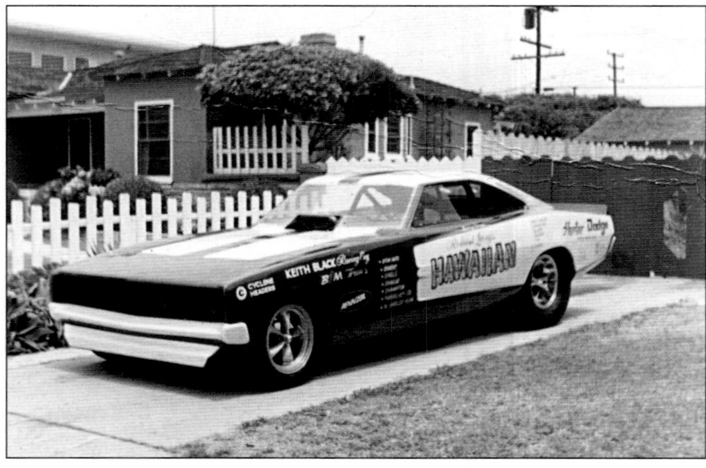

Imagine how awesome it would have been growing up next door to Leong and coming home from school or work to see the Hawaiian *parked in the driveway. (Photo Courtesy Roland Leong Collection)*

CHAPTER 7

1970: THE HAWAIIAN REINSTATED TO "LEGAL" STATUS FOR NHRA FUNNY CAR ELIMINATOR

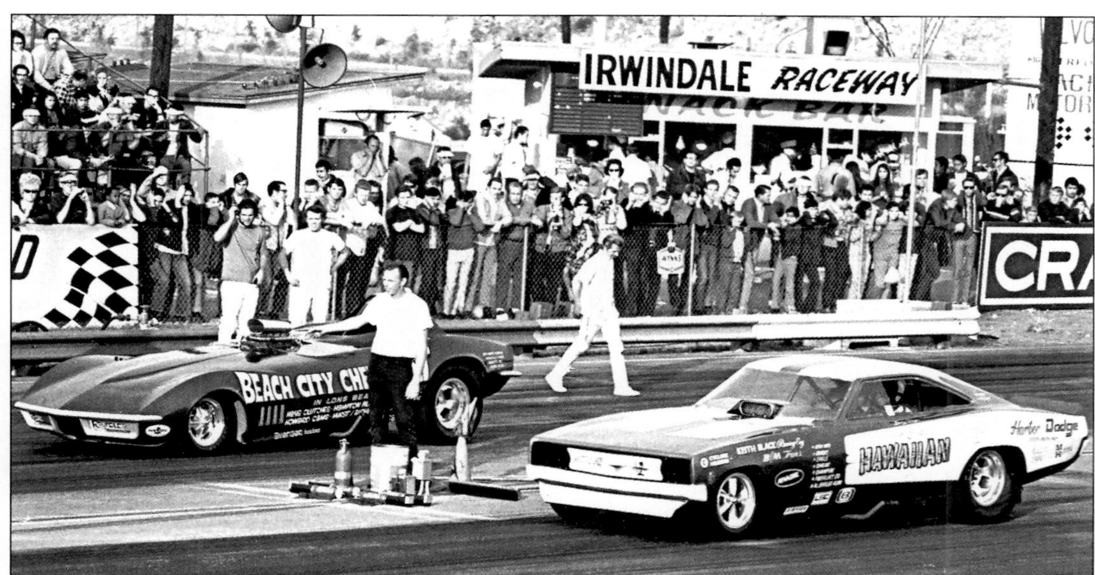

New Year's Funny Car Championship at Irwindale Raceway looked promising for Larry Reyes and the Hawaiian *with a first-round drubbing of Marc Susman. Round two wasn't as fortunate for Reyes. The* Beach City Chevrolet *with Don Hampton at the controls caught Reyes napping at the line and opened a huge hole-shot, sending the* Hawaiian *home. (Photo Courtesy Steve Delgadillo Photography)*

The *Hawaiian* was relatively unchanged from the previous year without any major modifications to the body or its appearance. The chassis was still relatively new, debuting in May 1969. Larry Reyes remained in the seat with Roland Leong making the calls on the tuning and upkeep on the Keith Black Hemi Elephant. The main factor for 1970 was the rule change from the NHRA that made the mini-bodies legal to compete at all national events.

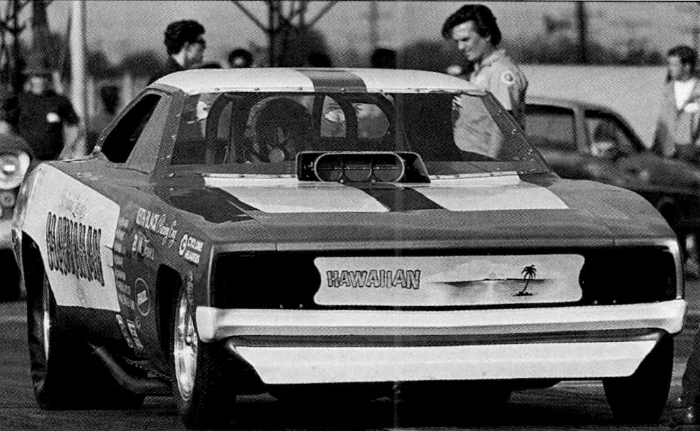

There were 14,600 Funny Car fanatics on hand to witness the battle of more than 40 floppers for Lions Drag Strip's two-day PDA Funny Car Nationals. Larry Reyes powered the Hawaiian *into the third position, running a 7.24 ET at 190.67 mph. Sunday's eliminations resulted in the upset of the meet in the first round when Jess Tyree, driving the* Bad Bascomb's Ghost*, took down the* Hawaiian*. Reyes lost traction on a damp track with a 15.66 ET at 148.88 mph. (Photo Courtesy John Ewald Photography)*

New Year's Day Championships

The *Hawaiian* opened 1970 at Irwindale Raceway's annual New Year's Day Championships and wasted no time. Reyes dropped

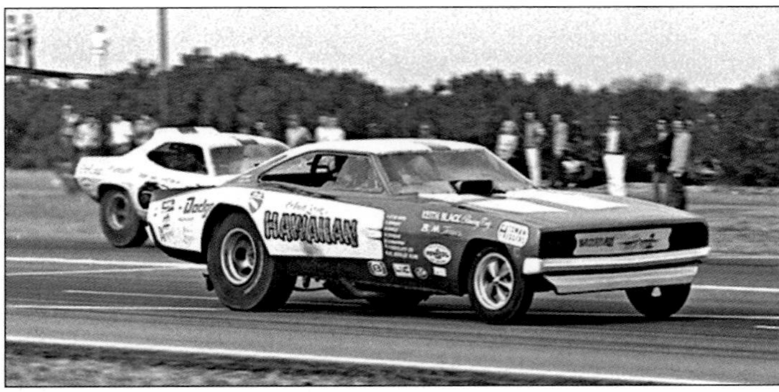

Back in the same class for the first time since 1968, Roland Leong's* Hawaiian *met Don Prudhomme in his new* Hot Wheels *Funny Car. Larry Reyes put the car in the show with 7.61 ET at 192.70 mph and put his old friend on the trailer early. (Photo Courtesy Steve Reyes)

Marc "the Kid" Susman in the opening frame. Round two, facing the *Beach City* Chevrolet Corvette driven by Don Hampton, Hampton displayed his unreal reaction time when he dropped an unforgettable hole-shot on Reyes, opening up an insurmountable lead over the *Hawaiian*. Reyes's valiant 7.57 ET at 198.66 mph could not gain ground on the roadster, losing to Hampton's 7.48 at 201.

It wasn't long after that Leong and Reyes regained their top form at Lions Drag Strip's two-day PDA Funny Car Nationals. At OCIR's All-Pro Series opener, Reyes brought the fans to their feet when he ran low ET and top speed of the meet with a 7.27 at 202.70 mph.

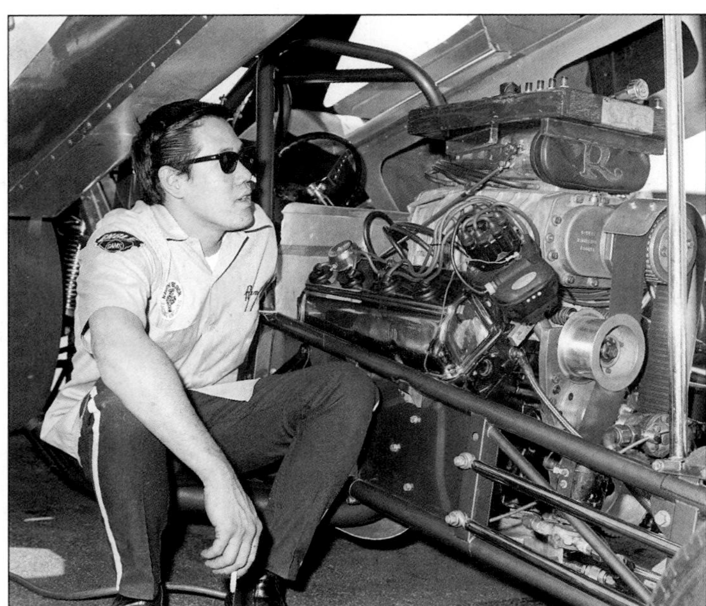

Leong relaxes from of his rigorous last-minute adjustments before going to the starting line. The iconic tuner and owner knew how to understand the engine by just listening to how it ran. (Photo Courtesy Roland Leong Collection)

1970 AHRA Winter Nationals

The *Hawaiian* showed up at Bee Line Dragway with minor body modifications around the rear wheel wells to house the newer, larger 18.00x16-inch M&H Racemaster slicks. Reyes stood in the overall third spot after Friday night's qualifying session at the 1970 AHRA Winter Nationals at Bee Line Dragway. The four-day event spanned from January 22 to 25.

Sunday's first-round encounter in Funny Car eliminations played into a major matchup when ex-*Hawaiian* dragster driver Don Prudhomme made his Funny Car debut at a national event, wheeling his new *Mattel Hot Wheels* Plymouth 'Cuda against the seasoned *Hawaiian*. The "experienced" Reyes had no trouble disposing of the "rookie" Prudhomme. The *Hawaiian* made it to the semifinals but tripped the red bulb against the eventual winner, Tommy Grove.

1970 NHRA Winternationals

In February, drag racing's Super Season kicked off at the 10th-annual Winternationals at the Los Angeles County Fairgrounds, drawing 45 Funny Cars that all wanted a slice of the $265,000 classic. Leong, Reyes, and Black put the unforgettable memories behind them after the previous year's devastating accident and focused on returning to the winner's circle at Pomona.

Leong once again proved that determination overshadows defeat, as the team handled all comers and won the highly competitive Funny Car Eliminator title. Leong had now won five major NHRA Championship Eliminator titles (three at Pomona), with this one being his first ever in Funny Car.

Larry Reyes put the* Hawaiian *into the elite field of 16 floppers with a 7.73 ET at 192.71 mph. This was nearly two-tenths of a second slower than the number-one qualifier, Dick Bourgeois, driving Don Cook's Chevrolet-powered Corvette (7.58 ET at 194.38 mph) at the 1970 NHRA Winternationals. (Photo Courtesy Tom Nelson Collection)

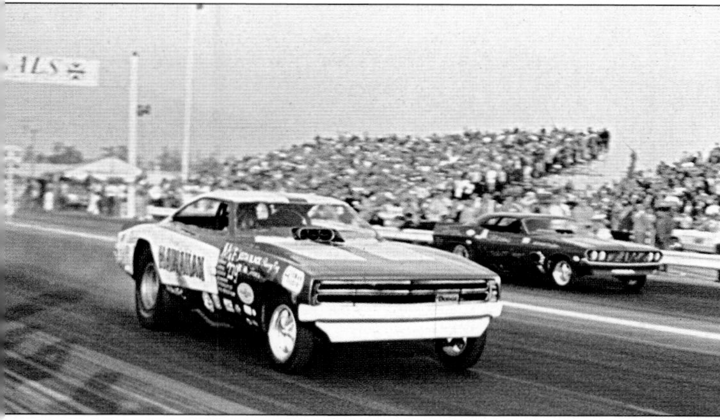

Larry Reyes dropped a hole-shot over Gene Snow in the final round of Funny Car Top Eliminator. The Hawaiian *won with a 7.67 ET at 195.22 mph to Snow's 7.83 at 184.43. Supporting Reyes was the crew of the* Hawaiian*, which included Leong and longtime friend Don Prudhomme. (Photo Courtesy Roland Leong Collection)*

The 1970 winner's circle celebration at Pomona featured Larry Reyes, "Miss Hurst" Linda Vaughn, and car owner Roland Leong after the team upset the greatest Funny Car field ever assembled for a national event. Over his career as a car owner and tuner, Leong won five major NHRA championship titles—three Eliminator titles alone at Pomona. (Photo Courtesy Roland Leong Collection)

Not all the congratulatory kisses are collected by the winning driver! In this case, Leong, the car owner and tuner, receives a kiss from "Miss Hurst" Linda Vaughn, making winning the Winternationals all the more special. (Photo Courtesy Roland Leong Collection)

Larry Reyes receives the congratulatory handshake from John Raffa, the publisher of Car Craft *magazine, while Leong, the Winternationals' race queen, and Keith Black look on. Along with collecting the coveted "Wally" trophy, Leong and Reyes earned more than $10,000 for the Funny Car Eliminator victory. (Photo Courtesy Roland Leong Collection)*

Sunshine State Dominance

After having won Pomona, Leong decided to bypass the NHRA Gatornationals at Gainesville and the long-running Bakersfield Gas Championships for fresh new paint and graphics to the body.

He sent the car over to painter George Cerny for the color change and re-lettering. It wasn't long after his

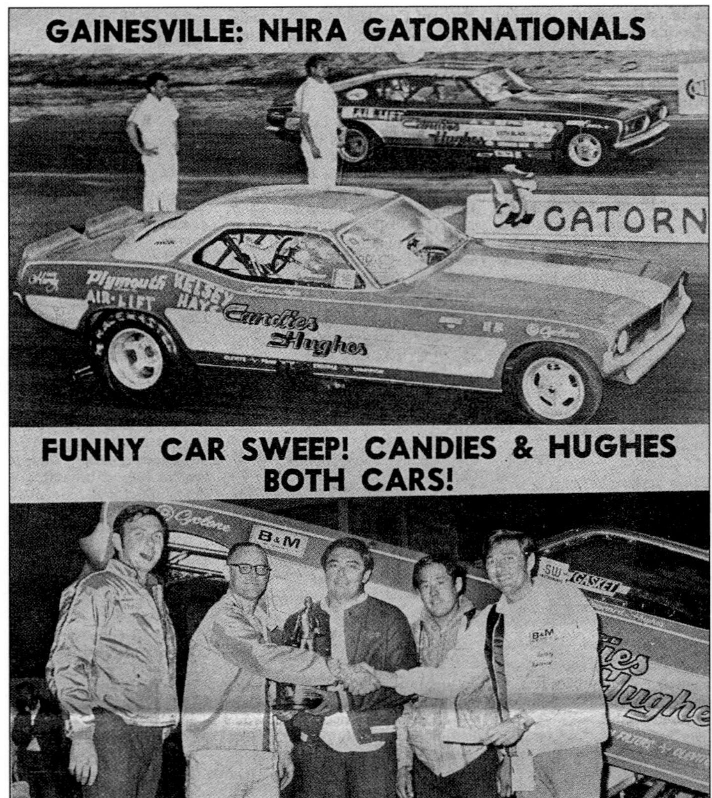

GAINESVILLE: NHRA GATORNATIONALS
GATORN
FUNNY CAR SWEEP! CANDIES & HUGHES BOTH CARS!
B&M

After both of the Candies and Hughes entries took top honors at the NHRA Gatornationals, Paul Candies, Leonard Hughes, Larry Reyes, and Roland Leong celebrate with congratulatory handshakes and a check from a B&M Transmission representative. With Leong wrenching and Reyes driving the team's "old car," they put together runs of 7.21, 7.15, 7.12, and 7.10 at 207.85 to 208.51 mph. These were the most consistent and quickest Funny Car times officially recorded. Hughes, driving the 1970 'Cuda, recorded his best time of 7.29 at 202.24 mph in the finals.

MEMORABLE MOMENTS:

Roland Leong

"After last year's crash at Pomona, we came back to win the 1970 Winternationals with basically the same 1969 version of the car we brought back over the Memorial Day weekend," Roland Leong said. "Right after winning Pomona, I decided to sit out the Gatornationals and the March Meet to get the car repainted for the 1970 season. I received a call from Leonard Hughes, and he told me that he built a new car. He asked me if I would like to run and maintain their old car at Gainesville and asked if Larry would come to drive it. I called Larry and he said 'Okay,' so we went racing.

"The car ran 0.20 of a second quicker than it had ever run before. We lowered our times and ran faster with each run. We earned our way into the final round against Leonard Hughes. Right away, I whispered to myself, 'Well, we know who's going to win in the finals!'

"In the finals, Leonard shot off the line with a car-length hole-shot, but Larry reeled him in and drove right past him. Reyes opened up a sizable lead when suddenly, the car shut off just past half-track! Hughes caught and drove past the coasting Barracuda and took the win. When I got to Larry down at the end of the track, we both looked at each other and didn't say anything. While we didn't win the Gators, we set low ET and top speed for the weekend."

decision not to attend the Gators that Leong received a call from Leonard Hughes and Paul Candies to see if he and Reyes would be interested to run their "old" Barracuda at the Gatornationals, as they wanted to run their brand-new 1970 Plymouth 'Cuda. Leong and Reyes agreed and took a red-eye flight to Florida.

On Friday morning, racing was underway. Leong and Reyes had the Barracuda running on a rail, besting the field with a quick time of 7.23 for the overall number-one position. Behind Reyes stood Leonard Hughes with their new 1970 'Cuda with a first-ever run of 7.30.

At the end of Saturday's final qualifying round, Hughes lowered his time to 7.28. Leong and Reyes dropped their time to 7.21 while at the same time ran top speed of the meet at 208.88 mph.

In each round of eliminations, both team cars improved on their times and increased the chances for facing each other for the all-important Eliminator title. Holding true to form, the double team cars of Candies and Hughes faced each other. Hughes grabbed the lead on a hole-shot, but Reyes caught and passed him at half-track. Suddenly, Reyes's Barracuda went silent. Hughes grabbed the win light, running a 7.29 ET at 202.24 mph to the losing but quicker Reyes (7.12 at 191.08). Leong and Reyes settled for the runner-up spot but set low ET and top speed at the Gators with a 7.10 ET at 208.81 mph.

Horsing Around at Lions

The weather in Southern California is known for its abundant sunshine and comfortable temperatures, but every now and then, Mother Nature can throw in a curveball and make a mess of well-laid-out plans. One such episode that hampered the decision of many racers was when downpours washed out the AHRA Grand American scheduled for February 28 through March 1 at Lions Drag Strip. The meet was postponed to the following weekend,

MEMORABLE MOMENTS: Larry Reyes

"Tom Prock and Jay Howell's Logghe Research Funny Car, the *War Horse* Mustang, was brought out to the West Coast in late 1969 for three to four weeks of testing," Larry Reyes said. "The new car just wasn't where it should have been, and they were trying to get the elapsed time lower. With Tom remaining back in Michigan, Jay not driving, and Roland and I being good friends with them, we parked the 'freshened' *Hawaiian* and raced their car at the Grand American Championships at Lions.

"The car was so small for me (with Jay being a small person) that I had a hard time getting in and sitting in the car. To drive it, the steering wheel needed to be much smaller. We had to modify it by cutting it down like a dragster wheel.

"I made a time-trial pass first before attempting to qualify. I finally placed the car high into the field, but at the same time, I was still trying to get accustomed to being inside the car. We went on to win in the first round, but I wound up facing Gene Snow in the second round and lost. Overall, it was a challenge to drive it but a fun time for both of us as well."

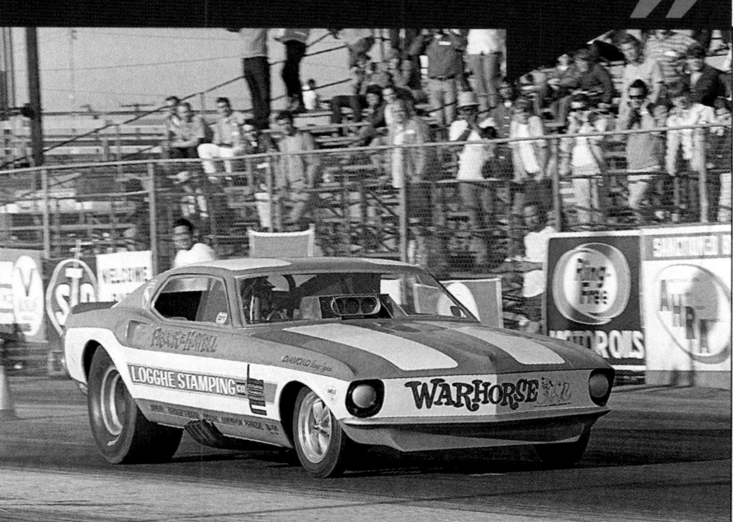

Ron and Gene Logghe, Jay Howell, and Tom Prock built their own rolling research and test vehicle, the Hemi-powered LSC War Horse *Mustang. Howell was assigned to drive while Tom Prock maintained and wrenched on the* War Horse. *With Prock back in Michigan and Howell unavailable to drive, the one-time driver/tuner combination of Larry Reyes and Roland Leong powered the Mustang into the 16-car field at the second-annual AHRA Grand American at Lions Drag Strip. With Leong observing his driver, Reyes put Marv Eldridge on the trailer with a strong 7.35 ET at 196.59 mph in the opening round of eliminations.*

March 7 and 8, which was the same scheduled slot occupied by the NHRA-sanctioned U.S. Fuel and Gas Championships at Bakersfield.

Both parties were aware of the precarious situation and had to make the best of it, possibly with a coin flip. Leong had already entered the newly improved *Hawaiian* at Bakersfield but opted to run the Prock & Howell LSC *War Horse* Mustang at Lions when both Tom Prock and Jay Howell were not able to attend.

With Leong's tuning and Reyes's expertise behind the wheel, expectations were high for the *War Horse* after a first-round win running a 7.35 ET over Marv Eldridge. In the second round against the *Rambunctious* Dodge of Gene Snow, Reyes went down in defeat, running on the *Rambunctious* bumper with a 7.42 ET at 193.13 mph to Snow's slightly better 7.34 at 193.54.

The *Hawaiian* Takes a Fresh New Look to Sears Point

The freshly revamped *Hawaiian* rolled onto the grounds of Sears Point for the second-annual Northern National Invitational. Disappointingly, only eight spots were filled in Funny Car Eliminator to run for the posted $2,000 top prize. Among the entries were Bakersfield Champion Hank Clark, Clyde Morgan, Mike Snively, Marv Eldridge, and Junior Brogdon.

Larry Reyes led all qualifiers at the Invitational with a low ET of 7.589 that set a new strip record. The first time out with the freshly painted *Hawaiian*, Reyes defeated Bob Pickett's *Mr. Pickett's* Javelin in the first round of eliminations.

Larry Reyes led all qualifiers at the second-annual Sears Point National Invitational with a low ET of 7.53, which set a new strip record. The first time out with the freshly painted Hawaiian, *Reyes defeated Bob Pickett's* Mr. Pickett's *Javelin in the first round of eliminations. (Photo Courtesy Paul Johnson Collection)*

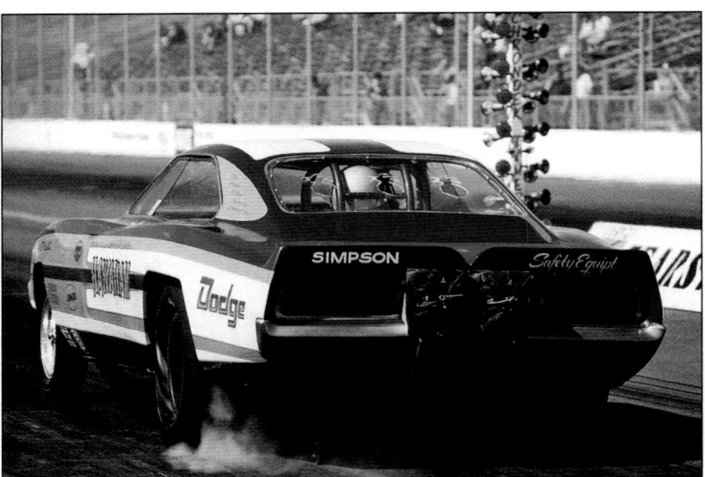

Larry Reyes disposed of up-in-smoke March Meet champ Hank Clark in the semifinal round at Sears Point. The finals pitted Leong's former Top Fuel driver, Mike Snively, driving "Diamond" Jim Annin's Dodge Challenger against Reyes. Unfortunately for Reyes, he had to settle for the runner-up position when the blower banged coming off the line. (Photo Courtesy Steve Reyes)

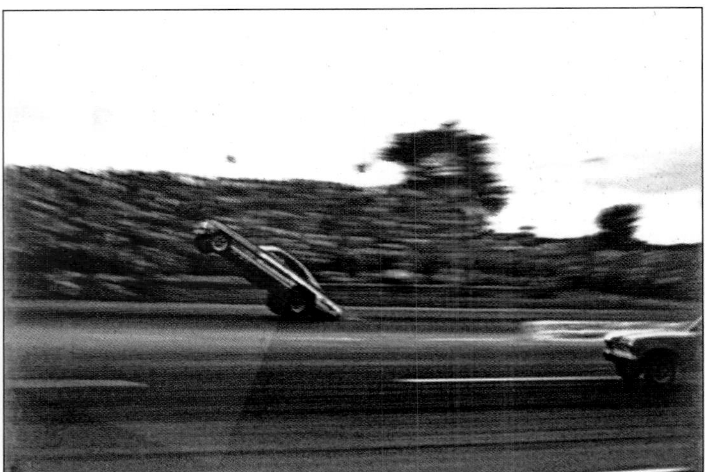

Funny Cars aren't supposed to do wheel-stands like their Pro Stock counterparts. However, the Hawaiian *looks like it's ready to take flight and head back to Hawaii. (Photo Courtesy Roland Leong Collection)*

The second round brought the March Meet and Winternationals champs, Clark and Reyes, up to the line. Reyes turned a strong 7.62 ET, as Clark skated around and lifted with an 8.05.

After Larry Reyes and Mike Snively surveyed the starting conditions, Reyes in the *Hawaiian* and Snively in the "Diamond" Jim Annin Challenger fired up for the all-important final round. Reyes was off the line first when he dropped a hole-shot on Snively, but the *Hawaiian*'s blower let go at 100 feet, allowing Snively to motor past for the $2,000 prize.

The Wheel-Standing *Hawaiian*

The summer touring schedule brought the *Hawaiian* up the Pacific Coast to Canada with a series of match races with Terry Hendrick and his *Super Shaker* Chevy II.

As Reyes and Hendricks came off the line, the *Super Shaker* Chevy became crossed up, accelerating into the *Hawaiian*'s lane, which could have been disastrous. At the same time, Reyes brought all four wheels (the back wheels as well) off the drag-racing surface, masquerading as the *Hemi Under Glass* wheel-stander. Reyes landed the Charger hard, which resulted in a bent front axle. The wheel-stand also tore up the rear bumper and the chute pack.

Fans came from over the fences and onto the track to help get the car off the strip. Fortunately, they were able to make the repairs and continue to race Hendrick in the next round. It was later determined that the pins holding the wheelie bars in position were inadvertently left out.

The *Hawaiian* Heads East and Scores at York

The sixth-annual Super Stock Magazine Nationals at York Dragway on July 17 to 19 was a huge drag racing success by anyone's standards. The three-day extravaganza kicked off Friday night with a spectacular Coca-Cola Cavalcade of Stars show that was followed by two days of points competition for all classes: Funny Car, Pro Stock, and Super Stock. There was $175,000 up for grabs.

Leong and Reyes had the *Hawaiian* running on a rail during the three-day affair. The first day of competition on Saturday featured qualifying and eliminations for the field of 20 Funny Cars. Qualifying was led by the Plymouth 'Cuda of Leonard Hughes and Paul Candies with a 7.24 ET, followed by Larry Reyes's 7.40 that was strong enough for the second position.

The *Hawaiian* was on a mission, running low 7.40 ETs during the elimination rounds before setting up a repeat of the Gatornationals final with Hughes and Reyes. The Funny Car final had the crowd on its feet. Both cars performed their burnouts well short, stopping before the six red-marker flags to avoid fouling out. As they staged carefully at the green, both cars were off the line at a dead heat. The *Hawaiian* held on to a slight lead all the way through the lights with a 7.35 ET at 210.34 mph to the 'Cuda's 7.24 at 200.34.

Leong and Reyes earned eight Enduro points for winning while Hughes collected four Enduro points for round wins and one point each for top speed and low ET.

Sunday was a near repeat of Saturday night only with

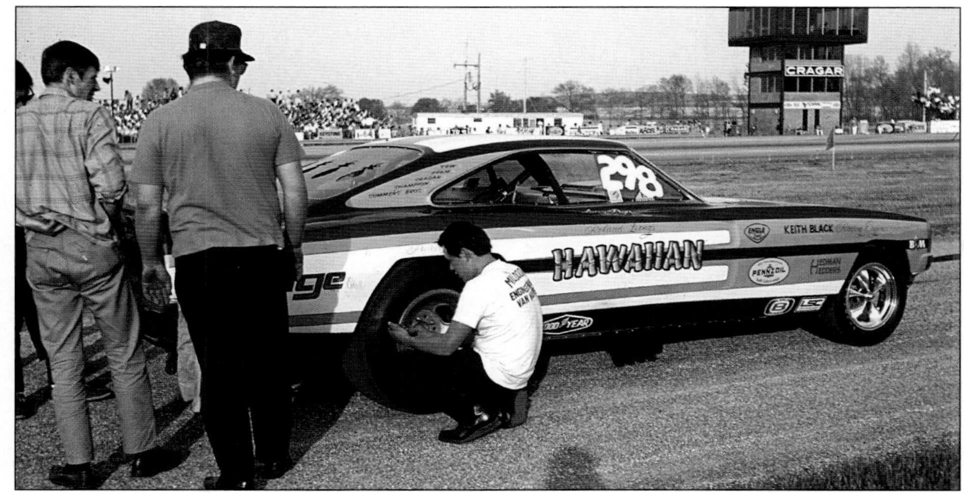

Leong checks and adjusts the air pressure at York's 1970 Super Stock Nationals. The Hawaiian *went on to dominate the two-day weekend event, taking the win on Saturday night and running a 7.25 ET at 201 mph. On Sunday, Reyes nearly duplicated the performance from the night before, but a transmission malfunction knocked the* Hawaiian *out in Sunday's finals against Leonard Hughes. (Photo Courtesy Bob Wagner Photography)*

switched results. Reyes defeated Phil Castronovo and Hughes took down alternate Gene Altizer in the semifinals, so the final round brought the two strongest runners to the line. At the go, Hughes got out first and led all the way as Reyes suffered a broken transmission that stopped the *Hawaiian* on the track. Hughes ran a 7.35 ET at 202.76 mph that was good for low ET and top speed of the meet. In winning the event, Candies & Hughes were declared the Enduro Eliminator Points winner in Funny Cars for 1970, and the *Hawaiian* finished second in points due to advancing into the finals in both days.

Dragway 42 brought in some great Funny Car match racing during the summer months. (Photo Courtesy Roland Leong Collection)

The *Hawaiian*'s Success Continues

Leong enjoyed a successful run from July 1 through 4, first besting the field of eight at Union Grove on Thursday night. The *Hawaiian* defeated Paula Murphy, Ron Rivero in the K&G Mustang, and Don Schumacher and the Ramchargers, en route to setting the low ET (7.22).

Returning on Friday night to Union Grove, Reyes drove the *Hawaiian* to the runner-up spot. He once again recorded the low ET of 7.25.

Saturday's race at Martin, Michigan, produced another low ET of 7.22 of the meet. The *Hawaiian* took out Terry Hendrick in the final round by running a 7.27 ET.

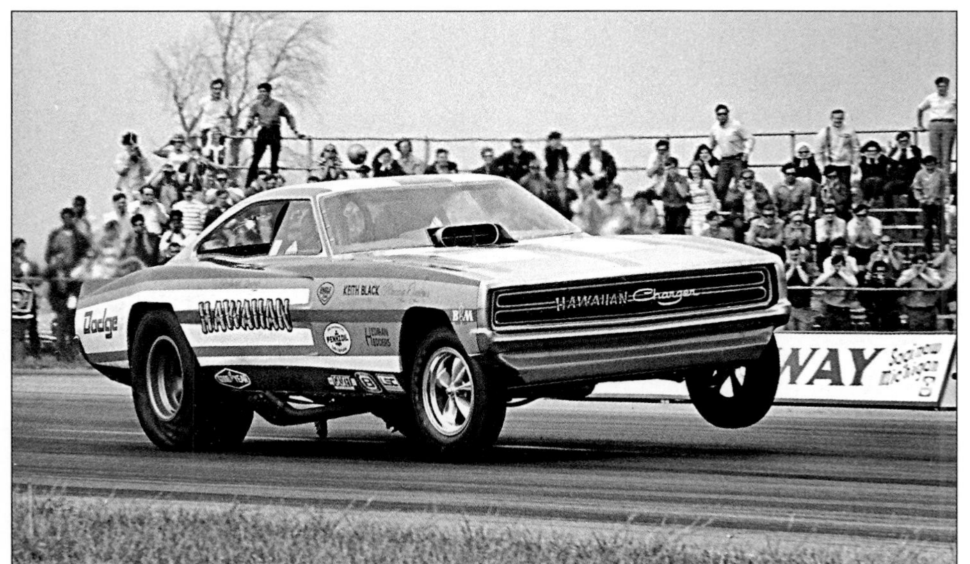

Tri-City Dragway was a state-of-the-art quarter-mile drag strip that was built by Saginaw GM dealership owner Reed Draper. The strip brought in the big-name racers and top-running cars from across the country, including the Hawaiian. *(Photo Courtesy Roland Leong Collection)*

MEMORABLE MOMENTS: Roland Leong

"In those days, many racers didn't have a lot of money to stay home and support their families and pay their race-car bills," Roland Leong said. "Winning a few nationals events didn't pay the money a racer would win out on the road. Match racing several days during the week in the summer months against other Funny Cars was our bread and butter."

MEMORABLE MOMENTS: Larry Reyes

"I just didn't enjoy traveling," Larry Reyes said. "Roland kind of wanted to go a different way, and there were no hard feelings–still aren't. He's been a good friend over the years. I had a good time and learned a lot. If I had to do it over again, I might have stayed longer."

Closing out the weekend on Sunday, July 4, at U.S. 30, the *Hawaiian* produced another meet win. Once again, Leong and Reyes reset the track elapsed time record with a 7.14 ET. Both Leong and Reyes were a model of consistency.

Reyes Steps Away from the *Hawaiian*

The winning streaks continued for Leong when the *Hawaiian* won the NHRA Circuit Meet at Maple Grove, in Norwalk, Ohio. Leong's *Hawaiian* dumped Tommy Ivo in three straight shots in a digger-versus-flopper match race at Norwalk, Ohio. Larry Reyes turned in a 7.39 ET and a 7.35, and he saved his best for the last round, where he ran his quickest time of 7.32. All three runs were over 200 mph.

Lastly at Hartford, Connecticut, Reyes (also known as "Mr. Consistency") took three straight over fan favorite "Jungle" Jim Liberman, setting new ET records of 7.33, 7.26, and 7.22.

As fans, we love the excitement and glamor of attending the local strip in the summer months, taking in a full event or a heavyweight best-of-three grudge match race, but behind the scenes, car owners and drivers take on the burden of demanding schedules. In August 1970, Reyes decided that he'd had enough of touring and announced his retirement from the *Hawaiian* after the year's tour.

Leong and Reyes parted ways on friendly terms before the U.S. Nationals. Jay Howell, who was driving the Logghe *Stamping Warhorse*, was named by Leong to succeed Reyes. In a last-minute flash, ex-Mickey Thompson shoe Pat Foster was listed as the driver for the Nationals when Howell, the official driver of the *Hawaiian*, was recruited by Don Prudhomme to handle the *Hot Wheels* 'Cuda for Indy.

Leong Collects Another "Ollie" Award

Roland Leong found Pat Foster available and hired Foster to drive at the U.S. Nationals. There, the *Hawaiian* advanced to the quarter finals when Foster lost to Leroy Goldstein driving the Ramchargers' entry. Foster stayed on to drive for Leong for the rest of the season.

On another note, at drag racing's answer to Hollywood's Academy Awards, Leong once again was voted to *Car Craft* magazine's All-Star Drag Racing Team as the Funny Car Crew Chief of the year for 1969.

The conclusion of the Nationals at Indy usually marked the migration of the touring pros to head out to the West Coast for the warmer fall racing months. The *Hawaiian* stayed east of the Mississippi River with stops at U.S. 13 Dragway, Blaney Dragstrip, and Phenix Dragway in Georgia. At Phenix, Leong took home the $2,000 purse, setting a new ET record with a 7.34.

After a lengthy stay away from home, the

Weeks before the 1970 NHRA U.S. Nationals at Indy, Larry Reyes finally had his fill of touring and decided he wanted to stay closer to home. Leong and Reyes parted company on friendly terms. Leong found ex-Mickey Thompson driver Pat Foster to fill the vacancy. At Indy, Foster advanced to the quarterfinals before bowing out to Leroy Goldstein and the Ramchargers. (Photo Courtesy Paul Johnson Collection)

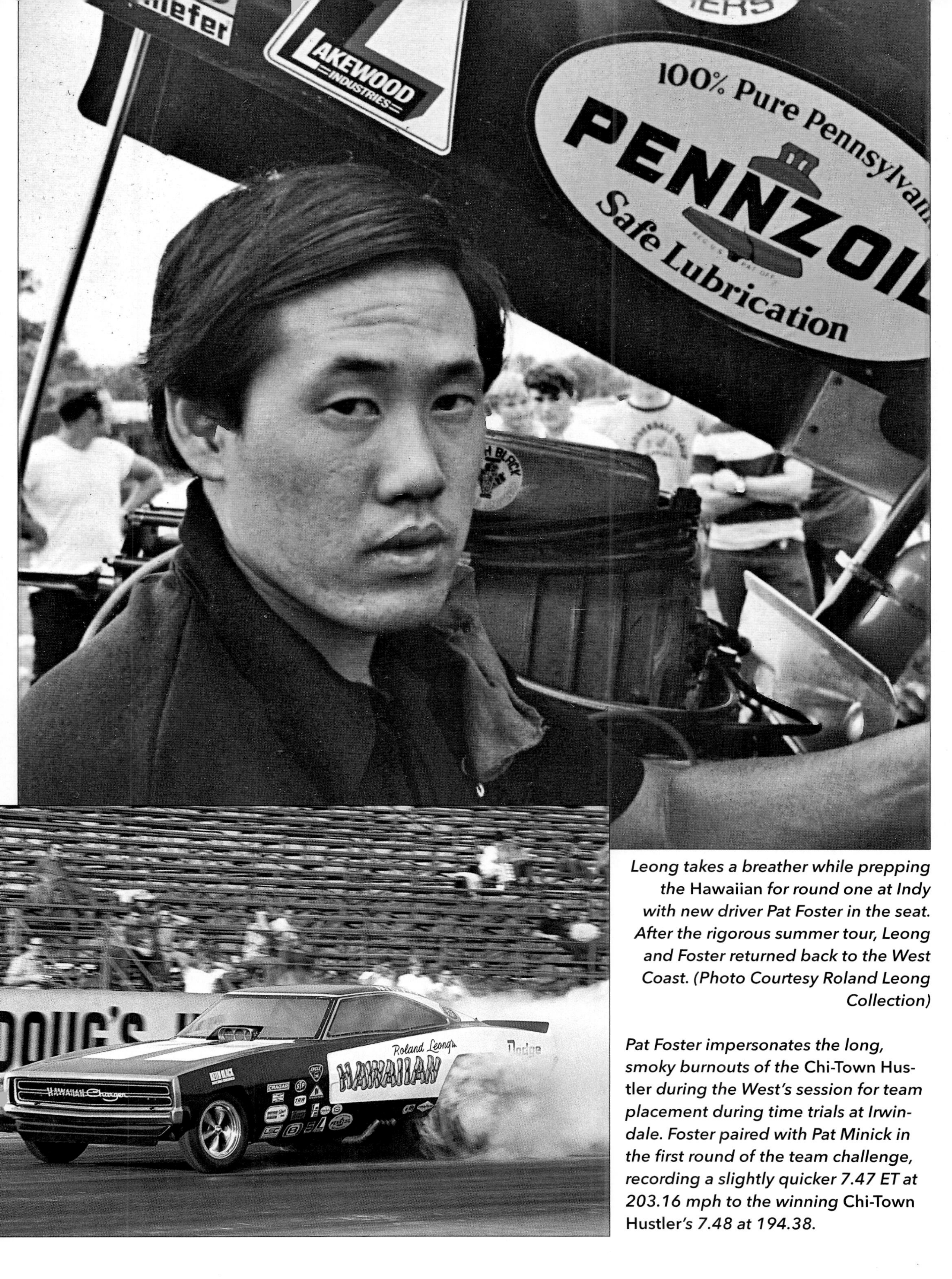

Leong takes a breather while prepping the Hawaiian for round one at Indy with new driver Pat Foster in the seat. After the rigorous summer tour, Leong and Foster returned back to the West Coast. (Photo Courtesy Roland Leong Collection)

Pat Foster impersonates the long, smoky burnouts of the Chi-Town Hustler during the West's session for team placement during time trials at Irwindale. Foster paired with Pat Minick in the first round of the team challenge, recording a slightly quicker 7.47 ET at 203.16 mph to the winning Chi-Town Hustler's 7.48 at 194.38.

season wrapped up in California and featured Fremont's East-West Funny Car event.

For Leong, the *Hawaiian* was running down the clock of being competitive. He contacted Logghe Stamping Company and placed his order for an ultra-modern Stage III digger-style chassis for the upcoming 1971 racing season.

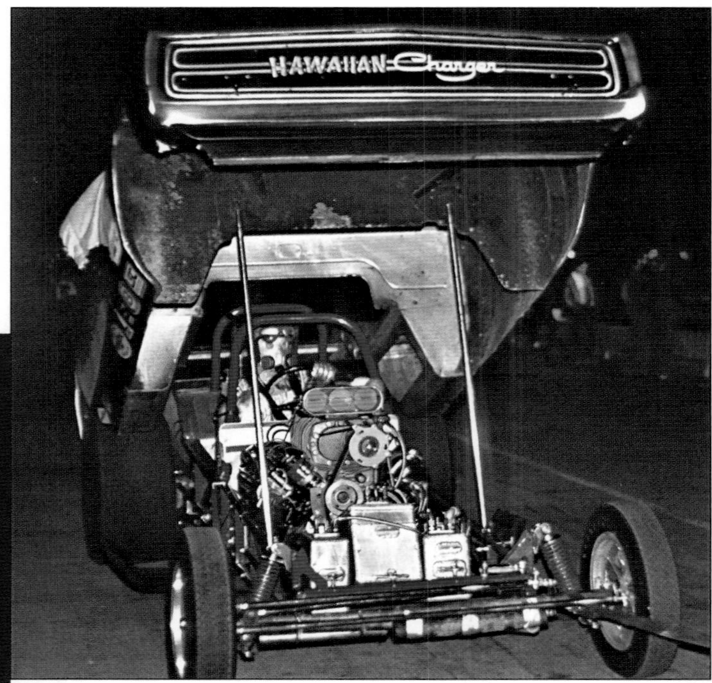

Pat Foster rolls up in front of the grandstands at Irwindale for his encounter with Ed "the Ace" McCulloch in the Division 2 bracket. McCulloch's 7.32 ET at 206.42 mph was good enough to hand Foster his second straight defeat when the Hawaiian *laid down a losing 7.55 at 199.70 mph.*

MEMORABLE MOMENTS: Pat Foster

"I remember when Roland and I were at Irwindale qualifying for one of the Funny Car shows," said Pat Foster, who drove the *Hawaiian* Funny Car. "When I launched from off the line, I thought I was on a great run, but when I was about 1,000 feet out, the pinion gear broke that over-revved the engine.

"At the same time, the blower banged and exited off of the manifold and the drum within the Lenco transmission exploded. At this point, there was oil everywhere inside the car, which ignited a blinding fireball that burned off the chute.

"Well, this led me in the direction toward the gravel pit, traveling around 200 mph! I reached for the brakes and of course, *nothing*. No brakes! The explosion sheared the master cylinder and mounting bracket off the chassis, leaving the whole assembly dangling. I sailed off the end of the track, which at Irwindale was like a desert, littered with rocks, bushes, and boulders. The safety crew got to me and got me out quickly, and luckily, without major injuries, but the Charger was banged up pretty good.

"When Roland got to the car, he looked it over and looked over to me, asking in his broken English, 'Foster, why didn't you stop?'

"I told Roland, 'Look, there's no master cylinder mounted to the frame, it's just hanging there.'

"Roland looked it over again and asked, 'Why didn't you pump 'em?'"

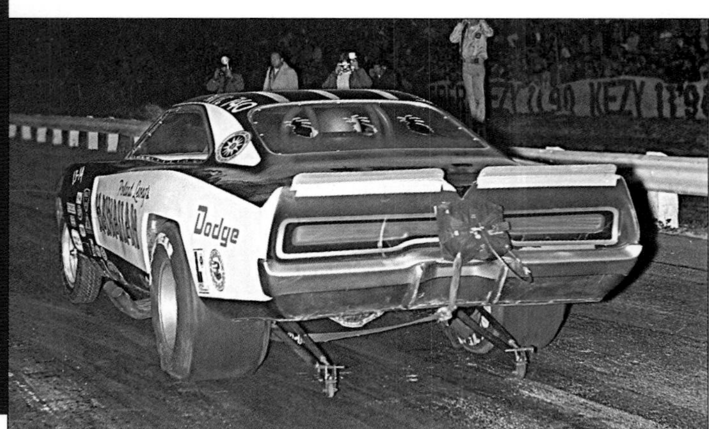

Pat Foster advanced past Stan Shiroma in the third round-robin frame, which earned a point for the Dodge team at the Manufacturer's Team Funny Car Meet at Orange County. Team Dodge was heralded by Gene Snow, Dave Beebe, Kenny Safford, Pat Foster, Pat Minick, and Kenny Goodell. The team finished second overall with 14.6 points, but that was overshadowed by team Plymouth's 20.

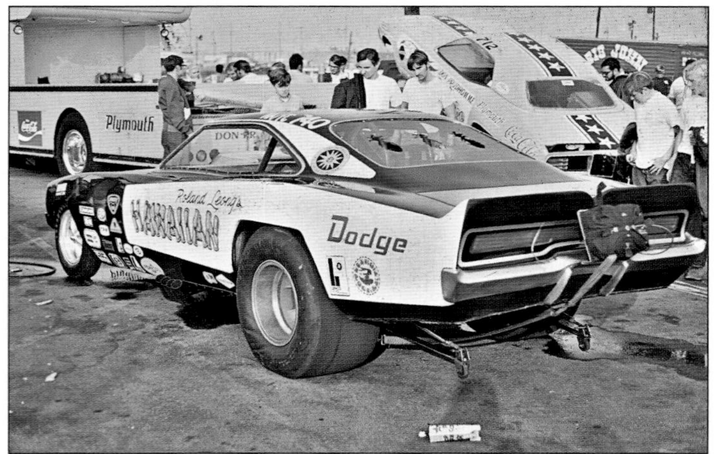

It was originally reported that fuel pilot Bill Tidwell had signed with Leong to drive the Hawaiian *instead of Pat Foster for Irwindale's East-West Funny Car event, but Leong changed his mind and stuck with Foster as the scheduled driver. As far as the timing went at the East-West show, Foster could be out and two others in. Only Leong knew.*

CHAPTER 8

1971-1972: A NEW CAR, NEW DRIVERS, AND A STRING OF WINS

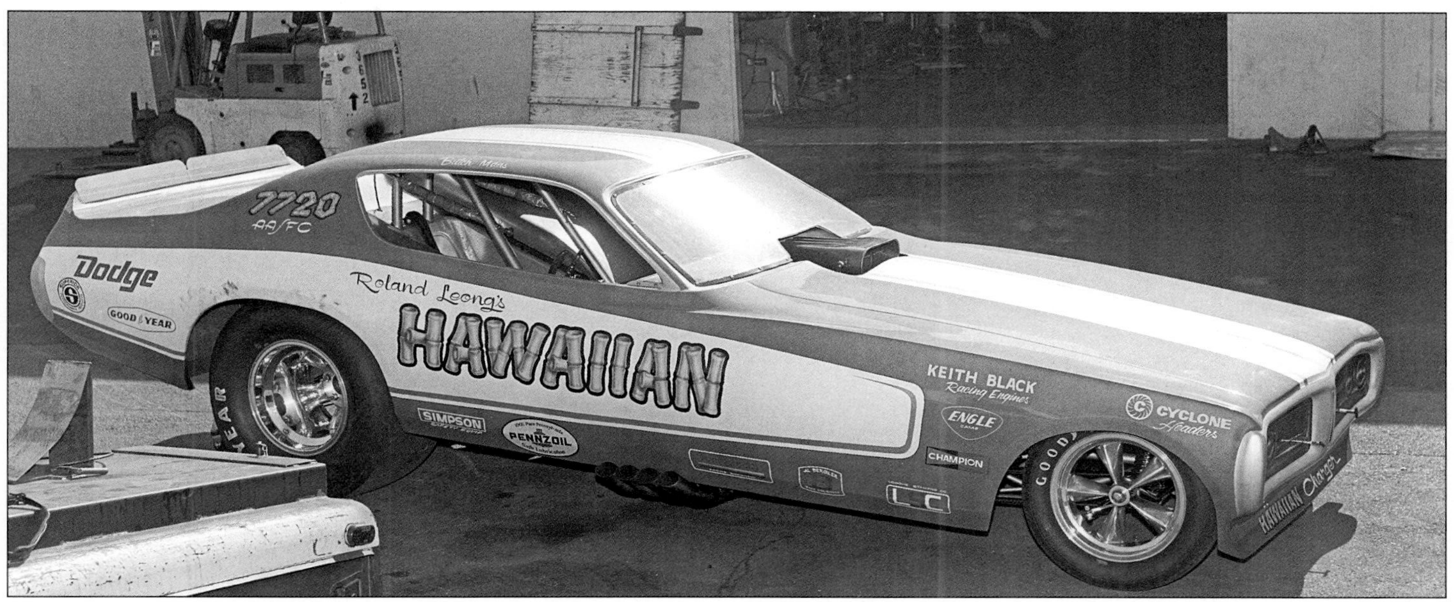

Signature tin work by Al Bergler and a new Fiberglass LTD 1971 Mini-Dodge Charger body that was mounted perfectly over the tubular frame topped off the new build. The uncharacteristic evidence to be found on any of Leong's super-sano race cars was the "greasy" finger and handprints that were left behind by the busy crew aligning the body to the chassis.

Roland Leong's rich history of building and owning the most super-sano race cars on the planet spanned from his early Dragmaster gasoline rails to the 200-mph-plus nitro-burning dragsters and Funny Cars that were high-speed masterpieces of drag-racing art. The end of the 1970 season saw another driver change with Pat Foster leaving to go drive for Don Cook. A few different drivers auditioned for a shot to drive for Leong, but when it came down to the decision, Butch Maas was given the reins.

Maas gained notoriety when Don Prudhomme pegged him to drive his *Mattel Hot Wheels* dragster at the NHRA Supernationals. Prudhomme was justified in his selection when Maas scored the low ET of the meet in qualifying. Many of the California racers who knew the prowess and skills of Maas (an outstanding veteran dragster pilot) understood that Leong would once again be a major threat in the Funny Car category.

Leong, known for his meticulous care and detail, set the bar even higher for 1971. He ordered a newer, super lightweight, digger-style Stage III chassis from the Logghe Stamping Company. Al Bergler worked his magic once again, hand forming the aluminum work. A more powerful Keith Black 426 Hemi of pure muscle loomed under the Fiberglass LTD 1971 Dodge Charger shell.

With a few trial runs at OCIR and the pre-Winternationals warmups at Irwindale, Leong was once again ready to make his presence known at drag racing's official curtain raiser at Pomona. Aimed for another victory at the "Big Go West," Leong was already accepting bookings from all over America for the summer.

Behind Keith Black's shop was Leong's newest mount: a Logghe's Stage III super-detailed, digger-style chassis with a Keith Black Elephant Hemi.

The might and power of the Hawaiian *fits tightly in between the tubular moly pipes of the Stage III chassis. It was Keith Black's latest form of motivation: a new 426 Chrysler Hemi fitted with a Bowers magnesium blower.*

Leong left no detail undone on the new Charger, which included many chromed parts and pieces down to every nut and bolt, the fuel pedal, and the steering linkage. Bill Simpson provided the safety blanket wrapped around the Crowerglide clutch setup and 2-speed gearbox that worked with Maas's vast dragster experience. Every SEMA-approved safety feature was built into the Hawaiian *to protect the driver, including pressurized fire bottles, high-temperature disc-brake pads and rotors to prevent brake fading, and Simpson lap and shoulder belts.*

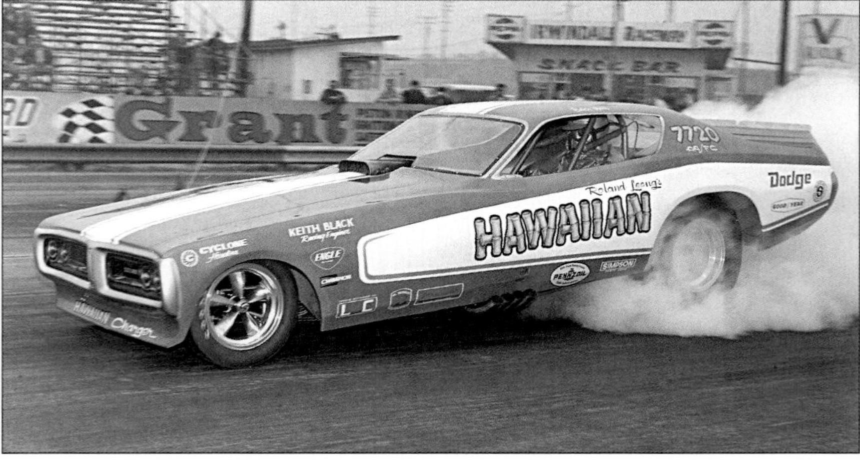

Irwindale hosted its annual Tuesday and Wednesday night pre-Winternationals warmups prior to Thursday's opening day at Pomona. Butch Maas put the new Hawaiian *in the number-one position with a 7.02 ET at 210.28 mph. That ET stood up for the low ET both days of the meet.*

The *Hawaiian*'s Legacy Reigns Supreme at Pomona

From the shores of New Jersey to the beaches of San Diego, a count of 47 star-studded Funny Cars battled for a spot in the 16-car field at the NHRA Winternationals at Pomona. Saturday afternoon's last qualifying session placed Butch Maas and the new *Hawaiian* into the fourth overall position, posting a 7.12 ET.

Maas cranked it in the first round against Kenny Goodell, running a 7.16 ET at 204.54 mph for the win. Round two matched Maas with Richard Siroonian, who

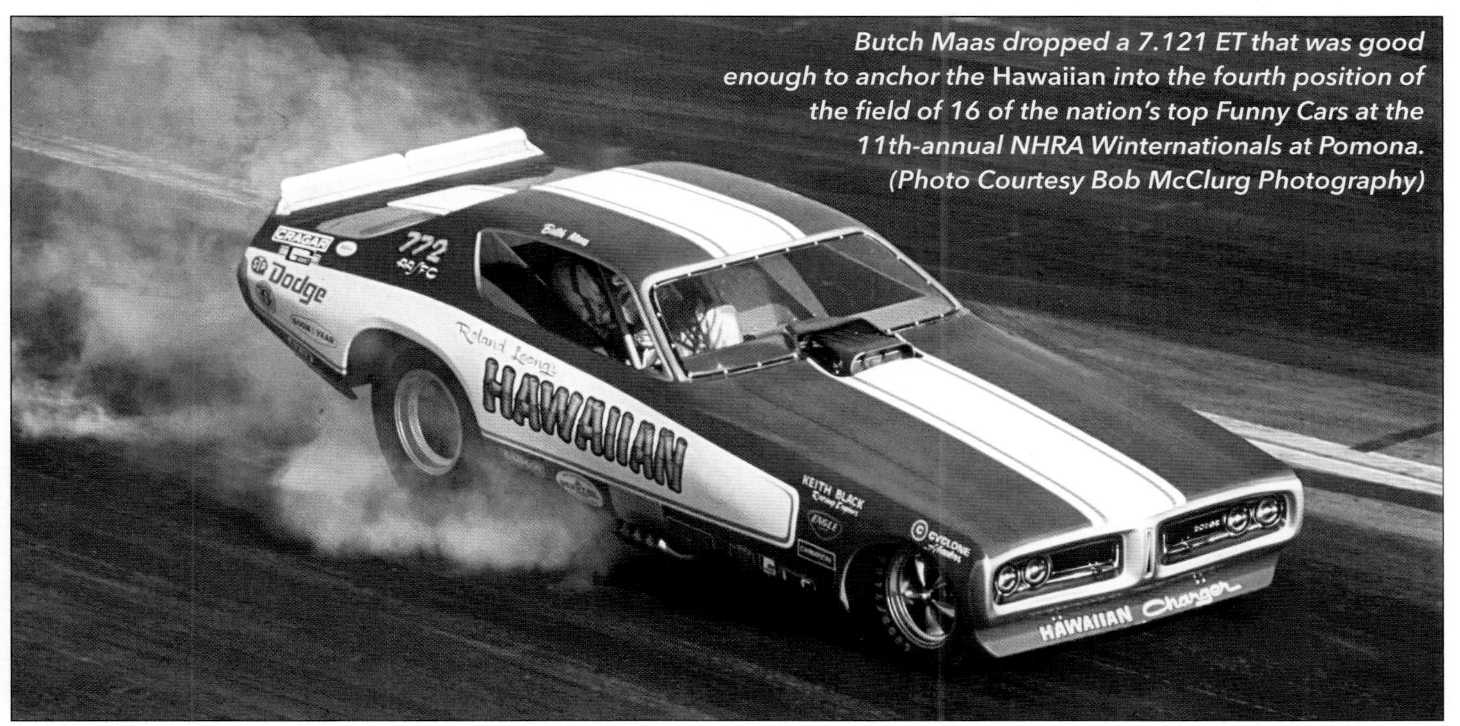

Butch Maas dropped a 7.121 ET that was good enough to anchor the Hawaiian into the fourth position of the field of 16 of the nation's top Funny Cars at the 11th-annual NHRA Winternationals at Pomona. (Photo Courtesy Bob McClurg Photography)

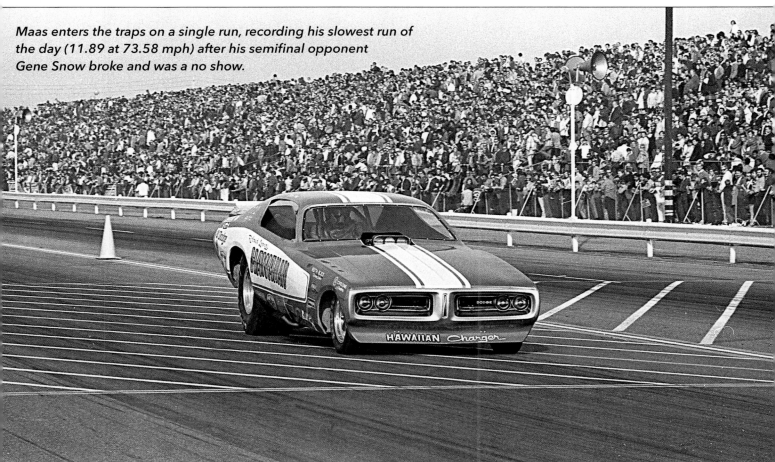

Maas enters the traps on a single run, recording his slowest run of the day (11.89 at 73.58 mph) after his semifinal opponent Gene Snow broke and was a no show.

The sellout crowd of more than 70,000 was on its feet for the Funny Car final. Butch Maas set low ET of the meet with a 6.93 ET at 212.76 mph, overtaking Leroy Goldstein (7.08 at 207.85) in the Ramchargers *Dodge Challenger. Maas's win marked the fourth time that Leong-owned machines had won fuel honors at Pomona. (Photo Courtesy Steve Reyes)*

"Big Daddy" Don Garlits (Top Fuel), Butch Maas, Walt Stevens (Top Gas), and Ronnie Sox (Pro Stock) clutch their prized "Wally's" in the winner's circle, sharing the spotlight as 1971 Winternationals Top Eliminator Champs.

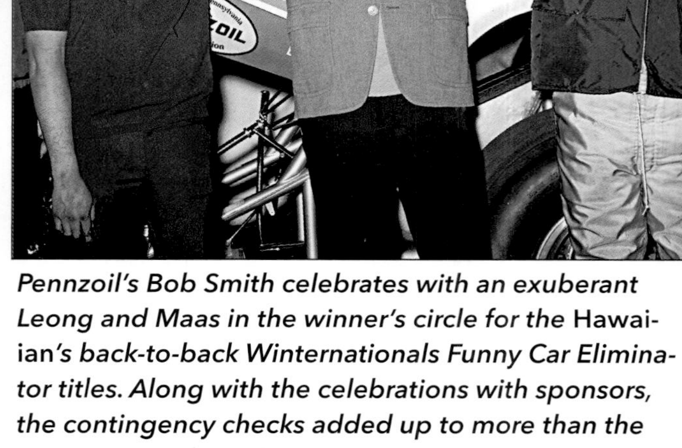

Pennzoil's Bob Smith celebrates with an exuberant Leong and Maas in the winner's circle for the Hawaiian*'s back-to-back Winternationals Funny Car Eliminator titles. Along with the celebrations with sponsors, the contingency checks added up to more than the purse money from the NHRA. (Photo Courtesy Steve Reyes)*

stood "Big" John Mazmanian's 'Cuda up on the parachute pack and crashed-landed back down on the track surface. This wheel-stand allowed Maas to cruise by, running a 7.26 ET at 209.30 mph.

Maas advanced to the final round when he received a bye, running an 11.89 ET at 73.58 mph when Gene Snow failed to show. In the final round, Maas lived up to his promise when he came from behind to overpower Leroy Goldstein in the *Ramchargers* Dodge Challenger. Maas had the low ET of the Winternationals with a 6.932 at 212.76 mph.

The *Hawaiian* Makes Noise at the March Meet

Butch Maas was overshadowed by "Big" John Mazmanian by two-tenths of a second when Richard Siroonian broke the 6-second barrier with a 6.95 ET to grab the pole at the 13th-annual March Meet at Bakersfield. Maas's 6.97 put him second in the field of 16.

The consistency of the *Hawaiian* powered Maas to the semifinal round when the underdogs Dave Condit and the Beaver Brother's *L.A. Hooker* Maverick upended the thundering Charger.

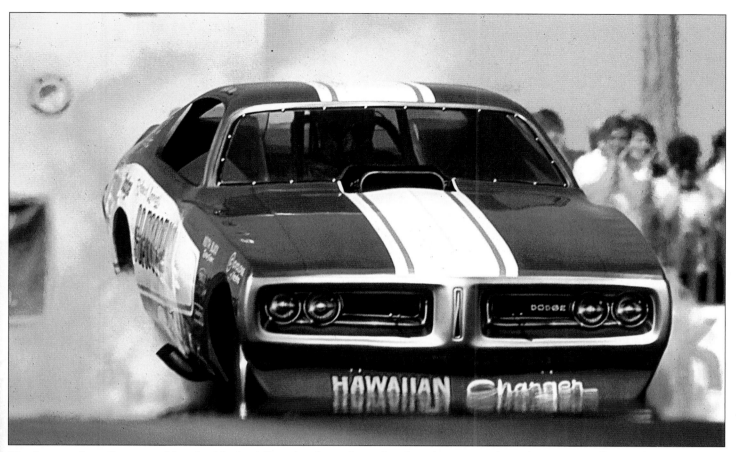

The hot track surface combined with the blistering heat from the Goodyears produced a mirage effect. Pilot Butch Maas advanced a few rounds in eliminations before losing to the eventual runner-up, Dave Condit, in the L.A. Hooker Mustang. (Photo Courtesy Bob McClurg Photography)

Maas reaches up for the chute release to deploy the laundry at the March Meet at Bakersfield. His 215-mph top speed reveals how pressure and stress flexes the fiberglass bodies.

Yamaha International Jumps on Board with Leong

After the conclusion of the March Meet, Leong penned a deal with Yamaha International to bring the giant corporation on board. The deal opened a window for Yamaha International to introduce its motorcycle performance products into drag racing. Coming off its fifth road-course 250-cc manufacturer's title, Yamaha was now a part of the influx of the Japanese Top Fuel motorcycles in NHRA drag racing.

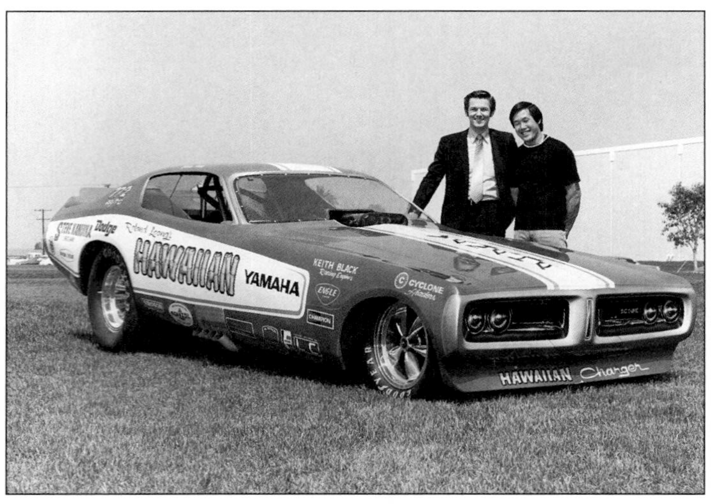

Leong added Yamaha International Corporation as a major sponsor to the Hawaiian *for 1971. The Yamaha name graced the side panels and the hood stripe that was added for the Mattel Hot Wheels Northern Nationals at Fremont. (Photo Courtesy Roland Leong Collection)*

Leong and Maas Shine at the Mattel Hot Wheels Nationals

After a three-week delay from rain-drenched conditions, 14,000 spectators were treated with clear, sunny skies from April 2 to 4, for the running of the Mattel Hot Wheels Nationals at Fremont. Qualifying runs were made prior to the postponement.

Maas simply outclassed the field when the ex–dragster pilot rewrote the Funny Car ET track record with a 6.77 ET in Saturday's qualifying. Because of prior obligations, three of the pre-qualified cars (Charlie Allen, Don Prudhomme, and Kenny Goodell) were unable to attend. Fremont still managed to field six great floppers.

The first round brought Maas against Larry Fullerton's *Trojan Horse*. The *Hawaiian* had no problems dropping Fullerton with a 6.86 ET at 207 mph to Fullerton's off-pace 7.27 at 192.70. Maas drew the odd-lot single in the second round. The money run brought the Corvette

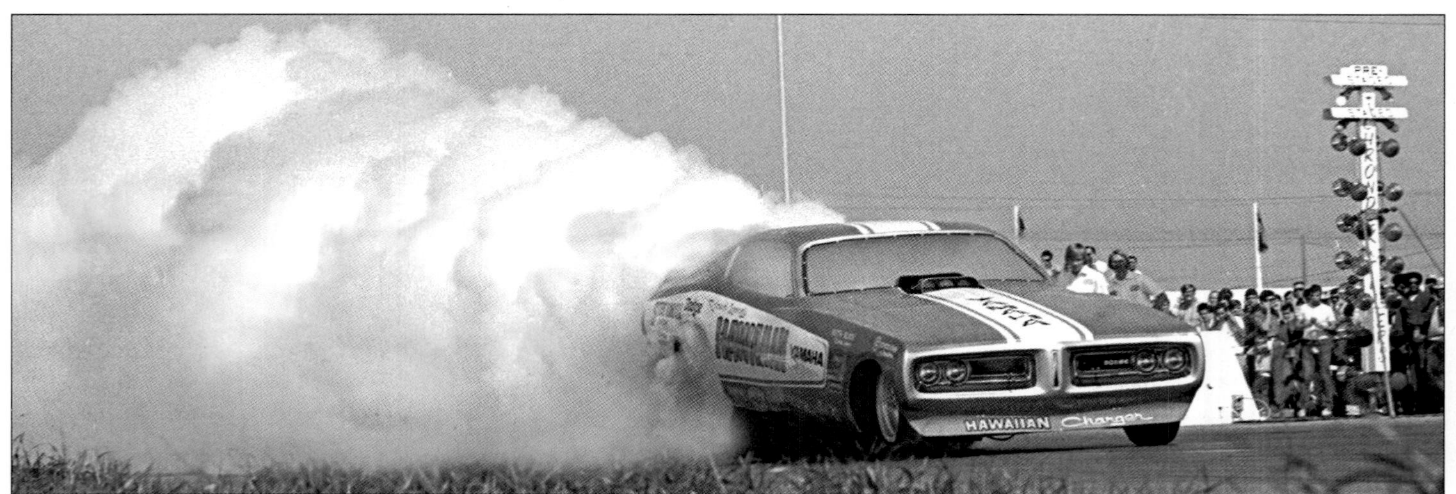

Maas nabbed Funny Car low ET with a 6.77 for the number-one spot at the Mattel Hot Wheels Northern Nationals at Fremont. After rain washed out Sunday's eliminations, racing concluded three weeks later. Maas and Leong returned to take top honors when the Hawaiian *dropped a 6.85 ET at 217.38 mph on Gene Conway in the finals. (Photo Courtesy Steve Reyes)*

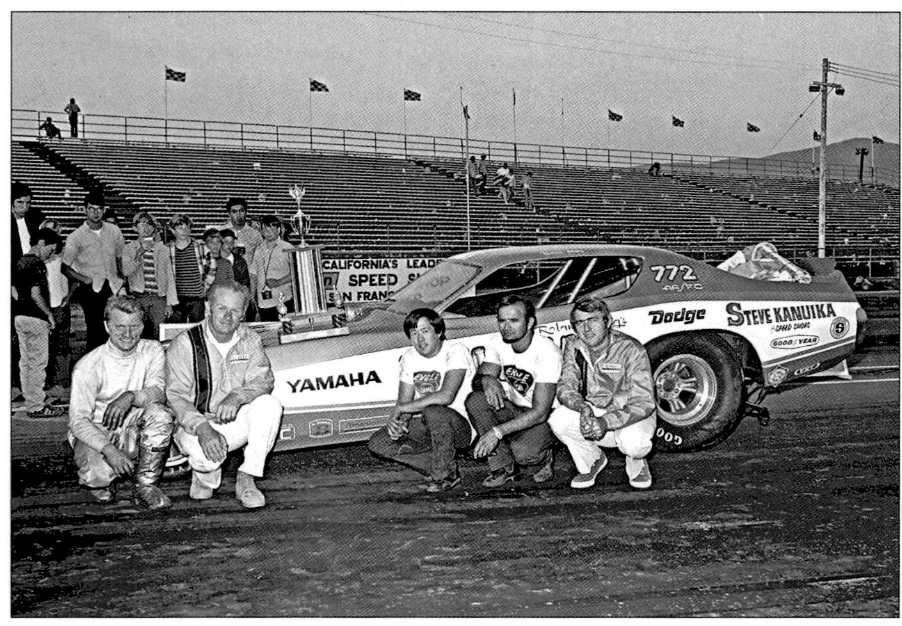

Butch Maas, Jim McLennan, Roland Leong, Dicky Watson, and track operator and announcer Steve Evans pose for photos around the Hawaiian*. Maas took top honors at Fremont's Mattel Hot Wheels Northern Nationals. (Photo Courtesy Steve Reyes)*

MAC's Car Care Products was now on board as an associate sponsor prior to the start of the* Hawaiian's *extended national tour. One tour stop was at Edgewater Park Dragway in Cleves, Ohio. Its annual Independence Day Factory Funny Car Fireworks Extravaganza gave the crowd more unexpected pyrotechnic excitement than they bargained for. Racing kicked off at dusk with the* Hawaiian *blasting the Goodyears out of the bleach box against the crowd-favorite "Jungle" Jim Liberman. Both drivers cut great lights, racing side by side until at mid-track, when the engine expired in the* Hawaiian *and exploded with the effects of a powder keg, erupting into a huge fireball. The car went off the end of the track and plowed into a field, where it finally came to a stop. (Photo Courtesy Roland Leong Collection)

of "Inglewood Flash" Gene Conway against the *Hawaiian* racer. Maas took the win with a 6.84 ET at 217.38 mph over Conway's floundering 7.64 at 126.05.

Head East, Young Man

The annual trek east this year came early, as the *Hawaiian* team made its way to Rockingham, North Carolina, for the International Hot Rod Association's Pro-Am drag race Championship on April 17 and 18. Maas sailed through the competition but ran into Mike Burkhart's Camaro driven by Charlie Therwhanger. Therwhanger blasted to a 6.91 ET at 208.33 mph, relegating the *Hawaiian* to a runner-up finish.

Team *Hawaiian* stayed on the Atlantic seaboard with stops at Phenix Dragway in Georgia and U.S. 13 Dragway in Delaware before moving inland to York U.S. 30 Dragway, Great Lakes Dragaway, Cordova Dragway, Rockford Dragway, Bristol, and back to Rockingham.

Fourth of July Explosion

One of the stops on tour was over the July 4 weekend at Edgewater Park Dragway in Ohio for a match race that ended in calamity for Leong. He lost his race car and driver to a fiery explosion. Driver Butch Maas was sent to the hospital with substantial second-degree burns to both of his wrists and legs as well as his back, which put him in the hospital and the *Hawaiian* out of action. During the run, the fuel tank exploded, igniting the car into a high-speed fireball when the onboard fire system failed to activate.

The chassis was repairable, but the body was turned into a blob of melted fiberglass.

Although the onboard fire system failed, the loss of the *Hawaiian* could have been avoided if the drag strip had the adequate fire equipment. There was only one

The Charger body was a total loss, but the chassis survived. Repairs to the car took three weeks to complete, but due to Maas's extensive injuries, he wasn't able to continue to drive. With Maas out, Leong hired the upcoming and talented Bobby Rowe to fill the vacancy. (Photo Courtesy Roland Leong Collection)

5-pound fire extinguisher on the property, which was at the starting line, and the fire was well past the finish line, off the track.

Don Prudhomme, not knowing that Butch Maas was already out of the burning car, jumped out of his idling race car to get to what he thought was a desperate Maas. Subsequently, Prudhomme's car had its own small fire that damaged some of the paint. At that point, the other racers refused to run, but the strip manager brought in several firefighters and trucks, and the racing continued.

The old cliché that "it makes no sense to lock the door after the horse has been stolen" fits well in this situation, as the damage had already been done.

Rowe Hired to Shoe the *Hawaiian*

With the repairs completed on the *Hawaiian* and Leong needing to fulfill his touring commitments, he hired his pal Bobby Rowe to replace the ailing Maas, who was unable to drive at that time. The first time back in action for the "new" *Hawaiian* was where it met its demise three weeks earlier at Edgewater Park.

Rowe, from Memphis, downed "Miss STP" Paula Murphy in the first round, which gave Leong a sigh of relief, as the car completed the run without incident. In round two, the *Hawaiian*'s "Pineapple Powered" 426 stroker was too much for Larry Arnold's *Kingfish*. The *Hawaiian* ran a 6.88 ET at 206.88 mph to advance to the finals. However, it was determined after the run with Arnold that the welding split in two different locations on the chassis and the transmission dropped and snapped the driveshaft at the top end. This ended the *Hawaiian*'s chance to face Pat Minick and the *Chi-Town Hustler* for all of the coins.

The following night at Maple Grove in Mohnton, Pennsylvania, Rowe powered the *Hawaiian* past an elite field of eight cars. He advanced to the final round against Jake Johnston in Gene Snow's *Ramhorn* Charger, only to come up short on the victory.

Thundering the Big Numbers

In the weeks to come, Bobby Rowe continued to live up to the *Hawaiian*'s past performances. For the first time, a Funny Car dipped into the 6s at Quaker City Dragway in Salem, Ohio. Not only firing to three straight wins, the *Hawaiian* also respectively ran times of 6.98 and 6.96. On a trip to Maryland at Budd's Creek, the *Hawaiian* reset the ET record at 6.802.

Leong and Rowe were back at Quaker City for the IHRA World Funny Car Championships. Rowe was one of six cars to qualify in the 6s (6.94) and one of five that ran over 215 mph (216.63). The racers were in full swing, warming up for Indy. Leong had the *Hawaiian* flying at the Popular Hot Rod Meet when Rowe stopped the clocks with a best ET of 6.56.

Hawaiian Lowlights

One of the lowlights in 1971 for Leong transpired during the 17th-annual NHRA Nationals. The *Hawaiian* failed to qualify for the Big Go.

At the third-annual International Hot Rod Association (IHRA) U.S. Open in Rockingham, North Carolina, Bobby Rowe bowed out against 16th-qualifier Bruce Larson in the first round. While backing up after his burnout, the steering box broke, allowing Larson an easy win on a single pass.

In early September, Leong and Rowe traveled north of the boarder to the Toronto International Dragway for a scheduled match race with veteran Funny driver Dick Harrell. Both cars launched from the line, and then Harrell's left front tire exploded just past mid-track. This sent Harrell into the guardrail, which knocked down a light pole. It landed on top of the car, fatally injuring the popular Chevrolet driver.

Over at the IHRA World Championships in Lakeland, Florida, Rowe

Leong, Sush Matsubara, and new shoe Bobby Rowe load up the revamped* Hawaiian *into the tow rig at Keith Black Racing Engines. They headed south to OCIR to burn tires and nitro, initiating Rowe into his new "office." (Photo Courtesy Roland Leong Collection)

Veteran Funny Car racer Dick Harrell was fatally injured on this run against Bobby Rowe in the Hawaiian during a match race at Toronto International Dragway in Ontario, Canada. Harrell's Camaro blew a front tire at over 200 mph. He lost control and slammed into the guardrail, hitting and knocking down a light pole that then landed on top of his Camaro. (Photo Courtesy Bill Hinton)

received the shock of his life in the first round of eliminations facing the Firebird of Charlie Wilson. The *Hawaiian* ran into a serious problem 30 feet off the line when both rear axles snapped off the car and spun Rowe around without hitting the guardrail. Rowe was unscathed, but the damage to the flopper was to the aluminum work and axles.

They gave the fans something to buzz about at Epping's fifth-annual Funny Car Championship when Rowe pulled off a rare feat with a tire-smoking, wheels-up burnout that's nearly impossible to perform with the clutch-equipped *Hawaiian*. Rowe and Leong had their share of problems when they lost to Jimmy King in the first round.

The seventh-annual East versus West Funny Car Championships at Lions was halted before the third round by a bolt of lightning. It hit a transformer around the starting-line area, which knocked out the power and all the lights at the starting line.

Home Cookin' Back on the West Coast

After the long road trip, members of team *Hawaiian* were looking forward to sleeping in their own beds. California had no shortage of events for the team, as their fall West Coast swing went into full effect.

Seventh-Annual East versus West Funny Car Championships

The first round of the seventh-annual East versus West Funny Car Championships was at Lions Drag Strip on October 16. The first race was between the *Hawaiian* and Gene Snow. Rowe lost the blower belt at the hit. The second round brought Shirley "Cha-Cha" Muldowney versus Rowe. Muldowney beat Rowe by a fender, as both ran identical 7.07s ETs, but her speed was several mph quicker, running 207.89 to Rowe's 200.88.

With the score all knotted up six to six after two completed rounds, the question was asked, "Will the quickest and fastest Funny Car come out of the east or from the west?" That question went unanswered until the beginning of the third round when the meet ended in a draw. A bolt of lightning struck a transformer close to the tower, taking out the public announcement system and all of the timing, staging, and Christmas-tree lights.

Fifth-Annual East versus West Funny Car Spectacular

The following week at Irwindale's fifth-annual East versus West Funny Car Spectacular, Rowe remained unbeaten after three round-robin wins. He advanced to the final round in Division 1 against Ed "the Ace" McCulloch. The Ace prevailed by taking the win over an out-of-shape *Hawaiian*.

Fifth-Annual Manufacturer's Funny Car Team Championships

From the time the gates opened for Friday's qualifying sessions till the last race run on Saturday night, a total of 24,600 fans went through the turnstiles at Orange County International Raceway for the two-day, super event of the year: the fifth-annual Manufacturer's Funny Car Team Championships. It was "Funny Car City U.S.A." at OCIR, where 66 of the nation's top Funny Cars competed for a share of the $50,000 prize and contingency money.

Each team's roster consisted of eight cars that would run a total of 48 round-robin races in team competition. Roland Leong and Bobby Rowe anchored the underpowered Dodge team with a team best 6.78 ET in qualifying. Winning two out of the three rounds of competition, Rowe ran four consecutive times in the 6.70s, which put the *Hawaiian* fourth in line to run against Pat Foster and "Big" Jim Dunn for overall top honors in the final round.

Both Rowe and Leong didn't go away unnoticed. They unloaded a 6.75 ET at 224.23 mph in the third round against Kelly Chadwick that notched top speed of the meet.

Friday Night Eighth-Mile Drag Championships

Irwindale Raceway presented its first-ever Friday night Eighth-Mile Drag Championships featuring a star-studded field of eight of the nation's top-name Funny Cars racing in a round-robin format on the short track. This was the first time that such an event had been staged in the Southern California area.

The lineup of the eight included Springnationals champ Don Schumacher, Connie Kalitta, Larry Arnold, the Ramchargers, the famed *Chi-Town Hustler*, Shirley "Cha-Cha" Muldowney, Ed "the Ace" McCulloch, and Roland Leong's *Hawaiian*. The final results were a repeat from a few weeks earlier. Ed McCulloch, who captured two Irwindale titles in October, grabbed another title win against his friendly rivals Roland Leong and Bobby Rowe. McCulloch set low ET once again in the finals, outdistancing Rowe with a 4.43 ET at 173.74 mph to the losing *Hawaiian*'s respectable 4.47 and top speed of the meet at 175.43 mph.

Bobby Rowe led the Dodge team in qualifying, where he nailed down the number-one spot with a 6.78 ET. It was a great day for Leong and Rowe, as they won all three of their team matchups and took home top-speed honors with a 6.75 ET at 224.23 mph to defeat Kelly Chadwick in the third round.

Leong debuted his new paint scheme for 1972 at OCIR's All-Pro Series opener in December 1971. Also, Rowe, Leong, and Leong's daughter Landa were sporting new "Hawaiian" crew shirts. (Photo Courtesy Steve Delgadillo Photography)

1972 Unexpected Changes in the Seat

The year 1971 was a first of firsts for Leong in trying to keep the seat occupied in his Funny Car. Butch Maas suffered multiple burns when his engine expired at the top end on July 4, forcing him out of the seat, and Bobby Rowe did a tremendous job filling in. The outlook was looking promising for both Leong and Rowe for the new year.

Lions Drag Strip was now under NHRA sanctioning for 1972, but its Annual Grand Premier continued as one of the strip's top events on the calendar.

Bobby Rowe paced the *Hawaiian* through the tough field to reach the finals against the *Revell Snowman* Charger of Gene Snow. The Funny Car final was the quickest ever recorded at Lions Drag Strip, as the number-one contender in the class, Snow, earned the win light with the time of 6.54 at 222.77 mph to Rowe's 6.55 at 226.13.

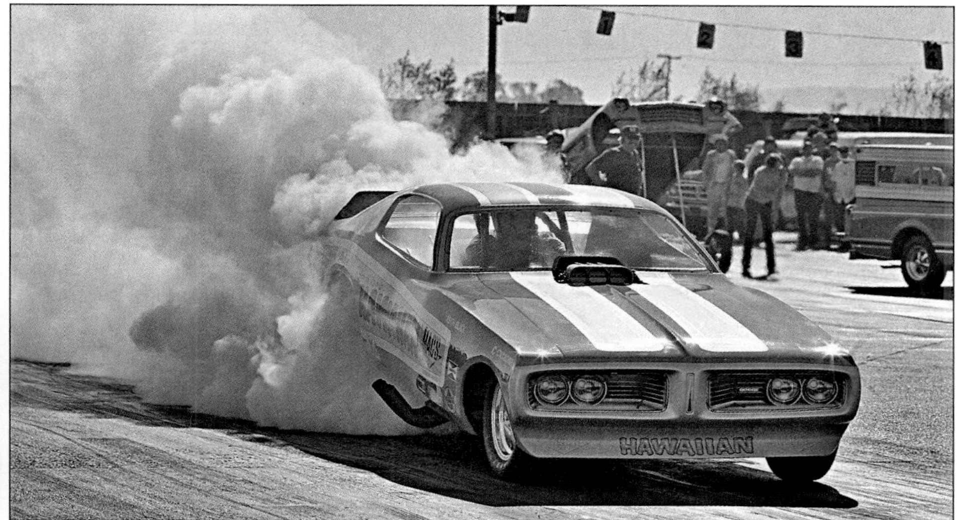

Bobby Rowe does his best **Chi-Town Hustler** *style-burnout at OCIR's All-Pro Series in the first of the four planned races for 1972. Leong refreshed his Dodge Charger body for 1972 with fresh paint and graphics, including dual hood, roof, and trunk stripes and color changes to the side body panels.*

All-Pro Series Championships

OCIR's 1972 All-Pro Series Championships four-race series kicked off on Sunday, December 26, under ideal weather conditions. Leong debuted the freshly repainted and re-lettered graphics on the 1972 Charger body. Rowe solidly placed the Charger into the show, but mechanical failure knocked him from contention.

After the final round concluded, Rowe announced that he was relinquishing his seat in the *Hawaiian*, leaving to drive one of Don Schumacher's new Butera-built cars.

With the new racing season already in motion, Leong scrambled to find a quality replacement. When word got out that ex-AA/Fuel Altered owner and driver Leroy Chadderton was available, Leong hired Chadderton, knowing he didn't have any experience behind the wheel in a fuel coupe.

Chadderton's reputation and his solid driving credentials (the first Fuel

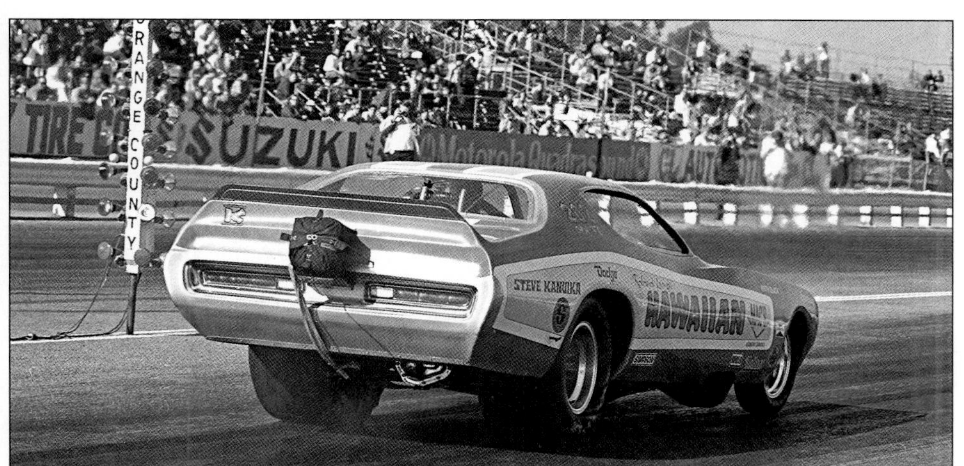

At the All-Pro opener, the **Hawaiian** *uncorks another 6-second run at 220 mph heading north toward the direction of Interstate 5.*

At the NHRA Grand Premiere at Lions Drag Strip, Bobby Rowe catapults off the line. Rowe waded through the field of 16 fiberglass flip-tops to meet the Revell "Snowman" Gene Snow in the finals. The finals were the quickest ever recorded in Funny Car. Snow got the jump on Rowe, stopping the lights with a 6.541 ET at 222.77 mph to the losing Hawaiian*'s 6.55 at 226.13. This was Rowe's last appearance driving for Leong, as Rowe went to drive Don Schumacher's second Plymouth 'Cuda. (Photo Courtesy Roland Leong Collection)*

Altered driver to break into the 6s) was an easy fit. Chadderton made his Funny Car driver's license runs at Lions Drag Strip on Saturday night, January 22. The very next day, Chadderton made his Funny Car debut at the second All-Pro Championship Series at OCIR.

Chadderton was put to the test right out of the gate when both he and Ron O'Donnell (driving the *Damn Yankee* of Don Cook) kicked off the first round of eliminations. Chadderton pocketed his first Funny Car round win when he scorched the asphalt with a 6.61 ET at 215.31 mph as O'Donnell coasted slowly through the lights with a 17.17 at 36.82 mph. Things were looking bright once again in the *Hawaiian* camp.

The Camera Car

The 12th-annual NHRA Winternationals brought Leong, Black, and new Funny Car pilot Chadderton to Pomona with the latest version of the *Hawaiian*. The team was there to attempt a Winternationals Eliminator three-peat.

Technology was now starting to play a significant role in racing and was a valuable tool used for the performance and handling of the highly powered race cars. With many focused on the *Hawaiian*'s search for another Funny Car title, it was unknown by many who installed a high-speed camera to the left rear of the Charger that was used in eliminations. Another question that went unanswered was, "With Chadderton running in the left lane, why was the camera pointed away from the car and track and turned toward the grandstands?"

Leong didn't recall the reason or purpose—or if the camera survived the 215-mph journey down the quarter mile.

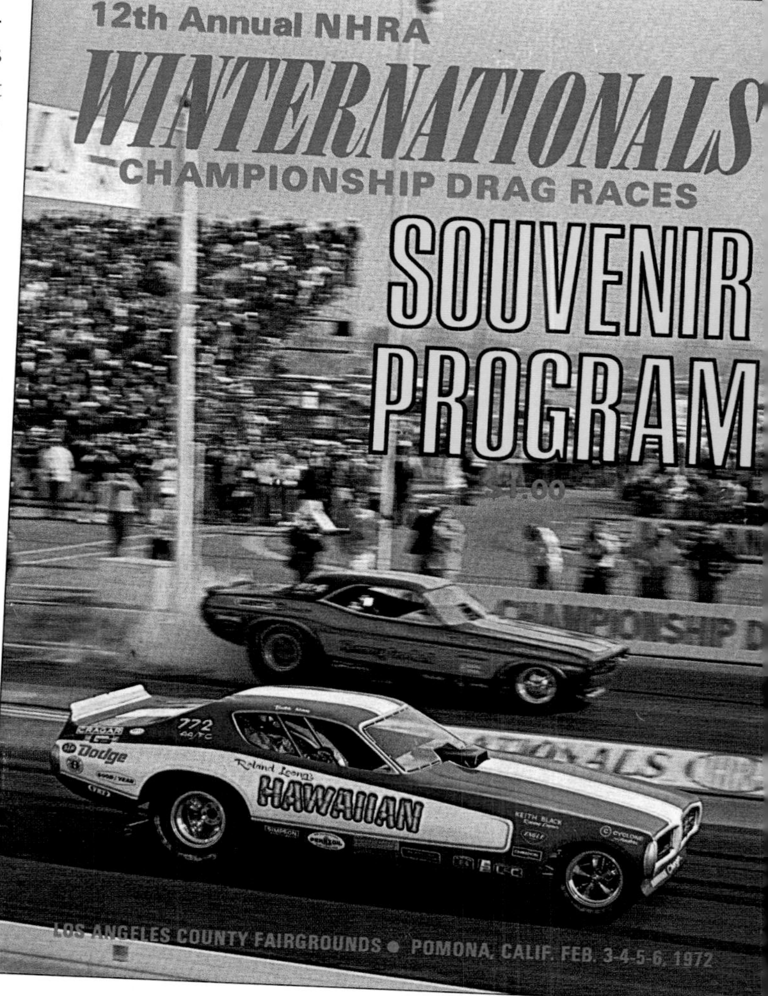

The NHRA honored the 1971 Winternationals Funny Car Champion Butch Maas and Leong by placing the Hawaiian *on the cover of the 1972 Winternationals program. Maas was the fourth driver for Leong to win a Top Eliminator crown at the Winternationals.*

New driver Leroy Chadderton immediately found his way into the spotlight during an unusual, one-time tire test session at the Winternationals. Using large amounts of duct tape, a high-speed movie camera was affixed to the driver-side rear of the car in the first qualifying session at Pomona. It was never determined who placed the camera on the car or why it was at that angle.

Chadderton Takes All-Pro Finale

Action in the Funny Car ranks was dominated by Leroy Chadderton when he defeated Gary Burgin in the finals at OCIR's All-Pro Series finale. Chadderton not only dropped the series champs Dave Braskett and Gary Burgin with a 6.59 ET at 219.51 mph to a losing 6.72 at 222.22 but also set a new OCIR ET mark of 6.56.

MEMORABLE MOMENTS:

Photographer Steve Reyes

"I remember that Roland had a camera (or cameras) mounted for a center spread or cover for either *Hot Rod* or *Car Craft* magazine for a shoot at OCIR," Steve Reyes said. "I know this because I was there shooting another car feature, and they got all pissed off at me being there, and I was asked to leave.

"They claimed that they rented the track, and I wasn't supposed to be let in to shoot my car feature. To be honest, I really didn't give a crap what they were doing. I felt bad for Roland, as from what I saw, they were running him around like they owned the car."

Leroy Chadderton releases the laundry after qualifying the Hawaiian *into the show in the number-two spot when he laid down a 7.04 ET at 212 mph at the 14th-annual March Meet at Famoso. Chadderton's day was over when he lost in the second round of eliminations to the overall winner, Ed McCulloch, who was driving Jim Murphy's* Holy Smokes *Plymouth.*

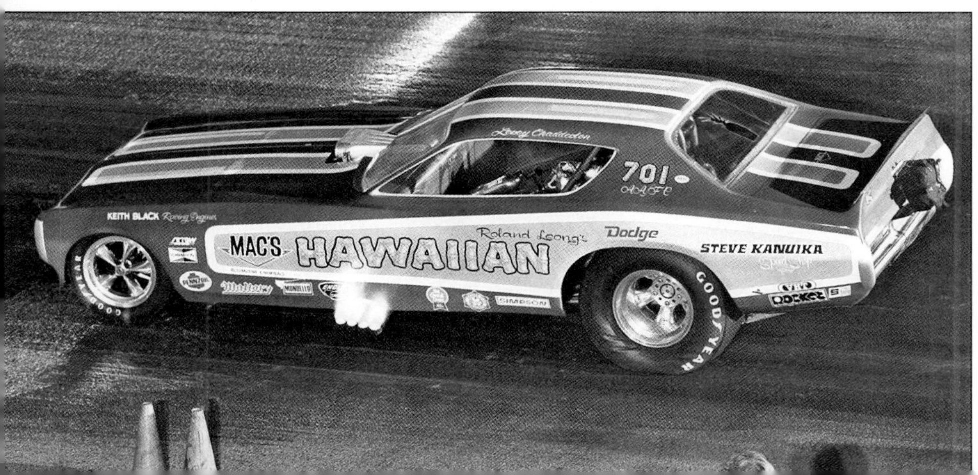

This rooftop view at OCIR shows the Hawaiian *in the staging beams at the 1972 All-Pro Series finale. This was Chadderton's best effort yet driving for Leong. In round two, Chadderton shut down a struggling Gene Snow, running an unreal 6.56 ET at 219.59 mph that was the first leg of the track's new ET record for Funny Cars.*

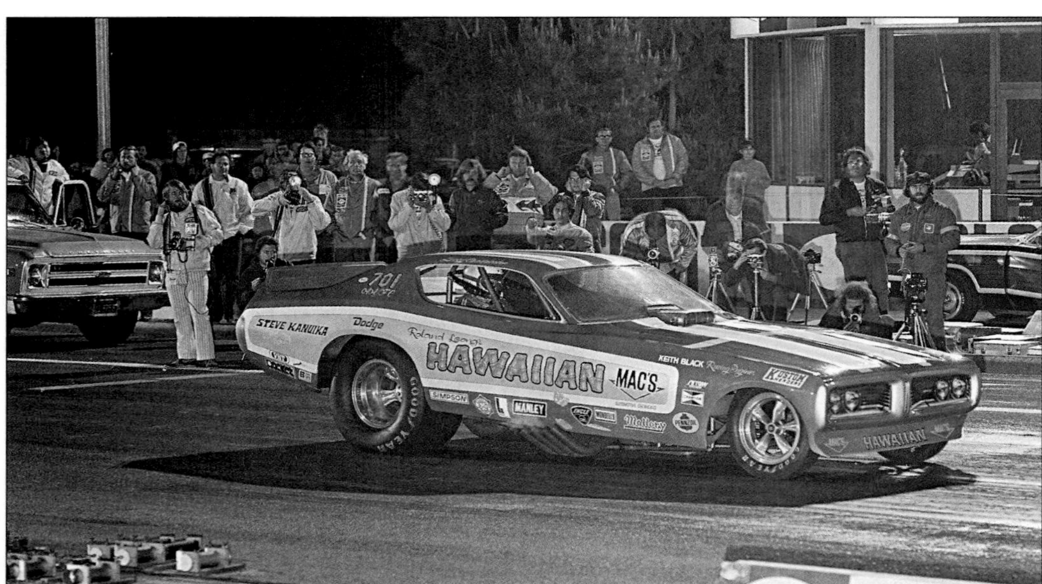

All cameras were on the Hawaiian *as photographers watched Leroy Chadderton take the win with a strong 6.59 ET at 219.54 mph over Gary Burgin's losing 6.72 at 222.22. Chadderton's 6.59 backed up his earlier run of 6.56 for the record. For Burgin, he outpaced the field during the four-race series for the overall Funny Car Championship. Shown in the photo were photographer greats Bob McClurg, Steve Reyes, Jere Alhadeff, and Tim Marshall getting their* Hawaiian *money shots. Engine whiz Ed Pink and chassis builder "Lil" John Butera were among the others checking out the action.*

Hawaiian Wins Pop Rod Championships

On Saturday night at U.S. 131 Dragway in Martin, Michigan, the Funny Car final was to be between the *Hawaiian* and the Snake. Unfortunately, the final was delayed until the following morning when pea-soup fog rolled in and blanketed the strip and the surrounding areas.

Both Leong and Prudhomme were booked into another contractual race later that Sunday afternoon at the same strip, so they agreed to race early Sunday morning for the title. Around 7 a.m., both cars fired up, completed their burnouts, and staged. Unfortunately for Prudhomme, he double-stepped the tree and fouled, giving the automatic win to Leong.

Super Stock Nationals

York U.S. 30 Drag-O-Way hosted one of the largest events in the East: the annual Super Stock Magazine Nationals. Drag racing's version of "Woodstock" featured the biggest names in Funny Cars and Pro and Super Stockers taking part in the three-day festival. Leroy Chadderton made a strong presence during the festival, delighting the Eastern folk with massive burnouts but fell short of taking the pot of cash.

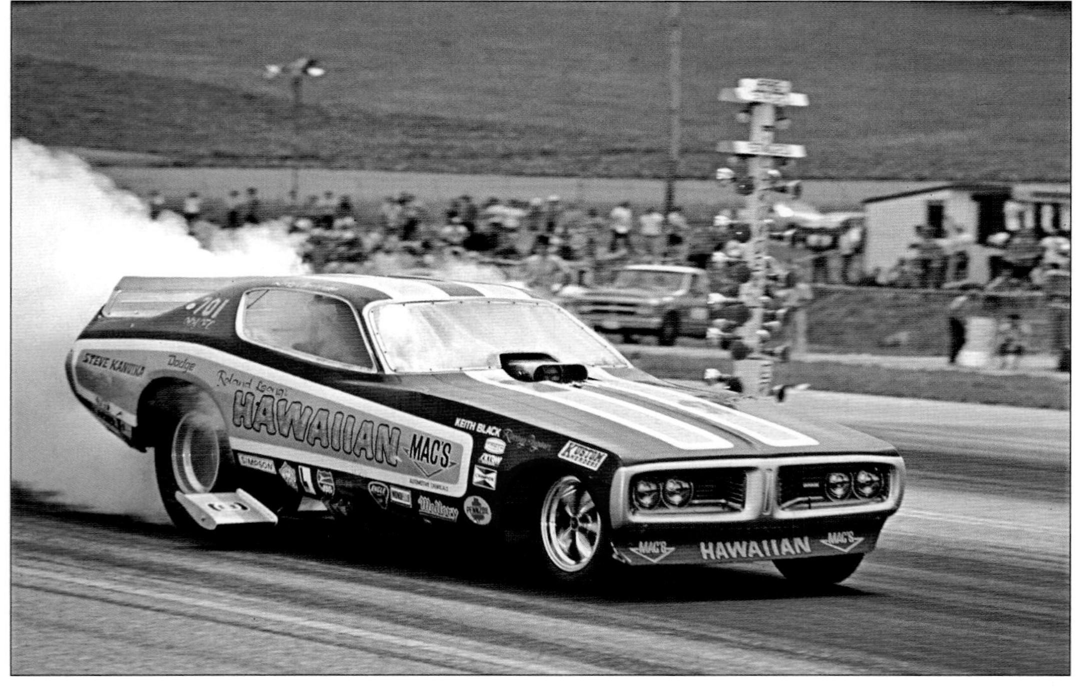

A stop at York U.S. 30 Drag-O-Way in Thomasville, Pennsylvania, for the 1972 Super Stock Nationals gave the Mid-Atlantic fans a close-up look at Roland Leong's Hawaiian.

MEMORABLE MOMENTS:
Photographer Steve Reyes

"I always said hello to Roland at the races but never hung out and bothered him," Steve Reyes said. "He was just like Prudhomme in that they were there to race, not to be anyone's good buddy. I think that's why both of them won so many races. They ignored the distractions at the racetrack and just focused on the race.

"The photo of the *Hawaiian* racing Prudhomme was shot about 7 a.m. on a Sunday morning at Martin, Michigan. The night before, the final between Roland and the Snake got fogged out, so they both came back and raced on Sunday morning. Well, Prudhomme red-lighted and Roland won. They both packed up and headed for a race at Union Grove. Boy, Prudhomme was pissed that he red-lighted, and I think he's still pissed today—50-plus years later."

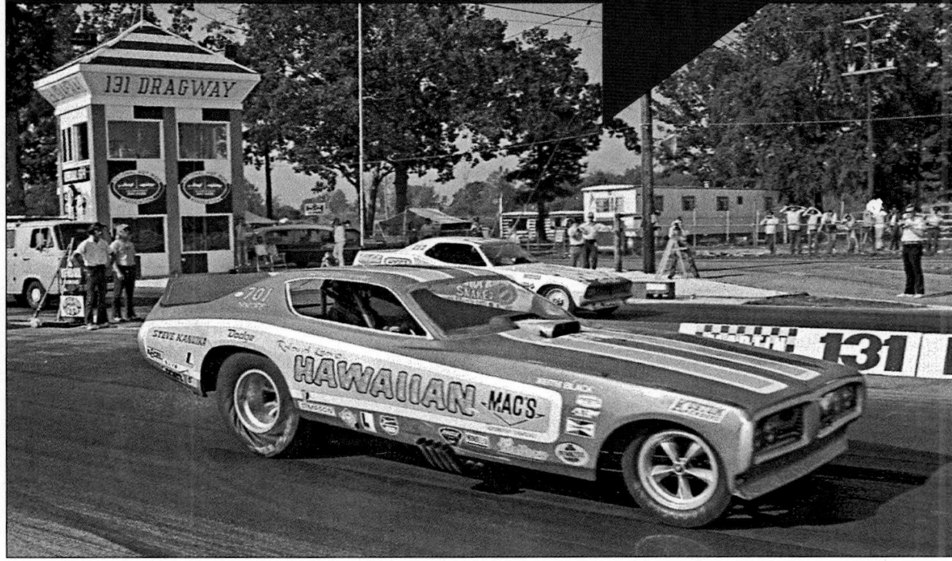

U.S. 131 Dragway in Martin, Michigan, was the site of the Funny Car final between the **Hawaiian** *and Don Prudhomme. After a delay due to fog, the racers battled the next morning. Prudhomme fouled, giving the automatic win to Leong. (Photo Courtesy Steve Reyes)*

Ed Pink (center) and Tom McEwen (right) swap stories during downtime with Leong at the Popular Hot Rod Nationals at U.S. 131. (Photo Courtesy Roland Leong)

Leong, Chadderton, Richie Okazaki, and Rayso Kobayashi accept the prestigious Popular Hot Rod Nationals trophy from the manager of U.S. 131 Dragway. They won the delayed final round on Sunday morning. (Photo Courtesy Steve Reyes)

Summer nights at Atco Dragway were filled with great times and memories that were shared by spirted fans. In the top-billed match races, the East's best took on the big hitters from the West Coast. In this instance, the Hawaiian *took three straight against the "Chicago Kid" Don Schumacher. (Photo Courtesy Tom Nelson)*

MEMORABLE MOMENTS: Jim Murphy

"Roland is a good person, he's very serious about what he does, and he's very, very good at it," said Jim Murphy, the owner and driver of the WW2 Racing Nostalgia Top Fuel dragster. "I've known Roland for 50 years. I first met him in 1972 through Keith Black when I bought my first Funny Car, the Holy Smokes 'Cuda. I didn't have my Funny Car license yet to drive at the 1972 Winternationals, so I hired Butch Maas to drive. Roland pulled double duty and assisted me with my car, helping with the tune-up along with maintaining his own car. I was at U.S. 30 in Indiana racing at the same time he was when his rig was stolen and talked to him to see if I could help with whatever he needed.

"In early 2017, I was running a Top Fuel dragster in the Nostalgia world and had been struggling a little bit getting the car down the track making runs. Roland offered to help, and he became the crew chief. Throughout the year, he had us running toward the top of the heap for the NHRA Heritage Nostalgia Top Fuel Championship.

"It came down to three cars battling for the crown at the final race of the year at the California Hot Rod Reunion in Bakersfield. Now, one thing about Roland was that I always referred to him as an 'engine whisperer.' He would always say to me, 'I can tell you what the engine wants to do just by listening. I think it speaks a different language to me.'

"He just looked at the thing without putting his hands on it, and he just knew what to do.

"In the semifinals, the engine blew up pretty hard, forcing the car up against the guardrail right after the lights and bending the front end. We won the race and won the championship after beating Adam Sorokin in the Champion Speed Shop car, which gave us the points that we needed. We didn't run the final because of the bent front end along with the blown engine. We just couldn't repaired it in time. I was pumped and excited about this championship, knowing how special this was for Roland—his first-ever drag racing championship!"

CHAPTER 9

1973–1974: THE REVELL YEARS

"I fight cars," Roland Leong said of drag racing. "When I'm thrashing between rounds, I feel like I'm the one who has to race the other car—not my crew or against the other crew or their car against my car. In a race, I *am* the *Hawaiian*!"

Leong, the top "wrench" in the business, had been drag racing for nearly a decade as an owner, builder, and tuner.

"The average spectator thinks that drag racing a quarter mile lasts six seconds, but many don't consider all the man-hours in the pits, the time out on the road away from families, the months in the shop, and the years spent learning," Leong said.

Leong and Chadderton opened the 1973 season with a brand-new Dodge Charger garnished in primer with shoe-polish lettering. John Buttera fabricated the lightweight chassis that anchored the Keith Black Hemi between the tubes. Expert painter

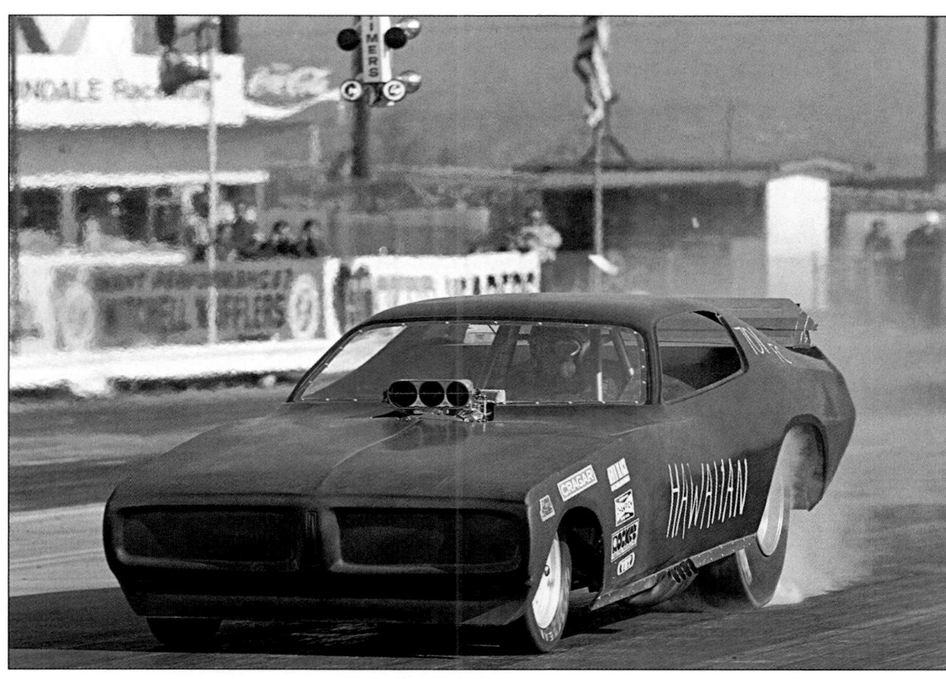

In January, the Hawaiian *began the 1973 racing season with high hopes at the Olympia Grand Premiere at the revamped Irwindale Raceway. With nearly a season under his belt driving the* Hawaiian*, Chadderton powered the car into the third overall slot with a 6.86 ET.*

One of the most sought-after pieces of memorabilia by drag racing modelers is this rare press kit of Roland Leong's Hawaiian *that was his 10th addition to the Revell Signature line. The kit was packed full of valuable information, including promotional black-and-white photos; race car, owner, and driver facts; a color giveaway handout card; and details about the Revell club. (Photo Courtesy Roland Leong Collection)*

Tom Stratton sprayed and lettered the body for the latest version of the *Hawaiian*.

On January 6, at Irwindale's Olympia Grand Premiere, Chadderton qualified in the third overall position with a 6.86 ET. The call to the racing grid for the first round brought a matchup between Gerry Glenn driving John Lombardo's Vega and the *Hawaiian*. Chadderton's potent Leong-tuned Charger took the win with a strong 6.79 ET to Glenn's respectable 6.94.

The second round pitted Mike Van Sant in the Stone-Woods-Cooke *Swindler* Mustang with the *Hawaiian*. In one of the closest races of the day, Van Sant got in front of the *Hawaiian* and held on for the win with a 6.82 ET at 212.26 mph to Chadderton's 6.86 at 219.56.

Positive Role "Models"

For 1973, Leong inked a contract with the plastic model company, Revell Inc., placing the popular hobby company's name on the side of his ultra-fast *Hawaiian*. The popular Charger became the model magnate's 10th car in the series that represented the company.

Leong's prediction for the year was to have one of his best years yet in racing. He entered the season loaded with a promising new car, a big-name sponsor, a seasoned driver, an inventory of three complete spare engines, and an abundance of spare parts. On the road, Leong, Chadderton, and the *Hawaiian* were crushing the opposition while smashing records with exceptional times and speeds.

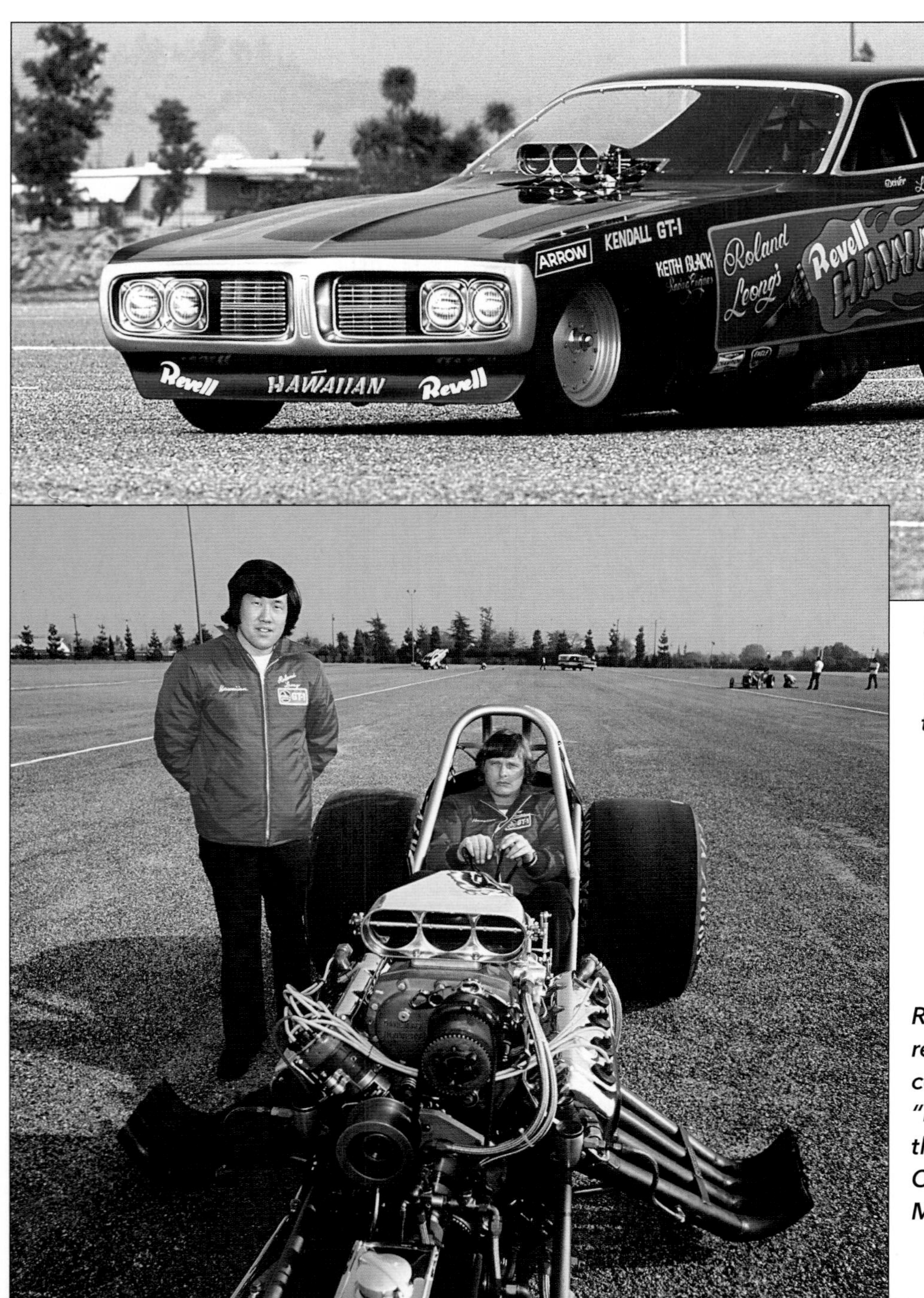

Leong's best-looking Hawaiian *Funny Car to date was the Revell Dodge Charger. It had the profile of a big cat that is ready to pounce on its prey. It's no wonder that the model fans were drooling to get their hands on the model kit. (Photo Courtesy Tim Pearl Collection)*

Roland Leong and Leroy Chadderton reveal the under-the-shell detailed construction and quality work from "Lil" John Butera that neatly housed the Keith Black 472 Black Elephant Chrysler Hemi. (Photo Courtesy Bob McClurg)

Leong, mechanic Rayso Kobayashi, and driver Leroy Chadderton pose for promotional photos in a parking lot that was adjacent to the NHRA Winternationals. (Photo Courtesy Tim Pearl Collection)

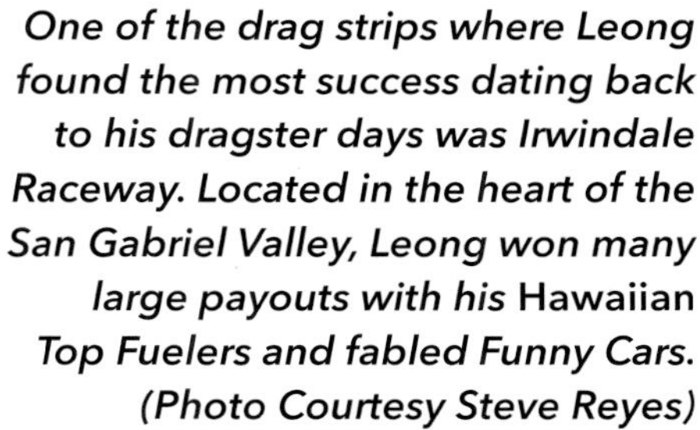

One of the drag strips where Leong found the most success dating back to his dragster days was Irwindale Raceway. Located in the heart of the San Gabriel Valley, Leong won many large payouts with his Hawaiian *Top Fuelers and fabled Funny Cars. (Photo Courtesy Steve Reyes)*

Leroy Chadderton rolls the Revell Hawaiian *into the staging beams on a cold, gloomy day at Pomona during the back-to-back rain-delayed NHRA Winternationals. The event was one of the longest-running events in NHRA history when heavy rain forced the postponement for three weeks before a break in the weather allowed racing to get underway.*

Ex-Fuel Altered shoe Leroy Chadderton mastered the knack of long, smoky burnouts from his days of piloting the Magnificent 7 *AA/FA. He now applied this trait to the Revell Dodge Charger at Bakersfield for the reincarnation of the fabled March Meet. (Photo Courtesy Roland Leong Collection)*

Fremont's AHRA Northern Nationals brought out a massive bevy of Funny Cars to the Northern California facility. One of the top hitters at Fremont was the Revell Hawaiian. *(Photo Courtesy Steve Reyes)*

Leong carefully lines up Leroy Chadderton back into his tracks at Fremont. One of the most important duties of Leong was to keep the car in the groove and staying clear of the "marbles." (Photo Courtesy Steve Reyes)

This is another angle of Chadderton putting the power down and exiting from the water box at Fremont. Fremont was known for its location and the heavy ocean air that provided superb traction to the fast track. Located 30 miles southeast of San Francisco, Fremont was one of the favorite stops of the touring professionals during the fall months on the West Coast. (Photo Courtesy Steve Reyes)

Leroy Chadderton piloted Roland's Revell Hawaiian *past a red-lighting Ed "The Ace" McCulloch's* Revellution *in a best-of-three match race in Sunday's main event at Firebird. McCulloch red-lit away two of the three matches, running top speed of 208.74 mph in spite of having a 25-mph headwind. (Courtesy Firebird Historical Photo Archives)*

The 1974 program cover of Seattle's Pacemaker International featured the 1973 winner, the Hawaiian.

Thieves Close Out the *Hawaiian*'s Season

In mid-June, the team competed at a Sunday afternoon race at nearby U.S. 30 in Hobart, Indiana. After the win, the crew headed back for the night to the Holiday Inn in Gary, Indiana. With the rig and crew staying at the hotel, Leong traveled up to Chicago to visit his old friend Kenny Hirata.

The next morning, the crew filed downstairs to begin preparing for the upcoming weekend's inaugural Springnationals at National Trail Raceway Park in Columbus, Ohio. When they went out to the parking lot, they found the tow rig missing. So, they placed a call to Leong to ask if he took it, and he said, "No!"

Leong immediately headed back to the hotel and filed a police report. Later that day, he received a call from the police. They found the abandoned rig in the middle of a vacant field.

"The truck was found, but nothing was inside of it," Leong said.

All of its contents were gone, including the car, spare engines, tools, and parts—basically everything that wasn't bolted down. Even all of the crew's clothing, gear, and jackets (racing and personal) were stolen.

Leong figured that the loss was between $60,000 and $70,000 for the famous car.

"I had about $12,000 in insurance on the car, so I returned home to Los Angeles to decide what I would do," Leong said.

What Now?

Leong took the summer off from thinking about racing, as he never was able to spend a summer at home. He did things such as take trips to the beach, amusement parks, movies, and museums—all the things one does with the family during the summer months. This worked well for a few months, but Leong had to decide to either go back to racing or go back to work.

Leong, who had been touring professionally since he was 19, returned to the sport with a used car that he bought from his good friend Ray Alley. Alley was selling his Funny Car operation, complete with an early John Buttera chassis with a nearly identical Dodge Charger body.

Leong spoke with Keith Black about what he was going to do. Black said that he'd help Leong with anything he needed regarding parts and engines until he got back on his feet and was able to pay him back.

Leong made a call to Don Prudhomme as well. As with Black, Prudhomme encouraged Leong to come by and pick up any parts he needed to help him get back on the track. Like family, the word even got back to Chrysler about Leong, who'd been associated with Chrysler since 1965. Revell stuck by Leong in keeping him as its major sponsor. After the long drought and stolen car, his then-driver Leroy Chadderton decided that he had enough of the road and quit.

The original 1973 box art of the Revell Hawaiian *1/16-scale model kit was one of the most sought after by many modelers. These original kits issued by Revell demand big money at online auctions, local collectable shows, regional hobby conventions, flea markets, and swap meets.*

"Ugly Car"

After rebuilding his race operation, Leong hired Gordie Bonin to pilot his secondhand Charger, dubbed the "ugly car." Bonin was available after the Pacemaker

Leong was eager to get back to racing along with his new driver, Gordie Bonin, when they debuted this no frills but improved Dodge Charger that was nicknamed "the ugly car" at Irwindale. Taking a seven-month break after the devastating theft of his original Revell Hawaiian, *Leong wanted to get back to racing. He purchased his longtime friend Ray Alley's fuel coupe with upgrades on the early-built John Buttera digger-style chassis. (Photo Courtesy Steve Reyes)*

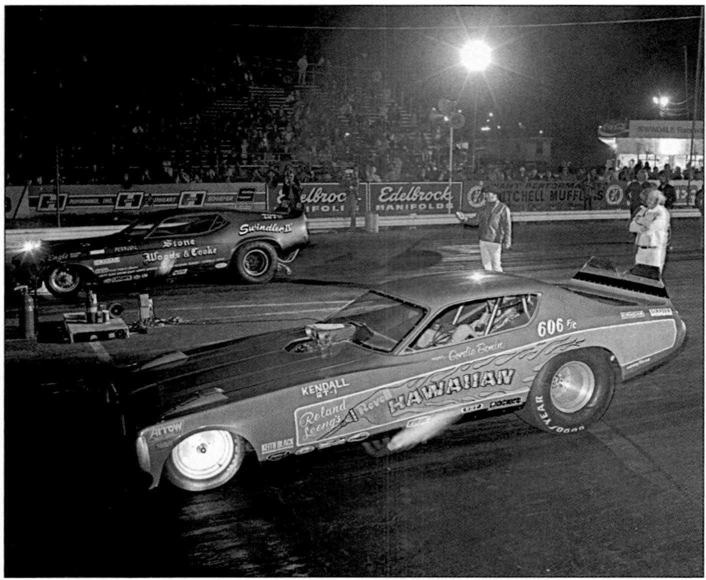

After its previous weekend debut, the freshly painted Revell Hawaiian *surprised all Funny Car comers with Gordie Bonin taking top honors at Irwindale's Grand Premiere. In the first round of eliminations, Bonin wheeled past "Mighty" Mike Van Sant in the Stone-Woods-Cooke* Swindler IV *Mustang with a strong 6.61 ET at 205.01 mph to Van Sant's valiant effort of 6.93 at 201.79. (Photo Courtesy Steve Reyes)*

LEONG REFLECTS ON HIRING GORDIE BONIN

"He was a good driver, and we got along pretty well," Leong said of his longtime friend Bonin. "When drivers left me, it was usually because of a personality conflict. I have to admit that back then, I felt like I'd had enough success that I wasn't going to let a driver tell me how to run my car. Right, wrong, or indifferent, it was my car, and a lot of times, the drivers had some strong opinions because of other cars they'd driven, but Gordie was really easygoing and upbeat, and we had real good communication.

"He didn't do stupid things behind the wheel, which can be hard not to do at times when you're driving a Funny Car. You just have a split second to decide, but he was pretty good at making the right decision."

team of Ron Hodgson and Gordon Jenner parked its car.

Leong and Bonin headed to Irwindale to shake off the rust to prepare for Irwindale's third-annual Grand Premiere that was scheduled for the following weekend.

At the Irwindale Grand Prix, Bonin powered Leong's new Dodge to its first big event win of the year. Bonin ran a 6.61 ET at 207.85 mph for a final-round win over, who else, Don Prudhomme. The Snake ran into problems at half-track and aborted the run against Bonin, resulting in an off-pace 8.19 ET at 111.24 mph.

Bonin lived with Leong during this time. Early in the tour, another setback occurred when Bonin totaled the body with an off-track excursion in Detroit in his second outing with the *Hawaiian*. With the body replaced, the racing continued without any more disruptions. Bonin stayed on throughout the remainder of the year and into the 1974 season before he left to return back to the Pacemaker team.

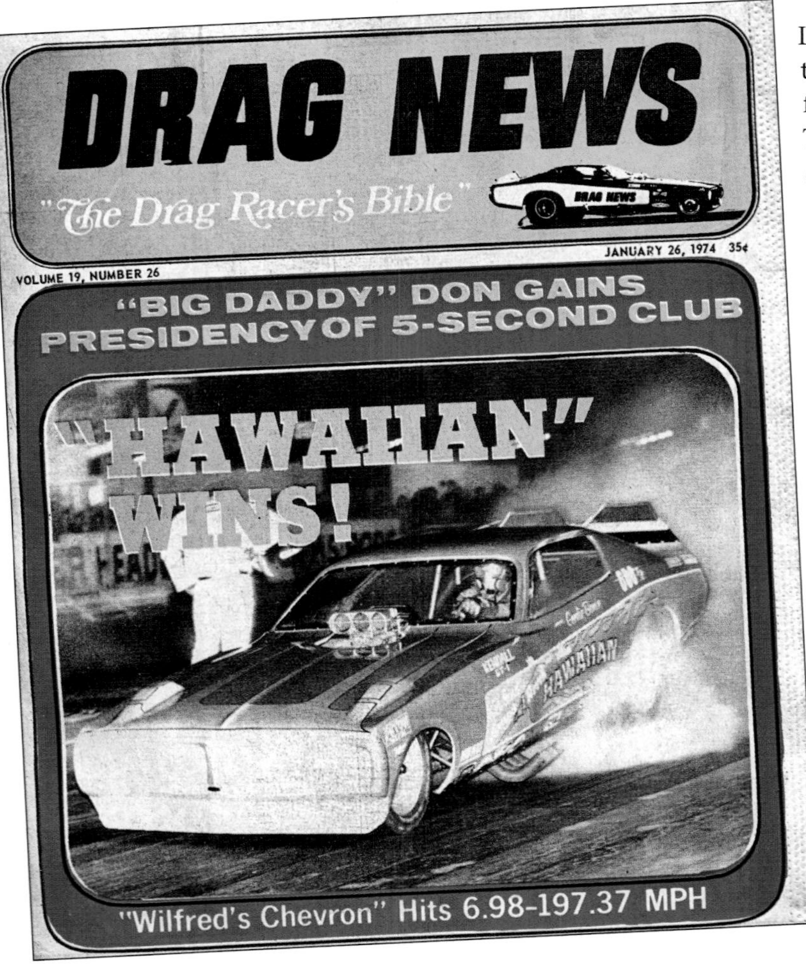

DRAG NEWS

"The Drag Racer's Bible"

VOLUME 19, NUMBER 26

JANUARY 26, 1974 35¢

"BIG DADDY" DON GAINS PRESIDENCY OF 5-SECOND CLUB

"HAWAIIAN" WINS!

"Wilfred's Chevron" Hits 6.98-197.37 MPH

After Leong and new driver Gordie Bonin won Irwindale's third-annual Grand Premiere, the Hawaiian *was on the cover of the January 26, 1974, edition of* Drag News. *Bonin defeated Don Prudhomme in the finals with a 6.61 ET at 207.85 mph to the aborted run of 8.19 at 111.24 for the Snake. It was extremely satisfying for Leong after his long wait to get back to the winner's circle at Irwindale, especially with a "used" Funny Car.*

The Federal Energy Crisis Cuts Field to 16

At the 1974 NHRA Winternationals, the field of racers was feeling the effects of the energy guidelines. They forced downsizing to a 16-car field, so the pressure to make each qualifying run count was on the minds of the Funny Car teams. Roland Leong and Gordie Bonin held their own but were a casualty of the shortened field when they failed to make the show for Sunday's elimination rounds.

This was the scene in front of the estimated crowd of 8,000 fans with the Hawaiian *under the lights at OCIR. Nothing could top mixing nitro and header flames together at night with the sounds of whining superchargers disappearing toward the finish lights. (Photo Courtesy Tom Nelson)*

Pat Foster streaks past Gordie Bonin during a best-of-three match race. Bonin, who totaled the body with an off-track excursion in Detroit in his second outing with the Hawaiian*, left later after this race to rejoin his former teammates Ron Hodgson and Gordon Jenner for the remainder of 1974. (Photo Courtesy Steve Reyes)*

Gordie Bonin kicked off the 1974 NHRA Winternationals at the helm of the Hawaiian*. Leong's* Hawaiian *was the former Ray Alley Charger that Leong purchased from Alley. The chassis was fabricated by Jon Buttera in his earlier days of building the digger-style frames. Buttera claimed that the chassis was one of his very first "original hot rods." With the downsizing at Pomona due to federal energy regulations, Bonin failed to put the* Hawaiian *into the show of the now 16-car field. (Photo Courtesy Bob McClurg)*

"Mighty" Mike Temporarily Fills the Seat Vacancy

After the departure of Bonin, Leong hired "Mighty" Mike Van Sant to fill the vacancy. The results paid off immediately for Leong with a midweek show at Fremont on May 1, 1974, at the first Revell Northern Challenge.

Six of the top Revell floppers made up the strong field that included Don "the Snake" Prudhomme, Tom "the Mongoose" McEwen, Pisano & Matsubara, Ed "the Ace" McCulloch, Keeling & Clayton's *California Charger* Mustang, and the *Hawaiian*. The six-car Funny Car show ran three round-robin matches that would overall bring the two quickest cars back to race in the final round.

Leong gestures to "Mighty" Mike Van Sant that he's staged and ready to "rock and roll" in another match race. Leong hired Van Sant after Gordie Bonin left to reunite with his former Canadian teammates, Ron Hodgson and Gordon Jenner, to finish out the rest of 1974. The hiring of Van Sant was the shortest stint for any of Leong's drivers. (Photo Courtesy Tom Nelson)

In the first round, Van Sant easily disposed of the Mustang of John Keeling and Jerry Clayton. In round two, Van Sant dumped Matsubara in the Pisano & Matsubara Vega. This brought the two quickest of the unbeaten cars to the line for the final: Don Prudhomme's *Army Cuda* and Van Sant in the *Hawaiian* Dodge Charger. When all was said and done, the win light hung for the *Hawaiian*.

This photo is a perfect example of what was said on the starting line. AHRA race director Don Wormsley, "Big Daddy" Don Garlits (eating a piece of fried chicken), and Mickey Thompson (glaring over Leong's shoulder) react to some words from Don Schumacher.

The next trip was up to the Pacific Northwest in Portland for the Rainier Oregon Open. Mike Van Sant made a respectable showing only to lose to the World Champion Frank Hall driving Jim Green's *Green Elephant* Vega. Van Sant posted a credible 6.75 ET at 212.76 mph to Hall's 6.61 at 214.79.

It wasn't too long after Portland that Leong was on the road, heading through the Midwest on his summer tour. Leong and Van Sant made a stop in Chicago, staying at Romeo Palamedes's shop to make repairs to the *Hawaiian*. Leong and Palamedes returned from lunch that same day and saw Dennis Petersavage (also known as Denny Savage) mounting a pair of new slicks by hand on the rims, which was no easy task.

Leong approached Savage and asked him, "You also work on everything on the car too?"

Leong was having difficulties with Van Sant not wanting to work on the car, so Savage earned his respect. Leong approached Savage at the end of the day and asked if he was willing to work for Leong. Without hesitation, Savage agreed! Van Sant's days in the *Hawaiian* appeared to be numbered.

Savage Makes It an Even Dozen

With repairs finished to the car, they loaded it up on the transporter and immediately left for Martin, Michigan, for a match race. On the first run of the night, Van Sant lifted the *Hawaiian* up into a gigantic wheel-stand,

Denny Savage rides the Race-masters out of the water box at OCIR. Leong changed the appearance of the Charger with the addition of red strips that accented both sides of the **Hawaiian.** *(Photo Courtesy Bob McClurg)*

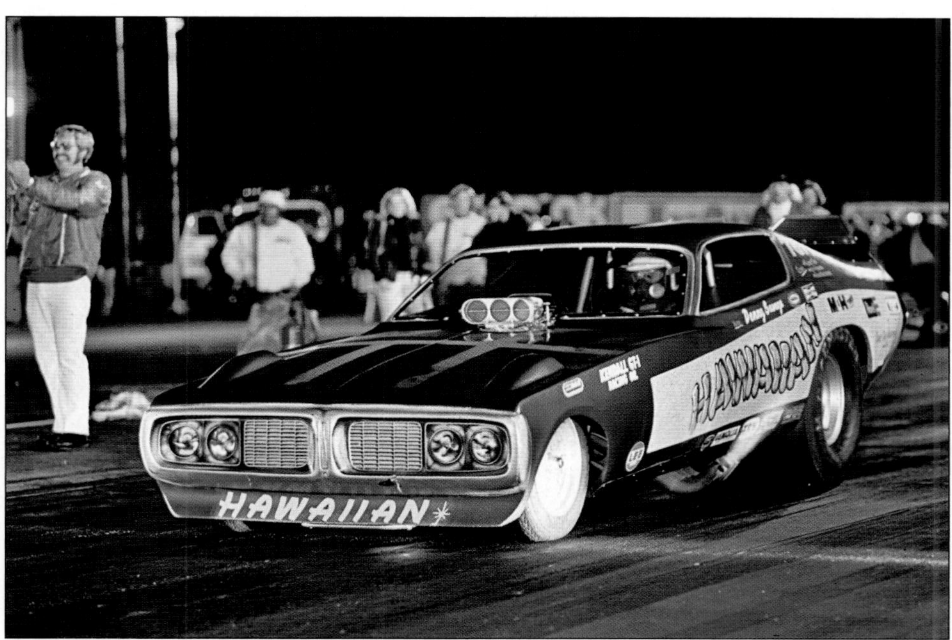

The Hawaiian ***made a strong showing for Dodge at the Manufacturer's Funny Car Team Championships at OCIR. Like his many drivers, Leong frequently changed the paint and lettering schemes for a fresh, new look throughout the season. Savage supported team Dodge by winning two of three rounds, collecting two valuable points. (Photo Courtesy Bob McClurg)***

landing back down hard, breaking all the frame rails in front of the motor. Leong was extremely angry because he was supposed to run the next day at Rockford Dragway in Byron, Illinois, for Rockford's sixth-annual Manufacturer's Funny Car Showdown.

Savage told Leong that he made the call to Palamedes and arranged to meet back at his shop around midnight. Arriving back in Chicago, they worked all night, re-halving the front of the car. Somewhere in all of this, Van Sant was sleeping in Palamedes's office.

Leong told Savage, "If the car gets fixed and we make it to Rockford in the morning, I want you to drive my car."

Well, they made it and raced it at Rockford.

Savage drove the *Hawaiian* to a 6.81 ET at 167.91 mph for a first-round win over the Kling & Gould Ford, which ran a 7.47 at 199.11. Round two began with the *Hawaiian* shutting off early at a 6.76 ET at 175.74 mph when Dale Pulde experienced an oil fire in Mickey Thompson's Grand Am. In the third and final round, Savage received a bye run when the Gretchko Brothers car lost fire on the line. The next day on the way back to Chicago, Leong dropped Van Sant off at the airport and sent him home.

Savage became the 12th driver for Leong. The duo had a solid second half of the 1974 season of the demanding match-race circuit. First was a late-October win at Blaney Dragstrip in Columbia, South Carolina, at the running of the seventh-annual Dixie Nationals. In the final round, Savage sank the *Flying Dutchman* Vega of Stan Bowman by running a 6.75 ET at 203 mph to the Dutchman's 7.03 at 184.72 mph.

Fire Sidelines Savage at OMS

Finishing the year at the fifth-annual Supernationals at Ontario Motor Speedway (OMS), there was a four-way battle for the Funny Car World Championship. Saturday's Funny Car qualifying became a series of all-out attempts to crack into the tough field of 16.

Looking outside in, Savage succumbed to the pressure in his last-ditch effort in Saturday's last session. The engine exploded past the finish line, erupting into an oil fire that forced the *Hawaiian* out of the race. Overall, the damage was minimal to the car and body, as the required onboard fire-suppression system extinguished nearly all the flames. Savage received moderate burns to his arms, hands, legs, and feet. This closed out the era for Leong's Charger-bodied *Hawaiian*s.

After nearly a month, Savage went to Leong's house to work on the car, and he saw Norm Wilcox working on the car. Leong told Savage that he hired Wilcox as his 13th driver. Leong had heard that the fire unraveled Savage and that he didn't want to drive anymore.

It was pure chaos during Saturday's final push in the last Funny Car qualifying session at the 1974 NHRA Supernationals at Ontario Motor Speedway. Several entries scrambled to make a last-ditch effort to race on Sunday. This included Savage, who pressed the limit when the engine gave up the fight. Hot oil ended up on the headers, resulting in a fire at the lights. (Photo Courtesy Steve Reyes)

Denny Savage suffered minor burns to his hands and legs when the engine expired in the Hawaiian, *turning the car into a raging ball of fire at the California Super Speedway. Savage rolled to a stop after activating the onboard fire system to extinguish the flame, but the car was a total loss. Unfittingly, this run was the end of Savage driving for Leong, as well as Leong's familiar association with Dodge Charger–bodied* Hawaiians. *(Photo Courtesy Steve Reyes)*

CHAPTER 10

1975–1979: THE GM YEARS

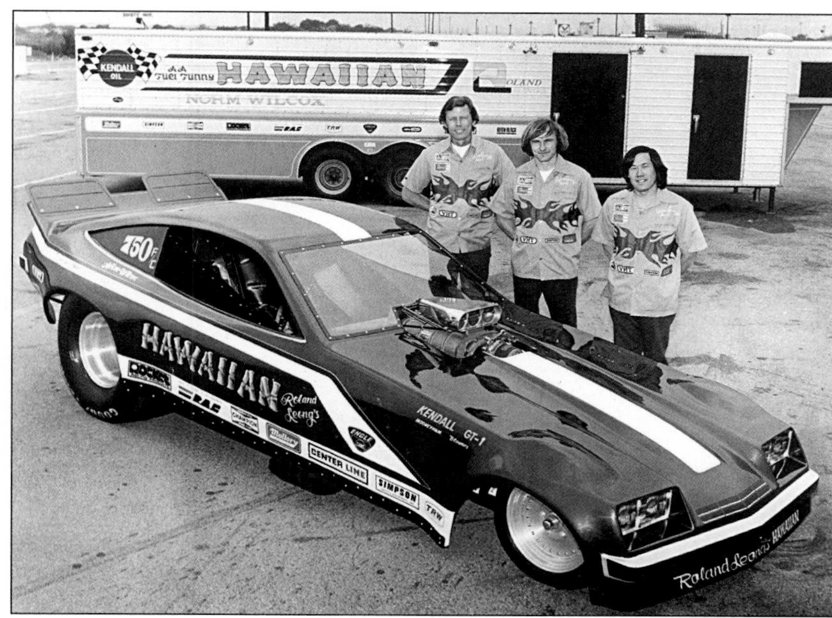

The crew of the Hawaiian *was ready to take on the competition for 1975. From left to right are an unknown crewmember, Norm Wilcox, and Roland Leong. For the 1975 campaign, the familiar Dodge-bodied* Hawaiian *floppers were replaced with a sleeker, compact Chevrolet Monza. (Photo Courtesy Roland Leong Collection)*

Leong, who had been touring professionally since he was 19 years old, returned to the sport in late 1974 with a used car. He did well enough to pay back all who came to his aid with parts and engines. During this duration, Leong was able to build a new Chevrolet Monza over the winter of 1974/1975.

For the first time in his career, Leong's association with Chrysler's fiberglass-bodied floppers ran its course when his contact at Chrysler expired. Leong decided to switch to General Motors with one of its newest models: the subcompact Chevrolet Monza.

Wilcox in for 1975

Along with running a new brand, Leong made another driver change for 1975. As was noted at the end of Chapter 9, he hired Top Fuel veteran Norm Wilcox of Culver City, California, to take over the controls of Leong's new supercharged, 484-ci Keith Black Hemi–powered *Hawaiian*.

The season started off slow for Wilcox. While at Fremont's New Year's Day Funny Car Championships, his first-round encounter was with Don Prudhomme. The hit of the gas resulted in both cars blowing off the tires past the 1,000-foot mark. Prudhomme recovered first before the finish lights, outrunning the *Hawaiian* with a 7.41 ET at 189.78 mph to a 7.59 at 176.44.

A few weeks later at Irwindale's Grand Premiere, Wilcox qualified in the 11th position of the 16-car field only to break right off the starting line against Bob Pickett in the first round. The bad-luck streak continued for Wilcox when the *Hawaiian* could only put together a best time of 6.77 at 178.21 mph. This failed to qualify him at Pomona for the Winternationals, which was a first for Leong in his illustrious career.

Eastern Swing

The team ventured out on tour in May with a stop in West Salem, Ohio, at Dragway 42 for the IHRA Grandnationals. Wilcox qualified 11th in the 16-car field, but when eliminations got under way, the performance picked up. A first round 7.08 ET gave Wilcox the win over Vic Cecelia's slower 7.97. In the second round, the *Hawaiian* advanced with a 7.12 ET over a troubled John Luna, who crawled down the strip with a 19.29. In the semifinals, Wilcox ran into the eventual winner, "Jungle" Jim Liberman, and transmission woes ended Wilcox's day.

During the trip to Freeland, Michigan, for the seventh-annual Manufacturer's Meet at Tri-City Dragway, the *Hawaiian* completed three runs, winning two of three against Twig Zeigler in the first round. After a no-start loss in the second round against Raymond Beadle driving the *Blue Max*, Wilcox rebounded in the third race, winning over a tire-smoking Terry Capp.

Leong was now running under the Bowtie banner with this 1975 Chevrolet Monza that was handled by veteran driver Norm Wilcox. Leong had been competing in Funny Car eliminator using Dodge-branded fiberglass bodies since 1969. Leong and Wilcox dealt with the usual learning curve with the Monza, which was limited in performance and technology, dealing with new combinations in an attempt to get the car up to speed. (Photo Courtesy Roland Leong Collection)

Wilcox experienced a devastating fire at the NHRA World Finals in Ontario when the supercharger backfired, blasting gaskets out of the engine and oil onto the headers. Wilcox had qualified number-two in one of his best efforts of the year. (Photo Courtesy Steve Reyes)

Wilcox tries to remain in control as flames engulf the entire cockpit of the Hawaiian*. The fire burned off the parachute pack and cords. Unfortunately, Wilcox lost control, crashing the car into the wall. Wilcox received extensive burns to his hands, legs, arms, and upper body. (Photo Courtesy Steve Reyes)*

The Low Points of Summer

Still, the *Hawaiian* was plagued with glitches throughout the touring season. There were off-par performances and unexpected breakages at the starting line, which were not the typical runs that one would expect from Leong and the *Hawaiian*.

A low point for Leong on the summer tour included not qualifying for the prestigious Popular Hot Rod Championships at U.S. 131 Dragway, where Leong experienced tremendous success in the past. A month later, on a return stop at Dragway 42 during the IHRA Nationals, Wilcox wound up 13th overall in the field of 16 cars. However, the surprising news was that the virtually unknown names of Roger Hamrick, Jackie Price, and Donny Plunkett sat well ahead of the *Hawaiian*. Wilcox went out in the first round in eliminations.

In an interview with reporter Jim Sims of the *Amarillo Globe-Times*, Leong said, "We had a lot of troubles with this car. I feel we've got them ironed out, but overall, this had been a learning season for us, and things look really good for next season."

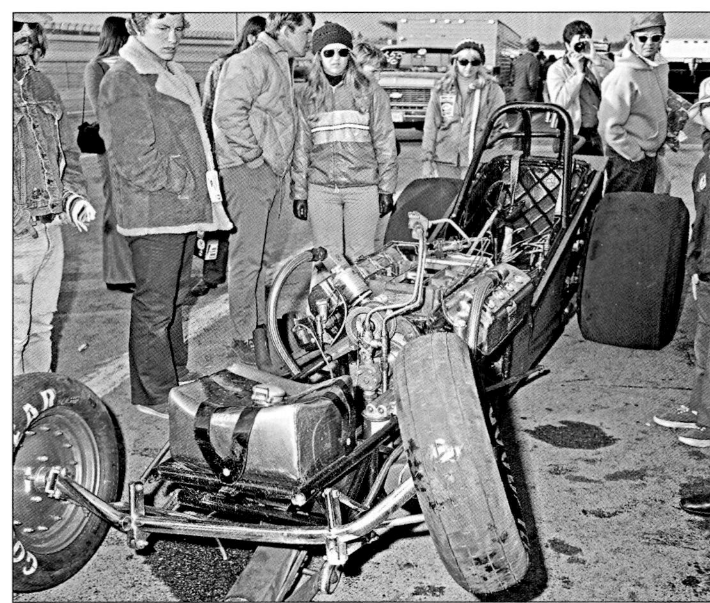

The mangled remains of the Hawaiian*'s bent and broken chassis drew the fans to the pits to survey the totaled carnage. The roll cage of the Sarte-built chassis kept Wilcox from sustaining more severe injuries other than the burns. (Photo Courtesy Steve Reyes)*

NHRA World Finals

By November, Leong got a handle on the car at the NHRA World Finals in Ontario. Wilcox qualified number-two with a 6.19 ET at 232.55 mph, right behind Don Prudhomme's 6.15 at 241.53. Wilcox improved on his qualifying time in round one when he defeated Jake

Johnston with a 6.16 ET at 218.97 mph to Johnston's 6.31 at 220.

In round two, disaster struck when the engine coughed up the blower, pushing several rods out of the block. It resulted in a horrendous fire that led to the destructive crash of the car.

1976

The new year kicked off at Irwindale Raceway's annual Funny Car Championships with Wilcox returning for another tour driving the new *Hawaiian*. However, he soon left for another ride. Larry Arnold took over in early 1976 before deciding to leave midyear to start his own crankshaft company.

The cover of the 1977 eighth-annual Governor's Cup Funny Car Championships program featured the previous year's Cup champion, the Hawaiian*, at Sacramento Raceway. (Photo Courtesy Roland Leong Collection)*

The bicentennial year kicked off on January 1 at Irwindale with the "Action Strip's" annual Funny Car Championships. Leong debuted his newest version of the Hawaiian *with returning driver Norm Wilcox back in the seat after the costly crash at Ontario.*

After the departure of Wilcox, Leong added new driver Larry Arnold (of King-fish *fame) to the long list of drivers that he employed. Arnold stuck around until midyear, when he left the seat to start his own crankshaft company. Leong's search to occupy the seat was short when he found the available Ron Colson to take over. (Photo Courtesy Roland Leong Collection)*

Looking for a temporary driver to fulfill several booking dates, Leong put Ron Colson in the seat on those terms. Colson stuck around and became the longest tenure of any of Leong's drivers from mid-1976 through the end of the 1980. Leong talked about drivers using this comparison: "Drivers are like a set of spark plugs. Just as you think you might need to find a new one, you screw out the old one and screw in the new one!"

Leong recalled that he and Colson worked very well with each other and that he was a good driver. "We got a couple of NHRA national event wins, including winning the Popular Hot Rodding Championships," Leong said.

With new sponsors Torco Oil Company and Power Gloss gracing the side of the Hawaiian, *Leong and Ron Colson returned to the low-6-second bracket, clocking speeds well over 230 mph. (Photo Courtesy Tal Barret Photography)*

Coconuts and Lightning Bolts in 1977

Roland Leong's 1977 Chevrolet Power Gloss *Hawaiian* Monza Funny Car was another creation from John Buttera that had a Keith Black Chrysler 488-ci aluminum Hemi engine. Bill Carter provided the striking Murano Pearl Electric Blue paint that was accented with intricate artwork from the brushes and spray guns of Kenny Youngblood. All of the painted, chrome, aluminum, and magnesium surfaces were fire resistant to 2,000 degrees. Backing came from the Torco Oil and Chemical Company.

Mark Vincent, then vice president of the Power Gloss division of Torco Oil Company, announced a trip for two to the NHRA Winston World Finals at Ontario Motor Speedway. The trip included airfare, a three-night stay at an exclusive hotel, track admission, pit passes, and an

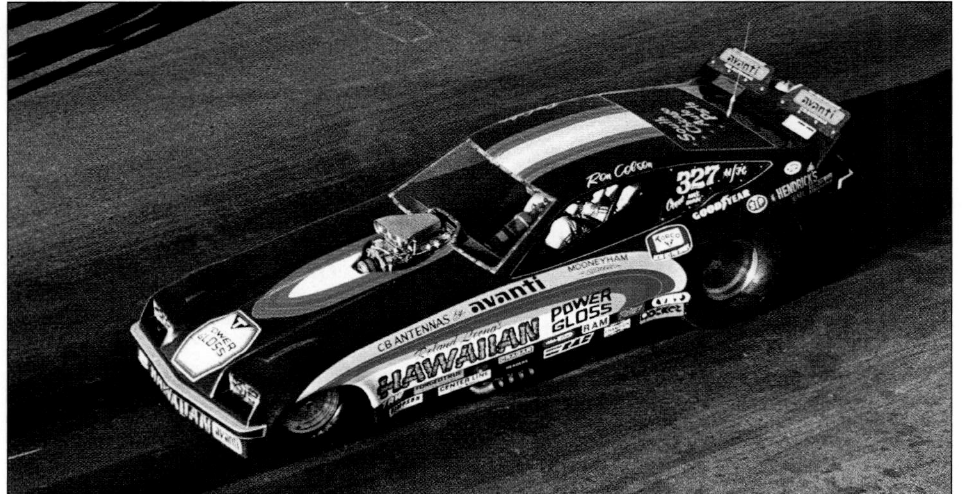

Six-time national champion Leong added Avanti CB Antennas as a secondary sponsor. The sponsorship opened the door to test the company's latest in CB antennas, a glass-mounted "Astro-Fantom" edition. This photo was taken from the rooftop of the tower at OCIR. (Photo Courtesy Roland Leong Collection)

Leong offers his insight during an interview with a local newspaper reporter between rounds of racing.

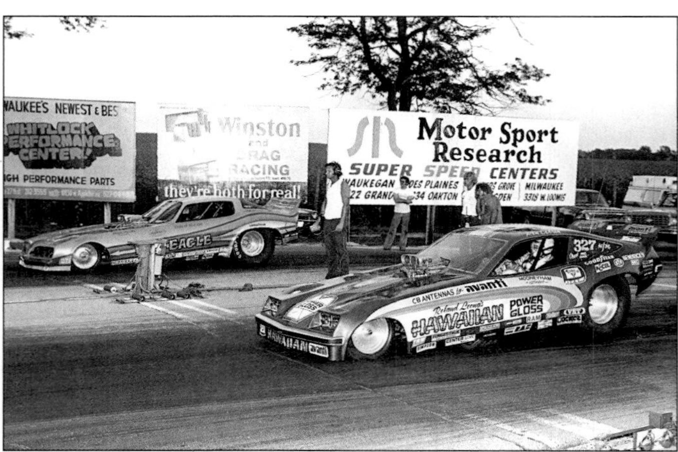

Dale Pulde and Ron Colson square off at Great Lakes Dragaway in Union Grove, Wisconsin. (Photo Courtesy Roland Leong Collection)

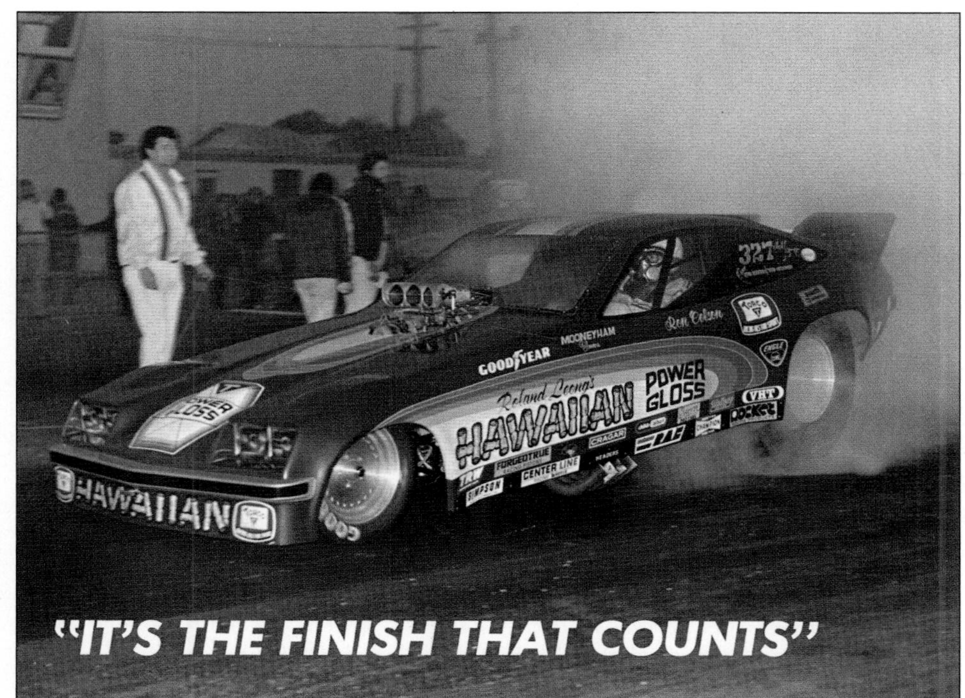

Power Gloss International's slogan "It's the finish that counts" had a double meaning. It referred to winning a race as well as the silicone surface coating that shines 20 times longer than regular car-wax products. Power Gloss was more than a sponsor for the Hawaiian. *Leong said, "The Power Gloss people had given me the authority to recruit my own network of direct distributors for their products and services. My group was known as Roland Leong's Power Gloss distributors." (Photo Courtesy Roland Leong Collection)*

honorary membership on the Power Gloss racing team. The promotion ran throughout the year with spectators filling out raffle tickets at the Power Gloss/Torco displays at each NHRA national event.

Making Progress

The rise back up to the top of the class for Leong had been a long journey. For 1978, the return could not have looked more promising. Ron Colson brought a ton of experience and competence to the wheel of the *Hawaiian*. Colson also brought in a bevy of new sponsors to aid in the operation, including the Avanti Research and Development Corporation, an Illinois-based company that specialized in manufacturing CB antennas. It also didn't hurt that Colson served as the company's national service manager.

Both Leong and Colson sorted out several initial problems with their new Jaime Sarte–built machine, which was motivated by 484 ci of Keith Black aluminum Hemi power. This was all too familiar for Leong's liking.

In addition, Leong hired young mechanic Mike Dunn, who was the son of Funny Car driver and owner Jim Dunn. The upside for Leong was Dunn's great engine knowledge, but he was also a licensed fuel driver too.

Among Colson's assets was his ability to receive and understand instructions given by Leong. Colson also

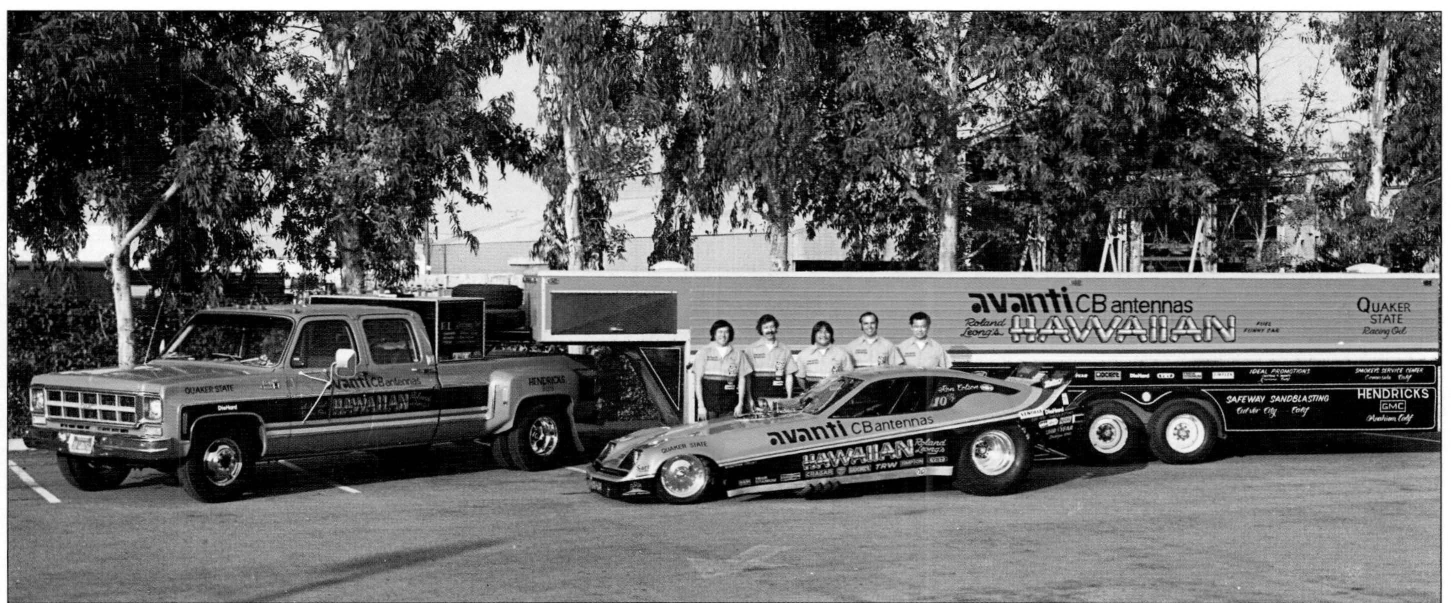

With Avanti CB Antennas being a full-time sponsor for the Hawaiian *for 1978, the new green, yellow, black, and magenta colors graced the team's racing operations.*

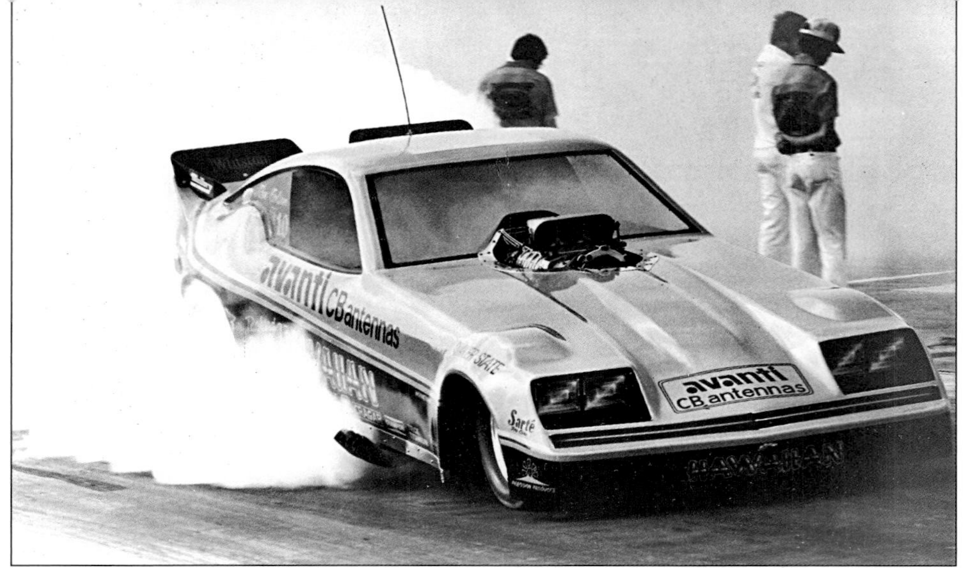

With the popularity of citizen radios running rampant across the country, the 240-mph Avanti Hawaiian *was the test bed for the company's unique glass-mounted "Astro Fantom" antennas at extremes of speed and vibrations. (Photo Courtesy Roland Leong Collection)*

barely crossed over the centerline, resulting in his disqualification.

If Leong had his way, Colson would have been dragged back up the return road by his thumbs.

"Ron had done a great job driving for me, and he only pissed me off twice in our years together," Leong said.

Colson's disqualification allowed Tom McEwen a single run in the semifinals that gave the Mongoose the tune-up to famously beat Don Prudhomme in the emotional final round. This came just weeks after McEwen's young son, Jamie, had died of leukemia. The rumor was that Colson claimed a part of the chassis broke,

offered precise explanations, dissecting each run on how the car performed and giving clear translations back to Leong.

Just When You Think You Have It Made

The 24th U.S. Nationals once again came over the Labor Day weekend. Colson turned in his best-ever run with a 6.03 ET, which was good enough to place the *Hawaiian* into the third overall position.

After a first-round win with a 6.18 ET, Colson and Leong got an incredible break when Kenny Bernstein couldn't return for the second round. Colson's luck ended when he got far out of shape on the single and

forcing the *Hawaiian* into crossing over the centerline, which added to the Hollywood script of McEwen's win.

Leong claimed that was not the case.

"I'm not totally convinced about the story of the broken chassis, but I'm sure he just lost control—plain and simple," Leong said said. "But on the other hand, if he didn't make that mistake, there might have not been the *Snake & Mongoose* movie."

Colson made up for his Indy blunder later in the season when he ended Leong's dry spell. He drove the *Hawaiian* to victory at the NHRA Fallnationals in Seattle over Dale Pulde in the final round. The win was Leong's first NHRA national event Funny Car win since 1971, when Butch Maas piloted his way into the winner's circle at Pomona.

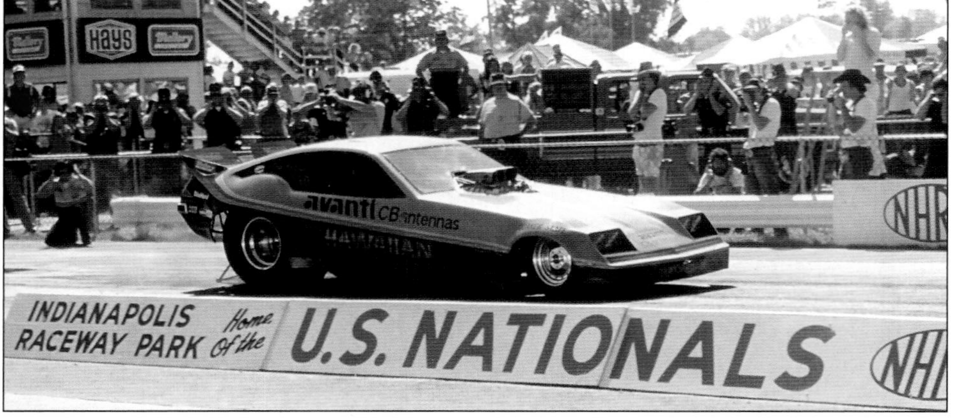

In the first round of eliminations at the 24th-annual U.S. Nationals, Ron Colson stopped the timers with a 6.18 win. He received a rare gift going into the second round when Kenny Bernstein, the tipster's favorite to win the Nationals, broke and couldn't make the call to the starting line. In what seemed to be an easy path to the semifinals, Colson negated all of his good fortune when he spun the tires, got out of shape, and crossed the centerline, resulting in an automatic disqualification. (Photo Courtesy Clinton Wright Collection)

1979

For 1979, the team dropped the Monza body and switched over to a Corvette, breaking two superstitious drag racing traditions. Green race cars were bad luck and Corvettes were cursed. In 1979, they found out if both of these superstitions held up.

NHRA U.S. Nationals' Silver Anniversary

The 1979 U.S. Nationals celebrated its 25th anniversary with Roland Leong and Ron Colson running the Avanti Corvette at peak performance. After an easy first-round win, Colson was matched up with

The beautiful new Avanti Hawaiian *was bodied with a 1979 Corvette that offered a sleeker and more aerodynamic design. The 2,400-hp missile set its sights on its third consecutive finish in the world points top 12. (Photo Courtesy Tony Thacker)*

Ron Colson demonstrates one of his patented smoky burnouts from his Revell **Chi-Town Hustler** ***days when driving for the super team of Farkonas-Coil-Minnick. Leong and Colson, his longest-tenured driver, enjoyed a lasting friendship.***

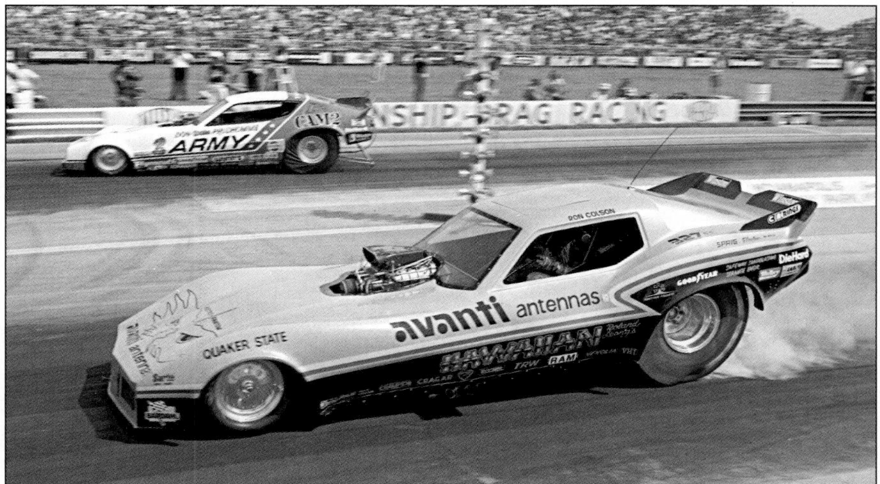

In the second round of Funny Car eliminations at the U.S. Nationals at Indianapolis Raceway Park, Ron Colson met low-qualifier Don Prudhomme, a four-time World Champion. With lane choice, Colson upset the Snake, as the Army entry got out of shape and lifted. (Photo Courtesy Steve Reyes)

Leong's great friend and former *Hawaiian* Top Fuel driver Don Prudhomme in round two. Prudhomme was the U.S. Nationals' number-one qualifier with a record-shattering 5.95 ET, but he got out of shape at the hit, allowing Colson to upset the low qualifier.

"This was the most difficult time that I ran against the Snake," Colson said in an interview with announcer Dave McClelland. "As I left the line, I overpowered the track and smoked the tires, breaking them loose. I got sideways, where I thought I was dead. I backpedaled and got some degree of control but didn't give up and made my way to the finish line for the win."

The *Hawaiian* went on to lose in the semifinal round against underdog Kosty Ivanof.

Overall, the *Hawaiian* still finished fifth in the 1979 NHRA World Championship points battle. As was mentioned earlier, Colson's other blunder took place at Ontario Motor Speedway for the season-ending World Finals. The World Finals was hampered when large amounts of oil were dumped on the track surface the prior weekend by a diesel truck.

Leong and Colson had the all-important lane choice coming into the semifinals with Gordie Bonin. However, Colson skated off the line and got out of the groove into the "marbles." He crossed over the centerline, disqualifying their chances of a sure win.

"On the run before in the second round, the front end was in the air, and we won, but it was hairy," Leong said. "I wanted to put weight on the front end, but Colson talked me out of it. He pulled the front end up again in the semifinals, and he had to lift, and we lost. That's the last time I've ever listened to a driver."

Not only was Colson an employee, driving and wrenching for Leong, but they also were very close friends. After Colson retired from driving, it wasn't uncommon for Leong to bring his entire *Hawaiian* team over to Colson's home for a few days before heading out to a match race in the Midwest. There was one time that Leong's 18-wheeler took out Colson's prized flower bed and several times that the neighbors heard the sounds of a nitro engine being fired in the driveway. It was all part of the racing experience.

CHAPTER 11

1980 AND 1981: A RACING LEGEND

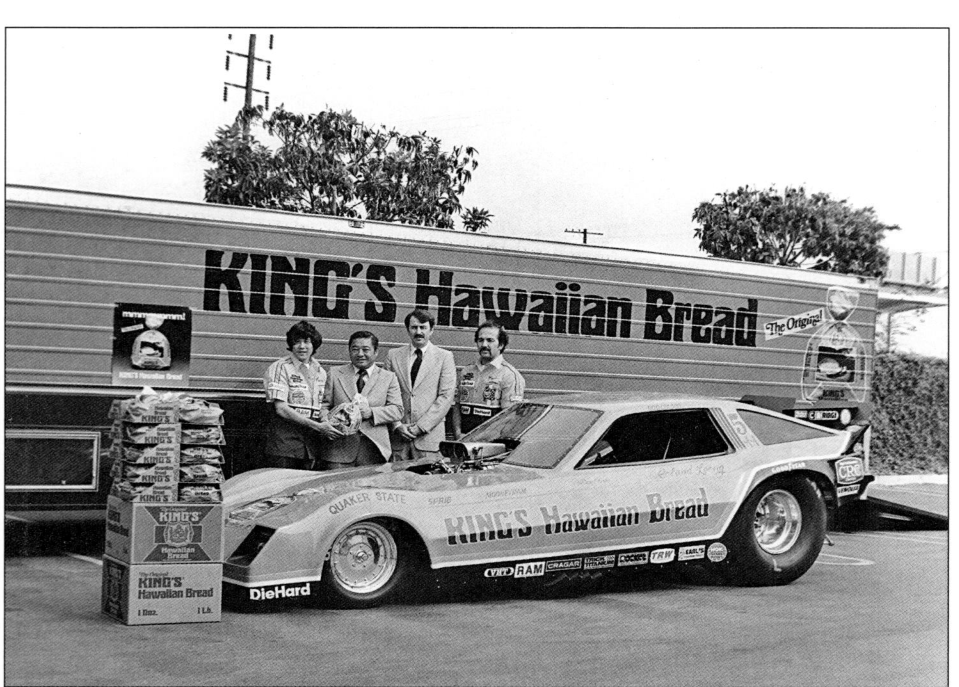

King's Hawaiian Bread of Gardena jumped into the race car business, sponsoring Roland Leong's 1980 Dodge Omni. Car owner Leong, King's owner Robert R. Taira, Earl Gurtner of King's, and chief wrench Danny Oliver are pictured at the King's Hawaiian Bread headquarters. (Photo Courtesy Roland Leong Collection)

Retrospectively, eight-time national-event champion Roland Leong had become a true legend in the sport of drag racing. Since 1959, he raced a series of gasoline-powered dragsters in Hawaii and on the mainland.

Leong won his first national title in 1963 with Danny Ongais as his driver. His career had been a mixture of bad luck and spectacular success. The bad-luck side included Leong's first brand-new Funny Car being destroyed on its first race at the 1969 Winternationals and the thievery of his entire race operation in 1972 with only the transporter being recovered. In addition, cars crashed and burned in 1971 and 1975, and there was another crash at the 1977 Springnationals, when the car seemed to be heading for another national-event title.

The bright side for Leong's dragsters and Funny Cars included track records that are too numerous to list: winning the U.S. Fuel and Gas Championships in 1967 and 1970; the 1967 Hot Rod Magazine Meet; NHRA Winternationals victories in 1963, 1965, 1966, 1970, and 1971; U.S. Nationals victories in 1965 and 1966; being crew chief for Don Prudhomme's 1969 win at the U.S. Nationals; the Popular Hot Rod Magazine Meet in 1972: the California's Governors Cup in 1976; and a spot in the top 12 in World Points for 1977 and 1978. The 1978 season was highlighted by an NHRA Fallnationals win over an elite field in Seattle, Washington.

The native of Honolulu had been the owner, crew chief, and tuner of a series of race cars for more than 16 years.

The Economic Side of Running a Nitro Funny Car

The 1970s had seen drag racing make phenomenal strides in technical innovation and the development of highly effective safety measures. It also was becoming a major force in the sports and entertainment industry.

Now into the 1980s, drag racing's major leaguers were more conscious in the economics department than ever before. It took larger amounts of money earned at the strip and through major sponsorships to keep the everyday operations running. Just the general cost of a barrel of nitro, extra tires, parts, and lubricants had doubled over the years. The old cliché that "you need to spend money to make money" was right on the mark. If you didn't have it (money), you didn't race.

In the early days, Leong made the bulk of his living on the match-race circuit. Racing at national events, the top stars were paid set amounts along with round money for winning. By adding in the merchandise awards from manufacturers and sponsors, the secondary cash was more than the racers actually earned from winning.

Since 1975, the R.J. Reynolds Tobacco Company backed the Winston World Championship Series. The series poured considerable sums of money in the competitor's pockets based on a season-long points series for the professional and sportsman racers.

Money, Money, Money

In the 1980s, prize money ran into the millions of dollars, leaving the homebuilt race cars a thing of the past. Investments into a professional race operation topped $100,000 annually, while operating expenses would exceed twice that amount.

A great example of that is what it cost Leong's Hawaiian Punch operation. Starting with the construction of a basic, competitive professional race car built from the ground up, the cost was more than $50,000. Spare engines (a minimum of three at $21,000 each) cost $63,000; spare engine components were $25,000; driveline spares were $11,000; spare tires and wheels cost $4,000; a tractor truck was $92,000; and a trailer was $52,000. This added up to a whopping $300,000-plus before the transporter even rolled out of the shop.

At the racetrack, Leong's nitro-burning Dodges consumed 12 gallons of nitromethane ($28 per gallon) on each quarter-mile run. This does not factor in the miscellaneous costs of diesel fuel, team uniforms, salaries, lubricants, and food to feed the entire crew, including hospitality programs for the local beverage bottlers and food-service vendors.

In the quest of keeping up with the cost of race car expenditures, the NHRA continually increased the prize and contingency money posted by more than 70 participating automotive factory and aftermarket sponsors annually.

1980–1981: Leong Mixes Dough and Nitro

In 1980, Roland Leong brought on board fellow Hawaiian Robert R. Taira, president and founder of the iconic bread company King's Hawaiian Bread. The partnership brought the Aloha spirit to Leong's all-new, 240-mph 1980 Dodge Omni AA/Funny Car.

Leong's Omni was powered by a 2,400-hp supercharged nitro-fueled Keith Black aluminum Hemi-head engine that was draped in a super-light chassis built by fellow Hawaiian Jaimie Sarte. The technology development had allowed the 1980s nitro-powered Top Fuelers and Funny Cars to exceed the scientific maximum level of pulling 1G, which translated to 9.4 seconds with a 144-mph terminal speed for a standstill start in the quarter mile.

Ron Colson was the longest employed driver for Leong. Colson inherited the seat from mid-1976 until his retirement from driving at the end of the 1980 season. (Photo Courtesy Steve Reyes)

Ron Colson, Leong's longest-tenured driver, was back behind the wheel of Leong's rocket for his final year as an active driver. Colson, a native from Rockford, Illinois, and a 23-year veteran in auto racing, announced that he would retire at the conclusion of the 1980 season. He wanted to focus full-time on running and owning his consulting business, Track Planning Associates.

1980 Winternationals

Leong's new *King's Hawaiian Bread* Dodge Omni debuted at the 1980 Winternationals. Colson made a strong run at Pomona with a 6.15 ET at 239 mph to qualify 11th, and he advanced to the finals against Dale Pulde. Unfortunately for Colson, he was disqualified after crossing the centerline, handing the automatic win to Pulde's *War Eagle*.

Ron Colson leaps out from the water box on Parker Avenue in Roland Leong's new Dodge Omni Funny Car with King's Hawaiian Bread as the primary sponsor. (Photo Courtesy Roland Leong Collection)

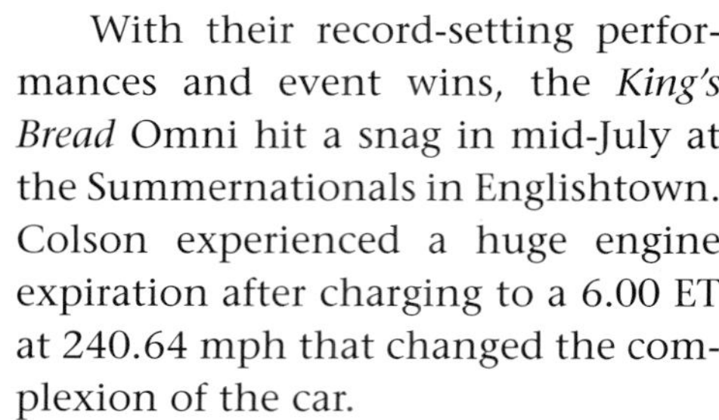

With their record-setting performances and event wins, the *King's Bread* Omni hit a snag in mid-July at the Summernationals in Englishtown. Colson experienced a huge engine expiration after charging to a 6.00 ET at 240.64 mph that changed the complexion of the car.

Without a spare body to complete the rigorous match-race schedule, Leong dispatched several of his crewmembers, including mechanic Mike Dunn. He sent them back to Los Angeles to pick up the leftover Avanti Antenna Corvette body and haul it back to Chicago.

Within the week, the Corvette was repainted by Hank Buk to sport new orange, gold, white, and black colors. The team finished the year running

Ron Colson scorches the Goodyears on a bright, sunny, cool winter day at the 1980 NHRA Winternationals at Pomona. The crowd in the grandstands roared its approval of Colson's expert long, smoky burnouts that carried him from his earlier days piloting the Revell Chi-Town Hustler.

Getting a handle on the surface at Pomona, Ron Colson transfers heat to the Goodyears prior to meeting Dale Pulde in the final at the 1980 Winternationals. It was an impressive debut for Leong, his new sponsors, and the King's Hawaiian Bread *Dodge Omni. (Photo Courtesy Steve Reyes)*

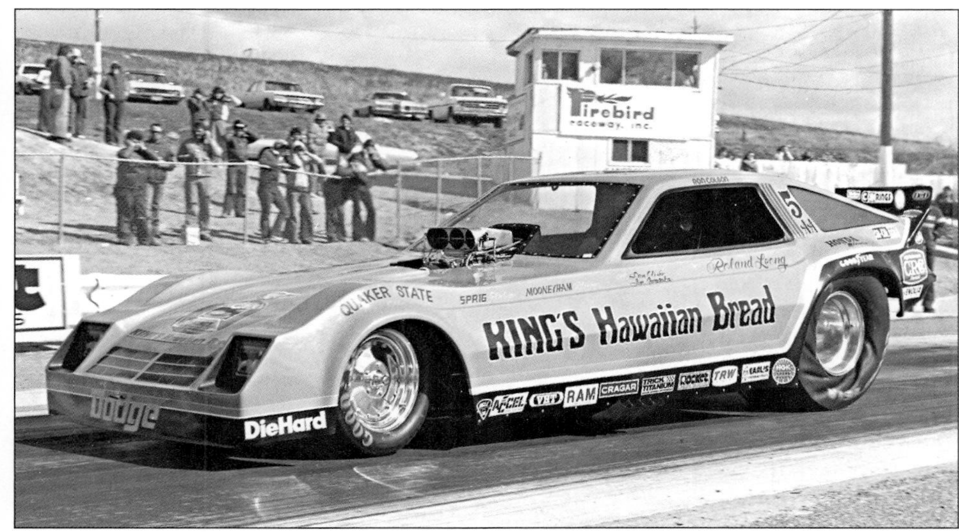

Ron Colson drove the King's Hawaiian Bread *Dodge Omni to the AA/Funny Car title for car owner Roland Leong at the 1980 Ignitor Nitro Opener at Firebird Raceway. (Courtesy Firebird Historical Photo Archives)*

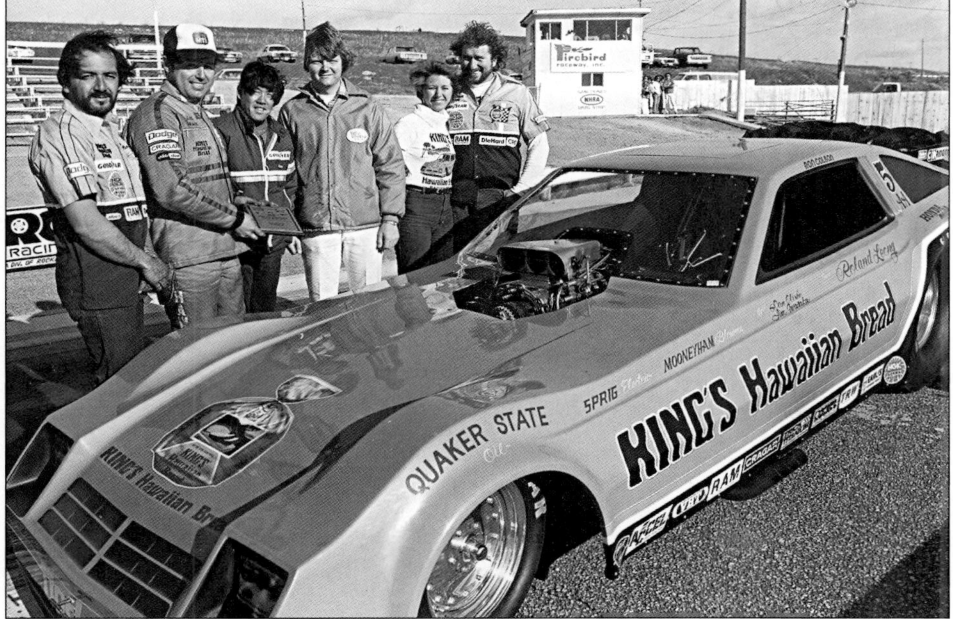

From left to right are chief wrench Danny Oliver, Ron Colson, Roland, Firebird's Scott New (the present-day General Manager of Firebird), and an unknown one-race volunteer crewman and his girlfriend after winning the 1980 Ignitor Nitro Opener at Firebird Raceway. Colson put away an elite field of funny cars on a cool, windy Sunday in April driving the King's Hawaiian Bread *Omni. In 1968, Firebird Raceway was founded by Bill New and his wife, Ellinor, and it is still owned and operated by the New family. (Courtesy Firebird Historical Photo Archives)*

After a massive engine explosion at Englishtown that completely destroyed the one and only Omni body that he had, Leong scrambled to keep his match-race and national-event obligations. He dispatched two crewmen from Chicago to Los Angeles to pick up the ex-Avanti Corvette body and hightail it back to the Windy City for paint and graphics. Back at Indy, Colson puts the Corvette through another round of rigorous qualifying sessions.

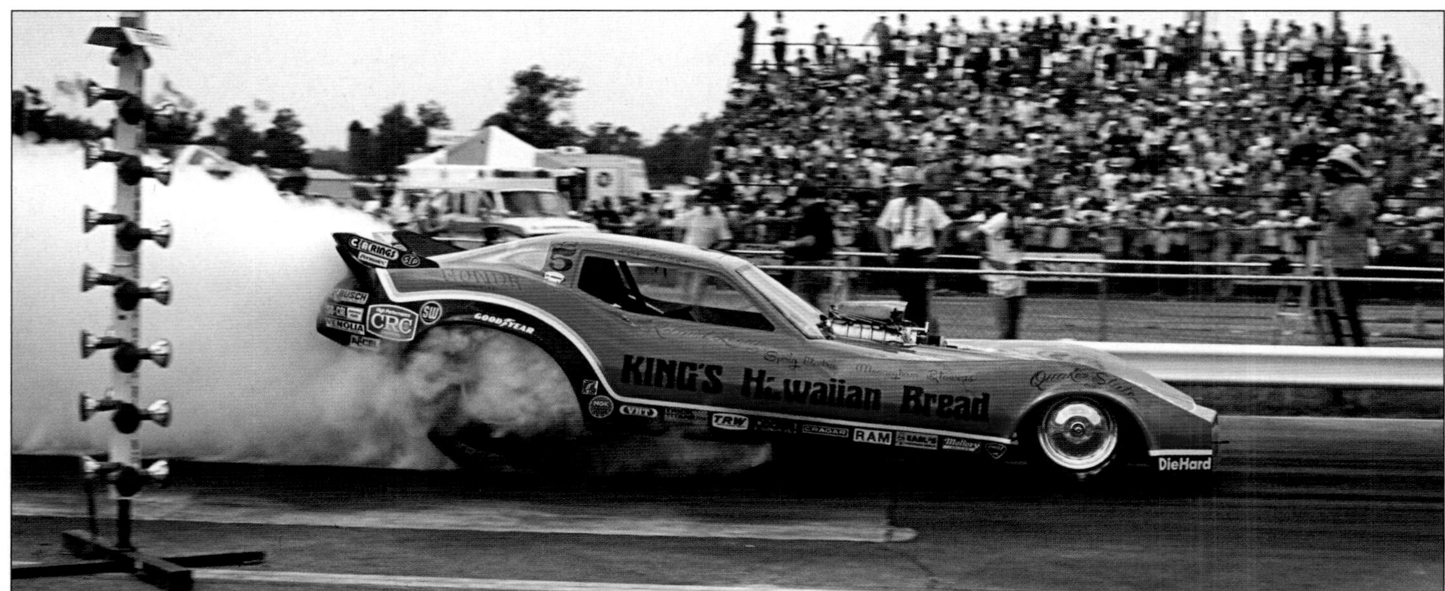

Ron Colson qualified the King's Hawaiian Bread *Corvette at Indy in the second position when he ran a 6.00 ET, behind Raymond Beadle's* Blue Max *at 5.98. The 16-car field was separated by only 0.141 second, making it the quickest in the history for Funny Cars at the Indy Nationals. A first-round disappointment set in for Colson when he lost to Leong's long-time friend and former driver Don Prudhomme. The* Hawaiian *could not produce the power, running an off-pace 7.07 ET.*

the Corvette. Colson and Leong clicked in winning the reputable NHRA Popular Hot-Rodding meet in Martin, Michigan, and later, the last NHRA World Finals at Ontario.

Phil Burgess, the *NHRA National Dragster* editor, sat down to interview Ron Colson regarding how the Dodge Omni body was destroyed at Englishtown.

"The windshield posts snapped in the lights (we didn't use side windows then), and the roof came down and pinned my hands to the steering wheel," Colson said. "Obviously, I couldn't see at all, but after years in a front-engine Fueler, I was used to that. I did get my right hand free, and I could get to the brake lever at about the middle, which translates to half braking leverage.

"Fortunately, as the lower half of the body was exploding (we gathered up 218 pieces, but not enough to put the puzzle back together), the chutes deployed from the disintegration. One tangled, and one, fortunately, opened. When the Safety Safari guys removed the roof off of me, I could see that I was within 100 feet of going off the end of the track."

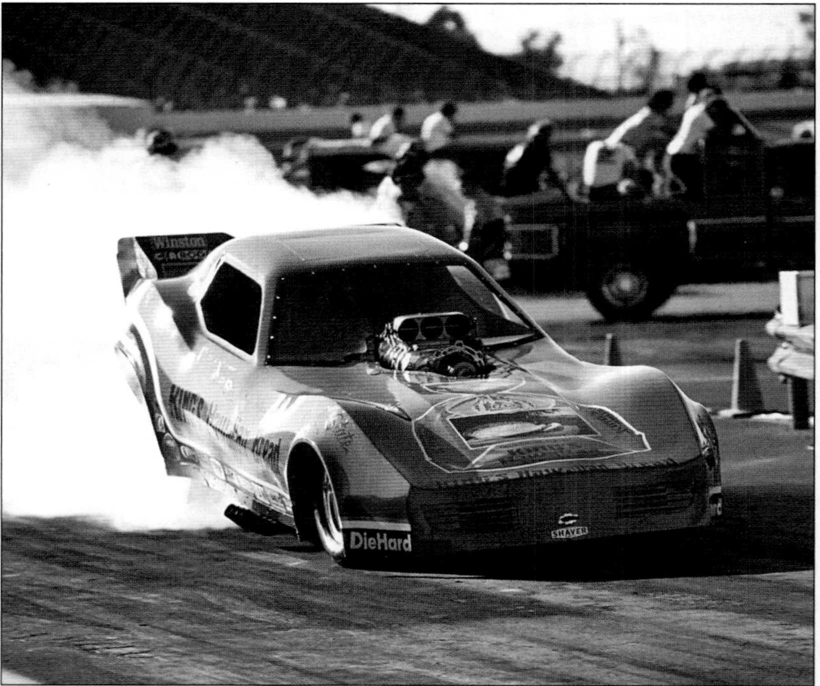

Ron Colson qualified the King's Hawaiian Bread *Corvette in the number-one overall position in the 16-car field at the NHRA Supernationals. Prior to the event, Colson announced his retirement from active driving to concentrate full time on his business. (Photo Courtesy Bob McClurg)*

Colson Exits by Winning in Style

Roland Leong and Ron Colson enjoyed their last weekend together at the 1980 NHRA Supernationals at Ontario Motor Speedway. Colson dimmed the lights at OMS, relishing the moment in one of the last AA/Funny Cars to run down the 1320 at the superspeedway, as the facility was slated for demolition in the early months of 1981.

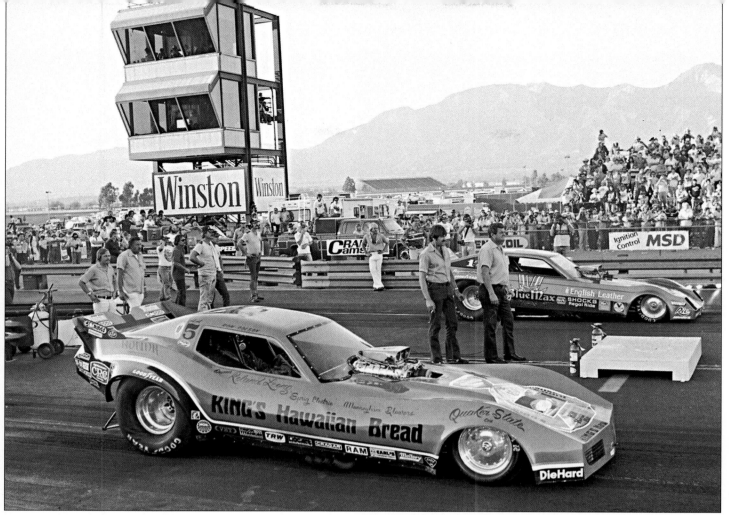

It was the end of an era for both driver Ron Colson and the Ontario Motor Speedway during this final-round pairing of AA/Funny Cars. Colson began his day on the pole only to finish his day in the winner's circle. Round victories came against Dale Armstrong, Kenny Bernstein, Roy Harris, and Raymond Beadle. (Photo Courtesy Steve Reyes)

In another move, Colson officially retired from his illustrious driving career and the sport that he really loved. In what could have been a well-scripted Hollywood movie, Colson closed his distinguished career in high style when he defeated world champion Raymond Beadle. Beadle's *Blue Max* Arrow got out of shape, nearly crossing the centerline in the final round.

Leong's *King's Hawaiian Bread* Corvette began the day from the number-one qualifying spot and took strides to the winner's circle. Colson had victories against Dale Armstrong, Kenny Bernstein, Roy Harris, and finally, Beadle. The victory sealed a career-best third-place finish in points for the year.

1981: Dunn Drives the *Hawaiian* to New Career Records

Mike Dunn, who had been working for Leong since 1977, was now his full-time driver for the 1981 campaign. Dunn began piloting the *King's Hawaiian Bread* Dodge after Ron Colson retired at the end of 1980.

With Dunn, the *Hawaiian* set several strip records throughout the country. It also won its share of trophies and gold, including the NHRA Popular Hot Rodding Meet in Martin, Michigan. Dunn recorded a career-best ET of 5.85 at 245 mph at OCIR for a Funny Car. Just a week later at Sacramento, Dunn lowered the mark with a 5.84 ET.

In 1981, Mike Dunn was now the full-time driver for the *King's Hawaiian Bread* Dodge.

MEMORABLE MOMENTS:

Mike Dunn

"I was told recently by Roland's daughter, Landa, that I had worked for Roland longer than just about anybody, which was just over seven years," driver and mechanic Mike Dunn said. "I started as a crewmember in June of 1977 on the Power Gloss Monza for Roland, which came about after I had a falling out with my dad.

"I had gotten my Funny Car license in my dad's car in April that year. Bill Doner, a promoter who ran events at OCIR and Seattle International Raceway, among others, told my dad that he would throw in some extra money if I drove at his events. The deal was to drive my dad's car for a whole season and then go out and get my own ride. He felt that I was a good enough driver, and if I drove for the full season, I could go out and get a ride in 1978.

"But after one race, he changed his mind. My dad told me his dad didn't give him a race car, so I needed to go out and get my own deal, which made me pretty mad.

"I was working for Henry Velasco at his Crankshaft shop. Henry was my dad's old partner back in the Altered days. I put the word out that I was looking for a position on a touring team, and Roland was the first to reach out to me.

"Two weeks later, I was on a plane to Chicago to start working for Roland as a mechanic, and I ended up doing that for three seasons.

"I learned a lot from working with my dad for years, but my dad didn't have the patience that Roland had. Roland was more trusting and willing to throw me into the fire with regard to working on the car, and I learned a lot more.

"One of the reasons I stayed with Roland was because during one of our initial conversations he said, 'You're the backup driver if Colson can't make it. You're in there.'

"There was a situation in 1978 or 1979 when we were on the Western Swing and Colson was having trouble getting a flight out from Chicago. Instead of me, Roland decided to put Gordie Bonin in as a standby, but in the end, Ron was able to make the race. I told Roland that was kind of BS and mentioned that it was just a hook to have me work on the car for next to nothing.

"We laugh about it now because I even turned down a job with Billy Meyer, who offered me a decent amount more money (more than Roland was paying me), but I stuck around because I thought I was the backup driver.

"In 1980, Roland actually helped get me the ride in Bill Schifsky's *Bear Town Shaker* by recommending me. He wanted me to get experience driving a car, as Ron Colson was ready to retire soon, and he wanted me to possibly be the next driver.

"Bill didn't have the budget to run national events, but it was a very good match-race car. I got to learn how to drive on the slick, lousy tracks and do long, smoky burnouts. It was a really good experience."

Mike Dunn advanced to the second round at the Gatornationals, where he met Tom Ridings, who was driving for Joe Pisano. (Photo Courtesy Steve Reyes)

Touring throughout the summer, Leong and Dunn won their share of match racing with the *Hawaiian* at the top strips and at the smaller, back-country venues.

One of his best showings was at the Popular Hot Rodding Nationals at U.S. 131 in Martin, Michigan. Dunn won his first national event at Fremont at the inaugural Golden Gate Nationals. This was Dunn's best showing driving any of Leong's cars.

"After the Golden Gate Nationals, it seemed like everything after that was a complete disaster," Dunn said.

Cameo by Colson at Sacramento

In mid-1982, Leong booked the *King's Hawaiian Bread* Dodge in a rare pair of back-to-back weekend match races at OCIR and the following weekend at Sacramento. Unfortunately for Dunn, he received a concussion in a crash at OCIR that kept him from driving the next weekend at Sacramento. Ron Colson was lured out of retirement by Leong for the race. Colson blew away his competitor Jim Dunn in the first round, driving the backup *Hawaiian* to a 6.18 ET at 233.17 mph.

Colson was more than a match in his next round, breezing past a smoking Mike Van Sant in the *Invader* with a 6.21 ET at 227.85 mph to Van Sant's 10.46 at 101.47. Showing no signs of rust, Colson saved his best run for the finals with a return encounter against Jim Dunn, the La Mirada fireman. Dunn's valiant effort of 6.30 at 221.89 mph couldn't overcome the *Hawaiian*'s overpowering 6.15 ET at 233.17 mph, as Colson reset both ends of Sacramento Raceway Park's time and speed records.

Leong backs up his driver, Mike Dunn, into the tracks made by the King's Hawaiian Bread Omni AAFC at Martin, Michigan. Dunn, a longtime crewman for Leong, earned the assignment behind the wheel when Ron Colson retired from driving. (Photo Courtesy Steve Reyes)

Tom McEwen congratulates Leong on the Hawaiian's record-breaking performances and win during the Popular Hot Rodding Nationals at U.S. 131 Dragway. (Photo Courtesy Roland Leong Collection)

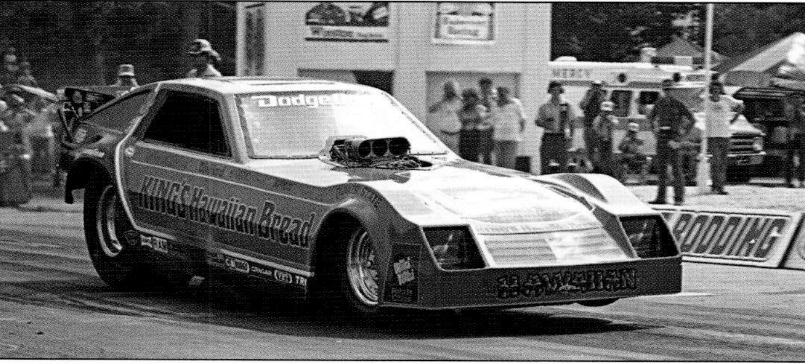

Mike Dunn carries the front wheels off the line at the 1981 Popular Hot Rodding Nationals at U.S. 131 Dragway in Martin, Michigan. U.S. 131 was one of Dunn's favorite venues to race.

Mike Dunn made track history by being the first driver at U.S. 131 in Martin, Michigan, ever to record a 5-second pass. This took place at the 1981 Popular Hot Rodding Nationals, as Dunn drove Leong's King's Hawaiian Bread entry. The run also put Leong's Dodge back into the winner's circle.

MEMORABLE MOMENTS:

Mike Dunn

"Right after Indy in 1980, Roland picked me up in Des Moines, Iowa, after I rode a Greyhound bus from Sioux Falls, South Dakota, where I drove the *Bear Town Shaker* in a match race," Mike Dunn said. "We headed back home to California for three more races: one at Orange County, the second at Ontario (the World Finals which Colson drove and won), and the other at Sacramento.

"I remember the first race at OCIR, where we went out with 10 or 12 cars. Each made two runs, and the quickest two cars came back for the finals to run against each other. We ended up being the quickest along with my dad as the next quickest car. I was nervous racing against my dad.

"Roland told me at the beginning of the day, 'If the car goes into a wheel-stand, pull the shifter into high gear, and the front end will come down.'

"It picked up the front end about 200 feet out, and I pulled it into high gear and went on to win the race, running 6.10 for low ET and the win. That was the highlight of my year and helped me become the full-time driver of the *King's Hawaiian Bread* Funny Car in 1981."

CHAPTER 12

HEY, HOW 'BOUT A NICE HAWAIIAN PUNCH?

Roland Leong was a businessman on the move. He wore two hats: one as a business executive of his brand and one with roots of a racer. He carried a briefcase and talked on the telephone endlessly. He jetted around the country meeting with corporate CEOs, officers, lawyers, and accountants. At first glance, anyone would conclude he was a high-pressure businessman on his way to the top of a corporate ladder. At the age of 40, Leong was the driving force, manager, and corporate officer of his own professional racing team in the United States.

However, 1982 was a rough year for Leong and Dunn. First, the *Hawaiian* started the year racing without a major sponsorship. While they were out on tour, Dunn encountered a serious tire shake at a strip in the Northeast that completely knocked him out cold, which resulted in a crash. Afterward, Dunn added extra padding to the roll cage and lowered it down closer to his head to help control the bouncing around in the cockpit. No matter how bad things were looking, it was all about to change.

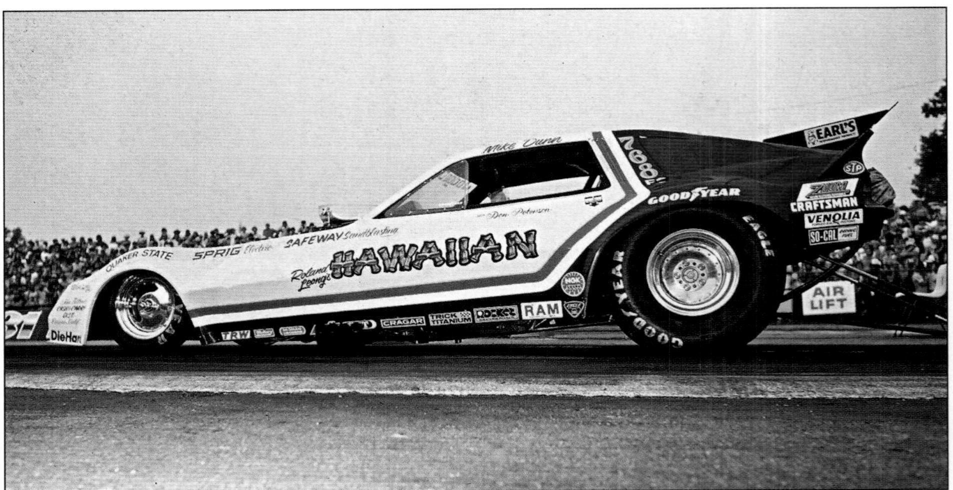

This ground-level view shows the aerodynamic lines and color scheme on the 1982 Hawaiian *Dodge Charger that Leong campaigned without having major sponsorship. Leong and driver Mike Dunn made a lot of noise and money on the match-race circuit. (Photo Courtesy Steve Reyes)*

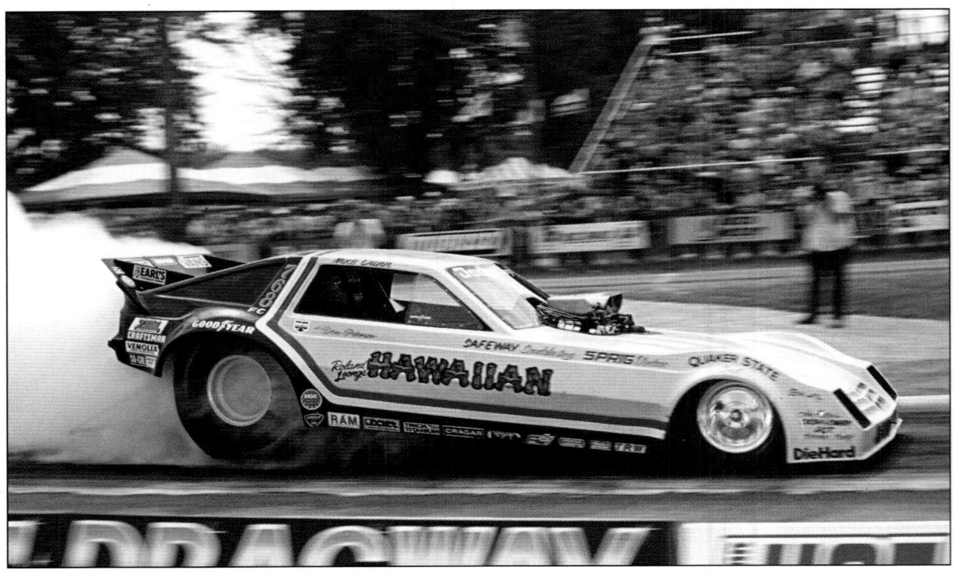

Mike Dunn was a tough competitor and was known as being one of the top runners at the 1982 Popular Hot Rodding Nationals at U.S. 131 in Martin, Michigan. (Photo Courtesy Steve Reyes)

Leong Lands a Big Punch

Leong's aggressive awareness landed him a deal with one of largest non-automotive sponsorships: the Del Monte Corporation. He inked a lucrative one-year deal with the food magnate.

In January 1983, OCIR announced Leong's new association with Del Monte and Hawaiian Punch's juicy fruit drink during a press release before the Winternationals at Pomona. In the press cover photo, Mike Dunn launches the Hawaiian Punch Charger down the OCIR track. (Press Kit Photo Courtesy Roland Leong Collection)

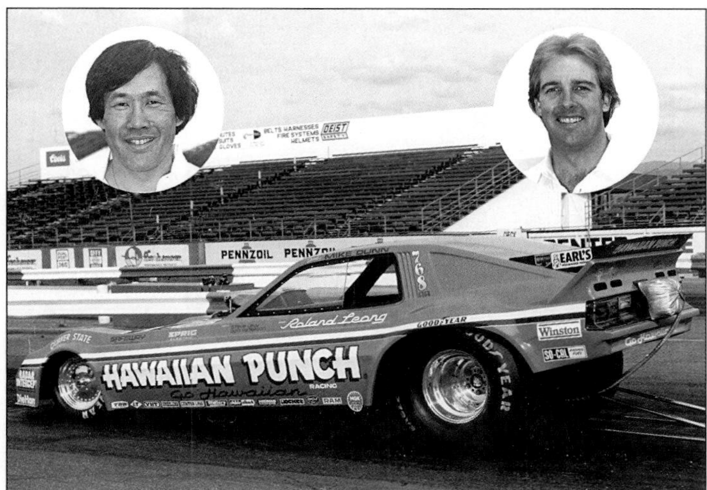

Car owner, crew chief, and super tuner Roland Leong and driver-mechanic Mike Dunn make up half of the team of the Hawaiian Punch Charger. Crewmen Steve Levy and Don Peterson (both not pictured) filled out the rest of the roster for the new "super team" of Leong. (Photo Courtesy Roland Leong Collection)

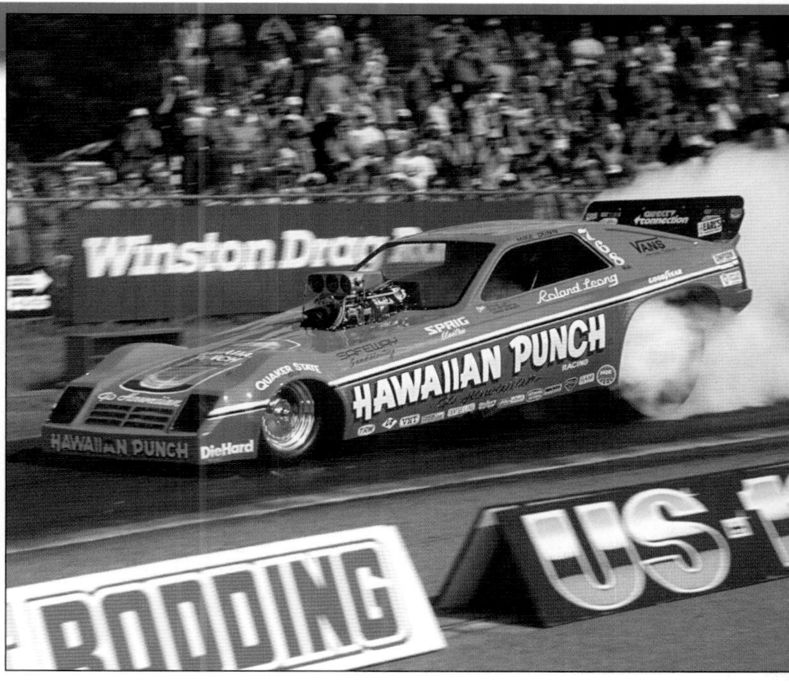

Mike Dunn transferred the Roland Leong/Keith Black power down onto the asphalt at U.S. 131 in Martin, Michigan, during the Popular Hot Rodding Nationals.(Photo Courtesy Steve Reyes)

Leong's 1983 press kit offered detailed team information on support team vehicles, car specifications, and performance predictions.

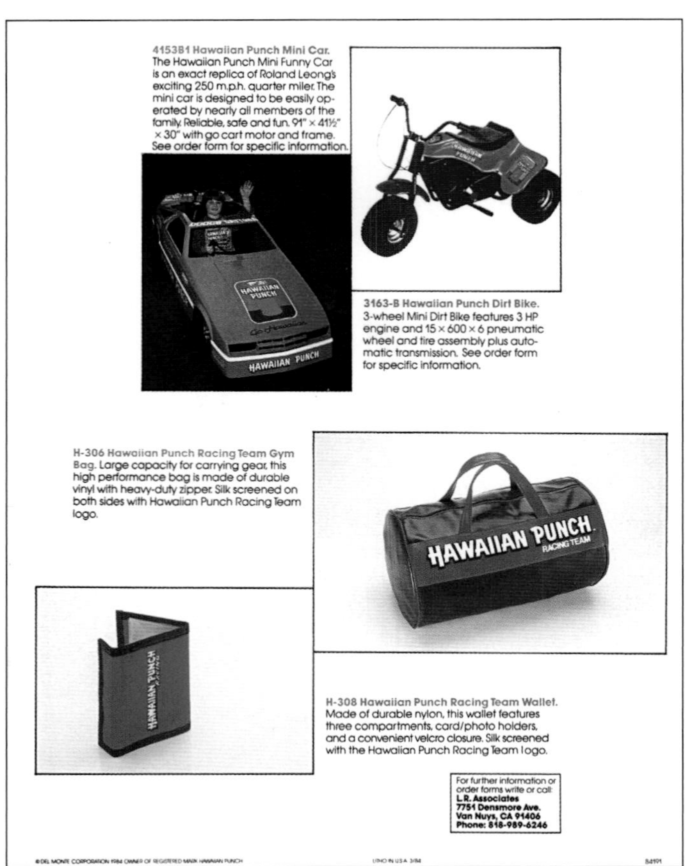

The Del Monte Corporation offered a catalog of promotional apparel and recreational vehicles, including a three-wheeler and mini* Hawaiian Punch *car. (Press and Advertising Materials Courtesy Roland Leong Collection)

It was a perfect merger for both Leong and Del Monte, as Leong pitched and negotiated with the makers of the Hawaiian Punch fruit-based brand drink for a one-year contract. His budget for the operation entailed a fuel-burning, tire-smoking, 2,500-hp Dodge Charger Funny Car; an 80-foot trailer that cost more than $200,000; a supply of spare parts; and a few spare Keith Black Hemi engines.

With big business now being an integral part of professional drag racing, Leong was aware of the responsibilities to his sponsors. He called on his years of racing experience to keep the *Hawaiian Punch* car brand aware. When you're at the top, the exposure for the sponsor needs to be at its highest level. It's a tough team assignment, but Leong had been down the road of toughness and had paid his dues over the years.

1983: A Forgettable Year

Mike Dunn and Roland Leong began 1983 on a promising note when they nabbed top honors at the March Meet at Bakersfield. Soon after that, things went downhill quickly.

Springnationals

At the 19th-annual Springnationals in Columbus, Ohio, the *Hawaiian Punch* Dodge was a total loss. Dunn stopped the clock with a 6.37 ET, but the engine detonated, turning the car into a rolling inferno. The right rear tire exploded, breaking the body in half. The car ended up snared into the aircraft-style catch net (a safety device made of nylon). Dunn was unharmed after he released his safety harness and ran from the burning wreck.

When Dunn was asked if this was the worst crash he'd been involved in, he quoted with a laugh, "Well, it wasn't that bad. The net definitely played a part in what could had been a sad situation. The throttle hung wide open, I reached for the fuel cutoff, and it backfired and blew up. Everything just went wrong on what could go wrong."

The most amazing feat that resulted from the crash was that Leong was able to keep his bookings for the following weeks. Leong purchased Steven Chrisman's Alcohol Funny Car two days after the fire and crash. The car was immediately refitted to accept Leong's nitro-burning setup with the help of many of his friends on the West Coast. The paint on the Dodge Charger was likely still wet when Leong loaded up the car and headed to Martin, Michigan.

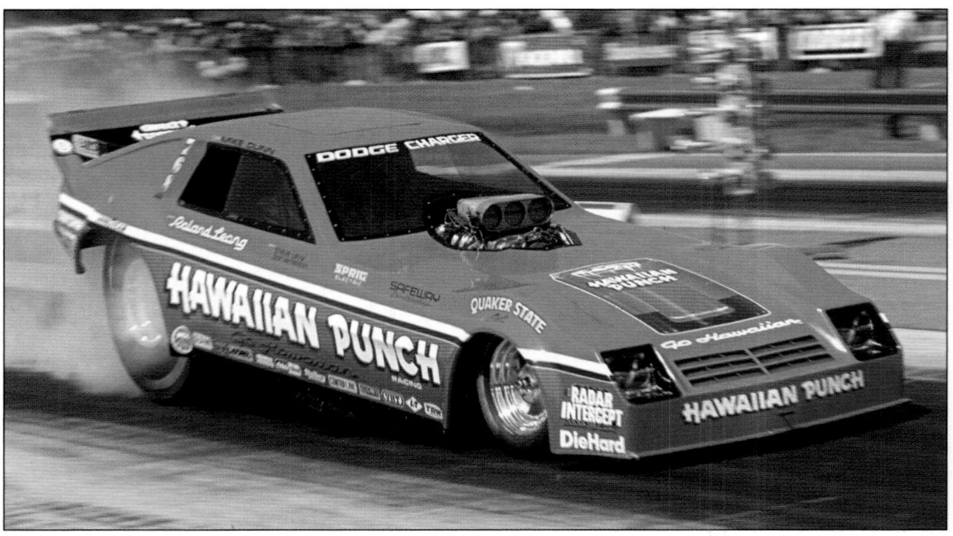

At the Springnationals in Columbus, Ohio, Mike Dunn posted a 6.37 ET when the engine detonated in the lights. The car was completely engulfed in fire, which caused the right rear slick to explode, destroying the body. The speedy 200-mph fireball wound up in the catch net. (Photo Courtesy Steve Reyes)

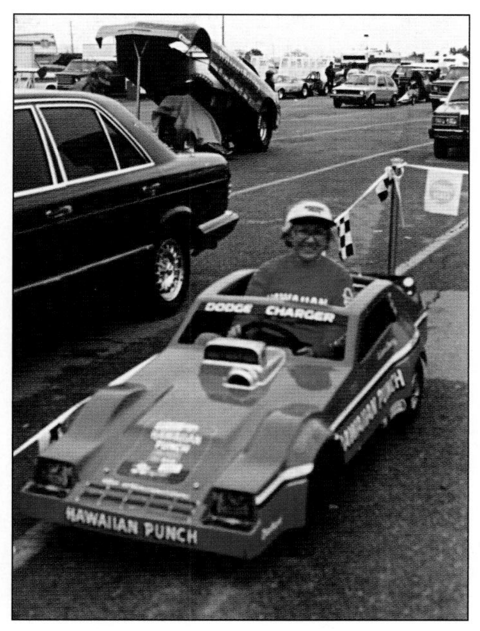

Teddy Leong takes a spin around the pits in a mini Hawaiian Punch *replica Funny Car. Hawaiian Punch offered racing fans and spectators several versions of the brightly colored red and blue car throughout the years of sponsoring Leong. The mini cars were available for purchase or as a raffle giveaway at strip and store appearances. (Photo Courtesy Roland Leong Collection)*

NorthStar Nationals

A few months later, at the NorthStar Nationals in Brainerd, Minnesota, Mike Dunn experienced another fire at half-track during the Thursday-afternoon qualifying session. This time, he got the fire out after 2 seconds of discomfort. The car was repaired and qualified later with a 6.04 ET at 240 mph.

From 1982 to 1983, Leong lost a total of three $50,000 Funny Cars in fiery crashes. Thanks to the drag racing safety standards, Mike Dunn wasn't hurt seriously in any of the crashes. Leong's outlook remained positive through it all.

"Mike Dunn has been a very consistent driver," Leong said. "All we have to do is find another tenth of a second in the car, and we'll be okay and back into the winner's circle."

Final Days of OCIR

Dunn experienced one of the most violent engine explosions in the history of Funny Cars at the NHRA World Finals at OCIR. Dunn entered the top-end lights well above 240 mph when the crankshaft broke in a violent engine explosion and exited the engine.

Instantly, the body turned into a jigsaw puzzle, exploding into hundreds of pieces. Hot oil covered Dunn's goggles, hindering his vision and causing him to crash hard into the guardrail. The impact launched the engine out of what was remaining of the car. Dunn continued to bounce down the strip, and then he barrel-rolled several times before coming to a complete stop. Dunn was out cold and didn't remember anything about the crash.

"Plain and simple, we just didn't have any luck," Dunn said. "Nothing went right. I was known for being upside down and on fire a lot!"

It was unfortunate timing for Leong. In two weeks, OCIR permanently closed with the Last Drag Race, which was presented by Hawaiian Punch. The fabled facility opened in August 1967 and closed on October 29, 1983, which was nearly 28 years. Formerly billed as the "Super Track," the closure brought the end of an era, as it was the last weekly, fully operating dragstrip in Southern California.

Leong scrambled to make the repairs for the Last Drag Race. He sent the damaged chassis over to Steve Plugger, who re-fronted half of the chassis. Leong borrowed a Ford EXP body from Billy Meyer and had the body sprayed in the Hawaiian Punch colors. They painted "DODGE" across the top of the windshield, and many didn't realize that it wasn't a Charger.

Mike Dunn remarkably qualified fifth into the show with a 6.05 ET. This was the first time in his stellar career that Leong was running a Ford-bodied race car.

Unlike the riotous closure of Lions Drag Strip 11 years earlier, the Last Race ran well past midnight into Sunday morning. Roughly 200 tired, die-hard fans were still hanging around, occupying the nearly empty stands.

Leong recounted racing at OCIR.

"I was there for the first race, and I was also there for its last race," he said. "We won many races there with both the dragsters and Funny Cars. There were a lot of memories and good times there!"

Even without a major win for the year, Hawaiian Punch sales were up more than 30 percent, according to Frank R. Cheli, marketing director for Hawaiian Punch beverages. "Obviously, we can't directly link sales with drag racing, but with the exposure of roughly 600,000 annually at the drag strip, along with the addition of network television, the promotion certainly hasn't hurt."

MEMORABLE MOMENTS:

Mike Dunn

"1982 and 1983 were bad years running the *Hawaiian*," Mike Dunn said. "I got knocked out when I went off the end of the track, hit a bunch of parked cars, ended up tangled up into the catch net at Columbus, and the debacle at OCIR. We just didn't have any luck. Nothing went right."

In 1983, Mike Dunn experienced one of the worst engine explosions and crashes in the Funny Car category that year. It unfolded in the Hawaiian *Dodge during the NHRA World Finals at OCIR. The engine detonated like a bomb when the crankshaft split into two pieces and exited out the bottom of the engine, crumpling the oil pan just as Dunn entered the finish lights. A split second later, the body disintegrated into fragments. The explosion sent Dunn into the guardrail, sheared off the engine mounts from the chassis, and launched the engine over the front end of the car onto the strip surface.*

The once-mighty 2,800-hp aluminum Black Elephant engine in the Hawaiian Punch *Dodge was reduced to scrap after an explosion. (Photo Courtesy Don Gillespie Collection)*

The fans at OCIR got a close-up view of the mangled remains of the Hawaiian *when the car hit the guardrail, launching the engine out of the frame. Astonishingly, driver Mike Dunn walked away after being knocked out briefly. He also suffered a sprained finger and a ringing headache from the devastating crash. (Photo Courtesy Roland Leong Collection)*

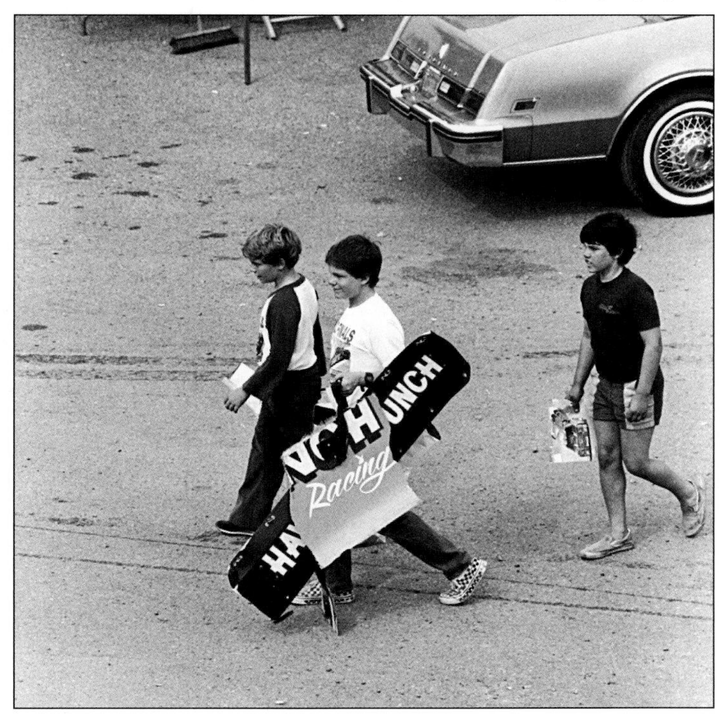

This band of three happy souvenir hunters carted home some treasure from the Hawaiian Punch *Dodge explosion. The chassis went through extensive repairs and returned back to OCIR two weeks later for the Hawaiian Punch's Last Drag Race event at OCIR. (Photo Courtesy Don Gillespie Collection)*

1984: The Breakout Year for Hawaiian Punch

Early-season performances indicated that 1984 would be a lot rosier for the *Hawaiian Punch* car. The team debuted a brand-new Dodge Charger Daytona at the NHRA Winternationals, where it qualified quickly with a 5.98 ET at 242.58 mph. Subsequent match races in Northern California resulted with ETs moving into the 5.80s. A week later, in Gainesville, Florida, Dunn dropped the times down into the 5.70 range on the ultra-quick Gatornationals strip.

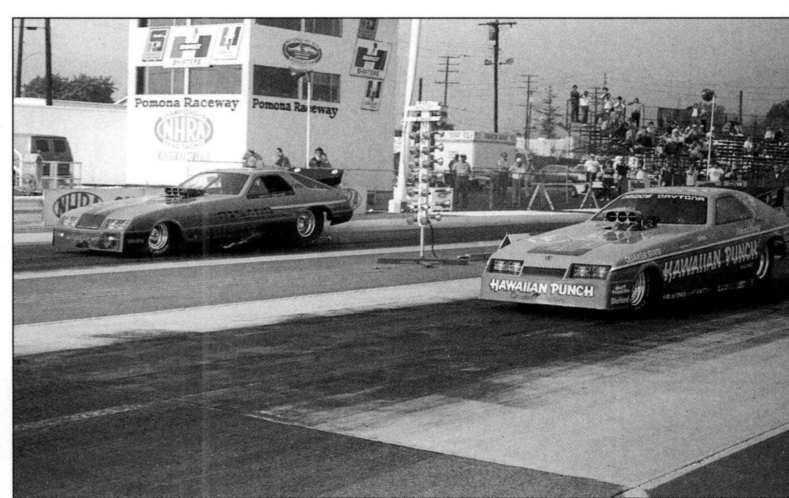

Mike Dunn squared up with Leong's former Hawaiian *Funny Car driver Denny Savage, who was behind the wheel of Joe Pisano's flopper at the NHRA Winternationals. (Photo Courtesy Tony Thacker/TorqTalk.com)*

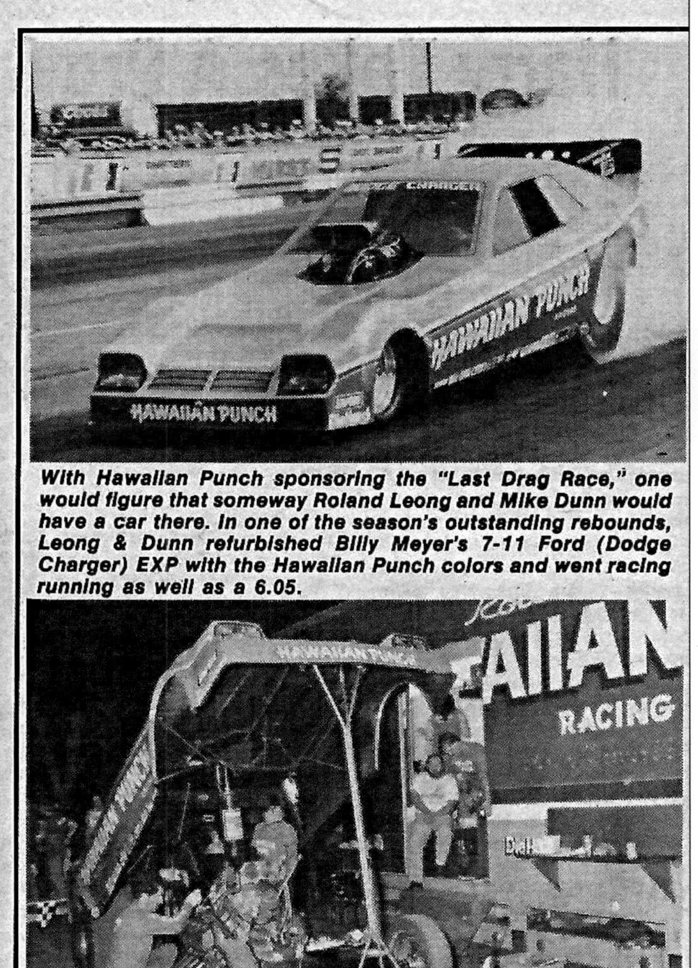

With Hawaiian Punch sponsoring the "Last Drag Race," one would figure that someway Roland Leong and Mike Dunn would have a car there. In one of the season's outstanding rebounds, Leong & Dunn refurbished Billy Meyer's 7-11 Ford (Dodge Charger) EXP with the Hawaiian Punch colors and went racing running as well as a 6.05.

These photos and the caption from National Dragster *highlight the Last Drag Race with Leong's Hawaiian Punch entry. It was fitted with a borrowed Ford EXP body from Billy Meyer. The "Charger" pulled it off so well that many fans overlooked the transformation. The quickly revamped car ran a best 6.05 ET! (Image Courtesy* NHRA National Dragster*)*

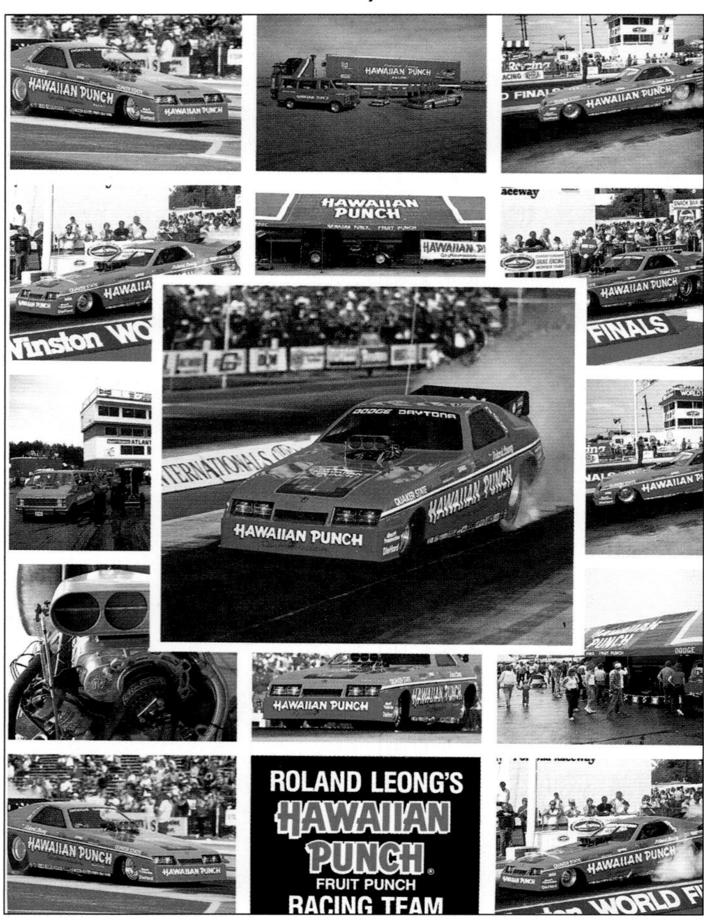

The 1984 Hawaiian Punch Racing Team's press kit shows the new* Hawaiian Punch *Dodge Daytona. (Photo Courtesy Roland Leong Collection)

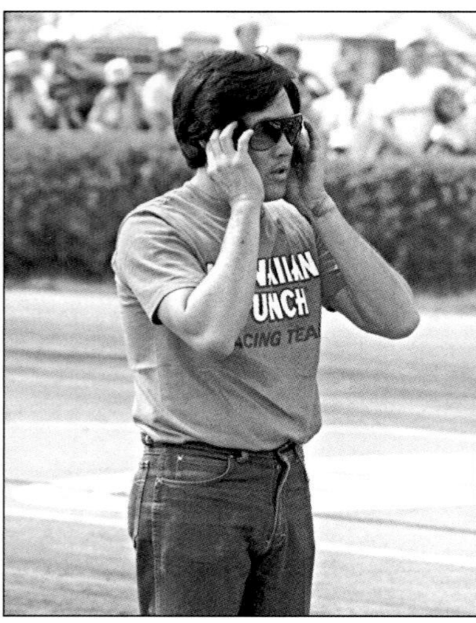

At the U.S. Nationals in Indianapolis, Leong keeps a sharp eye on Mike Dunn as he blasts down the quarter-mile on another 260-mph run. (Photo Courtesy Steve Reyes)

Manufacturer's Meet

The 14th-annual Manufacturer's Meet at Byron Dragway went to Billy Meyer driving his Pontiac Trans Am over Mike Dunn in Roland Leong's *Hawaiian Punch* Dodge Charger. With rain falling on and off during the event, the finals took place under a dark, threatening sky with a heavy mist falling on the track.

All parties agreed to run, as other race dates in the future would prevent a race on some other date. The final was less spectacular, as it resulted in a slip-n-slide affair. Both cars spun the tires and skated around. Meyers crossed the finish line first, running a 17.70 ET to an 18.27. Not only did Dunn take second place but he also reset the track record for top speed, hitting 241.28 mph.

Popular Hot Rodding Championships

The 15th-annual Popular Hot Rodding Championships at U.S. 131 Dragway in Martin, Michigan, was an NHRA's Pro Bonus Points Event presented by Winston.

Dunn put the *Hawaiian Punch* entry into the field with a 6.075 ET at 245.23 mph. The red and blue machine of Leong powered its way to the semifinals. Dunn kicked off the semifinals by getting out ahead of Tom Hoover, but Dunn broke at mid-track, handing the win to the *Showtime* Corvette's 6.11 ET at 233.16 mph to the coasting Charger's 8.37 at 90.45.

Injury Knocks Dunn Out of the Hawaiian

Both Roland Leong and Mike Dunn survived several calamities together, from the trip into the catch net at Columbus to Dunn's infamous barrel-roll at the World Finals at OCIR. Later in the year, at a match race on August 4 in Kansas City, Missouri, Dunn was seriously

If there was an award for who had the most popular pit area at the old St. Louis Dragstrip, it would go to Roland Leong. The* Hawaiian Punch *Funny Car was accented with 11 bikini-clad contest beauties surrounding the car. According to driver-mechanic Mike Dunn, he doesn't remember who won the race, but he remembered that it was difficult for the crew to concentrate while working between rounds. (Photo Courtesy Roland Leong Collection)

Rick Johnson, known for his fast reaction times at the line, was hired by Leong to fill the vacancy left by Mike Dunn after the Kansas City incident. Johnson had worked for Gene Snow, Bill Schifsky, and Fred Castronovo. In addition, Johnson drove "TV" Tommy Ivo's four-engine Buick exhibition car at one time. (Photo Courtesy Roland Leong Collection)

injured when the car's rear end broke. The coupler shattered and pierced his left leg and broke the bone. Ironically, his opponent, Jim White, never left the line due to engine gremlins of his own. Dunn would have won the round and advanced had he not been at the hospital. The injury left Dunn unable to drive, so Leong hired 32-year-old Rick Johnson to finish out the year.

Two Dunns Are Better Than One

When strip promoters, team public relations agencies, and owners arranged bookings months ahead for their big money-making schedules in the summer months, many strips demanded the popular Funny Cars that not only drew in the spectators but also made large payouts. Owners had to choose which venue to race at, as it was impossible to be in two places on the same day. More often, some dates were double-booked.

On one occasion, Leong had two conflicting bookings in two different states on the same weekend. Mike Dunn was committed to match racing at two strips in the East region, while out in the Northwest at Seattle International Raceway (SIR), the NHRA held its four-day Rainier Brewery/KISW-FM 100–sponsored U.S. Funny Car Championships. Up for grabs at Seattle was a share of the $125,000 purse and valuable NHRA Winston points. The big guns who entered were John Force, Tom "the Mongoose" McEwen, John Lombardo, and Roland Leong.

With driver Mike Dunn fulfilling the match-race commitment, "Big" Jim Dunn filled in for his son. He borrowed a *Hawaiian Punch* Dodge Daytona body from Leong and mounted it on Dunn's *Fireman's Quickie* Funny Car chassis. Dunn, who had enjoyed success at SIR in past years, posted two runner-up finishes at the NHRA Fallnationals between 1977 and 1979. Leong and Jim Dunn ran a few more races together in the Northwest under the red and blue Punch banner.

"I'm looking forward to the SIR race and the chance to drive the *Hawaiian Punch Express* Dodge Daytona for Roland Leong," Jim Dunn said. "While Mike is racing back East, I'll be representing the Hawaiian Punch team here in the Northwest."

1985: The Bernstein Rule

Rick Johnson began the year being retained by Leong with high hopes of returning the *Hawaiian* back to consistency. Nine days before the NHRA Winternationals, Kenny Bernstein and Ray Alley met with NHRA officials to debate the legality of Bernstein's brand-new Ford Tempo *Budweiser King* AA/FC. The super-slippery body had a twist: it was possibly the most radical departure from the previously approved bodies ever seen for Funny Cars. The new body measured 40 inches in the front and 56 inches in the rear and had a much lower blower "bubble."

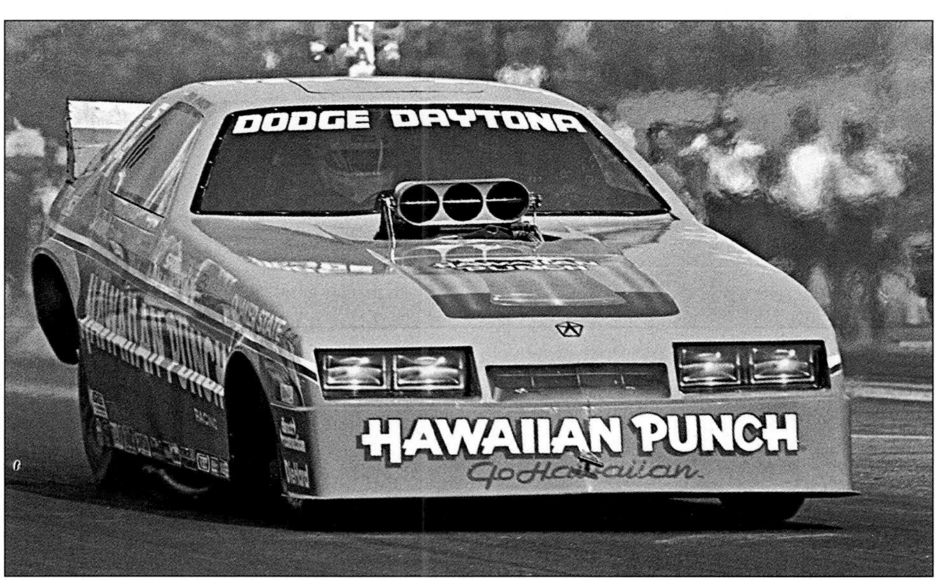

Rick Johnson competes in the first round of qualifying at the 1985 Winternationals. With the Bernstein Rule now approved by the NHRA technical officials, every Funny Car team at the L.A. County Fairgrounds immediately went to work modifying for the allowed aerodynamic body updates, attempting to level the playing field even with Bernstein's Budweiser Tempo. (Photo Courtesy Tony Thacker Photography/TorqTalk.com)

When the new Tempo rolled out of the trailer on Thursday, fellow fuel racers were shocked and could not believe that the swoopy Tempo even passed tech inspection. None of the other Funny Car entrants were informed of the rule changes until a published copy of the January 25, 1985, issue of the NHRA's *National Dragster* magazine displayed diagrams with the new rulings. Bernstein's first run on the Tempo netted an unreal 5.66 ET at 259 mph.

Immediately, all of the Funny Car teams were able to compensate for the changes. This forced Leong to tack on a new "beam breaker" nose protrusion that gained 10 extra inches of the front end, which was allowed by the new rules.

The Hawaiian *Stuns the Drag Racing World*

Rick Johnson made history at the 1985 NHRA Winternationals driving the *Hawaiian Punch* Dodge Daytona. Johnson and Leong shocked the Funny Car community, unloading a 5.66 ET at 259.81 mph and following it up with a quicker charge of 5.588 at 263.62. This was by far the quickest and fastest that a fuel Funny Car had ever run!

The hopes for another Winternationals Eliminator title ended in the semifinal round when clutch problems took the *Hawaiian* out of contention. However, notice was served on their competitors.

ADRA Winter Nationals

Fresh off a 5.58 ET at 263 mph in Pomona, Johnson gave Leong his first win of 1985 at the inaugural ADRA Winternationals at Gerald John's Tucson Dragway in Arizona. The *Hawaiian Punch* Dodge ran a steady stream of 6.10s throughout eliminations to win the first ADRA national-event AA/FC title.

Johnson narrowly defeated a slowing Paul Smith, who burnt a few pistons before the lights in the *Capt. Crazy* Tempo, running a 6.14 ET at 238.72 mph to Smith's 6.16 at 224 mph. The race was too close to call, as Johnson actually congratulated Smith for what he thought was the win.

Striking Molson Gold

Qualified in the sixth position with a 5.76 ET, Rick Johnson overcame a hole-shot to score his first major NHRA win at the wheel of the *Hawaiian Punch* car. He defeated Kenny Bernstein with a 5.72 ET at 260 mph to 5.79 in the finals at the 15th-annual NHRA Molson Grandnationals at Montreal, Canada.

Johnson was more than ready to deal with Bernstein for the final when he came blasting out of the chutes, clocking an unreal 5.72 ET at 260.26 mph (setting a new top speed track record and Canada's first Funny Car 260 mph), eclipsing Bernstein's 5.79 at 250.13.

Johnson was interviewed from the winner's circle on driving for his tuner and owner.

"Roland is a professional in every sense of the word," he said. "His cars are always first rate. It is easy for a driver to do his best in a car that he can have complete confidence in."

Understanding Body Language

Leong was one of the growing number of drag racers to use the advanced technology of wind-tunnel testing. The information learned in the tests aided the Funny Cars in reaching higher speeds as well as improving stability at those speeds.

Leong had known that Funny Cars had the horsepower to run the big numbers and low ETs, but the issue was pushing the car through turbulence over 250 mph. So, he took a page from the textbook used by both Formula One and Indy car builders on aerodynamics and applied them to his new 1985 Dodge Daytona body shell. He brought the car to test in the wind-tunnel facility of Lockheed Martin in Marietta, Georgia.

Investigating video tapes of his 1984 version of the *Hawaiian Punch* Dodge, the team noticed that the body was extremely distorted by air pressure to the rear body panels. They were forced onto the slicks, along with the front fenders and hood showing distress.

"Using the air correctly is the key to performance," Leong said.

The Lockheed engineering team, aided by Roland Leong and Chris Christenson of Odyssey Engineering, added a tail to the new spoiler of the Odyssey Daytona body. Results from the wind tunnel changed the base car-spoiler drag-hp rating at 200 mph from 593 to 682. (Photo Courtesy Roland Leong Collection)

Chief mechanic Don Peterson positions the experimental injector cover during wind-tunnel testing. This helped Leong's Hawaiian Punch *Dodge Funny Car run the class's quickest times and fastest top speeds. Leong (upper left) secures one version of the rear spoiler before a 205-mph blast of air provided an evaluation of drag and lift effects. A Chrysler engineer (upper right) uses a smoke stream for visual evaluation and tuffs of yarn taped to the Daytona body to show how the wind passes over it. (Photo Courtesy Roland Leong Collection)*

Changes for 1986

Several important changes for the 1986 car included switching over to a stronger, more durable carbon fiber body; replacing the heavier fiberglass models that had been in use from the mid-1960s; and the hiring of veteran shoe Johnny West. West's Funny Car career spanned back to the 1970s.

Hawaiian Punch Turns 50

In March 1986, Leong was in New York to celebrate the Del Monte Corporation's 50th anniversary of its popular Hawaiian Punch–brand drink and to announce the latest generation of the sugar-free Hawaiian Punch drink mix. It had a "retrospective" 50-year-old look at the color red in fads and fashion. Sharing the stage with Leong was American jazz vibraphonist, pianist, percussionist, and bandleader Lionel Hampton and a mini version of Roland's *Hawaiian Punch* Dodge Daytona Funny Car.

Roland Leong and jazz musician Lionel Hampton share the stage at a New York press conference in March 1986 to celebrate the Del Monte Corporation's new Hawaiian sugar-free drink mix. Displayed with Hampton and Leong was a go-kart that mimicked the fabled Hawaiian Punch *Dodge Daytona. The popular soft-drink brand had sponsored Leong for the past four years. (Photo Courtesy Roland Leong Collection)*

Rick Johnson and Roland Leong recheck the measurements of the new revolutionary whale-tail rear wing on the Hawaiian Punch *Dodge. The new tail was one of the factors that aided in the incredible times and speeds on the Daytona. The new wing extended behind the car and offered less drag and more downforce. (Photo Courtesy Roland Leong Collection)*

MEMORABLE MOMENTS:
Johnny West

"The first time I started driving for Roland was after the World Finals in 1984 at Pomona," Johnny West said. "I knew I was going to take over driving, and after we packed up after we were done on Sunday afternoon, we got into the truck and left the track. Roland said we're going down to Florida for three match races at West Palm Beach, Bradenton, and somewhere else–I can't recall.

"Keith Jackson and I headed down the road to go to these three match races. I didn't really have too much of an idea on what to expect for what I was going to get paid, which wasn't too much of a concern right then. After making two runs in the first race, Roland handed me a check for $1,800, and I thought, 'I didn't get paid *that* for running my own Funny Car!'

I didn't even have to come up with one penny to drive, and he paid me all that money for three weeks in a row! You always had the fear of being a contract driver to fulfill his expectations. I was the most brutal on myself to make sure that I did everything right."

1987: The Onboard Computer System

In 1987, Leong brought in a new tool of technology to the team that was also made available to the professionals in drag racing. When the *Hawaiian Punch* Daytona and Johnny West blasted down the drag strip, Leong was able to track valuable data with a new advanced onboard computer system manufactured by Ram Automotive Industries.

Leong's L201/Logix computer carried 28 channels that monitored raw data, including measuring the engine and driveshaft RPM, shift points, blower pressure (boost), crankshaft pressures, and the speed of the car when the engine was at full throttle.

The computer system was very sophisticated and sensitive, measuring the time lapse between full-throttle and the movement of the car off the starting line. The L201/Logic was also IBM-PC compatible, where unlike many other onboard systems, data on the IBM-PC displayed graphs and charts that also could be stored on a floppy disc.

Having to perfect the computer was like having another member of the crew, but as Leong put it, "The computer can't tell you everything on how to run 5.50 at 260 mph. You have to have the basic knowledge on how to set up the car and engine before you can even turn on a computer. You need to set up a baseline for the engine setup, tires, transmission shift points, and clutch and fuel settings. Then, go out and make your run and collect the data. The information the computer provides is invaluable but thrown in was the 25 years or so of gut-level experience needed to make a successful run."

The computer age had come to drag racing.

Strong Finish in Florida

The *Hawaiian Punch* Dodge turned in a strong performance at the Motorcraft NHRA Gatornationals in Gainesville, Florida, where Johnny West finally made it past the "three-round blues" to solidify his spot in the final round. Leong's opponent was longtime friend, ex-driver, and four-time Gatornationals winner, Don Prudhomme.

The Snake took a sabbatical from drag racing for the entire year of 1986, but when he came out to the races, you could almost bet on seeing him riding in Leong's push car.

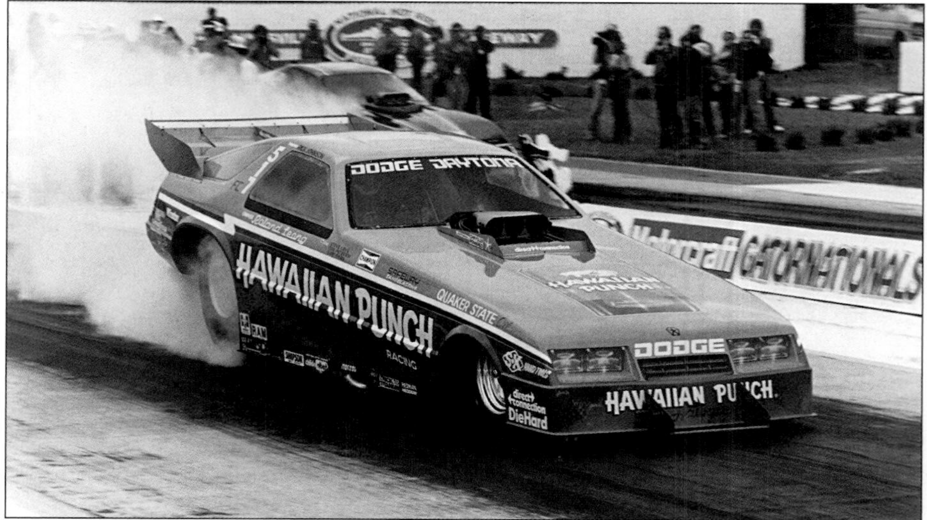

The quickest run in the history of drag racing for a Funny Car was recorded by Rick Johnson, who was driving Roland Leong's Hawaiian Punch *Dodge Daytona on February 3 at the NHRA Winternationals. Johnson stopped the Chrondeks with a time of 5.588 at 263.62 mph. Johnson defeated Kenny Bernstein's* Budweiser King *Ford in what was deemed to be the quickest side-by-side Funny Car race in history. Later in the year, Johnson took home his first NHRA trophy when he powered the* Hawaiian Punch *Dodge past Kenny Bernstein at the Molson Grandnationals in Montreal, Canada. Shown here at the Gatornationals are the aerodynamic additions that were added two weeks earlier at Pomona. (Photo Courtesy Roland Leong Collection)*

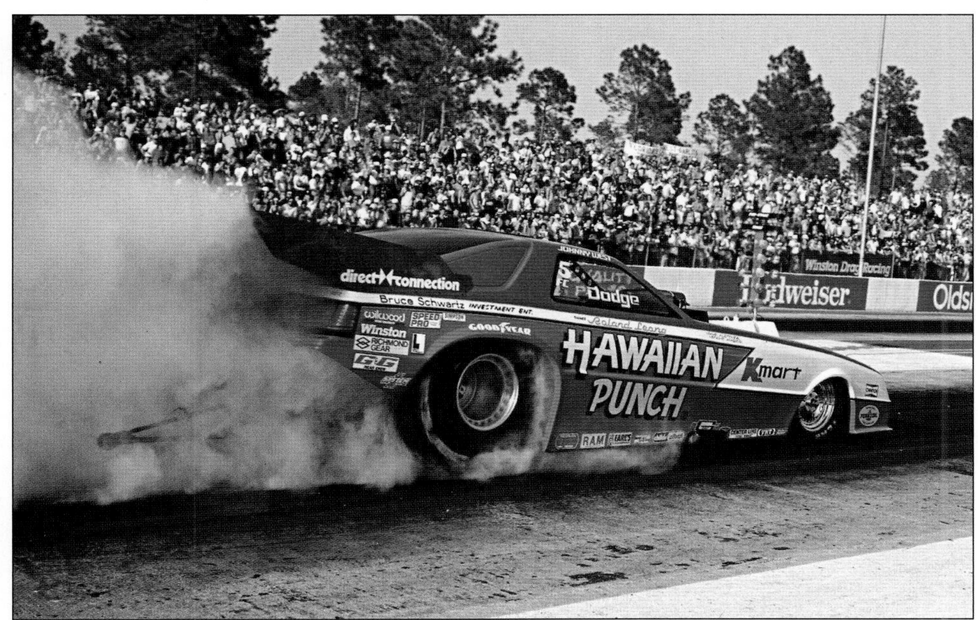

Johnny West applies heat to the clutch and the Goodyears at the Gatornationals during Sunday's elimination rounds. West advanced to the finals, where he met up with former Gatornationals champ Don Prudhomme.

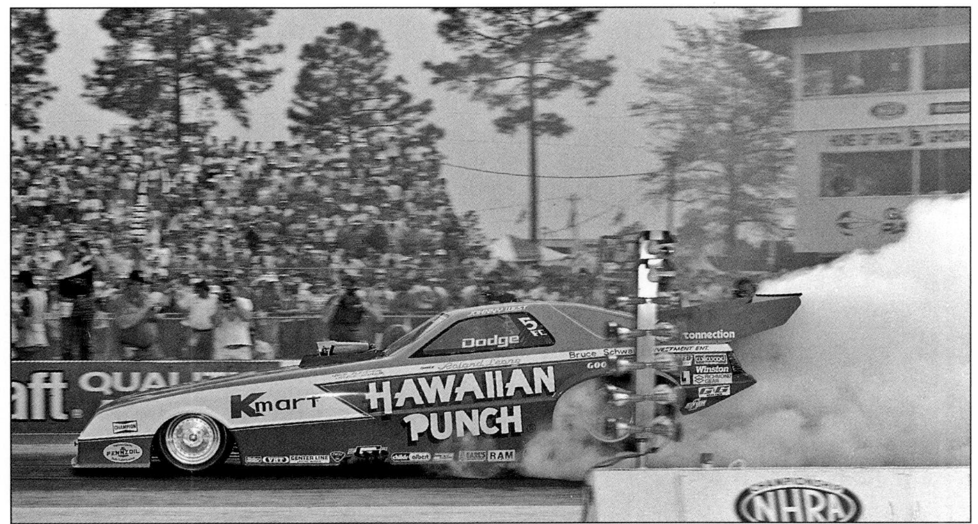

It didn't take long for Chandler, Arizona's Johnny West to make it to his first final round driving for Leong. It took place in Gainesville against the Skoal Bandit of Don Prudhomme. This was one of countless times where the long-time friends faced each other in final round. At the hit, West was out roughly 50 feet from the line when the blower banged, causing a flash fire under the car. Prudhomme went on to capture his fifth Gatornationals Eliminator title.

"You were only as good as your last time slip, not the one before that one or the one you set a world's record," West said before the final round facing against Prudhomme. "All of that goes out the window when you race Prudhomme."

Leong trusted West.

"He was the hardest-working driver working on the car that I ever had," Leong said.

In the final, both cars left evenly off the line. When West was out roughly 50 feet, the supercharger backfired, letting out a huge fireball from under the car. Prudhomme's *Skoal Bandit* Firebird sailed home and took the easy win.

Atlanta Gives It Up and Takes It Back

With Funny Cars demanding far more traction with the engines in front of the driver and not nearly enough weight over the rear wheels, lane imbalance can change in minutes, going from the "good" lane to the worst in just a matter of moments. Johnny West had driven on more slick tracks than any other driver, since most of the drag strips in Arizona had a coating of sand at some point.

At the 1986 NHRA Southern Nationals at Atlanta Dragway, the number-two qualifier, John Force, found out the track was slick the hard way against Johnny West in the second round of eliminations. Force, in the better lane, led off the line. Simultaneously, both cars struck the tires and both drivers backed off the pedals. After they recovered, it appeared to be a sure win for Force. However, it was determined that Force crossed over the centerline, and West was declared the winner.

West's 6.86 ET at 244 mph proved that he was a skillful driver on less-than-desirable track surfaces. In the post-round interview, Johnny West was asked if he knew he beat Force.

"No, not really," West said. "Both of us smoked the tires in low gear, and all of a sudden, I got out of my groove and tried to get back into it when I finally was catching up to him still in low gear. I strung it out as long as I could, where I just barely caught him in the lights. I thought he beat me, but apparently, he crossed the centerline."

In the semifinal round against Jim Head, West left too soon, red-lighting his chance to race Ed McColloch in the finals. Overall, that was a shock to Leong.

Atlanta Dragway hosted the annual NHRA Southern Nationals with some unfavorable racing conditions. Many didn't have a handle on the traction. A second-round matchup saw Johnny West face the favorite, John Force. Force and West left evenly off the line, but both instantly lost traction and went up in smoke. Force crossed over the centerline, handing West and Leong the win.

Half of the field of the eight quickest cars in the Big Bud Shootout (Kenny Bernstein, Ed McCulloch, Mark Oswald, and Johnny West) present their well-earned Budweiser participation plaques for photo ops prior to the first round of the Shootout at Indy.

This Bud's for Leong

In conjunction with the support of Budweiser and the NHRA, the Big Bud Shootout was created in 1982 as a bonus race for Top Fuel dragsters and Funny Car divisions. A collective points system started from the beginning of the year at the Winternationals and concluded at the race two weeks before the U.S. Nationals at Indy.

Each team accumulated points during national events based on qualifying. With enough points tallied, teams earned a position in the eight-car field. The higher the points, the better position in the ladder the team would be placed. The 1987 Big Bud Shootout was on Sunday on the grand stage of the Nationals in Indianapolis, where all eight combatants competed for the $50,000 prize.

For Leong and the *Hawaiian*, this was his second straight year in the Shootout with driver Johnny West. A first-round defeat knocked West out of contention.

Going Home: Hawaii's First 5-Second Run

The annual South Pacific Championships or "Hawaiian Punch: Race for the Rainbow" event was generally held over the first weekend in December. It was also the homecoming for the former local racer, Roland Leong. Leong raced predominantly on the national event circuit but split his summer months match racing across the mainland.

Leong brought home his latest *Hawaiian Punch* Dodge Daytona

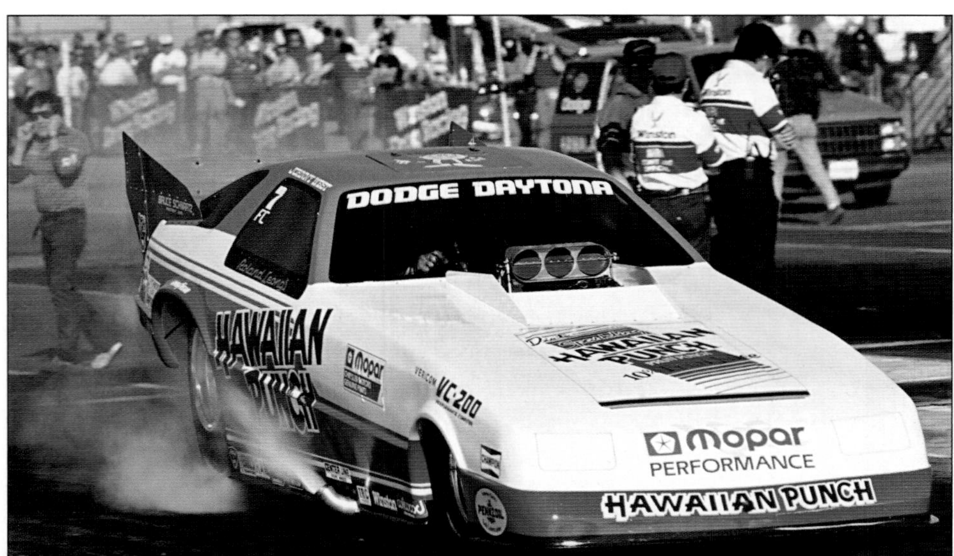

Behind the wheel at Pomona, Johnny West releases the 4,000-hp-plus of Keith Black power through the water box at Pomona, transferring heat to the track through the Goodyears. (Photo Courtesy Bob McClurg)

HAWAIIAN PUNCH

SAVE $3.00
AL EARLY BIRD PROMO
$3.00 OFF ALL 3-DAY EVENT TICKETS
HURRY... LIMITED TIME ONLY

"RACE FOR THE RAINBOW"
FRIDAY, SATURDAY & SUNDAY
NOVEMBER 27-29, 1987
HILO DRAGSTRIP
TICKETS AVAILABLE AT ALL
SURE SAVE LOCATIONS

ADULTS' 3-DAY ADMISSION + PIT PASS $25.00
CHILD'S 3-DAY ADMISSION + PIT PASS $15.00
ADULTS' SAT. 11/28 + PIT PASS $15.00
ADULTS' + PIT PASS $20.00
CHILD'S 1 DAY + PIT PASS $5

Hawaii will always be home for Roland Leong. The Hawaii Tribune-Herald *ran this advertisement in preparation for the* Hawaiian Punch *car and Leong's return to the islands.*

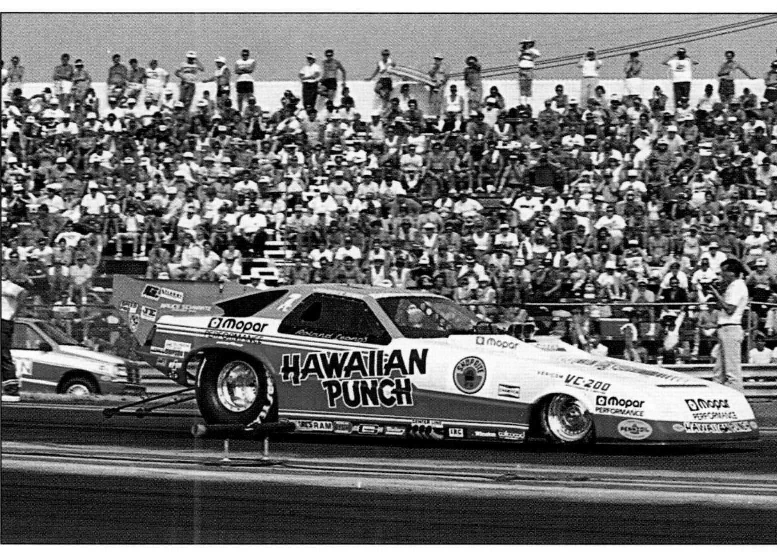

Under tremendous acceleration, the Hawaiian Punch *Dodge pulls nearly 4 Gs coming off the starting line. Leong and West discussed what they should do round by round to keep consistently running 5.40s at 270 mph. (Photo Courtesy Paul Johnson Collection)*

Funny Car with driver Johnny West to put on a show for the hometown fans. California fireman Jim Dunn was brought along with his *Fireman's Quickie* Oldsmobile Firenza to match race the *Hawaiian Punch* Dodge. Many local fans who followed Big Jim were on hand for his third visit to Hawaii. Races were held at both Hilo Dragway and Hawaii Raceway Park.

The match races between the *Hawaiian Punch* Daytona and Dunn's *Fireman's* Firenza meant more to Leong than the matter of winning. It was the matter of coming home after 20 years of pursuing a successful, national career and racing in front of hometown fans that meant a lot to him.

West and Dunn exchanged round wins in the special best-of-three match race, but it was the *Hawaiian* prevailing at Hawaii Raceway Park. They won the finale in grand style with West and Leong resetting the track record with a 5.84 ET at 250 mph.

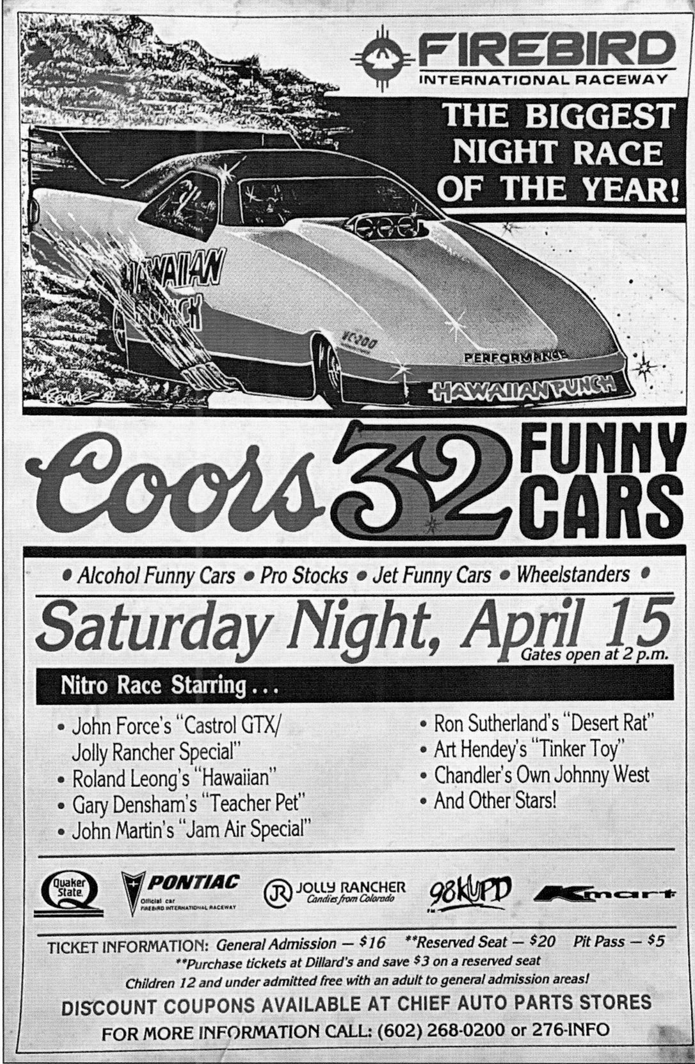
FIREBIRD
INTERNATIONAL RACEWAY
THE BIGGEST NIGHT RACE OF THE YEAR!

Coors 32 FUNNY CARS

• Alcohol Funny Cars • Pro Stocks • Jet Funny Cars • Wheelstanders •
Saturday Night, April 15
Gates open at 2 p.m.
Nitro Race Starring...
• John Force's "Castrol GTX/ Jolly Rancher Special"
• Roland Leong's "Hawaiian"
• Gary Densham's "Teacher Pet"
• John Martin's "Jam Air Special"
• Ron Sutherland's "Desert Rat"
• Art Hendey's "Tinker Toy"
• Chandler's Own Johnny West
• And Other Stars!

Quaker State · PONTIAC Official car Firebird International Raceway · JOLLY RANCHER Candies from Colorado · 98KUPD · Kmart

TICKET INFORMATION: General Admission — $16 **Reserved Seat — $20 Pit Pass — $5
**Purchase tickets at Dillard's and save $3 on a reserved seat
Children 12 and under admitted free with an adult to general admission areas!
DISCOUNT COUPONS AVAILABLE AT CHIEF AUTO PARTS STORES
FOR MORE INFORMATION CALL: (602) 268-0200 or 276-INFO

In 1989, Firebird International Raceway, in conjunction with Coors, held its biggest Funny Car race of the year. More than 40 nitro and alcohol big-name floppers raced in the valley of the sun.

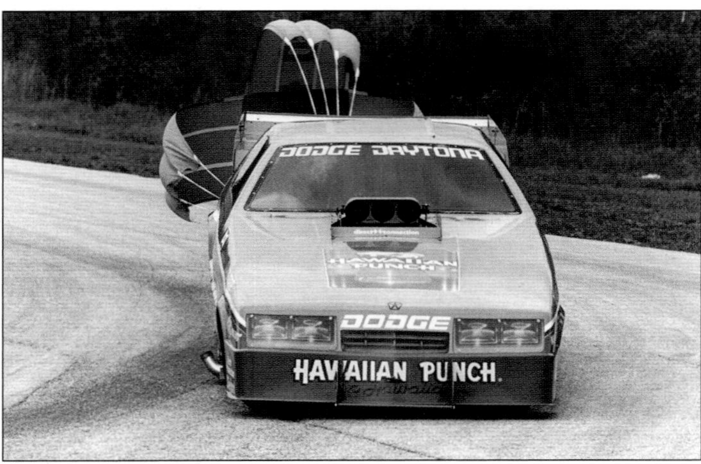

Rick Johnson makes the wide, sweeping turn out of the shutdown area at the NHRA Gatornationals at Gainesville. The surface of the strip at the Gatornationals was found to be to Johnson's liking after running another 5.66 ET at 259.09 mph. (Photo Courtesy Roland Leong Collection)

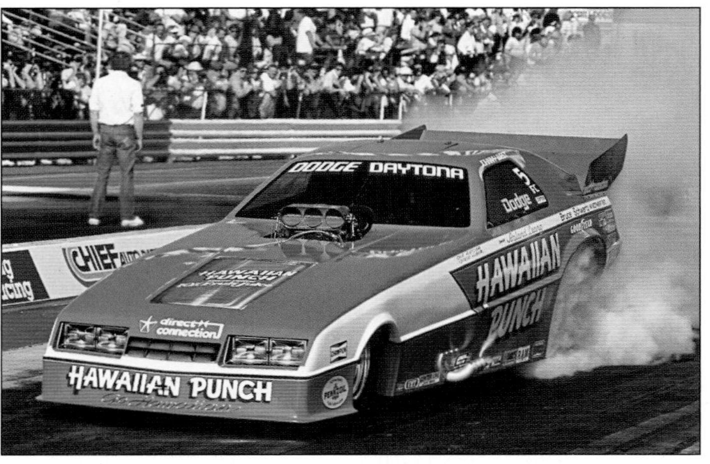

Johnny West made his driving debut for Roland Leong at the NHRA Chief Auto Parts Winternationals in Pomona. West took over the seat after Rick Johnson left the **Hawaiian** ***at the end of 1985, where he finished fifth in the points hunt.***

During one of his quieter moments in Hawaii, Leong sat down with members of the Hawaiian Cruisers. He sat for a one-on-one interview of a local young man who left home, became a success story and national legend, and came back home.

"It's good to be racing in Hawaii and to be back home," Leong said. "Local fans want to understand what Funny Car racing is all about, and I hope we have shown them after they leave the strip. Many people asked questions, since they are unfamiliar with this type of racing. The aerodynamics of the car draws a lot of attention, as this is the only Dodge Funny Car that has been put into the wind tunnel to help with its design. The time in a wind tunnel averages $1,800 per hour, which is serious business.

"The future may slow down a little from the fast growth of the past five-to-seven years, however the sport of professional drag racing will keep getting bigger and bigger. As for myself, I want to be involved in drag racing until the day I don't want to do it anymore. When and if that day comes, I'll move on to something else. A lot of people have been forced to give up for financial reasons—I've been fortunate."

Johnny West went on to drive the *Hawaiian Punch* for three seasons for Leong. He ended up in several runner-up positions, multi-appearances in non-point bonus races including the Big Bud Shootout, and three top-10 finishes.

"In the '60s, '70s, and throughout the '80s, lots of us match raced, but I don't think there were a lot of drag racers making a living with just their cars," Leong said. "At the time, there weren't very many people who made a living drag racing. That's all I did."

1987–1990: Proctor and Gamble Ends Nine-Year Run

Jim White took over driving duties in 1988 after Johnny West decided to leave to pursue other racing interests. White raced three seasons under Leong's guidance and raced with greater success than his predecessors.

In 1990, Leong read the writing on the wall when the unconfirmed

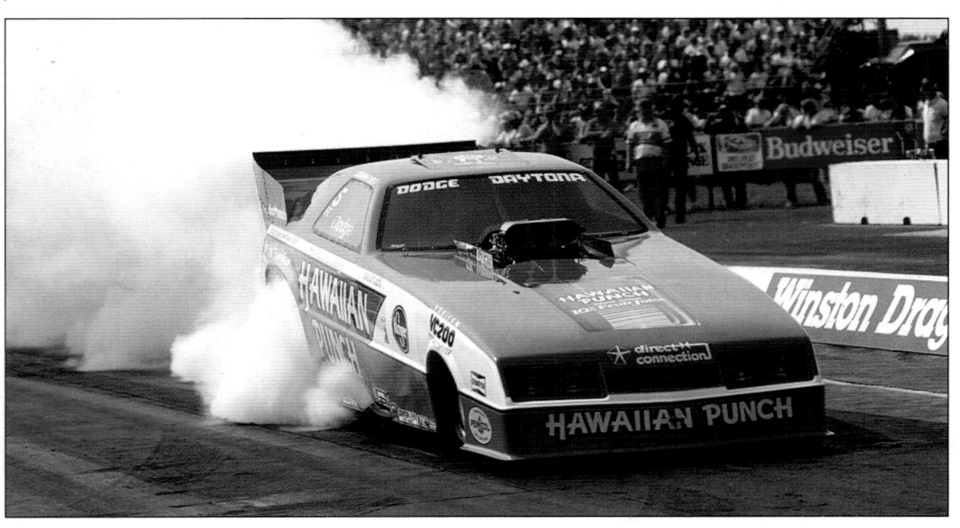

Roland was a stickler on being meticulous with every one of his race cars, dating back to his earlier Dragmaster days. His **Hawaiian Punch** ***cars were no exception. He built his*** **Hawaiians** ***with pride and perfection along with the best available components.***

rumors became reality that Del Monte was bought out by Proctor & Gamble (P&G). Leong's one-year contract with Hawaiian Punch was honored by P&G, allowing him to continue racing under the Hawaiian Punch banner in 1991. P&G's marketing group then made the business decision to go in another direction, advertising in the other sporting fields, focusing more on the larger markets, such as golf, tennis, figure skating, basketball, etc. instead of drag racing. The plug was pulled on the *Hawaiian*.

MEMORABLE MOMENTS: Roland Leong

"I had been sponsored by Hawaiian Punch for nine years, which was nearly as long as Kenny Bernstein had with Budweiser," Roland Leong said. "Unlike Bernstein, I never had multi-year deals or contracts. At the end of each year, I needed to renegotiate my contract with the Del Monte Corporation, owners of the Hawaiian Punch brand soda.

"On my end, not only was I the car tuner, parts manager, and owner but I was also the agent, promoter, business manager, and an HP representative who had to go out and prove to Del Monte every year that its investment was well spent."

"I organized and put together programs that included team and car appearances at the local supermarkets, department and convenience stores, and malls prior to racing on the weekend at the area drag strip.

"In late 1990, Del Monte was sold to Procter & Gamble, So, I feared for the worst. In 1991, a lot of things changed because the marketing people decided to go in other directions. They figured the typical sports fan followed basketball, baseball, golf, tennis, or whatever, and not drag racing. That's how Prudhomme lost his Miller deal, too; they got bought out.

"After the buyout, I knew my tenure with Hawaiian Punch would not be renewed, but when I sat down with the Proctor and Gamble marketing group, they told me they would honor my last year for 1991 with the name Hawaiian Punch on the side of the car. Well, as it turned out, 1991 was one of my best years of making some memorable racing.

"I had hired Jim White to drive for me, and we struggled at first but then we set the national speed record four or five times during the year. We went out and won four races, including doubling up at the U.S. Nationals at Indy, winning both the celebrated Big Bud Shootout and the Funny Car Eliminator title. We also recorded low ET and set the new national top speed record.

"At the end of the campaign, we ended up overall number-two in the points for the year. If the NHRA had given points for top speeds during national events and setting a national record, we might have won the championship, but unfortunately, they didn't give out points for top speed. Today, they still don't."

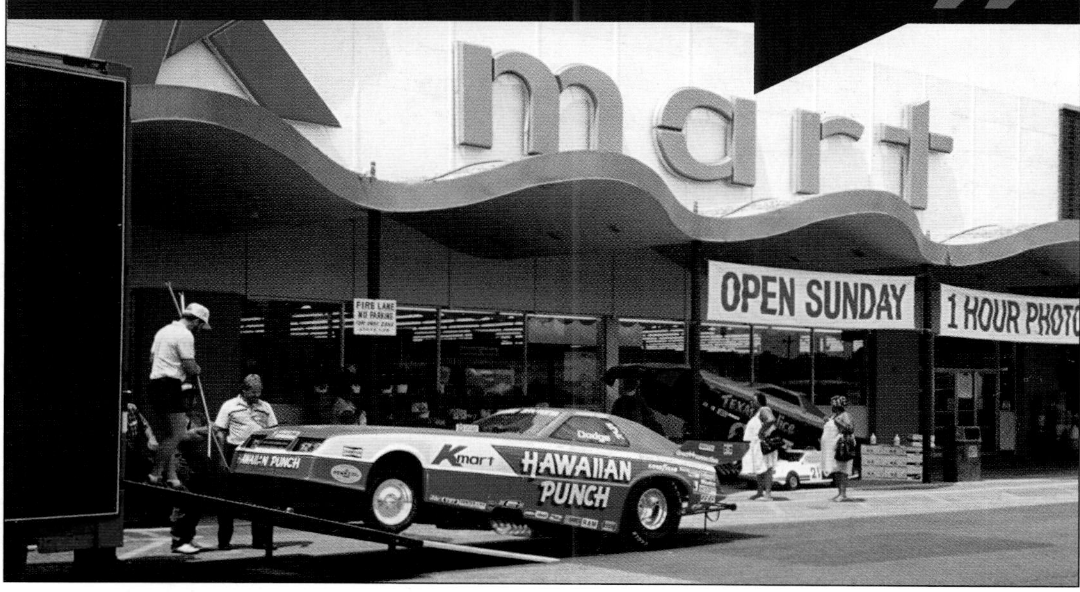

Outside of a Baton Rouge, Louisiana, Kmart, curious onlookers gather to check out Roland Leong's crew unloading the Hawaiian Punch *Funny Car out of transporter for a display promoting the NHRA Kmart/Citco Cajun Nationals. There was a strong possibility that these shoppers got their first close-up view of a 260-mph fuel Funny Car. Also displayed in front of Kmart was the* Texas Justice *Funny Car and a Citco exhibit. Over at the racetrack, Johnny West took on the responsibility of temporary crew chief when Leong was a no-show during the weekend. Leong was relaxing on the beach in the Bahamas. West went on to a final-round runner-up finish, losing to Kenny Bernstein. (Photo Courtesy Roland Leong Collection)*

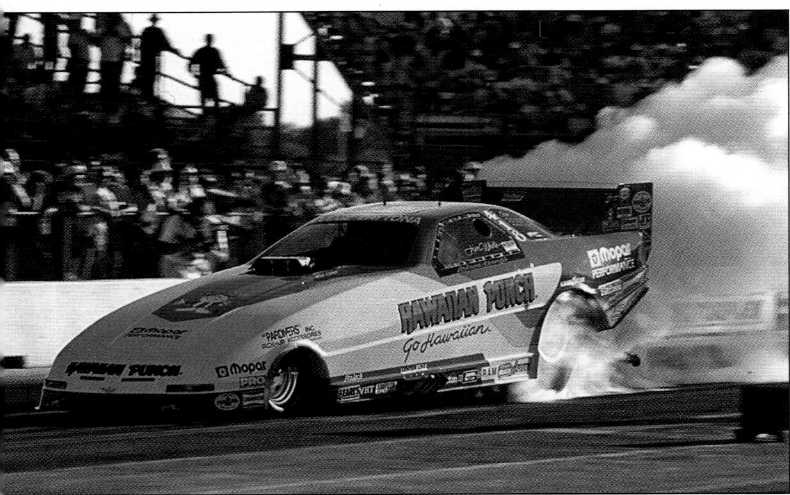

The Hawaiian brought a whole different look with special one-race-only paint and graphics at the 1990 NHRA Winston Invitational at Rockingham, North Carolina. White, who qualified number-three for the Winston, now had tuner Wes Cerny in his corner. White's first round against Mark Oswald ended up with a peddle fest.

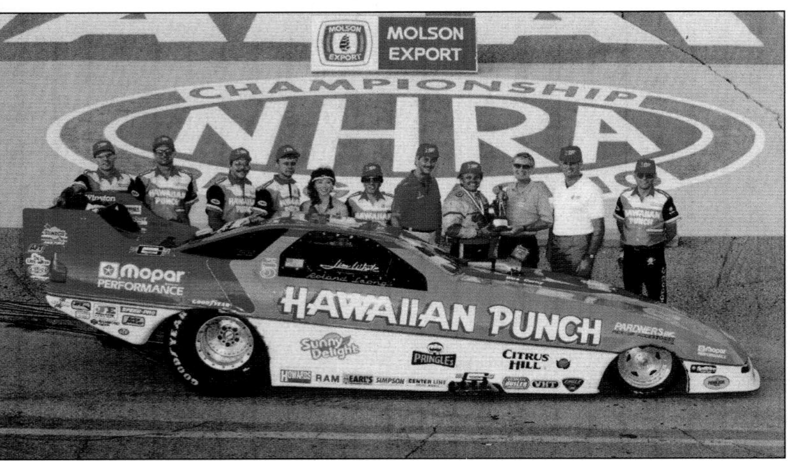

Jim White brought home his second "Wally" for Leong after White amazed the fans with an unreal 5.18 ET at 289.94 mph for the fastest time ever at the Le Grand Molson Export Nationals at Sanair. The victory snapped John Force's 7-0 winning streak against White, as White and Cerny finally put away Force and the domination of Austin Coil in the final round. (Photo Courtesy Roland Leong Collection)

1991 Hawaiian Punch: The Best Year Yet

In a nutshell, 1991 was the best year yet during Leong's association with Hawaiian Punch. He was continuing a nine-year relationship with Del Monte, which was his longest successful tenure by far. He won five national events, having his best year yet. The team reset numerous speed records, including running the fastest run ever of 289.94 mph at Sanair.

The Magic of Cerny

If there was anyone qualified to find a path to get the most in RPM, it was Wes Cerny! Cerny was the shop foreman at Engle Cams before going to work for Keith Black. He was an expert, taking the quantum leap in camshaft design that vigorously assisted his efforts to build driveshaft speed. Trying all types of combinations with the fuel-delivery system, the clutch, and the cams, he found the right chemistry that got the car to accelerate all the way to the end of the track.

The performance of the amazing *Hawaiian Punch* Dodge could be traced back to 1989 when Wes Cerny, the shop foreman at Keith Black Racing Engines, had agreed to offer his insight. He would tell Leong why all the extensive parts failure had taken place in 1989. Cerny took it one race at a time to check things over.

"Despite all the grief, we believed we had a strong car," Jim White said. "At the 60-foot mark, it was like there was no tomorrow; we got a 0.911 and 0.920s. But the combination was too violent.

"Coming out of that season, Cerny felt that the car was too volatile off the line—that we needed to soften it up a little in the beginning and then pick it up in the middle and top end. After all, we probably were averaging in the mid-260s for speed back then. We charged at the start and fell over on the top end."

Given the issues, Cerny didn't want to make immediate, massive changes. Instead, he wanted to take gradual steps to make sure everything was done correctly.

By mid-1990, the forecast was low for a Funny Car championship, with the *Hawaiian* being 5,000 points off the lead. The team had made decent strides, but it was at that point that Cerny began to get more aggressive. He had several radical ideas and changes, which boosted the level of performance to a whole different level.

1991 NHRA Chief Winternationals

At the 1991 NHRA Chief Winternationals, Jim White laid down a 5.14 ET at 278.89 mph in qualifying. He later backed it up with a 5.17 at 275.39 for a new national ET record.

The speeds were the best of White's career, which continued to improve in each elimination round. Along with the increased speeds, times steadily progressed: 5.25 at 279.93, 5.24 at 278.89, and 5.20 at 278.03. This was before the blower belt made its untimely exit from the car in the final round against Mike Dunn, crowning Dunn the event winner.

With the positive results from the Winternationals, the next stop was at the Arizona Nationals. There, White took the triple crown, taking a low ET of the meet (5.25), resetting the NHRA national speed record (284.62 mph), and winning his first "Wally."

The streak continued with the trip to Gainesville for the Gatornationals. White proved both Pomona and Arizona were no flukes when he set a low ET of the Gators: a 5.17 at 279.62 mph right off the trailer.

With the times and speeds improving at each national event, much work was still needed with the clutch system to advance further into the elimination rounds. John Force went to his fourth-consecutive final round at Gainesville, which expanded his points lead.

Hughes Adds Final Piece to the Puzzle

With John Force pulling away in the points race, the team was able to bring in Cerny's longtime friend Leonard Hughes for his cylinder-head knowledge and setups for the big top-end speed numbers that he used on the Candies & Hughes Funny Cars.

Leong figured that Hughes's heads, along with the performance of Cerny's cam, fuel, and clutch package would bring more life to the *Hawaiian Punch*.

Shedding light on the heads, Leong contacted Steve Potsek to purchase four blocks of solid aluminum to build and machine four cylinder heads. The heads were prepped by Hughes and Cerny. Cerny, Hughes, and Leong decided to try their theories, so the custom-made, one-of-a-kind parts were ordered in April. They became available in late May, which was in time to test in June at the Springnationals.

Springnationals

The planned scheme taken at the Springnationals was simple: qualify early and place solidly into the show, put on the new parts, and roll the dice.

White qualified number-one on Friday with the regular parts and equipment with a 5.25 ET. Then, it was time to test the new secret parts on Saturday. The first outing wasn't what they were hoping for. White shut the car off at 300 feet after the engine incinerated the heads, damaging the combustion chambers and burning up all 16 spark plugs. The experiment was put on hold for the rest of the Springnationals and all of the Le Grandnationals before taking another try at the Summernationals.

The results were an exact copy of the Springnationals. They qualified into the show, put on the new pieces, and shut off at half-track with the new parts burned up. Not giving up, Cerny continued to switch around combinations to the engine, fuel, and clutch systems. Finally, at the Northwest Nationals in Seattle, things started to fall into place. In the 90-degree heat, White recorded the *Hawaiian*'s first outstanding pass of 5.22 at 264.31 mph in qualifying. Although the heads once again suffered damage, that was the team's best run to date with the new parts, which made the team ecstatic.

A small event unfolded at Seattle when both Cerny and Hughes studied the computer data. Dale Armstrong (Kenny Bernstein's *Budweiser King* crew chief) joined in the summit and suggested putting Armstrong's ignition parts in their combination. The results were positive.

Mystery at Indy

With the U.S. Nationals looming, Cerny was more confident about the program and decided to duplicate the parts (adding cylinder heads, fuel pumps and nozzles, and camshafts) to run them at Indy. The plan remained the same that was used for the Springnationals and Northwest Nationals: qualify with the proven parts and go all out.

White put the Dodge Daytona into the number-one position on Friday's qualifying round with a 5.27 ET and then made the switch over to the secret parts for Saturday morning's sessions. White unloaded with an incredible 5.26 ET at 288.18 mph!

Right away, the NHRA tech officials ruled that the

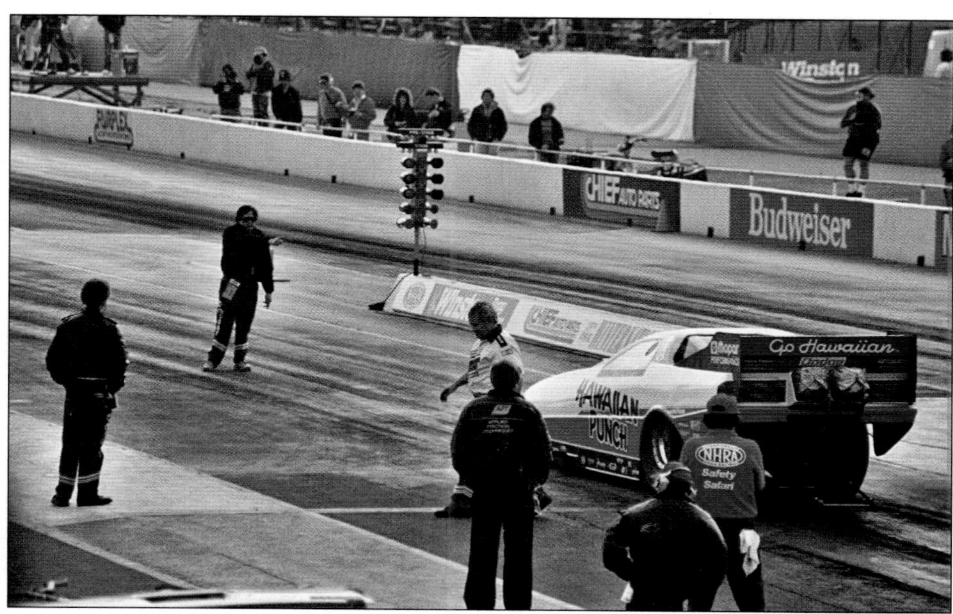

Leong directs his driver, Jim White, back into the groove at the 29th NHRA Winternationals. The camaraderie between Leong, White, and Cerny instantly forecasted great things to come for the Hawaiian Punch team in 1991. (Photo Courtesy Bob McClurg)

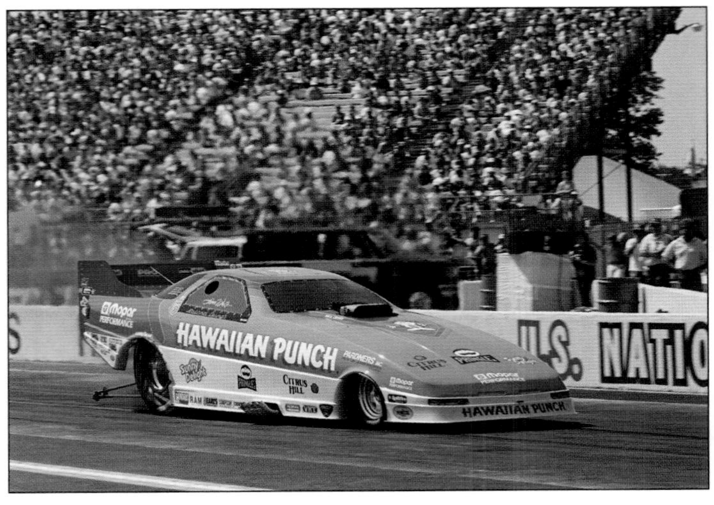

The 37th running of the NHRA U.S. Indy Nationals was the one to remember for Leong. He won everything that weekend. He swept the Big Bud Shootout on Sunday, qualified number-one in Funny Car, and won the Funny Car Eliminator title on Monday. His Hawaiian Punch *Dodge Daytona ran both top speed and low ET of the race, and he reset the NHRA Top Speed Funny Car record. (Photo Courtesy Richard Shute Photography/autoimagery.com)*

rear spoiler was out of spec (being too long). Cerny took it in stride but wasn't fazed, telling the team it didn't matter, as he had it under control.

The "Mystery at Indy" had all the Funny Car teams mumbling and scratching their heads on why Jim White put up that unbelievably big number (288.18 mph). Various conclusions were made by others: cheating, hiding nitrous, the clocks were off, etc.

The team of the Hawaiian Punch *Dodge celebrates after winning the Big Bud Shootout at the U.S. Nationals. The Hawaiian team was the model of consistency, which was the name of the game by Leong's standard. The win earned driver Jim White a huge payday from the King of Beers: the $50,000 paycheck. (Photography Courtesy Roland Leong Collection)*

Unfortunately for the opposition, there was no letting up for the Hawaiian Punch team. White kept the pressure down on the pedal, running stronger on each and every run. His 287.71-mph blast in the first round of the Budweiser Big Bud Shootout led to winning the remaining two rounds. White raised the bar when he rocketed to an unbelievable 5.16 ET at 288.27 mph in the final over a slower John Force (5.34 at 273).

Roland Leong brought Steve Potsek to Indy for cylinder head repairs (as needed) at the track. After each run using the trick heads, they were immediately removed, checked for damage, and sent over to Potsek, where he rushed to repair them for use in the following rounds. While Potsek had no issues with the repairs, he was unhappy that he didn't get to catch more racing during the weekend.

"All of the other drivers and teams and different people would love to know what we were doing," Leong said. "I don't see where this limit of speed will stop. I've been hearing that for over 25 years, and so far, I haven't seen it, so maybe there isn't any."

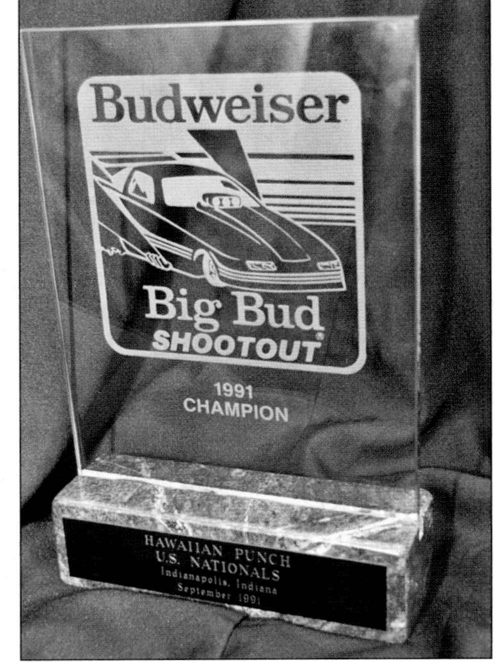

Leong's 1991 Big Bud Shootout trophy is on display at the Lions Automobilia Museum along with other rare memorabilia that honors his accomplishments and legacy.

White Hot!

The NHRA U.S. Indy Nationals was the most memorable one for Leong in all his racing career. They won everything that weekend at Indy including the Big Bud Shootout and the Funny Car Eliminator title when Jim

White outran John Force and Austin Coil in the final round.

Jim White began his dream matchup with Force when he defeated Al Hoffman in the second round. He then drove past an up-in-smoke Mark Oswald's *In-N-Out* entry in the semifinal before meeting John Force in the finals for the second time during the weekend.

Wes Cerny was awarded $1,000 from Craftsman tools as crew chief of the race. White recorded both top speed and low ET of the race, and he reset the NHRA Top Speed Funny Car record. But for Leong, it was more meaningful because his mother was able to attend and see him win the weekend.

Jim White closed in on the elusive 290-mph mark with runs of 288.18 and 288.27 mph to win the Budweiser Big Bud Shootout and the U.S. Nationals titles.

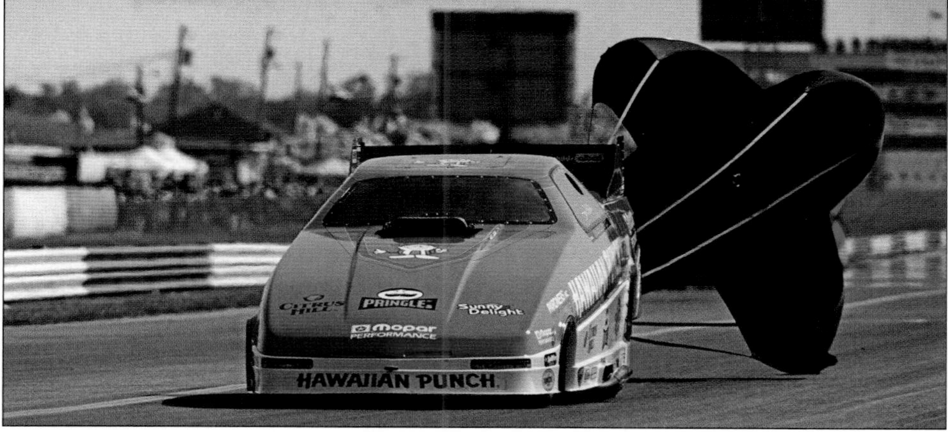

Jim White drops the laundry and hits the brakes after recording the fastest speed in Funny Car history at the NHRA Indy U.S. Nationals with a 288.27-mph blast. At one time, the Hawaiian Punch *Dodge was the fastest nitro-fueled car in drag racing. It was quicker than any Top Fuel dragsters or fuel coupes. (Photo Courtesy Richard Shute Photography/autoimagery.com)*

For the third time in his career, Roland Leong added his name to the Top Eliminator award for winning the U.S. Indy Nationals, his first in the Funny Car category. It was a special moment for Roland and Jim White, who celebrated in the winner's circle. This was White's first-ever U.S. Nationals win. For Roland's sister Marilynn, mom Teddy, Roland himself, and Susie, it was more meaningful for the family because this was the last race that his mom ever attended. (Photo Courtesy Richard Shute Photography/autoimagery.com)

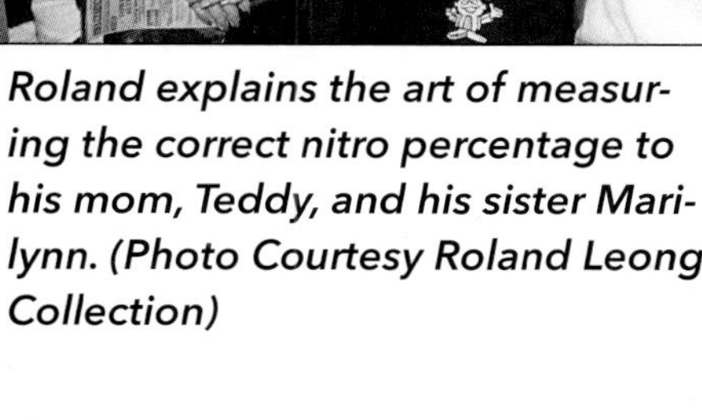

Roland explains the art of measuring the correct nitro percentage to his mom, Teddy, and his sister Marilynn. (Photo Courtesy Roland Leong Collection)

Jim White and Roland Leong receive their congratulatory handshakes from Wally Parks, the founder, president, and chairman of the NHRA. They dominated the U.S. Indy Nationals. (Photo Courtesy Richard Shute Photography/autoimagery.com)

Battle of the Crew Chiefs

At the next race at the Sunoco Keystone Nationals at Maple Grove, in Reading, Pennsylvania, the team didn't skip a beat after leaving Indy. Jim White made it two races in a row qualifying number-one with a 5.15 ET.

It seemed to become the battle of the crew chiefs. Wes Cerny and Austin Coil put both of their drivers into the final round. White made it look like a cake walk when he beat John Force with a 5.18 ET at 289.94 mph.

NHRA Winston World Finals

The *Hawaiian* finally broke the 290-mph barrier at the Texas Motorplex when White reeled off an incredible run of 290.13 mph. The *Hawaiian Punch* entry closed out the year at the NHRA Winston World Finals with the quickest blast ever in the history of drag racing: 291.82 mph, which was faster than any Top Fuel dragster on the planet.

The end of the year concluded at Pomona at the NHRA Winston World Finals. The *Hawaiian* was the odds-on favorite with the fans to see if the high-end performances would be reset once more. In the second round of eliminations, White once again smashed the top-speed record when his *Hawaiian Punch* blasted past the traps at 291 mph.

The *Hawaiian* outperformed nearly every Funny Car after Indy, dropping the big numbers on the opposition. In the second round of eliminations, White set the drag racing official top speed of 291.82 mph at Pomona, becoming not only the world's fastest Funny Car but also the fastest fuel dragster in the history of the NHRA.

The second round of competition hurt the engine, so a switch was made. In most cases, a crew chief

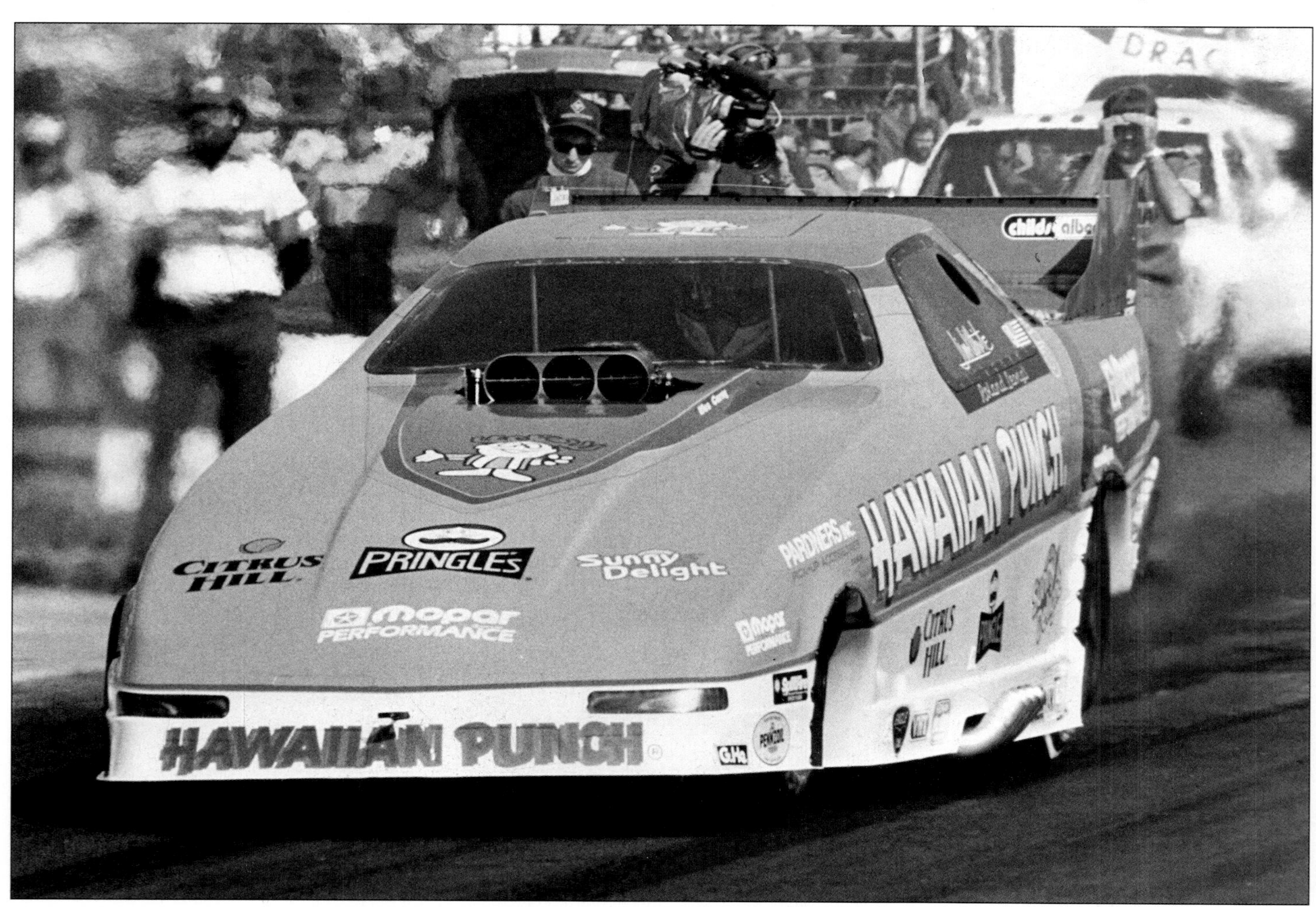

The Hawaiian Punch *Dodge with driver Jim White recorded the official top speed of 291.82 mph at Pomona, becoming not only the world's fastest Funny Car but also the fastest fuel dragster in the history of drag racing. The* Hawaiian Punch *Dodge was the favorite to win it all at the World Finals, but after hurting the engine in the second round, the block was replaced with a fresh one. Ed "Ace" McCulloch and Jim White faced each other in the semifinals, when the phenomenal run of the world's fastest Funny was over for Leong and White. Sadly, the nine-year run with Hawaiian Punch was finished as well. (Photo Courtesy Bob McClurg)*

MEMORABLE MOMENTS:

Roland Leong

"One of my biggest thrills happened in 1991 when World Champ John Force was the man to beat," Roland Leong said. "We celebrated a double victory when we won the Big Bud Shootout and the U.S. Nationals on the same weekend. I had confidence in the car. [I thought that] if we didn't mess up or make a mistake, the car should outrun Force, which it did."

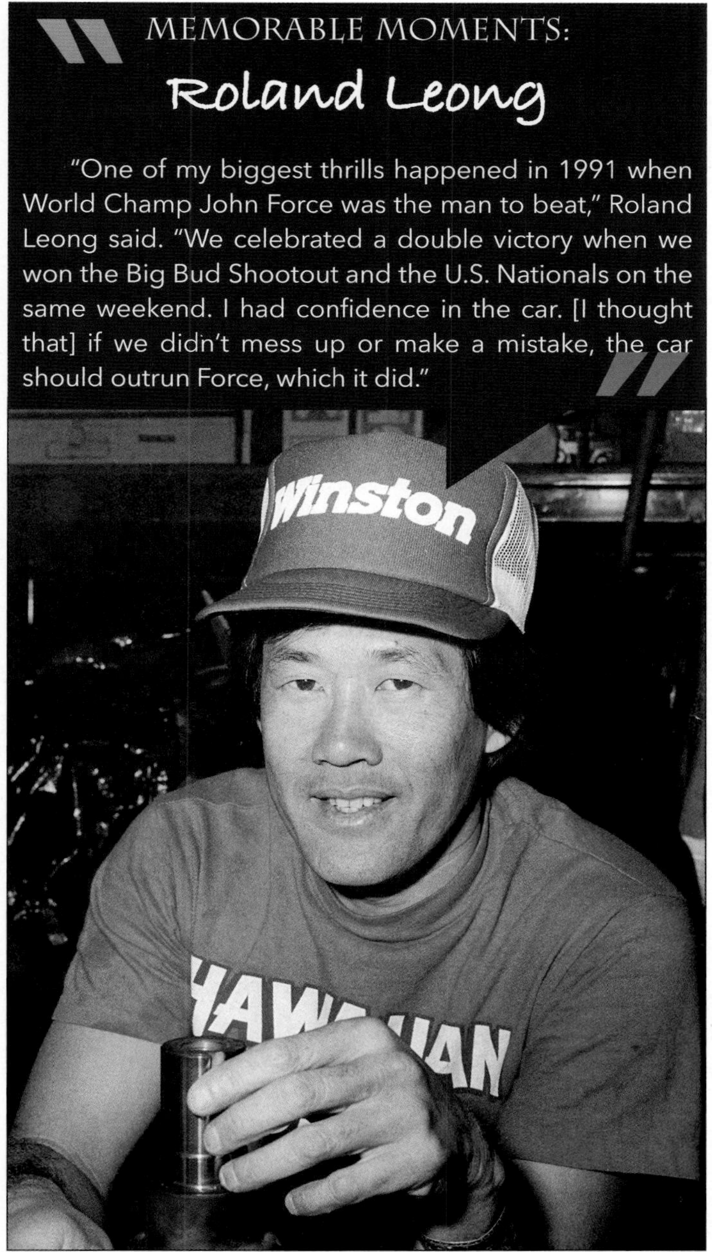

When you drove for Roland Leong, you drove for the best owner and tuner in the business. Looking back at those who drove for Leong is like a list of Hall of Famers. Danny Ongais, Don Prudhomme, Mike Snively, Larry Reyes, Butch Maas, Leroy Chadderton, Ron Colson, Gordy Bonin (two tours), Mike Dunn, Rick Johnson, Johnny West, and Jim White were all propelled into stardom behind the wheel of a Hawaiian *race car. (Photo Courtesy Roland Leong Collection)*

automatically assumes that having a fresh, new engine in the car will be fine, reassuring the driver that it's going to be better than the first engine. However, in the semifinal round, Ed "the Ace" McCulloch and Jim White faced each other, and the new engine broke around the 1,000-foot mark. The run didn't give White enough speed for the big numbers, and he lost to McCulloch.

It was an extraordinary year for the world's fastest Funny Car for Leong and White, but now Hawaiian Punch's relationship from the last nine years with Leong had come to its end. Without secured sponsorship for 1992, Leong was forced to park his race-car operation.

Without financial backing to continue racing, Leong went on to spend six months in 1992 applying his tuning expertise on his friend Don Prudhomme's Top Fueler.

Vacation Minded

While he was performing his magic on Prudhomme's Top Fuel hot rod, his heart was yearning to return as an owner and operator of a fuel Funny Car. In September 1992, Leong reached out to his homeland Hawaii for what would be a perfect fit for both parties.

Leong arranged a meeting with Hawaii state senator Dennis Nakasato, head of the senate Tourism and Recreation subcommittee. He convinced Nakasato to take a personal visit to the NHRA World Finals at Pomona. It was a gamble for Leong. Even with the senator's tight schedule, both men took a red-eye flight to Los Angeles to take in one day of racing.

Senator Nakasato was able to take in only one round of the Budweiser Classic. Then, he immediately returned to Hawaii. Nakasato was thoroughly impressed with the abundance of fans and with the sponsors of the cars. He asked Leong to come to Hawaii to make a proposal for a sponsorship.

What was originally thought to be four days of talks with the prospective idea and persuading the Tourism and Recreation subcommittee became a three-week endeavor. Leong pitched his idea with many politicians of the value and exposure of drag racing over on the mainland.

Leong and Senator Nakasato mentioned that the money spent for 30 seconds of television exposure and the usual newspaper and magazine ads averages nearly $500,000 per year. They suggested that the same money in drag racing sponsorship would provide exposure throughout the country of the racing faithful, translating to fans spending their vacation dollars in Hawaii.

Speaking in front of the tourism and recreation subcommittee, Leong said, "Out of 10 months a year, we travel between 60,000 to 75,000 miles across the country, through 42 states. Now, imagine the image of the colorful Hawaiian vacation scheme painted on the side of the transporter that would be seen by millions of drivers traveling on the interstates. This is more a marketing and advertising effort than a sponsorship."

CHAPTER 13

HAWAIIAN VACATION

TOURIST BUREAU "DRAGS" VISITORS OFF TO PARADISE

In early February 1993, Hawaii State Senator Dennis Nakasato, head of the senate Tourism and Recreation subcommittee, acknowledged the idea of using a race car in promoting tourism to the Hawaiian Islands. Realizing that there would be some ridicule and heavy criticism of the state-sponsored car for Hawaii, as funding was already tight for the year, Nakasato said, "When you look at the numbers from a strictly business standpoint, it's a damn good deal!"

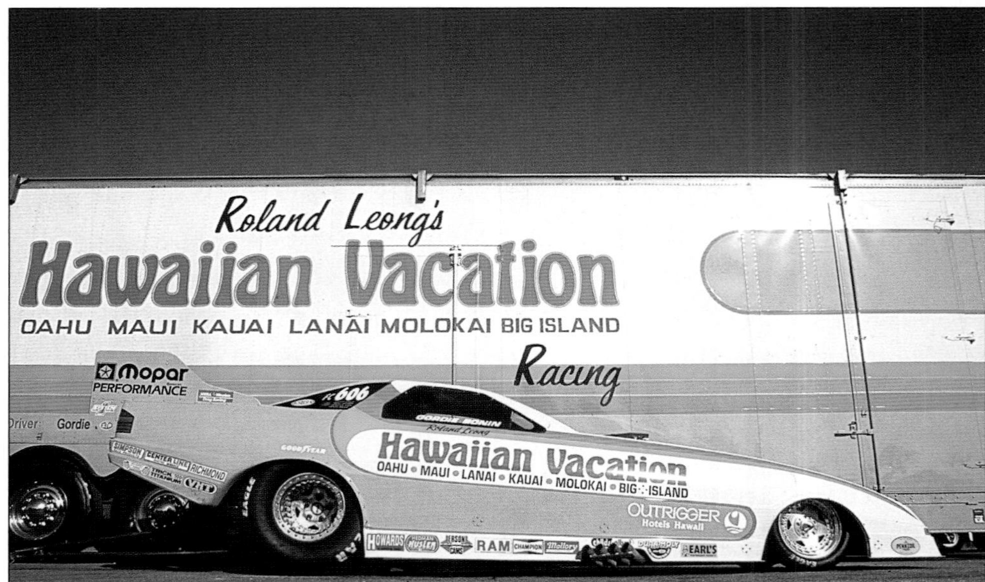

Roland Leong's quest for another NHRA Winston Funny Car title was supported entirely by the state of Hawaii, the Hawaii Visitors Bureau, Outriggers Hotel Hawaii, Hawaiian Isles Kona Coffee Company, and Mopar Performance Parts. Leong was back at the helm with his record-setting Dodge Daytona that produced a thundering 5,000 hp. (Photo Courtesy Jeff Burk Photography)

With racetrack appearances, magazine and television coverage, and personal appearances and displays at shopping centers throughout the nation, this deal would generate 200 million favorable impressions valued at over $600,000 for Hawaii. Just over $200,000 alone of advertising was paid by the NHRA before the races. Only $600,000 for 200 million impressions? Exposure across the United States with television and radio ads (some free time and some paid), plus the $200,000 paid by NHRA, along with advertising with billboards, newspapers, etc. was available to the population of 256,514,224.

Each race offered an incentive with a Hawaiian vacation giveaway for two. With the convention center on the minds of the Hawaiian Vacation Bureau (HVB), the idea was to woo the motorsports world, aftermarket manufacturers, and Detroit's automakers to come and have their conventions in paradise.

Mufi Hannemann, the department director for the HVB, was highly skeptical at first, but the more he looked at it, the more it made sense.

"It's a promotional vehicle, pardon the pun," said Hannemann.

What more would tune in their interests with Hawaii's own son, drag-racing figure Roland Leong. As head of the Hawaiian Vacation Dodge Daytona Funny Car, Leong was paid $225,000 from the HVB to immediately begin the campaign that would carry the car through the end of June. Another $700,000 would need to be sought to sustain the title sponsorship that would carry throughout the second half of the season.

One of Leong's first moves was rehiring veteran driver Gordie "240-Something" Bonin, who had been in retirement for the past six years. Bonin, who'd been friends with Leong for more than 20 years, drove the *Hawaiian* Dodge Charger Funny Car to numerous wins in 1974.

Gordie "240-Something" Bonin reunited once again with his old boss Roland Leong. Bonin returned from a six-year hiatus. (Photo Courtesy Jeff Burk Photography)

Slick 50 Nationals

Kicking off the program from March 4 to 7 at the Slick 50 Nationals in Houston, Bonin blazed the *Hawaiian Vacation* Dodge Funny Car down the quarter mile, promoting isle travel. Bonin did not qualify, but a violent explosion and fire on Saturday to Jim Dunn's driver, Kenji Okazaki, put Bonin in as first alternate. After the lengthy six-year absence, Bonin breezed past the first round against Gary Bolger but lost in the second round against old-foe John Force.

Outrigger Hotels Hawaii

Roland landed an additional $1-million corporate Maui vacation package from Outrigger Hotels Hawaii along with the Hawaii Visitors Bureau. Outrigger Hotels Hawaii supplied 20 giveaway holiday trips of six nights, one for each national event that the *Hawaiian Vacation* car appeared at. Leong's longtime association with Mopar (Chrysler Corporation's automotive parts division) also sent 91 of the nation's top-selling dealers and families to Hawaii.

Roland Leong's return to Funny Car took place at the fifth-annual NHRA Slick 50 Nationals at Houston Raceway Park. After a year's absence from the sport, the Hawaiian Vacation *Dodge failed to qualify. It earned a spot to race on Sunday as an alternate when driver Kenji Okazaki experienced a disastrous fire in qualifying the day before. (Photo Courtesy Roland Leong Collection)*

Outrigger Hotels marketing also paid and printed out 200,000 postcard handouts that included coupons for an inexpensive $70-a-night stay that included a free rental car that was handed out by the crew.

The crew of Todd Okahara, Bonin, an unidentified crewman, Leong, and crew chief Leonard Hughes finish up the necessary maintenance and adjustments for the next round of eliminations. (Photo Courtesy Roland Leong Collection)

Rockin' It at the Rock

Rockingham Dragway had been hosting the NHRA non-points Winston Invitational since 1988. It awarded only prestige and a huge amount of cash. There, Gordie Bonin qualified the *Hawaiian Vacation* Daytona into the sixth position, running a 5.37 ET. During the final elimination round against Al Hoffman, the Daytona overpowered the track and went up in smoke against the eventual winner.

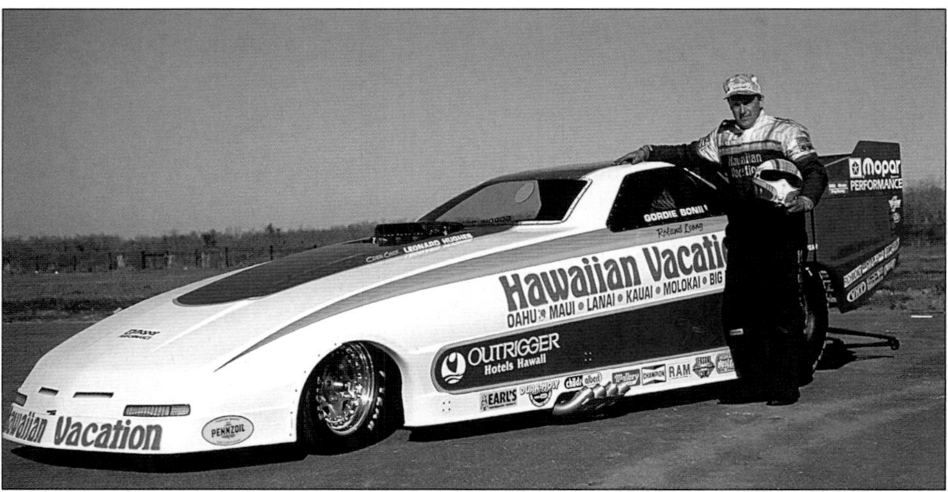

Gordie Bonin is shown with the special one-time purple-and-white-paint-schemed* Hawaiian Vacation *Dodge Daytona for the prestigious 1993 NHRA Winston Invitational. The All-Star non-points race was the most lucrative event on the NHRA Winston Drag Racing tour, awarding $25,000 to the champions in Top Fuel and Funny Car. (Photo Courtesy Jeff Burk Photography)

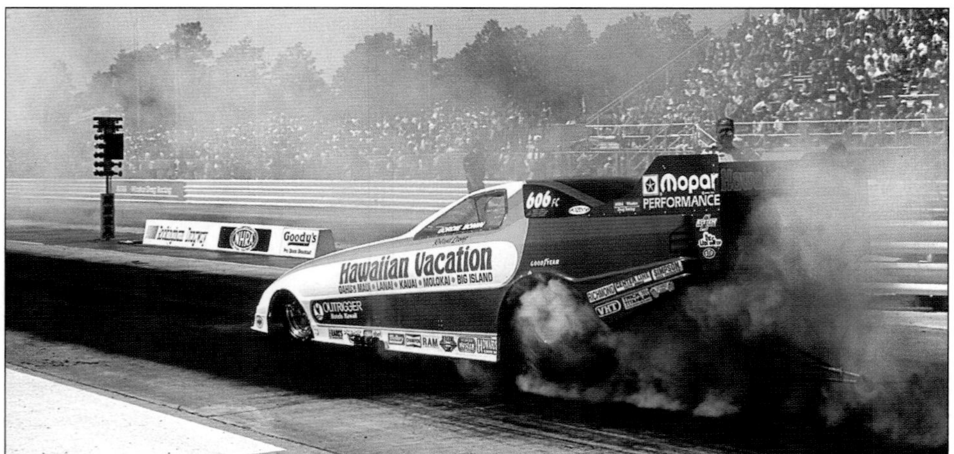

Gordie Bonin drove Leong's Dodge Daytona into the sixth position, stopping the clocks with a 5.37 ET at the Rock. Bonin took a bye run into the second round, where he ran a 5.42 ET at 268 mph against a broken Chuck Etchells. Bonin stepped up in the semifinals with a 5.33 ET at 237 mph against Wyatt Radke before meeting the NHRA's tough guy, Al Hoffman, in the final. The dream of cashing in the $25,000 bounty for both Leong and Bonin literally went up in smoke as the Funny Car lost traction in the final round against Hoffman. (Photo Courtesy Jeff Burk Photography)

Funds for the Season

At one time, Leong's biggest worry was how to sneak his mom's 1959 Oldsmobile out of the garage to take it for a spin down the Kahuku strip. Since then, he'd faced many challenges and conquered many of his fears, but as chief entrepreneur of the state-sponsored *Hawaiian Vacation* flopper, Leong needed a plan. He would need to bargain for an additional $700,000 from the state of Hawaii to continue to race on the NHRA circuit for the remainder of the year.

"People in Hawaii associate racing with Hawaii Raceway just as a hobby, but they mostly didn't realize how the overall picture was in drag racing," Leong said.

Springnationals

In mid-June, the controversial *Hawaiian Vacation* Funny Car took home the gold, glory, and the coveted Wally trophy at Kirkerville, Ohio, during the running of the 29th-annual Springnationals at National Trails Raceway. Bonin ran the fastest speed of the day when he hit 289.48 mph before heading back to victory lane for the first time since 1981.

Bonin posted an easy single pass when he clicked it off early, turning a 5.60 ET at 194.34 mph in Leong's Dodge Daytona when "Flash" Gordon Mineo couldn't make the call in the final round.

Western Auto Nationals and Mopar Mile-High Nationals

Continuing his winning ways, the stop at the Western Auto Nationals in Topeka, Kansas, Bonin made it through three elimination rounds only to lose in the final. A week later, at the Mopar Mile-High Nationals at Denver, Leong managed to get Bonin down the track to win three rounds, despite the battle of bad track conditions and the altitude, before losing to Cruz Pedregon in the final.

Bonin was "Mr. Consistency" at Atlanta, where he ran a series of mid-5.30

Bonin cuts loose on another 5.38 at 262-mph blast at the Fram Southern Nationals at Atlanta. (Photo Courtesy Roland Leong Collection)

The Hawaii State Bureau's goodwill ambassador, Gordie Bonin, and Miss Hawaii, Pamela Kimura, give the lowdown to Mike Lewis regarding how easy it was to enter for a Hawaiian getaway presented by the Outrigger Hotels Hawaii and the Chrysler Cooperation's Mopar parts division. Bonin, the popular driver for Roland Leong's Hawaiian Vacation race team, returned for a second stint in the driver's seat. (Photo Courtesy Roland Leong Collection)

at 260 mph runs at the Fram Southern Nationals. Bonin made it all the way to the semifinals.

Pulling the Plug

The majority of sponsorship was funded by the Hawaii State Department of Business, Economic Development and Tourism (DBEDT). The initial funding of $225,000 was set to run out at the end of June, and Leong needed an additional $700,000 to keep the car going until the end of the year.

Critics of the advertising program said that the money could be better spent on other types of marketing. On the other hand, supporters of the program maintained that sponsoring drag racing was one of the most innovative tools that produced results.

With time running out on the state-backed promotion, the hard-charging Bonin was climbing up the ladder rapidly and racing stoutly. The *Hawaiian* won one of its last four events and made it to the finals in the other three.

Heading into the next event for the Autolite Nationals at Sonoma, California, Bonin shrugged it off and said, "Whether we will run or not depends on what happens between the HVB and DBEDT."

Leong felt strongly that if they had raced through the whole season leading up to the World Finals, the Hawaiian Vacation team would have likely finish in the top ten of the point standings. Unfortunately, both time and funding ran out. Leong had no choice but to park the car in August.

Leong ran the *Hawaiian Vacation* Dodge from the third race of the year in March through August for a total of 10 NHRA national events. During that time, the car won one national event and produced four runner-up finishes.

"The bottom line is that one of the politicians lied to me," Leong said. "I was given just enough money to get off the ground and was told that he'd get us the money for the rest of the year later. Well, it turned out that he never had any intentions of following through. That was the end of my time as a car owner.

"I sold my Funny Car along with everything to Ray Higley, who was a friend of mine when we worked together back in the Dragmaster days. He was just a regular guy who didn't really have that much money. Several people wondered why I helped him. He paid me, but he didn't have that much money. He helped me to build my dragsters after work at Dragmaster. Ray asked me to help him run the car, so I did for a little while."

Ending the Full-Time Career

Throughout the years as owner and tuner of all his famed *Dragmaster Hawaii* Gas and *Hawaiian* Top Fuel Dragsters and Funny Cars, Roland Leong employed 21 top talented drivers. That list included Don Prudhomme, Danny Ongais, Mike Snively, Larry Arnold, Mike Sorokin, Larry Reyes, Pat Foster, Butch Maas, Bobby Rowe, Leroy Chadderton, Norm Wilcox, Johnny West, Rick Johnson, Gordie Bonin (twice), Ron Colson, Mike Dunn, Mike Van Sant, and Jim White. As one of the top crew chiefs in NHRA drag racing, Leong also tuned and guided Ron Capps, Ray Higley, and Jim Epler.

Leong's remarkable career as an iconic owner had now finally run its course.

MEMORABLE MOMENTS:

Ron Capps

"My first year with big sponsor Copenhagen driving for Don "the Snake" Prudhomme, we were in Richmond, Virginia, not having any kind of luck getting down the track all year," said Ron Caps, a three-time NHRA Funny Car Champion. "I had to peddle the car in Richmond when it lifted up the front end and came down hard, breaking the front end, but we did get the round win. Rain postponed the race for a week. This was when Don made the move where he released crew chief Tom Anderson.

"I knew that Don and Roland were friends and had stayed friends. I had heard stories from Larry Dixon that no matter what, they were like a band of brothers. When Don told me that he was bringing Roland in to be my crew chief, I was excited. I grew up idolizing Don and Roland but just didn't realize at the time how much Roland would change my life!

"Two weeks later, at the inaugural race in Dallas, Texas, the first thing Roland said was that he was going to make things as simple as possible, which allowed me to get my confidence back again. I previously had no confidence at all in the car, having to peddle on every run. It was tough!

"Right away, Roland and I hit it off. We spent every minute together. We didn't room together, but I felt like I had a new roommate. We rode in the same rental car and ate breakfast, lunch, and dinner together. He gave me a lot of confidence. It was a huge time in my career.

"We also had a lot of fun. The crew also had a lot of fun, as he was the reason they stayed when they wanted to quit. I could tell the difference in the car right away. The mood changed, the car was running better, and I was driving better too.

"In St. Louis, at the Inaugural Craftsman Nationals at Gateway, I took my first career win as a Funny Car driver. After St. Louis, we were consistently running into the later rounds as the car became an instant threat. We won twice in three final rounds and climbed up in the points. I was driving my rear-end off, and Roland tutored me by teaching lessons that helped me become a better driver and racer. We even joked that it was like Mr. Miyagi in *The Karate Kid*. There is no way that I would have been where I was in my early career without Roland in 1997.

It was fun being in the middle of this group, growing up as a kid in the sport of drag racing, now having dinner with Don and Roland, and celebrating a win after a race. To me, it was like being at home."

Miss Hawaii Pamela Kimura and Roland Leong take a moment out of their schedules to promote the Hawaii Visitor Bureau. Miss Kimura went on to become an actress and appeared in numerous productions, including several remake episodes of Hawaii Five-O. *(Photo Courtesy Roland Leong Collection)*

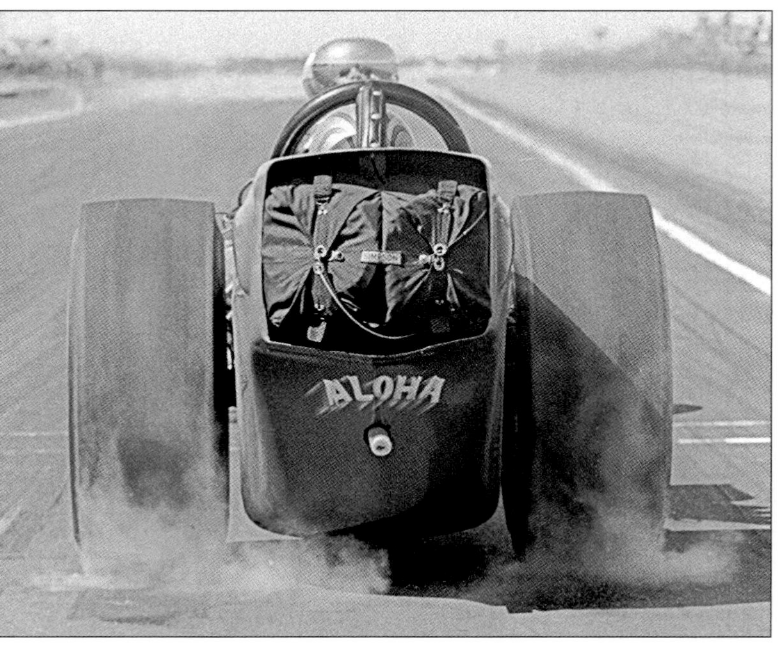

This friendly greeting was all too familiar, as it was seen by many competitors trying to catch the Hawaiian *throughout the years. (Photo Courtesy Steve Reyes)*

EPILOGUE

HONORING A HAWAIIAN LEGEND

On September 6, 1959, Roland Leong walked out of a classroom on his first day of his senior year of high school and never looked back.

Fifty-five years later, he couldn't have imagined that after being a high-school dropout, he would be receiving two of Hawaii's highest honors given by the state.

On November 19, 2019, Roland was honored with two proclamations: one by the 30th Legislature of the State of Hawaii and the other from the Office of the Governor from the State of Hawaii. The ceremony was inside the chambers of the Hawaii State Capitol, as Governor David Ige saluted Roland's 55 years of being a worldwide, at-large ambassador for his work in motorsports. Roland was presented with the decrees in honor of his many drag-racing accomplishments.

In addition, as one of Hawaii's most-recognized sports icons, Roland was enshrined into the Hawaii Sports Hall of Fame for his motorsports contributions during a ceremony on Thursday, August 25, 2022, in the Hibiscus Room at the Ala Morna Hotel in Honolulu. Leong, one of three inductees from the 2020 induction class, (late surfing great Ben Aipa and racquetball world champion Egan Inoue) shared the podium with two other members from the class of 2021 (contributors Dr. Larry Price and National volleyball champion Reyan "Tita" Ahuna). These five inductees brought the total number of Hawaii Sports Hall of Fame fraternity to 160 members.

"The 2020 Induction Class covered a wide variety of pursuits, exemplifying Hawaii's unique and profound impact on the sports world," said Larry Price, Hawaii Sports Hall of Fame's Chair. "It is our honor and privilege to welcome Ben Aipa, Egan Inoue, and Roland Leong."

Hawaii is proud of their "Hawaiian!"

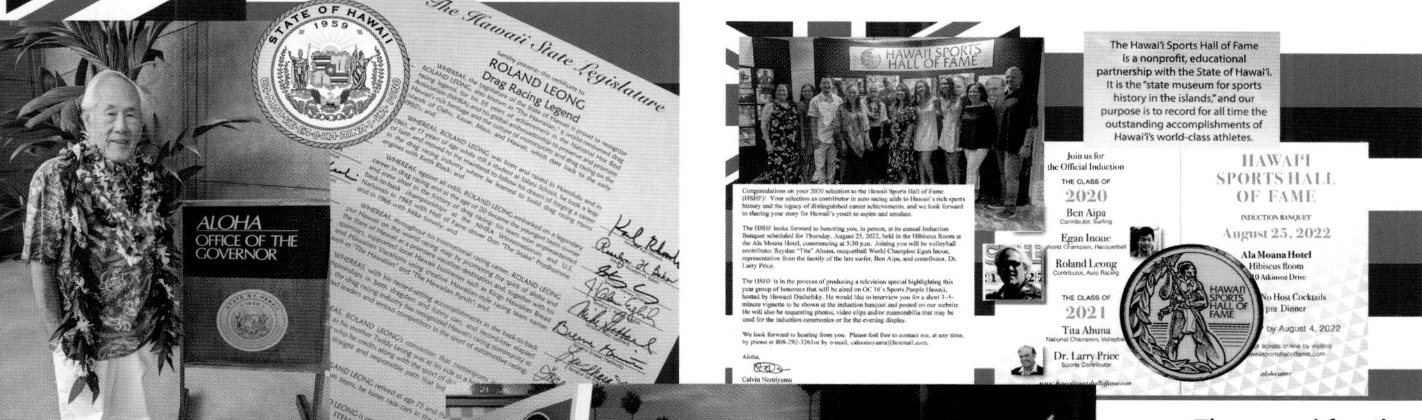

Roland Leong was recognized by the Hawaii State Legislature for more than 50 years of contributions and accomplishments as he represented the state of Hawaii in organized drag racing. (Photo Courtesy Jerry Inouye Photography/Ross Howard Graphic Designs)

The proud family of Roland Leong celebrates Roland's enshrinement into the Hawaii Sports Hall of Fame. They are (from left to right) Roland's daughter Landa; granddaughter Rachael; grandson Collin; Suzy Leong; Roland; granddaughters Jade, Kaya, and Natalie; and Roland's youngest daughter Lani and her husband Troy. (Photo Courtesy Jerry Inouye Photography/Ross Howard Graphic Designs)

Inseparable friends Roland Leong and Don Prudhomme, sit together at the Lions Automobilia Foundation Museum on December 3, 2022, at the 50th anniversary of the Lions Drag Strip Last Drag Race and hall of fame inductions.

ROLAND LEONG'S FAMILY GALLERY

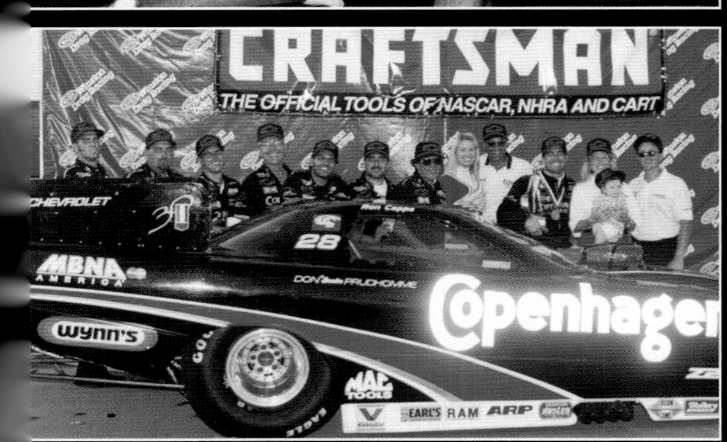